D1608857

# Gastrow
# Injection Molds
# 108 Proven Designs

# GASTROW
# Injection Molds
## 2nd Edition
### 108 Proven Designs

2nd updated and revised edition with new mold designs

Edited by

E. Lindner and P. Unger

Hanser Publishers, Munich, Vienna, New York, Barcelona

The Editors:
Dipl.-Ing. Edmund Lindner, Kassel
Dr. Peter Unger, Büttelborn

The examples of molds contained in this book represent to a large extent designs that have been proven in actual operation or those that have been prepared in accordance with current technical standards.
Nevertheless, neither the authors, editors or publishers can provide any guarantee that the designs are free from error and will function without difficulty if design details or the design itself are used.

Translated by Dr. Kurt A. Alex, Rumford RI, USA

**Die Deutsche Bibliothek – CIP-Einheitsaufnahme**

**Gastrow, Hans:**
Injection molds : 108 proven designs / Gastrow. Ed. by E. Lindner and P. Unger. – 2., updated and revised ed. with new mold designs. – Munich ; Vienna ; New York ; Barcelona : Hanser 1993
ISBN 3-446-15682-8

Cover design by Kaselow Design, München
Printed and bound in Germany by Sellier GmbH, Freising

# Preface to the second edition

The second English edition of Gastrow is now here. Since the appearance of the 1st (German) edition of this interpretative collection of tested and proven mold designs more than twenty-five years ago, this book has served two generations of designers and mold makers as a reference work and problem solver. This is also the intent of this new edition of Gastrow. It was not supposed to be a text book either then or now.

This new edition has been revised extensively. A large number of new molds representing the state of the art has been included. The computational methods given in earlier editions have been eliminated completely, since these are treated in a more up to date fashion and in greater detail in other literature (e. g. in Menges, Mohren "How to Make Injection Molds", 2nd edition, Carl Hanser Publishers). Whenever possible, the particular tool steels used have been listed with the respective examples. Accordingly, it appeared necessary to add a new chapter on material selection and surface treatment methods.

The 2nd edition is easier to use: an overview (p. 17) with references to the particular design employed for a given mold simplifies the use of the book. Following the previous tradition, the spectrum of molds presented extends from the simplest design to those exhibiting the highest degree of difficulty. Nevertheless, all molds have one thing in common: each contains some special know-how, and they demonstrate the high technical standards moldmaking has reached today. The editors wish to thank all authors for their contributions to this new "Gastrow" and especially the translator Dr. Kurt Alex who prepared this English edition.

Fall 1992                                                                                      The Editor

# Preface to the first edition

*Hans Gastrow* has been publishing examples of mold construction for injection molding since the mid-fifties. These were collected and published in 1966 in the first German edition of this book, which was widely acclaimed because there had been, until then, no other collection of its kind. The injection molding industry stood at the beginning of its great upturn and ideas for constructing good and economically feasible molds were received with great interest. Shortly after the publication of the first edition, Gastrow died. The second edition, published in 1975, kept the objectives set by the first. It does not aim to be a textbook but illustrates selected problems of injection mold construction with interesting and commercially tested solutions. Some of the examples from the original *Gastrow* were retained; others, from younger specialists, were added. The present English translation of the third German edition remains true to this principle. Along with a large number of new examples, principles of construction are also treated. At the time of the second edition's publication, some of them did not possess their present topicality, as for example, hot-runner molds. The solutions to the problems illustrated include molds from the simplest technology to the most complex multi-stage molds.

Summer 1983                                                                                      The Editor

# Contents

# 1 Principles of mold design

Critical analysis of a large number of injection molds for parts from all areas of application leads to the realization that there are certain classes and groups that differ from one another in some basic manner. Naturally, such a classification cannot contain all possible combinations of the individual classes and groups if it is to remain clear. It is conceivable that new knowledge and experience will require expansion and reorganization.

Nevertheless, such a classification fulfills its purpose if it conveys the previously collected experience with regard to mold design as clearly and thoroughly as possible. When working on a new problem, the mold designer can then see how such a mold is to be designed or was designed in similar cases. He will always, however, make an effort to evaluate the previous experience and create something even better instead of simply keeping to what was done previously. One basic requirement that must be met by every mold that is intended to run on an automatic injection molding machine is that the molded parts be ejected automatically without the need for secondary finishing operations (degating, machining to final dimensions, etc.).

From a practical standpoint, the classification of injection molds should be accomplished on the basis of the major features of the design and operation. These include:

– the type of gating/runner system and means of separation,
– the type of ejection used for the molded parts,
– the presence or absence of external or internal undercuts on the part to be molded,
– the manner in which the molded part is released.

Fig. 1.1 shows a procedure to methodically plan and design injection molds.

The finite element method (FEM) along with computational methods such as Cadform, Cadmould, Moldflow, etc. are being used increasingly to design and dimension parts and the associated injection molds. With these methods, development time and costs can be saved, while the serviceability of the molded parts is optimized.

The final mold design can be prepared only after the part design has been specified and all requirements affecting the design of the mold have been clarified.

## 1.1 Types of injection molds

The German standard DIN E 16 750 "Injection and Compression Molds for Molding Compounds" classifies molds on the basis of the following criteria:

– standard molds (two-plate molds),
– split-cavity molds (split-follower molds),
– stripper plate molds,
– three-plate molds,
– stack molds,
– hot-runner molds.

There are also cold-runner molds for runnerless processing of thermosetting resins in analogy to the hot runner molds used for processing thermoplastic compounds.

If it is not possible to locate runners in the mold parting line or each of the parts in a multiple-cavity mold is to be center-gated, a second parting line (three-plate mold) is required to remove the solidified runner or

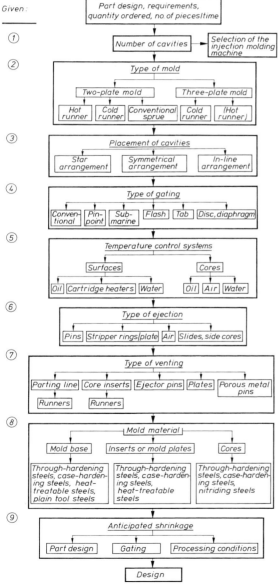

**Fig. 1.1   Flow chart for methodical designing of injection molds**

melt must be conveyed by means of a hot runner system. In stack molds, two molds are connected one behind the other for all practical purposes without the need for doubling the clamp force. A prerequisite for such molds is a large number of relatively simple as well as shallow parts. Low production costs are the particular advantage of operating such a mold. Today, stack molds are equipped exclusively with hot runner systems that must satisfy quite stringent requirements with regard to thermal homogeneity in particular.

Ejector pins are used most often to eject the molded parts. They also often serve to vent the cavity. With electrical discharge machining (EDM) having become so common, proper venting has become increasingly important. Whereas cavities were previously built up from several components with the possibility of incorporating effective venting at the respective mating surfaces, it is possible today by means of EDM to produce cavities in a solid block in many cases. Special care must thus be taken to assure that the melt displaces the air completely. Measures must also be taken to assure that entrapped air is avoided at particularly critical locations. A poorly vented cavity can lead to the formation of deposits in the mold, burning (the so-called diesel effect) and even corrosion problems. The size of a vent is determined primarily by the melt viscosity. Vents are generally between 0.01 mm and 0.02 mm in size. With extremely easy-flowing resins, vents on the order of $\geq$ 0.001 mm in size may already be adequate. It should be noted, however, that effective cooling is generally not possible wherever a vent is placed.

Moving mold components must be guided and located. The guidance provided by the tiebars for the moving platen of an injection molding machine should be considered as rough alignment at best. "Internal alignment" within the injection mold is necessary in any case.

Tool steels are the preferred material for injection molds. Selection of the material should be made quite carefully on the basis of the resins to be processed. Requirements that must be met by the tool steels include:

– high wear resistance,
– high corrosion resistance,
– high dimensional stability, etc. (see also Section 1.10).

## 1.2 Types of runners and gates

### 1.2.1 Solidifying systems

According to DIN 24 450, a distinction is made between the:
– runner as part of the injection molded shot that does not belong to the molded part,
– runner system as the channel through which plasticated melt is conveyed from its point of entry into the mold up the gate,

– gate as the cross section of the runner system at the location where it feeds into the mold cavity.

The flow path of the melt into the cavity should be as short as possible in order to minimize pressure and heat losses. The type and location of runner/gate are of importance for:

– economical production,
– properties of the molded part,
– tolerances,
– weld lines,
– magnitude of molded-in stresses, etc.

The following provides an overview of the most commonly encountered types of solidifying runner systems and gates.

– Sprue (Fig. 1.2)
  Is generally used for relatively thick walled parts or for gentle processing of highly viscous melts. The sprue must be removed from the molded part after ejection takes place.

– Pinpoint gate (Fig. 1.3)
  In contrast to the sprue, the pinpoint gate is generally separated from the molded part automatically. If the gate vestige causes problems, the gate "d" can be located in a lens-shaped depression in the surface of the molded part. Commercially available pneumatic nozzles are also used for automatic ejection of a runner with pinpoint gate.

– Diaphragm gate (Fig. 1.4)
  The diaphragm is useful for producing, for instance, bushings with the highest possible degree of concentricity while avoiding weld lines. The necessity of having to remove the gate by means of subsequent machining is a disadvantage, as is the support of the core on only one side.

– Disk gate (Fig. 1.5)
  This is used preferably for internal gating of cylindrical parts in order to eliminate disturbing weld lines. With fibrous reinforcements such as glass fibers, for instance, the disk gate can reduce the tendency for distortion. The disk gate must also be removed subsequent to part ejection.

– Film gate (Fig. 1.6)
  To obtain flat molded parts with few molded-in stresses and little tendency to warp, a film gate over the entire width of the molded part is useful in providing a uniform flow front. A certain tendency of the melt to advance faster in the vicinity of the sprue can be offset by correcting the cross section of the gate. In single-cavity molds, however, the eccentric location of the gate can lead to opening of the mold on one side, with subsequent formation of flash. The film gate is usually trimmed off the part after ejection, but this generally does not impair automatic operation.

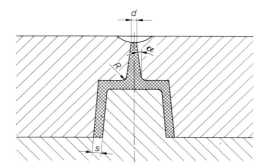

**Fig. 1.2    Conventional sprue**
a = draft, s = wall thickness, d = sprue (diameter), d ≧ s, d ≧ 0.5

intended gating location

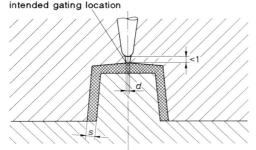

**Fig. 1.3    Pinpoint gate, d ≦ 2/3 s**

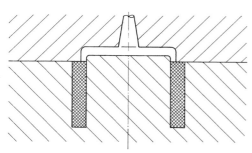

**Fig. 1.4    Diaphragm gate**

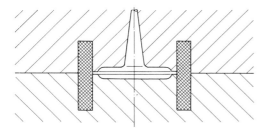

**Fig. 1.5    Disk gate**

– Submarine gate (Fig. 1.7)
Depending on the arrangement, this gate is trimmed off the molded part during opening of the mold or at the moment of ejection by means of a specified cutting edge. The submarine gate is es-

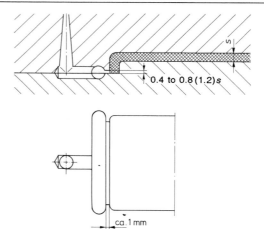

**Fig. 1.6    Flash (film) gate preferred for large-area parts**

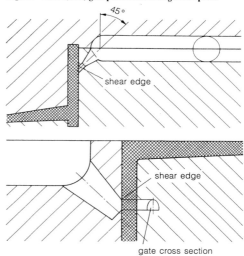

**Fig. 1.7    Submarine (tunnel) gate**

pecially useful when gating parts from the side. The lower part of Fig. 1.7 shows a submarine gating formed as a truncated cone. This design permits longer holding pressure times because of its greater cross section than the conical pointed gating in the upper part and prevents jetting during injection. With abrasive molded compounds, increased wear of the cutting edge in particular is to be expected. This may lead to problems with automatic degating.

Runner systems should be designed to provide the shortest possible flow paths and avoid unnecessary changes in direction while achieving simultaneous and uniform filling of cavities regardless of position in multi-cavity molds (assuming that all cavities are the same) and assuring that the duration of holding pressure is identical for each cavity.
Star- as well as ring-shaped runner systems (see Fig. 1.8) offer the advantage of identical and shortest possible flow paths. They are a disadvantage, however, when slides must be employed. In this case, in-line

runner systems (see Fig. 1.9 A) are useful, but have the disadvantage of unequal flow path lengths. This deficiency can, however, be offset to a very high degree by artificially balancing the runner system with the aid of a Moldflow analysis, for instance. This is achieved by varying the diameter of the run-

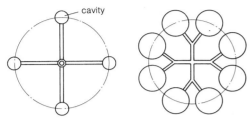

**Fig. 1.8   Star-shaped runner**

ner channels, but not the cross section of the respective gates. A naturally balanced in-line runner system is shown in Fig. 1.9 B. This arrangement, however, generally leads to a relatively unfavorable ratio of molded part volume to runner system volume.

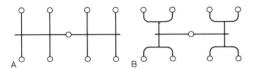

**Fig. 1.9   In-line runners**
A: unequal flow path lengths, B: equal flow path lengths

### 1.2.2  Hot-runner systems

Hot-runner systems are employed for so-called "runnerless" injection molding of parts in thermoplastic resins. It is also advantageous to use partial hot-runner systems, i. e. those with secondary runners. With proper design, lower pressure losses can be achieved in hot-runner systems than in comparable molds with solidifying runner systems. Thus, it is possible to produce extremely large parts such as automobile bumpers with suitable hot-runner systems.

Economical production of parts in stack molds has become possible only through the use of hot-runner technology.

By completely eliminating the solidifying secondary runners, the injection capacity of an injection molding machine can be better utilized. This may also result in a reduction in the filling time, which can be a reduction in cycle time. In principle, however, hot-runner systems do not reduce the cycle time.

The design principles employed for various hot-runner systems can differ considerably. This applies to both the hot-runner manifold and the hot-runner nozzles, the type and design of which can have a consider-

able influence on the properties of a molded part (Table 1).

The various hot-runner systems are not necessarily equally well suited for processing of all thermoplas-

**Table 1   Types of hot-runner systems**

| Component* | Type |
| --- | --- |
| Hot-runner manifold | externally heated<br>internally heated |
| Manner of heating the hot-runner nozzles | externally heated, direct<br>externally heated, indirect<br>internally heated, direct<br>internally heated, indirect<br>internally and externally heated |
| Type of hot-runner nozzles | open nozzles, with or without torpedo; needle shutoff |

\*  Designations as per DIN E 16 750, issued July 1988

tics, even though this may be claimed occasionally. Thermally gentle processing of the melt to the greatest degree possible should be considered a particular criterion. From a heat transfer standpoint, this requires very involved design principles. Accordingly, hot-runner systems satisfying such requirements are more complex, more sensitive and possibly more prone to malfunction than conventional injection molds. As for the rest, the guidelines of precision machining must be observed to a very high degree when manufacturing such molds. When processing abrasive and/or corrosive molding compounds, the hot-runner system must be suitably protected. For instance, it may be necessary to take into consideration the incompatibility of the melt with respect to copper and copper alloys, which may lead to catalytically induced degradation. Suitably protected systems are available from suppliers. For the sake of better temperature control, hot-runner systems with closed-loop control should be given preference to those with open-loop control.

In medium-sized and, especially, large molds with correspondingly large hot-runner manifolds, "natural" or "artifical" balancing of the runners is successfully employed with the objective of obtaining uniform pressures or pressure losses. With "natural balancing", the flow lengths in the runner system are designed to be equally long. With "artifical balancing", the same result is achieved by varying the diameter of the runner channels as necessary. Natural balancing has the advantage of being independent of processing parameters such as temperature and injection rate, for example, but means that the manifold becomes more complicated, since the melt must generally now be distributed over several levels. An optimum hot-runner system must permit complete displacement of the melt in the shortest possible period of time (color changes), since stagnant melt can degrade thermally and thus result in reduced molded part properties.

Open hot-runner nozzles may tend to "drool". After the mold opens, melt can expand into the cavity through the gate and form a cold slug that is not necessarily remelted during the next shot. In addition to surface defects, molded part properties can also be reduced in this manner as well. In an extreme case, a cold slug can even plug the gate.

With the aid of melt decompression (pulling back the screw before opening the mold), which is a standard feature on all modern machines, or with an "expansion chamber" in the sprue bushing of the hot-runner manifold, this problem can be overcome. Care must always be taken, however, that the decompression always be kept to a minimum in order to avoid sucking air into the sprue, runner system or region around the gate (avoidance of the diesel effect).

Although hot-runner technology has generally reached a high technical level, the user should be aware that more extensive maintenance by properly trained personnel is unavoidable.

### 1.2.3 Cold-runner systems

In a manner analogous to the so-called "runnerless" processing of thermoplastic resins, thermosets and elastomers can be processed without the loss of a runner system in cold-runner molds. This is all the more important, since crosslinked, or cured, runners generally cannot be regranulated. The objective of a cold-runner is to keep the thermoset or elastomer at a temperature level that precludes the possibility of crosslinking. As a result, the requirements placed on a cold-runner system are very stringent: the temperature gradient in the cold-runner system must be kept to an absolute minimum and optimum thermal separation of the mold and cold-runner must be provided in order to reliably prevent crosslinking of the resin. If, nevertheless, difficulties occur during operation, the mold must be so designed that the difficulty can be corrected without a great deal of work. Various types of cold-runner molds are described in greater detail in Sections 1.12 and 1.13.

## 1.3 Temperature control in injection molds

Depending on the type of resin to be processed, heat must be introduced to or removed from the injection mold. This task is handled by the mold temperature control system. Water or oil is usually employed to convey heat, while electrical heating of the mold is generally provided when processing thermosetting resins. A great deal of importance should be given to optimum temperature control. It has a direct influence on the functionality of the molded parts. The design and type of temperature control system influence:
- the warping of molded parts. This applies especially to semi-crystalline resins,

- the level of molded-in stresses in the part and thus its susceptibility to failure. With amorphous thermoplastics, the susceptibility to stress cracking can increase,
- the cooling time and thus also the cycle time.

The economics of a mold can be influenced significantly in this manner. Molds intended for the processing of amorphous thermoplastics are not necessarily equally well suited for the processing of semi-crystalline materials. The greater degree of processing shrinkage of semi-crystalline thermoplastics must be taken into account in most cases by providing a more uniform and higher-capacity temperature control system. This often means separate temperature control circuits in corner regions, for instance, keeping in mind that the temperature control circuit cannot be interrupted by the position of ejectors, slides or the like. The temperature difference between the inlet and outlet of the temperature control medium should not exceed 5 K. This often prevents series connection of temperature control circuits. Parallel connection or, even better, the use of several temperature control circuits each with its own temperature control unit is the preferred alternative in most cases. The magnitude of processing shrinkage is a direct function of the cavity wall temperature. Temperature differences in the mold and/or different cooling rates are thus responsible for warpage, etc. If water is employed as the temperature control medium, corrosion and calcium deposits in the temperature control circuits must be prevented, as otherwise the heat transfer and thus the effectiveness of the mold temperature control can be reduced.

## 1.4 Types of ejectors

As a consequence of the processing shrinkage, molded parts tend to be retained on mold cores (this does not necessarily hold true for parts molded of thermosetting resins). Various types of ejectors are used to release molded parts:

- ejector pins,
- ejector sleeves,
- stripper plates, stripper bars, stripper rings,
- slides and lifters,
- air ejectors,
- disc or valve ejectors, etc.

The type of ejector depends on the shape of the molded part. The pressure on the surface of the section of the molded part to be ejected should be as low as possible in order to avoid deformation. Profiled ejector pins should be prevented from turning.

Usually the mold cores and thus also the ejector mechanisms are located on the movable platen of the injection molding machine. In certain cases, it may be advantageous to attach the core to the stationary platen. In this case, special ejector mechanisms are required. To release undercuts, slides are generally needed. Internal undercuts can be released by collapsible cores or internal slides. Threads may be released by:

– slides,
– removable inserts,
– collapsible cores,
– unscrewing cores, etc.

Undercuts which are intended to act, for instance, as snap fits can also be (forcibly) released directly, i. e. without the use of slides, lifters etc. It must be ensured, however, that the ejection temperature is considerably above room temperature and that the material stiffness is correspondingly low. The ejection forces must not lead to stretching of the molded part nor should ejectors be forced into the molded part. The permissible deformation during such forced ejection depends on the physical properties of the particular resin at the ejection temperature and on the design of the undercuts. A general statement with regard to the possibility of using (cost-reducing) forced ejection cannot be made. In principle, however, forced ejection should be taken into consideration when laying out a suitable mold.

Textured or grained surfaces generally act like undercuts. They thus require a certain minimum draft which, if not provided, can result in visible damage to the surface. As an approximate guideline to avoid such damage, the following value applies: per 1/100 mm of texture depth, approximately 1 degree of draft is needed. Ejectors serve not only to release the molded parts, but are also needed to vent the cavity. Inadequate venting can lead, for instance, to

– incomplete filling of the cavity,
– inadequate welding where flow fronts meet,
– the so-called diesel effect, i. e. thermal degradation (burning) of the molded part, etc.

Problems with venting occur far from the gate especially.

## 1.5  Types of undercuts

Release of undercuts (see Section 1.4) generally requires additional design features in the mold such as opening of the mold along several planes, for instance. Additional release surfaces can be provided by slides and split cavities. Molds with slides release **external** undercuts with the aid of
– angle pins,
– cams,
– hydraulically or pneumatically actuated mechanisms.

Release of **internal** undercuts can be accomplished through the use of

– lifters
– split cores, which are actuated by means of a wedge,
– collapsible cores, which have smaller outside dimensions in the collapsed state than in the expanded state.

If release of threads is not possible by means of split cavities or slides, or if the witness line is undesirable, unscrewing molds are employed. These may utilize

– replaceable cores that are unscrewed outside the mold,
– threaded cores or threaded sleeves that release the threads in the molded part as the result of rotation during ejection. Actuation is accomplished either through the opening motion of the mold (lead screws, gear racks, etc.) or through the use of special unscrewing units.

Release of undercuts for short production runs can also be accomplished through the use of so-called "lost cores" (see also Section 1.6.1). When threads intended for fastening are involved, it is often more economical to mold throughholes instead of threads and then use commercially available self-tapping screws.

## 1.6  Special designs

### 1.6.1  Molds with fusible cores

Fusible core technology is employed to produce molded parts with cavities or undercuts that could not otherwise be released. Low melting point, reusable alloys on the basis of tin, lead, bismuth, cadmium, indium, antimony are employed. Depending on the composition, very different melting points result (lowest melting point approx. 50 °C). By introducing heat, e. g. inductive heating, the metallic core can be melted out of the molded part, leaving almost no residue.

### 1.6.2  Prototype molds of aluminum

The heat-treatable aluminum-zinc-magnesium-copper alloy (material no. 3.4365) has proven useful as a material for injection molds used to produce prototypes or small to medium production quantities. The advantages of this material, such as weight reduction, ease of machining, good thermal conductivity compared to tool steel, must be compared with the lower strength, reduced wear resistance, low stiffness as a result of the low modulus of elasticity and the relatively high coefficient of thermal expansion. In some cases, the properties of aluminum can be used to advantage in combination with steel.

### 1.6.3 Prototpye molds of plastics

To largely save on the cost-intensive machining need-ed to produce the part-forming surfaces in molds, cur-able casting resins can be employed. When strength-ened by metal inserts or when reinforced with glass fibers, etc., such casting resins can also meet more stringent requirements within certain limits. The low wear resistance of casting resins must always be taken into consideration. Generally, such molds are used to produce prototypes or only small quantities of parts by means of injection molding.

## 1.7 Standard mold components

In order to produce injection molds economically, a large number of standard components that have been premachined to near-finished dimensions is available. These include (replaceable) mold components such as

- mold plates, clamping plates,
- inserts,
- guiding and locating elements,
- ejector pins and sleeves,
- latches,
- quick-clamp mechanisms,
- hot-runner manifolds,
- hot-runner nozzles,
- heating elements,
- positioning cylinders, etc.

Depending on requirements, some of these compo-nents are also available in different materials. The part to be molded as well as the injection mold itself can be designed with the aid of appropriate computer pro-grams such as Cadform and Cadmould. Standard blanks of graphite or electrolytic copper are available to produce molds by means of electrical discharge ma-chining (EDM).

## 1.8 Status of standardization

### 1.8.1 Standard components

The continued development of molds for the produc-tion of molded plastic parts is also reflected through standardization. In accordance with German standard DIN E 16 750, issued July 1988, the following mold components, among others, are standardized (Table 2).

### 1.8.2 Injection mold for producing test specimens of thermoplastic resins

In order to directly compare the physical properties – as determined from test specimens – of thermoplastic

**Table 2    Standard components as per DIN E 16 750**

| Designation | DIN standard |
|---|---|
| Guide pins | 9825, Part 1 |
| Sprue bushings | 16 752, Part 1 |
| Sprue retainer bushings | 16 757 |
| Ejector sleeves with a cylindrical head | 16 756 |
| Ejector pins with a cylindrical head | 1530, Part 1 |
| Ejector pins with a cylindrical head and stepped-down shank | 1530, Part 2 |
| Ejector pins with a tapered head | 1530, Part 3 |
| Ejector pins with a cylindrical head and rectangular shank (blade ejector) | 1530, Part 4 |

resins from different material suppliers, the so-called Campus data bank (Kunststoffe/German Plastics 79 (1989) 8, p. 713) was developed in 1988. As a supple-ment, a corresponding standard for an injection mold to produce test specimens in a uniform manner is be-ing prepared by the Plastics Technical Standards Committee 304.2. The mold consists of a frame with interchangeable inserts in which the cavities to pro-duce the respective test specimens (e. g. 2-cavity ten-sile bar) are located. The mold is equipped with self-closing couplings for the temperature control system so that rapid and problem-free replacement of the inserts is possible. In order to process high-temperature resins characterized by relatively high melt and cavity wall temperatures, only tool steels with suitable properties are to be used (see also Section 1.9). The inserts can be preheated to pro-vide the necessary cavity wall temperatures in a separate preheating station so that replacement of one mold insert with another involves the least pos-sible amount of time.

## 1.9 Material selection

### 1.9.1 General

With the objective of achieving high functionality, dif-ferent requirements are placed on the materials used to produce injection molds:
- *High wear resistance*
   In order to increase the stiffness of molded parts, for instance, reinforcements in the form of glass fibers, mineral fillers, etc. are used extensively. These, as well as some pigments, promote wear. Se-lection of suitable materials and/or surface treat-ment is thus of great importance.

- *High corrosion resistance*
   Aggressive components such as flame retardants or even the melt itself can chemically attack the part-forming surfaces. When combined with abrasive fillers and reinforcements, cumulative mold dam-

age may result. Corrosion-resistant steels or surface coatings, e. g. multi-layer chrome plating, are thus to be recommended.

– *Good dimensional stability*
The processing of high-temperature plastics, for instance, requires cavity wall temperatures that can approach 250 °C. Tool steels with appropriate tempering properties (so-called hot work steels) are a prerequisite for this. Non-compliance with this requirement can lead to a change of the microstructure with temperature and thus to a dimensional change in the mold.
The dimensional changes during heat treatment, e. g. case hardening, of the steel used must be small, but generally cannot be avoided (exception: maraging steels). Heat treatment of molds with large differences in cross section, for instance, is risky (distortion or cracking upon hardening, etc.). It is thus preferable to utilize prehardened steels that can be machined. Heat treatment after the machining can then, as a rule, be dispensed with. The strength and hardness of such steels however, is generally quite low. If, on the other hand, molds are produced by means of conventional electrical discharge machining, steels that have been tempered to the highest possible hardness can be employed.

– *Good thermal conductivity*
Good mold temperature control is of great importance when processing semi-crystalline thermoplastics in particular. In order to affect the heat transport in a particular manner, variously alloyed steels may be employed. The effect of this measure on the thermal conductivity, however, is relatively modest. The noticeably higher thermal conductivity of copper, wrought copper alloys, etc. must be judged in light of the relatively low modulus of elasticity, relatively low hardness and low wear resistance. Depending on the type and quantity of alloying components, the mechanical properties can, however, be varied within certain limits. With each change, however, the thermal conductivity is also affected. The wear resistance can be improved noticeably with surface coatings, e. g. electroless nickel plating. It must not be forgotten, however, that in the event of surface or Hertzian pressure a hard surface layer may be penetrated as a result of inadequate support from the (soft) substrate. In addition to these requirements, the materials must furthermore exhibit good machineability, high purity and good polishability, etc.

## 1.9.2  Tool steels

The stiffness of a mold is independent of the steel selected, since the modulus of elasticity is practically identical for all common tool steels. Nevertheless, depending on the importance given to the various requirements, different materials may meet particular requirements better than others:

– case-hardened steels,
– prehardened steels,
– through-hardening steels,
– corrosion-resistant steels,
– special materials.

### 1.9.2.1  Case-hardening steels

These are low-carbon steels ($C \leqq 0.3$ %) that are given a hard, wear-resistant surface through case hardening (Table 3).
During the case hardening or carburizing (treatment temperature approx. 900 to 1000 °C), carbon diffuses into the near-surface regions of the material. The depth of case is a function of temperature and time. After case hardening for a lengthy period of time (several days), a depth of case of approx. 2 mm can be achieved. A hard, wear-resistant surface is achieved by quenching the carburized workpiece, while the core – assuming adequate workpiece thickness – in general remains tough.

### 1.9.2.2  Heat-treatable steels

Quenching and tempering is a heat treatment used to achieved increased toughness at a certain tensile strength. The treatment involves hardening with subsequent tempering at temperatures between 300 to 700 °C depending on the material and requirements. The available steels that have been treated in this manner (Table 4) are machined in the prehardened state. There is no subsequent hardening of the mold components. In this way, the risk of heat treating cracks and distortion upon hardening in particular is avoided.

### 1.9.2.3  Through-hardening steels (Table 5)

In order to achieve a uniform microstructure throughout even larger cross sections, through-hardening (alloyed) steels are used the hardness/strength and toughness of which can be matched to the particular requirements through heat treating (quenching and tempering). By selecting the temperature at which tempering takes place, these properties can be optimized. The through-hardening steels have proven very well suited for processing of abrasive molding compounds, e. g. those with glass fibers as a filler.

### 1.9.2.4  Corrosion-resistant steels (Table 6)

To protect against corrosive plastics or additives, there is always the possibility of electroplating the molds. One possible disadvantage, however, is that

**Table 3   Case-hardening steels**

| Abbreviation | Material No. | Surface hardness Rockwell C | Remarks |
|---|---|---|---|
| CK 15 | 1.1141 | 62–64 | For parts subjected to low loads |
| 21 MnCr5 | 1.2162 | 58–62 | Standard case-hardening steel, good polishability |
| X6CrMo4 | 1.2341 | 58–62 | Preferred for hobbing |
| X19NiCrMo4 | 1.2764 | 60–62 | Very good polishability, ideal for stringent requirements with regard to surface quality |

**Table 4   Heat-treatable steels**

| Abbreviation | Material No. | Tensile Strength N/mm$^2$ |
|---|---|---|
| 40CrMnMo7 | 1.2311 | |
| 40CrMnMoS8 | 1.2312 | approx. 1000 |
| 54NiCrMoV6 | 1.2711 | |

the deposited layer may delaminate on shutoff edges, for example, as the result of high surface pressure. The use of corrosion-resistant steels is thus recommended in such cases. Nitriding of corrosion-resistant steels is not recommended because of the resulting decrease in corrosion resistance.

## 1.10   Surface treatment methods

The condition and the type of treatment given the surface of a mold component has a significant effect on its functionality. In mold making, surface treatments are employed to achieve certain properties such as

– increased surface hardness,
– increased compressive strength,
– increased wear resistance,
– improved corrosion resistance,
– improved sliding properties.

The following surface treatment methods have proven useful in mold making in particular:

– nitriding,
– carburizing,
– hard chrome plating,
– hard nickel plating,
– hardcoating.

### 1.10.1  Nitriding

Of the nitriding methods, bath nitriding (e. g. the Tenifer method from the Degussa Co., Hanau) has become quite common. Through nitriding, an extremely high (surface) hardness with excellent dimensional stability is attained as the result of a

**Table 5   Through-hardening steels**

| Abbreviation | Material No. | Strength N/mm$^2$ or hardness Rockwell C | Remarks |
|---|---|---|---|
| X38CrMo V5 1 | 1.2343 | 1450 | Standard hot work tool steel |
| X45NiCrMo4 | 1.2767 | 50–54 | Very good polishability, high toughness |
| 90MnCrV8 | 1.2842 | 56–62 | Normal wear resistance |
| X155CrVMo121 | 1.2379 | 58 | Good wear resistance, good toughness |
| X210Cr12 | 1.2080 | 60–62 | High wear resistance |
| X165CrMoV12 | 1.2601 | 63 | Highly wear resistant steel |

Note: For components subject to minimal requirements, the plain tool steel C45W3, Material No. 1.1730 is used in an unhardened state.

**Table 6   Corrosion-resistant steels**

| Abbreviation | Material No. | Hardness Rockwell C | Remarks |
|---|---|---|---|
| X42Cr13 | 1.2083 | 54–56 | Corrosion-resistant only when polished |
| X36CrMo17 | 1.2316 | 50 | Machining after heat treatment, high corrosion resistance |
| X105CrMo17 | 1.4125 | 57–60 | Rust- and acid-resistant steel, wear-resistant |

chemical change in the surface layers that considerably improves the wear resistance and fatigue strengths. Since nitriding takes place at a temperature of 570 °C, a reduction of the core strength is usually to be expected in accordance with the tempering diagram of the particular steel.

Nearly all steels commonly encountered in mold making can be nitrided. Nitriding of corrosion-resistant steels is not recommended because of the reduction in corrosion resistance.

### 1.10.2  Carburizing

Carburizing is employed with steels having a low carbon content (C $\leq$ 0.3 %). With this method, carbon diffuses into the near-surface region.

A (case-hardened) steel produced by such a treatment exhibits a significant increase in hardness of its surface while the core generally remains ductile.

### 1.10.3  Hard chrome plating

The electrolytic deposition of hard chrome layers is used especially to achieve hard and wear-resistant surfaces that have proven effective for mold components used for processing abrasive plastics. Moreover, the hard chrome layer serves to reduce the tendency to gall and considerably improves corrosion resistance (multi-layer chrome plating). Hard chrome plating also finds application for the repair of worn surfaces. In the event of repeated plating and deplating, hydrogen embrittlement of the near-surface regions must not be overlooked.

Along edges and the like, the formation of a raised bead and the possibility of delamination of the chrome layer are to be expected.

### 1.10.4  Hard nickel plating

During the chemical hard nickel plating process, nickel layers are deposited without the use of an imposed electric current. With this method, the formation of different film thicknesses along edges in particular (bead formation), which is characteristic of electrolytic methods, does not occur. This means that through holes, openings, profiled surfaces, etc. can generally be nickel plated without problem.

Electroless nickel plating is known by the names of Nibodur (Paul Anke KG, Essen), Kanigen (Heinrich Schnarr OHG, Aschaffenburg) and Durni-Coat (AHC-Oberflächentechnik, Kerpen/Erft).

The film thickness usually employed is approx. 40 µm. Nickel-phosphorus-silicon carbide dispersion coatings known by the name Kanisil (Heinrich Schnarr OHG, Aschaffenburg) have also proven useful for electroless deposition of coatings on surfaces to be protected. The above-mentioned methods are characterized especially by their good performance with regard to providing protection against corrosion and wear and can also be employed with nonferrous metals such as copper. It must not be forgotten, however, that the nickel layer, which is much harder than the substrate material, can be damaged under a compressive load and tend to delaminate.

### 1.10.5  Hardcoating

To achieve high wear resistance along with very good corrosion resistance, coatings based on titanium nitride and other similar materials have proven especially useful. Such coatings are provided by the following companies, for example: Mahler GmbH, Esslingen/Neckar; VACTEC-Systems GmbH, Weiterstadt near Darmstadt, and Deutsche Balzers GmbH, Geisenheim.

## 1.11  Special materials

### 1.11.1  Metal-carbide (Table 7)

Metal-carbide (sintered metals) with a high carbide content are employed to advantage especially for molds and sections of molds, e. g. the gate region, that

Table 7   Hard metal alloy

| Trade name | Hardness (Rockwell C) |
|---|---|
| Ferro-Titanit WFN[*] | Max. 72, hardness as annealed 48–50 |

Note: Hardness approx. 68 Rockwell C at normal plastics processing temperatures; high wear resistance

[*] Trade name of Thyssen-Edelstahlwerke AG, Krefeld.

are subject to high abrasive wear when processing reinforced plastics. These materials are characterized by:

– machinability in the as-delivered state,
– hardenable to approx. 72 Rockwell C, practically without distortion,
– good polishability,
– very high resistance to wear and corrosion.

Polishing to a mirror finish is possible to only a limited extent with this material.

### 1.11.2  Materials with high thermal conductivity

Optimum temperature control in a mold is of great importance. This essentially determines the cooling and thus the cycle time and for semicrystalline thermoplastics in particular has a great effect on the tendency for distortion as well as the dimensional stability, and thus on the quality of the molded parts.

In order to improve the heat transport, i. e. the thermal conductivity, of not only small regions, but also entire sections of a mold, nonferrous metals such as

– copper,
– beryllium-copper,
– beryllium-copper-cobalt,
– zirconium-copper-chrome, etc.

have proven useful. These materials generally have a thermal conductivity several times that of tool steels, but without reaching their hardness, wear resistance, compressive strength or fatigue strength. A suitable surface coating is often a necessary prerequisite for successful use of these materials.

## 1.12  Molds for processing thermosets

Molds for processing of thermosetting molding compounds are in principle comparable with those used for processing of thermoplastics, bearing in mind, however, that peculiarities specific to these molding compounds must be taken into consideration. The basic principles and nomenclature of these molds are specified in German standard DIN 16 750. Examples 62 to 66 show thermoset injection molds.

### 1.12.1  Mold construction

Molds for processing of thermosetting molding compounds are generally heated electrically. The heat needed for the crosslinking reaction is drawn from the mold. Once in contact with the cavity surface, the viscosity of the melt passes through a minimum, i. e. the melt becomes so low in viscosity that it can penetrate into very narrow gaps and produce flash. The molds must thus exhibit very tight fits, while at the same time providing for adequate venting of the cavity. These largely opposing requirements are the reason that formation of flash cannot be completely eliminated. Molds should be designed to be extremely stiff so that "breathing" and thus deformation that promotes the formation of flash are avoided. The use of pressure sensors to determine and monitor the injection pressures, on the basis of which the mechanical properties of the mold are calculated, is recommended. Approximate values for the injection pressure are 100 to 300 bar for unsaturated polyester resins and 30 to 400 bar for amino and epoxy resins. The actually required pressure depends on the size and geometry of the molded parts. Material selection is of great importance with regard to the life expectancy of the molds, a subject which must already be addressed during the quoting phase. What was said in this regard for thermoplastics applies analogously here. Through-hardening steels are to be preferred for the part-forming sur-faces and must exhibit a resistance to tempering consistent with the relatively high operating temperatures of the molds. For molding compounds that tend to stick, e. g. unsaturated polyester resins, steels with $\geqq$ 13 % chrome content have proven useful, e. g. tool steel no. 1.2083. Since the thermosetting molding compounds are modified with sometime abrasive fillers, special attention must be given to the resulting wear. Fillers such as stone flour, mica, glass fibers and the like, for instance, promote wear. In wear-prone regions of the mold such as the gate, for example, metal carbide inserts should be provided. Other wear-prone mold components as well should generally be designed as easily replaceable inserts.

### 1.12.2  Part-forming surfaces

Both the appearance of the molded parts and the life expectancy of the mold are determined largely by the part-forming surfaces. Often, textured surfaces on the molded parts are requested. In this case, adequate draft for part release must be provided; see also Section 1.4. Texturing of mold areas particularly prone to wear should be avoided, since rework of such areas is difficult. Hard chrome plating has proven useful as a means of increasing the wear resistance of part-forming surfaces. At the same time, a certain corrosion protection is achieved.

Titanium nitride coatings increase the service life of molds noticeably. Improvements by a factor of 5 have been reported. In addition to improved wear and corrosion resistance, the few micron thick layer facilitates part release and mold cleaning. Stainless steels with more than 18 % chrome are also suitable for corrosion protection, but are limited in terms of achievable hardness.

### 1.12.3  Ejection/venting

Depending on the geometry of the molded part and type of molding compound, different amounts of draft for part release must be provided, usually between 1 and 3 °. At the time of ejection, thermoset parts exhibit very little shrinkage because of the relatively high temperature (e. g. 170 °C). As a result, parts are not necessarily retained on the mold cores, but rather may be held in the cavity by a vacuum. To avoid problems during production, measures must be taken to assure that the parts can always be ejected from the same half of the mold. As a rule, thermoset parts are not yet fully cured at the time of ejection and are thus relatively brittle. Accordingly, an adequate number of ejector pins or suitably large surface area for other ejection means should be provided to avoid damaging the parts during ejection. In addition to ejection, the ejector pins must also provide for venting of the cavity during filling. For this reason, but not only, ejectors should be located behind ribs and other deep sections where air entrapment could be expected. Forced ejection of undercuts should be avoided because of the generally inadequate toughness of thermoset molding compounds. Undercuts should be released by means of movable cores or slides, which, in addition to being designed for long-term operation, should permit easy removal of any cured resin that might possibly collect. For complicated parts with internal undercuts, fusible core technology is employed. This involves the use of low melting point alloys for cores that are inserted into the mold and then subsequently melted out of the mold parts. The vent channels should have a height of approx. 0.01 to 0.03 mm and be highly polished, so that the flash that forms there is readily removed upon ejection.

### 1.12.4 Heating/insulation

Combination heating utilizing heater cartridges for the mold plates in conjunction with frame heaters has proven useful in achieving satisfactory homogeneity. The majority of the heat is provided by the cartridge heaters, while the heated frame serves as a heat shield against the surroundings. Depending on the mold size, 30 to 40 W/kg of mold weight have been found by experience to be adequate for the required heating capacity. This heating capacity should be installed uniformly throughout the mold by using a number of heating elements. Each heating circuit should be provided with its own thermocouple, which should be placed between the heating element and the part-forming surface.

As a general principle, molds should be provided with insulating plates to prevent heat losses and the resulting temperature differences. Besides being placed between the mold clamping plates and machine platens, such insulating plates can also be positioned between molds plates and possibly even other areas of the mold. It is further possible with the aid of computer programs to simulate heating of molds and thus specify the location of heating elements. It has also proven helpful to determine the mold temperature during operation by means of thermophotography and then to use this information to make any necessary changes in new molds.

### 1.12.5 Runner/gate design

Various aspects must be taken into consideration when designing runners for thermoset processing. In general, thermoset molding compounds are not regranulated. Accordingly, an attempt should be made to keep the size of the runner system small in relation to that of the molded parts. The gate should be located such that it can be easily removed without damaging the part. All of the gate types commonly used in thermoplastics processing can, in principle, be employed. As with thermoplastic molding compounds, the type

and location of gates will affect the physical properties of the molded parts. In contrast to gates for thermoplastic injection molding, which have to be as large as possible in order to avoid material degradation as the result of shear and friction, gates for thermoset processing are intended to increase the melt temperature via friction. Thus, the appropriate gate size and number of gates must be established on the basis of the type of part to be molded and the type of molding compound to be processed.

As a rule, the molding compounds are modified by the supplier to meet the set criteria, which means that joint discussions early in the planning phase for a mold are advisable. In multiple-cavity molds, the runner channels must always be equal in length and generate equal pressure drops in order to assure identical filling conditions and uniform molded part quality. This means that attention must also be given to the direction of melt flow in the cavities. Fig. 1.10 shows an improperly designed runner system for a 24-cavity mold in which the cavities fill at different times and thus cannot fill uniformly. Balancing of the runner system can only be accomplished here by varying the cross sectional area of the gates. To achieve uniform part quality, it would have been better to design the mold with only 16 cavities and a runner system as shown in Fig. 1.11. Even though injection molding may be the most economical means of producing thermoset molded parts, there is still interest in process variations such as injection compression, for instance, which can be employed to produce very high-quality parts automatically. Injection compression combines the advantages of compression molding and those of injection molding. Example 64 shows a single-cavity mold used to produce plates. Multiple-cavity molds utizling this technique are more complex, since the molding compound must be distributed uniformly among all cavities in order to obtain uniform product quality. Fig. 1.12 shows a multiple-cavity mold with runner pinch-off. With appropriate design of the runner system, runners are pinched off during compression. Multiple-cavity molds with a common filling chamber (Common Pocket System/Bakelite) as shown in Fig. 1.13 represent relatively simple-to-build, proven designs where the molded parts have minimal flash, which is ejected along with the parts, and the sprue bushing is designed to function as a cold runner. The three-plate design (Bucher-Guyer System; Fig. 1.14) is a relatively involved design, but does permit center gating of parts, which is particularly advantageous for round parts. The so-called HTM process (High-Temperature Molding/Bakelite) represents a development in which conditions in the cavity similar to those for injection molding of thermoplastic resins are achieved during injection of thermosetting resins. While the resin in the cavity briefly becomes more fluid through contact with the heated mold (e. g. 170 °C) and thus flows into the smallest gaps and creates flash during convention thermoset processing, with the HTM process the resin is overheated in the runner system so that it cures immediately upon entering the cavity. With

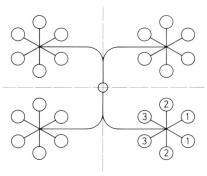

Fig. 1. 10    Improperly designed runner system for a 24-cavity mold

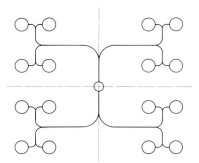

Fig. 1. 11    Runner system for a 16-cavity injection mold for parts as in Fig. 1. 10

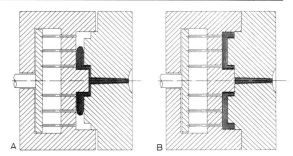

**Fig. 1. 12    Multiple-cavity injection compression mold with runner pinch-off**
A: during injection, B: closed mold

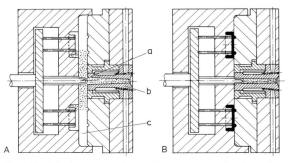

**Fig. 1.13    Injection compression mold (Common Pocket System/-Bakelite)**
A: during injection, B: closed mold
a: flow divider, b: sprue bushing, c: common pocket

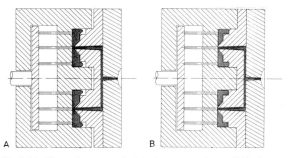

**Fig. 1. 14    Three-plate two-cavity injection compression mold (Bucher-Guyer System)**
A: during injection, B: closed mold

this type of runner system, also known as the hot-cone method, very dimensionally accurate, almost flash-free parts can be produced, above all in multiple-cavity molds. A significant reduction in cycle time is one major advantage of this technique. Fig. 1.15 shows finished parts molded using the HTM process along with the runner system. The HTM runner system is illustrated schematically in Fig. 1.16.

In a manner analagous to the use of hot-runner systems employed for processing of thermoplastic resins, so-called cold-runner systems are used to process thermoset resins. Whereas the mold plates and part-forming inserts of thermoset molds have, for instance, an operating temperature of 170 °C, which initiates curing of the material, the sprue bushing and runner channels in a cold-runner system are kept at a lower temperature by means of a circulating fluid. The temperature is set such that the material does not cure, yet still has a viscosity suitable for processing. For example, the temperature set in a cold-runner system may be $\leq$ 100 °C. Fig. 1.13 shows a sprue bushing designed to operate on the cold-runner principle.

The cold-runner system does not necessarily have to be part of the mold. It is often practical to design the machine nozzle to function as the cold runner. In this way, excellent thermal separation of the mold from the

cold runner is assured. This relatively inexpensive solution provides a well-defined break-off location and is furthermore easy to maintain. This principle is illustrated schematically in Fig. 1.17, where it can be seen how the nozzle extends into the mold, which must be suitably enlarged. With single-cavity molds, quasi-runnerless injection molding of thermoset parts is possible via this technique. In multiple-cavity molds, the cold-runner system is usually incorporated into the mold itself in a manner similar to that employed for hot-runner systems for thermoplastic injection molding. Fig. 1.18 illustrates a multiple-cavity mold with a cold-runner system located at the secondary mold parting line

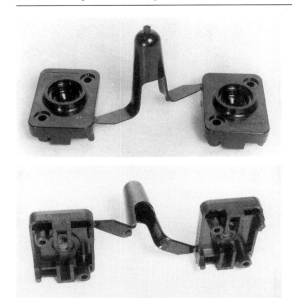

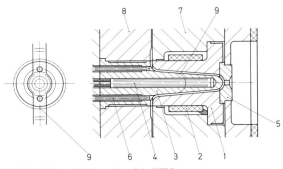

**Fig. 1. 15   Molded parts and runner system for the HTM (High-Temperature Molding/Bakelite) system; shot weight 96 g, runner 12 g, part size 45 × 70 mm**

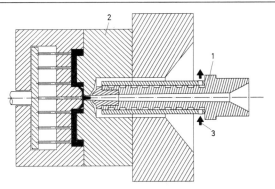

**Fig. 1. 17  Thermoset injection mold with jacketed (cold runner) machine nozzle (1) that extends into the stationary mold half (2); (3) inlet/outlet for temperature control**

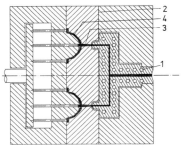

**Fig. 1. 18   Multiple-cavity mold with a cold-runner system (1) (Bucher-Guyer System) located at the secondary mold parting line (2), (3) sprue, (4) molded part**

**Fig. 1. 16   Schematic illustration of the HTM process**
1: sprue bushing, 2: spiral cartridge heaters, 3: cone, 4: heater cartridge with thermocouple, 5: locating ring, 6: ejector pin, 7/8: mold plates, 9: runner channel

(2), which can be released and opened to service the manifold block. A short sprue is required on the molded parts to connect the cold-runner system to the cavities. The gate dimension must be specified on the basis of the material to be processed. A smooth gate mark on the molded part would require use of pneumatically or hydraulically operated needle shutoff nozzles (valve gates), which entails not a few problems, however. A jacketed sprue bushing available as a standard mold component is shown in Fig. 1.19. To provide precise temperature control, the sprue channel (1) is enclosed in the cold-runner system (2) through which a fluid circulates. How the material in the sprue can be saved through such a cold-runner bushing is shown in Fig. 1.20 for a multiple-cavity mold. The contact area between the cold-runner bushing and mold should be kept as small as possible in order to reduce heat trans-

fer to a minimum. Likewise, the face of the sprue bushing should not be in contact with the movable mold half; an air gap of approximately 0.3 mm should be provided for thermal separation. Sprue bushings with an integral temperature-control jacket of the above type are also suitable for processing thermoplastics. By cooling the relatively thick sprue, which often determines the cycle time, it is often possible to improve molding efficiency in a relatively simple manner.

## 1.13  Molds for processing elastomers

Processing of elastomers is in principle comparable to processing of thermoset plastics. Both differ from processing of thermoplastics primarily in that the material is brought into heated molds, undergoes crosslinking (cures) and cannot be reprocessed. The statements made in Section 1.12 for thermoset molds thus also apply in general to molds for elastomer processing.
Nevertheless, the details of elastomer molds are special. A distinction must be drawn between processing of rubbers and silicones. For economic reasons, runnerless or almost runnerless automatic molding of largely flash-free parts with a perfect surface is expect-

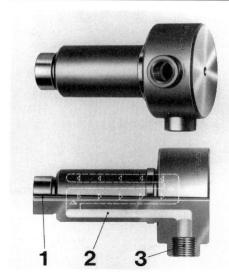

**Fig. 1. 19    Standard jacketed sprue bushing**
1: sprue channel, 2: temperature control jacket, 3: connection threads

ed here as well. The gating techniques and construction of the mold are thus of major importance and require a great deal of experience, as does compounding of the material. Today, injection molding is the dominate process for production of molded rubber parts. The state of the art as of 1987 is presented in depth in [1], along with extensive literature references.

As with thermoset processing, injection molding of elastomers developed from compression molding and transfer molding, both of which used vertical presses. For parts with fabric inserts such as automobile tires, for instance, conventional compression molding cannot be replaced even today. An injection mold for bellows made of silicone rubber is presented in Example 68. What type of mold should be employed is always a

matter of economic considerations and machinery availability. Some injection molding machines for elastomers operate vertically, which is important for mold design and removal of the molded parts. Generally, however, "normal" injection molding machines are employed, so that the mold parting line is vertical and molded part removal as well as mold cleaning during operation are facilitated. To avoid the formation of flash during processing of elastomers, which become very fluid upon injection into the cavity, molds must be very tight and ruggedly built, with clearances of less than 0.01 mm.

To vent the cavities, connections for vacuum pumps or overflow channels should be provided at all locations where material flows together. Computer-aided design of molds [2] offers significant advantages, since the items that are important for optimum process management can already be taken into consideration during the concept stage [3]. In multiple-cavity molds, the runner system must be balanced, just as with thermoplastic and thermoset molds. Cold-runner molds have, among other things, the advantage of operating at lower pressures and thus produce less flash, since the runner system is not located in the mold parting line, but in a separate manifold. Example 67 presents a 20-cavity cold-runner mold for rubber bumpers. The cold-runner principle as well as important details relating to the design of elastomer injection molds are described in [1].

Electric heating of molds is preferred, with heating elements divided into several circuits. Insulating plates should be provided between the mold and the machine platens as well as within the mold itself in order to keep the temperature within narrow limits. The mold steel must also be selected for the relatively high operating temperature of 170 to 220 °C. Chrome-alloy steels are used for part-forming sections. Often these are given an additional surface coating, e. g. chrome plating. The surface finish has an effect on the flow properties of the material processed as well as on release of the molded parts, depending on the part geometry and specific elastomeric material. A slightly roughened part-forming surface is often advantageous. Release of elastomeric parts is not without problems, since such parts are very flexible and often have undercuts. If positive ejection by means of ejector pins and air assist is not possible, the molded parts can also be removed from the cavity by an auxiliary device or robotic part extractor. For automatic production [4] of elastomeric parts in particular, positive ejection must be assured. Aspects of parts release/ejection as well as arrangement of parts in the mold in general and gating should be given consideration already when designing the parts, which can often be carried out successfully with the aid of a computer. While rubber materials generally require very high pressure because of their high viscosity in the cold runner and injection unit, processing of silicone materials, especially the addition-crosslinking two-component liquid silicones, can be accomplished with relatively low pressure (100 to 300 bar).

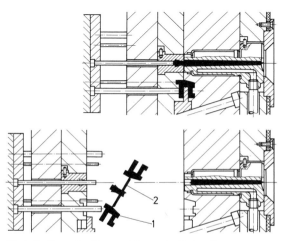

**Fig. 1. 20    Example of the use of the standard jacketed sprue bushing in a multiple-cavity thermoset injection mold**
1: molded part, 2: runner system

The low injection pressure somewhat offsets the even lower viscosity of silicones as compared to other materials as regards flash formation. Nevertheless, silicone molds must also be built extremely precisely and ruggedly. The cure times for silicones are very short, so that the cycle time is considerably shorter than for other types of rubber. Details based on practical experience are given in [5, 6] for economical production of injection molded silicone parts.

Molds for processing elastomers are in principle comparable to those for thermoplastics and thermosets. The special nature of elastomers, however, requires specific measures with regard to flow properties, temperature control and part release/ejection, so that elas-tomer processing still remains a case for specialists. With improved machine technology, optimization of material characteristics and increased use of computers, designing of molds for elastomers and processing of elastomers into precision parts poses no difficulties today.

## Literature references for Section 1.13

1 *Hofmann, W.:* Kunststoffe 77 (1987) 12, S. 1211–1226
2 *Benfer, W.:* Thesis, Aachen 1985
3 *Janke, W.:* Thesis, Aachen 1985
4 *Stegemann, U.:* Kunststoffe 73 (1983) 6, S. 295–296
5 *Merkt, L.:* Plastverarbeiter 34 (1983) 3, S. 227–230
6 *Steinbichler, G.:* Maschinenmarkt 91 (1985) 77, S. 1508–1511

# 2  Overview and classification of mold examples

| Design features | Examples |
|---|---|
| *Conventional mold* | |
| Two-plate mold | 3, 6, 7, 9, 95, 100 |
| *Split-cavity/side action mold* | |
| Split-cavity/external slides | 10 to 13, 15 to 23, 27, 29, 31 to 34, 37, 43, 44, 45, 47, 48, 60, 62, 66, 70, 76, 77, 85, 86, 89, 108 |
| Internal slides/lifters | 11, 15, 17, 37, 45, 73, 97 |
| Side cores | 12, 24, 25, 26, 45, 60, 81 to 84, 90, 96, 97, 99, 101, 106, 108 |
| Collapsible cores | 9, 72, 80, 107 |
| *Stripper plate mold* | 1, 8, 10, 14, 18, 22, 30 to 34, 41, 43, 49, 51, 55, 58, 59, 70, 72, 74, 75, 76, 79, 84, 85, 86, 102, 107 |
| Mold core on stationary side | 4, 21, 29, 46, 50, 55, 58, 75, 91 |
| *Unscrewing mold* | |
| Threaded core inserted | 27 |
| Unscrewing core | |
| Actuated via mold motion | 10, 74, 78, 81, 82, 86, 92, 102, 104 |
| Motor-actuated | 2, 18, 28, 46, 53, 65, 70, 71, 96, 98, 103 |
| *Three-plate mold* | 8, 32 to 35, 65, 66, 78, 86, 91, 92, 93 |
| *Stack mold* | 5, 15, 36 to 44, 99 |
| *Hot-runner mold* | |
| With naturally balanced runner system | 15, 36, 42, 44, 46, 49 to 55, 60, 88, 104 |
| With "conventional secondary runner system" | 11, 17, 21, 23, 26, 33, 37, 45, 47, 55, 56, 69, 75, 76, 89, 108 |
| With valve gates | 51 |
| With decompression | 36, 39, 40, 43, 44, 54, 58, 69 |
| Miscellaneous | 33, 38 to 41, 43, 48, 57, 59, 61, 70 |
| *Thermoset and elastomer molds* | 62 to 68 |
| *Special molds* | |
| Encapsulation of inserts | 16, 69, 88, 105 |
| Two-color injection molding | 87 |
| Injection-compression molds | 62, 63, 64, 95 |
| Assembly within the mold | 89 |
| *Design details* | |
| Pneumatic nozzle | 13, 73, 97 |
| Submarine gate | 2, 4, 11, 17, 21, 25, 28, 30, 32, 37, 47, 56, 69, 74, 75, 76, 81, 84, 89, 96, 101, 103, 105, 107, 108 |
| Multi-stage ejection | 1, 8, 16, 30, 45, 50, 51, 54, 56, 61, 66, 70, 85, 101 |
| Forced ejection of undercuts | 1, 11, 14, 40, 49, 50, 51, 61, 67, 68, 70 |
| Air ejection | 14, 22, 32, 36, 44, 54, 91, 94 |
| Centering of cores prior to injection | 4, 91, 101 |
| Copper/bronze inserts for cooling | 26, 32, 36, 44, 45, 48, 89 |
| Cooling pins | 26, 54, 96 |
| Core cooling via air blast | 54, 86, 101, 103 |
| Venting components | 2, 4, 12, 44, 69, 70 |

# 3 Examples

## Example 1, Single-cavity injection mold for a polyethylene cover

The cover with dimensions 141 mm × 87 mm × 12 mm high (Fig. 1) has an approximately oval shape. On the upper side, it has an inwardly projecting lip that forms an undercut around the entire part. The elasticity of polyethylene is used to release this undercut, thereby permitting release from the core without the use of complicated part release mechanisms.

### Mold

The cavity half of the single-cavity mold (Figs. 2 to 5) consists essentially of the mold plates (1, 2), the heated sprue bushing (41) and the cavity insert (46).
The mold is based on the use of standard mold components, except for the core backup plate (47), core plate (48), core ring (50) and stripper ring (49). Final and accurate alignment of the two mold halves is assured by four locating pins (37).

### Part release/ejection

The mold opens at I; the molded part is retained on the core as it is withdrawn from the cavity. As the knockout bar (14) is pushed forward, the ejector rods (33) attached to the ejector plate (7) actuate plate (3) with the attached stripper ring (49; parting line II). At the same time, plate (8) with the attached core (47, 48) moves forward through the action of the compressed springs (39).
Plate (4) with the attached core ring (50) remains stationary, because it is attached to the clamping plate (5) via the bars (6) (Fig. 5). Both the molded part and the core are now free of the core ring (50).
After a distance W, plate (8) comes up against plate (4); the core (47, 48) comes to a stop and the spring (39) is compressed further. The stripper ring, however, continues to move and can now strip the molded part off the core. During this stripping action, the rim of the molded part along which the stripper ring (49) acts is expanded. Accordingly, the stripper ring must not hold the molded part too tightly in order that this expansion not be hindered.

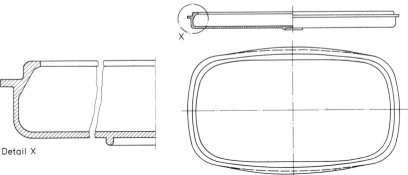

Detail X

**Fig. 1    Polyethylene (PE) cover**

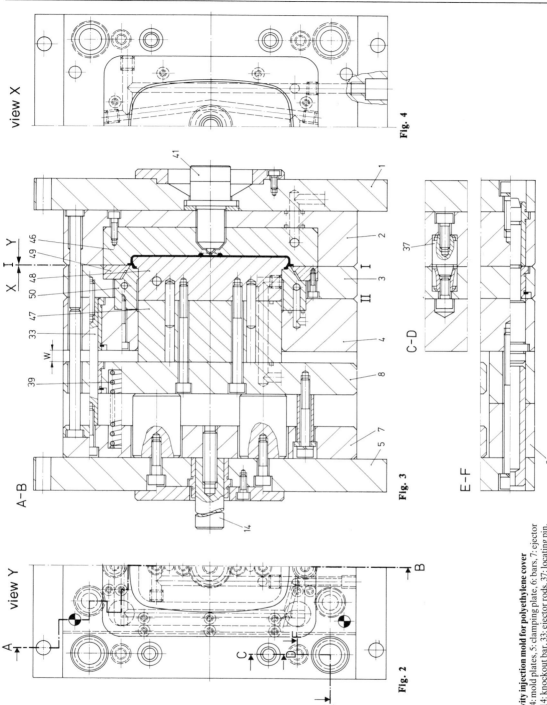

**Figs. 2 to 5    Single-cavity injection mold for polyethylene cover**
1: clamping plate, 2, 3, 4: mold plates, 5: clamping plate, 6: bars, 7: ejector plate, 8: ejector plate, 14: knockout bar, 33: ejector rods, 37: locating pin, 39: spring, 41: heated sprue bushing (Hasco), 46: cavity insert, 47: core backup plate, 48: core plate, 49: stripper ring, 50: core ring

## Example 2, Two-cavity unscrewing mold for glass-fiber-reinforced nylon (polyamide) threaded plug

The threaded plug (Fig. 1) consists of a top flange with a hexagonal recess in its upper surface. The underside of the flange has a pot-shaped section that encloses the hexagonal recess and to the bottom of which a stop pin is attached. This section is enclosed by an outer ring that carries the threads. In addition, the underside exhibits an annular groove "O" around the outer ring and intended to hold a seal. The annular space between the pot-shaped section and outer ring contains radial ribs.

**Fig. 1    Plug of glass-fiber-reinforced nylon**

### Mold

Release of the annular groove and threads is accomplished most easily by unscrewing the molded part from a threaded sleeve. The mold (Figs. 2 to 5) is designed with two cavities. Release of the threads is accomplished on the stationary mold half. The threaded sleeves (2) are located in guide bushings (10) and are driven by the gear (3) and spindle (4) of the unscrewing mechanism.

The annular core (9) forms the stop pin and, by means of a tubular extension, the annular space in the plug. A central core pin (18) provides for venting of the stop pin cavity.

The hexagonal recess is formed by the core insert (11), which also encloses an ejector pin (16). The other ejector pins (15) are used to knock out the sprue and runner.

### Gating

The location of the ejectors and unscrewing mechanism requires that injection take place into the mold parting line (5). Each plug has a single submarine gate (6) located at the flange.

### Mold temperature control

The mold plates on either side of the parting line have cooling lines encircling the mold inserts. The annular core (9) contains a double-threaded cooling pin.

### Part release/ejection

The latch (7) causes the mold to first open at parting line "I". This withdraws the annular core (9) from the underside of the plug and releases the stop pin. This motion is limited by the stop bolt (8).

The opening motion is now interrupted and the unscrewing begins. The treaded sleeve (2) is unscrewed while the hexagonal core insert (11) prevents the molded part from turning.

Upon completion of unscrewing, the main parting line "II" opens, shearing off the submarine gates. The molded part is still retained on the core insert (11); the sprue and runner are held by the undercut in the sprue puller (12). As the ejector plate (14) moves forward, the ejector pins (15, 16) eject the molded part and the sprue.

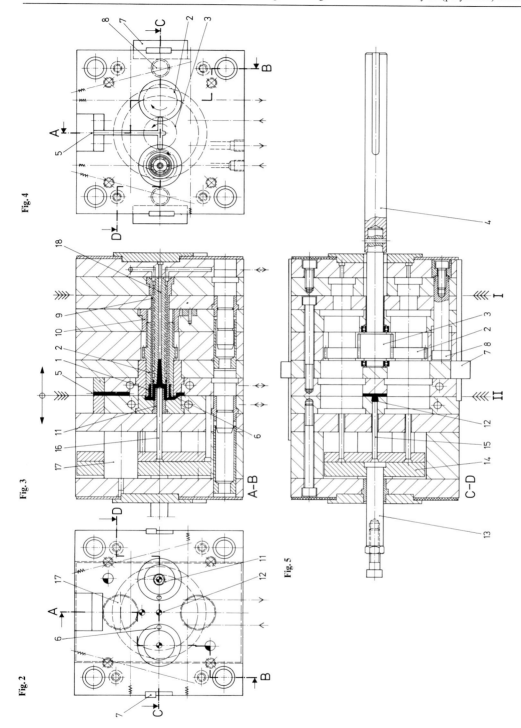

**Figs. 2 to 5    Two-cavity unscrewing mold for threaded plugs**

1: molded part, 2: threaded sleeves, 3: gear, 4: drive spindle, 5: mold parting line, 6: submarine gate, 7: latch, 8: stop bolt, 9: annular core, 10: guide bushing, 11: hexagonal core insert, 12: sprue puller, 13: ejector rod, 14: ejector plate, 15 and 16: ejector pins, 17: support pillar, 18: center pin

# Example 3, Eight-cavity injection mold for brush handles

Flat parts such as the shoe polish brush handle produced in the mold shown in Figure 1 require only a relatively simple mold design. It is practical to design the movable-side clamping plate and ejector housing (c) in such a way that it can also be used for other similar molds. The same applies to the ejector rod (d) and the ejector plate (e). The ejector retainer plate (f) will have to be made new each time, since the spacing between the ejector and push-back pins (g) and (h) respectively will differ depending on the size of the parts to be produced. In the present case, use of a sprue bushing and return pin bushing was dispensed with in order to further simplify the mold. In general, however, use of at least a sprue bushing is recommended, since the nozzle seat in the stationary-side cavity plate may be easily damaged if the machine is improperly set up and subsequent installation of a sprue bushing in this hardened plate will be difficult. With large mold plates, it is practical to have a separate locating ring (i) for the stationary-side cavity

plate (b). The advantage here is that both cavity plates can be ground flat and with parallel surfaces, which is important in view of the possibility of distortion on hardening. Because of their replaceability, guide bushings (k) should always be used, since especially in older machines that no longer provide exact guidance of the mold halves the guide pin bearing surfaces are subjected to considerable loads that may make replacement of guide bushings and guide pins necessary after a short period of time. A new bushing with a somewhat smaller inside diameter can be rapidly produced. The old guide pin can then usually be reground to be made serviceable once again. Keeping this wear in mind, the diameter of guide pins should not be smaller than 16 mm if possible. For reasons associated with grinding, a smaller diameter is also undesirable.

A locating ring for the movable-side cavity plate (a) on the clamping plate and the ejector housing (c) is impractical, because in the event of distortion on harden-

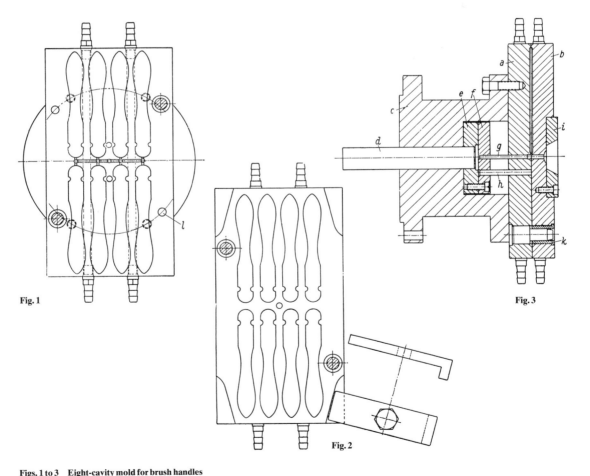

**Fig. 1**          **Fig. 3**

**Fig. 2**

**Figs. 1 to 3    Eight-cavity mold for brush handles**
a, b: cavity plates, c: movable-side clamping plate and ejector housing, d: ejector rod, e: ejector plate, f: ejector retainer plate, g: ejector pin, h: push-back pin, i: locating ring, k: guide pin, l: two locating pins

ing flat grinding of the recess is more difficult than flat grinding on a surface grinding machine. It suffices if the cavity plate ($a$) is held in the proper position on the clamping plate and ejector housing ($c$) by two locating pins ($l$). Because of their length, it is best to drill the cooling channels from both sides and provide hose connections at each end. This provides the opportunity to connect all cooling channels in series through the use of appropiate hose connections or to run them in parallel.

The well at the end of the sprue ejector pin should be provided with a slight undercut ($5°$) to ensure that the individual parts attached to the runner system are retained on the movable mold half and not in the stationary cavity plate ($b$).

# Example 4

**Fig. 1**

**Fig. 2**

**Fig. 3**

**Fig. 4**

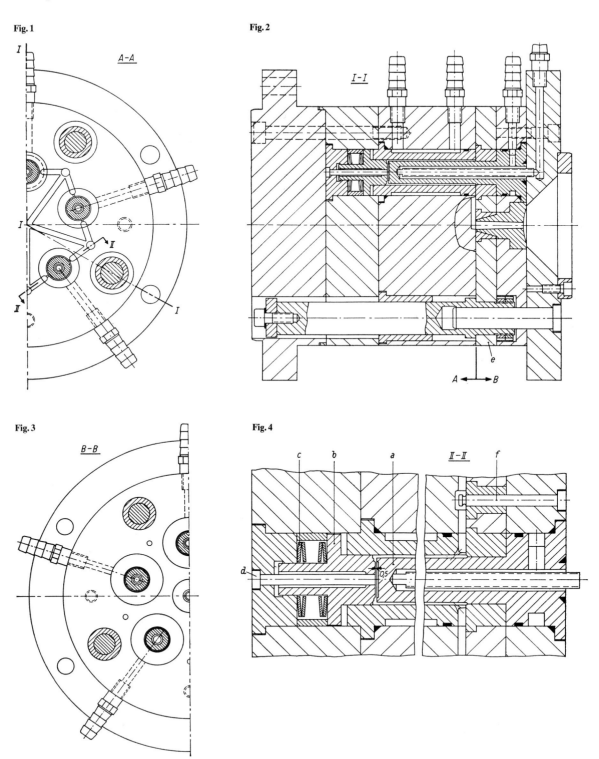

**Figs. 1 to 4    Five-cavity injection mold for long tablet tubes**
*a:* water-cooled core, *b:* movable core, *c:* spring washers, *d:* vent pin, *e:* stripper plate, *f:* sucker pin

## Example 4, Five-cavity injection mold for tablet tubes of polystyrene

It has been found that especially with tubes which are relatively long in relation to their diameter, it is extremely difficult to prevent displacement of the core and avoid the resulting variation of wall thickness with all the detrimental consequences. As the result of uneven melt flow, the core is displaced toward one side even when a centrally positioned pinpoint gate is used on the bottom.

In the following, an injection mold is described in which displacement of the core is reliably prevented. It has been determined that gating from two opposite points on the open end of the tube already leads to considerably less displacement of the core than occurs when gating on the bottom. It is useful to design these two points as tunnel gates so that they are automatically sheared on opening of the mold and eliminate the need for any secondary operations.

With long tubes, however, even this type of gating is not enough to ensure completely uniform wall thickness. The core must be held in position until the melt reaches the bottom.

This is accomplished in the mold shown in Figs. 1 to 4 as follows:

To avoid an unnecessarily long sprue, the water-cooled cores ($a$) are fastened on the stationary mold half. The face of the core has a conical recess about 0.5 mm deep into which a conical protrusion on the movable core ($b$) is pressed by means of spring washers ($c$) when the cavity is not filled. As soon as the plastics melt fills the cavity to the bottom and flows into the annular space around the protrusion, the injection pressure overcomes the force exerted by the spring washers and displaces the movable core ($b$) by an amount corresponding to the thickness of the bottom. The entire bottom now fills with melt. A vent pin ($d$) with running fit in the movable core ($b$) to permit the compressed air to escape is provided to ensure that the melt will flow together properly at the center of the bottom.

As the mold opens, the spring washers assist in ejecting the tablet tubes from the cavities as well as in shearing off the two tunnel gates. The tubes are supposed to be retained on the cores, from which they are stripped by the stripper plate ($e$) during the final portion of the opening stroke. The runner system is initially retained by undercuts on the sucker pins ($f$). However, as soon as the stripper plate ($e$) is actuated, the runner system is pulled off the sucker pins ($f$) and drops out of the mold separated from the molded parts.

## Example 5, Twelve-cavity injection mold for blouse hangers

So-called disposable hangers are part of the purchase with men's shirts, women's blouses, etc. They are produced by the injection molding process exclusively, as any other manufacturing means would prove far too expensive.

These hangers consist of as thin walled a carrier as possible, usually of T-section, with a central hole for the hook. In most cases the hole is arranged in the direction of the mold parting plane, which means that comparatively few hangers can be accommodated because the core pulling for the bore requires much space in the parting plane. As the hangers require relatively large tools due to their length and hence need correspondingly large machines, there is usually a striking disproportion between actual injection capacity required and the necessary machine size, which cannot even remotely be utilized.

The mold design according to Figs. 1 to 3 offers the advantage of incorporating as many hangers as possible in one tool, so that the injection capacity of the relatively large machine can be fully utilized. In this case hangers and hooks are produced in the same mold, resulting in considerable savings in mold-production costs.

The mold has been constructed as a stack mold, i.e., there are two parting lines. The runner system is located in the parting line facing the fixed half and the hangers are injected through pinpoint gates on the inside of the boss. The hangers lie in the moving-half plane with the hole axis in the direction of the ejector. This arrangement makes it possible to accommodate 12 hangers at approximately 18 mm spacing within the place available between the tiebars of the machine.

The upper sides of the hangers are profiled into plate ($a$), which is displaceable on the guide strips ($b$) in the opening direction of the machine until halted by stops on these strips. The hooks are partially profiled into the other side of plate ($a$). They are injected through their spheres by pinpoint gates from the runner situated in that parting line. The gates must be substantial enough to demold the hooks without breaking when this parting line opens and the runner is forcibly ejected.

The other halves of the hooks are partially arranged in plate ($c$), which also accommodates the runner man-

**Example (pages 26–27)**

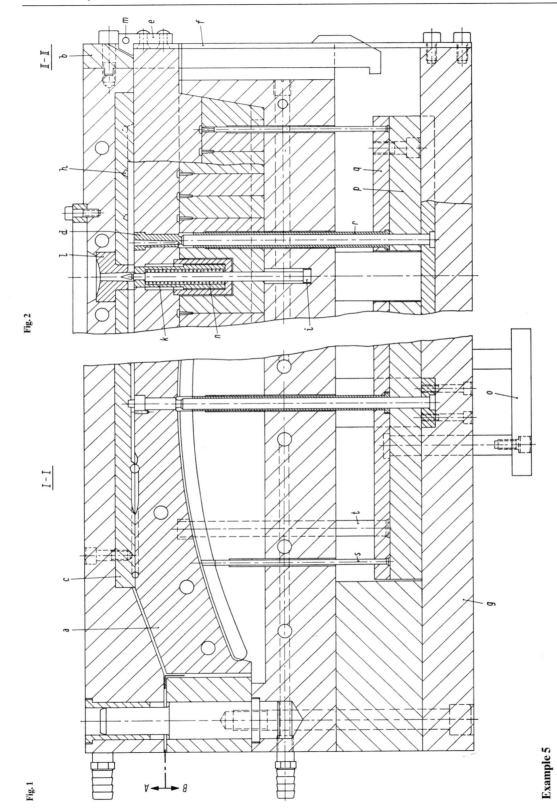

Fig. 2

Fig. 1

## Example 5

**Figs. 1 and 2   Twelve-cavity injection mold for blouse hangers, secs. *I – I* and *II – II***
For an explanation of terms refer to Fig. 3

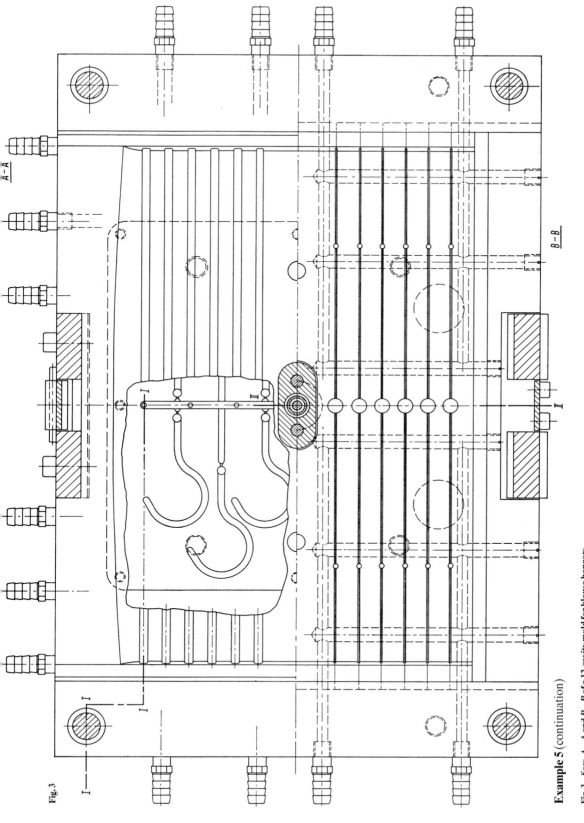

**Example 5** (continuation)

**Fig. 3    Secs. *A – A* and *B – B* of a 12-cavity mold for blouse hangers**

*a*: cavity plate, *b*: guide strips, *c*: runner plate, *d*: core inserts, *e*: interlocking latches, *f*: leaf springs, *g*: mounting plate, *h*: undercut bores, *i*: sprue retainer, *k*: ejector bushing, *l*: sprue bushing, *m*: release pins, *n*: spring, *o*: ejector bushing, *p, q*: front and rear ejector plate, *r*: sleeve ejector, *s*: ejector pins, *t*: push-back pins

ifold. Conical bores from this runner to the core inserts (*d*) lead right up to the bore of the hangers, where they enter the mold cavity through a pinpoint gate of approximately 1.2 mm diameter at less than 45°.

Plate (*a*) is interlocked with the moving mold half, when the tool is closed, via the locking latches (*e*) and the leaf springs (*f*) riveted to them. The leaf springs are bolted together with the mounting plate (*g*) on the moving mold half. During opening the mold therefore initially opens at the runner. The gates on the hanger are severed and the sprues pulled out of their bores. The runner is initially retained on the fixed half by undercut bores (*h*) in plate (*c*).

The center of the runner system is held captive by the sprue retainer (*i*) on the moving half. This retainer is allowed to move along for a distance approximately equal to the length of the secondary sprue before it contacts a stop. The ejector bushing (*k*) travels the same distance before it encounters its stop. The runner parting line continues opening for a distance of altogether approximately 150 mm, until the plate (*a*) contacts the stops of the guide strips (*b*). During this travel the main sprue is pulled from the sprue bushing (*l*).

After an opening distance of 150 mm in the runner parting line the latches (*e*) are released as the release pins (*m*) run onto the 45° cams on the guide strips (*b*) and the mold opens in the main parting line, which houses the hangers. From that moment on the sprue retainer (*i*) pulls out from the undercut in the main sprue and the runner is ejected by the forward movement of the ejector bushing (*k*) under pressure of spring (*n*). Once the mold has opened sufficiently far in the main parting line in which the hangers are positioned, the ejector plate (*o*) contacts the machine ejector and the ejector plates (*p*) and (*q*) are pushed forward. The hangers are now ejected by sleeve ejector (*r*) and ejector (*s*).

Push-back pins return the ejector plates when the mold closes. With three cycles per minute, which is easily attainable on a machine with screw plasticizing, 2000 hangers and hooks per hour can be produced.

# Example 6, Mold base with interchangeable inserts to produce standard test specimens

Component testing, product development and short production runs often require injection molded parts that have been produced under defined and reproducible conditions. Conventional molds have long mold change times, with the disadvantages of lengthly idle times and excessive residence time of the melt in the barrel. Purging of the melt would mean a material loss that could not be justified with the often small quantities of expensive experimental materials.

In order to avoid these disadvantages, a mold base was developed that meets all of the requirements with regard to processing, economy and reliability of operation. This mold base with interchangeable plug-in inserts is also suitable for production of flat molded parts, e. g. gears, small plaques etc., and is characterized by the following features.

The mold cavity is located in the interchangeable mold plate (1) on the ejector side (plug-in insert). The cavity is machined only into this plate, which seals against a flat mating plate (2) bolted to the stationary-side clamping plate. The plug-in inserts can be removed and stored without any aids within approximately one minute. The weight of each plug-in insert is approx. 6 kg.

## Mold temperature control

The cooling lines for mold temperature control are located in the plug-in insert and mating plate. Self-closing quick disconnects (3) in the supply lines facilitate replacement of the inserts. With a suitably sized mold temperature control unit, the insert reaches operating temperature after only 8 shots thanks to optimum positioning of the cooling lines.

## Cavity pressure and cavity wall temperature

Cavity pressure and cavity wall temperature are measured and recorded along with additional important process variables. Only similar test specimens are produced in a given insert. The mold design permits simultaneous filling of all cavities and is based largely on the use of commercially available standard mold components. The materials used, heat treatment (core 64 RC) and surface treatment (CVD for the mating plate, surface 72 RC) assure high wear and corrosion resistance.

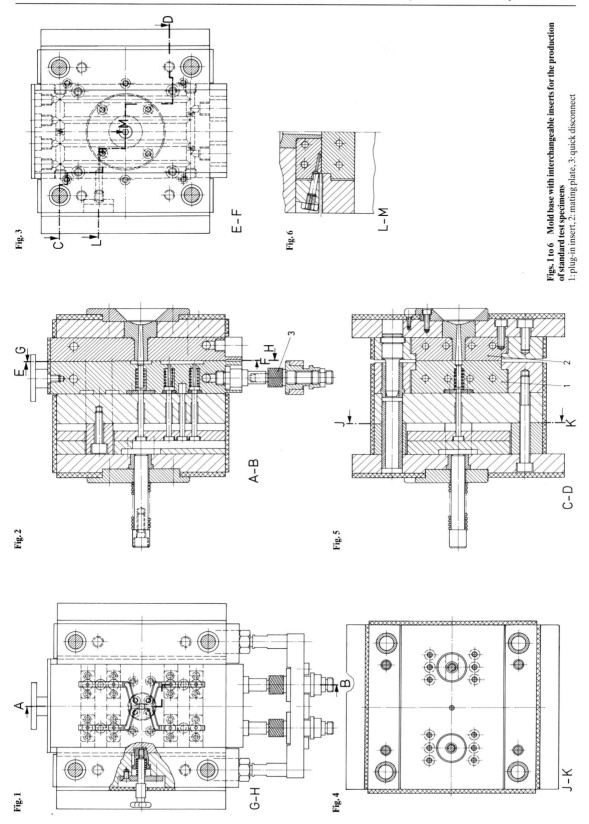

Fig. 3

E – F

Fig. 6

L – M

Fig. 2

E ↑ G

F ↑ H    3

A – B

Fig. 5

J

2

1

K

C – D

Fig. 1

A

G – H

Fig. 4

B

J – K

**Figs. 1 to 6    Mold base with interchangeable inserts for the production of standard test specimens**
1: plug-in insert, 2: mating plate, 3: quick disconnect

## Example 7, Injection mold for cover components of ABS

When designing a mold, not only the properties of the material to be processed but also constructional aspects should be taken into consideration in order to keep the mold costs low. In the present case, the objective is to build an injection mold for the production of cover components of ABS. The mold is to be designed using standard mold components. The molded part should exhibit as few changes in wall thickness as possible in order to facilitate filling of the mold.

The resulting design uses a sprue and runner with pinpoint gating (see Figs. 1 to 3). An additional requirement was to provide especially good cooling. Accord-

ingly, the inserts ($a$) and ($b$) in the stationary mold half were each provided with a peripheral cooling circuit ($k_1$). In addition, insert ($a$) was provided with spiral cooling ($k_2$) and insert ($b_1$) with bubbler-type cooling ($k_3$). The cores ($c$) and ($d$) in the movable mold half are provided with peripheral and bubbler cooling. To prevent deflection of the support plate ($e$), support pillars ($g$) are placed between the clamping plate ($f$) and the support plate ($e$). The return spring ($h$) retracts the ejector ($i$) from the mold parting line, thereby ensuring that the parts can fall freely.

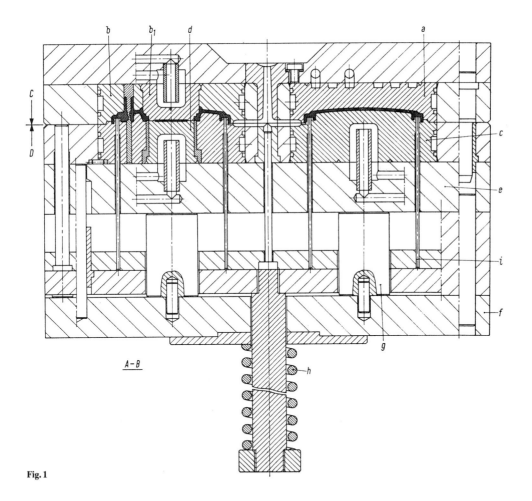

**Fig. 1**

**Figs. 1 to 3   Two-cavity injection mold for cover components of ABS, designed using standard mold components**
$a$, $b$, $b_1$: inserts in stationary mold half, $c$, $d$: cores in movable mold half, $e$: support plate, $f$: clamping plate, $g$: support pillars, $h$: return spring, $i$: ejector, $k_1$ to $k_3$: cooling channels

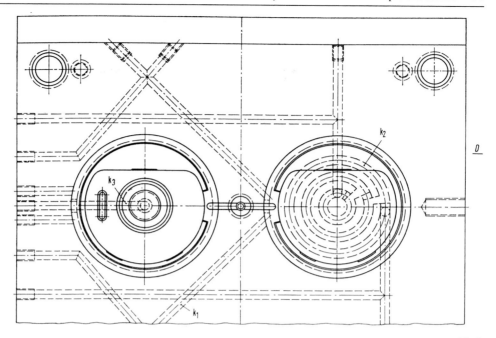

Fig. 3

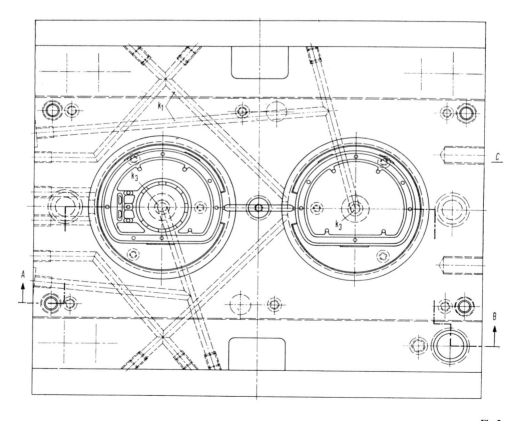

Fig. 2

# Example 8, Six-cavity mold for measuring spoons

The considerations that led to the design of a six-cavity mold for measuring spoons will be discussed in example 8.

The requirement was to achieve a guaranteed output of 1600 measuring spoons per hour from an automatic injection molding machine with a maximum plasticating capacity of 8 kg/h. For economic reasons, the number of cavities in the mold was to be kept as small as possible. For reasons associated with melt flow, the part had to be gated at the center of the bottom of the spoon, since after test molding with the gate on the handle the bowls of the spoons split too easily along the resulting weld line.

Although a four-cavity mold would have been adequate to produce the required quantity with a readily achievable seven shots per minute, a six-cavity mold was designed. This was done on the one hand with a view to providing a certain reserve capacity with respect to the required quantity, but above all because of the complicated part removal situation in the self-degating mold that was needed in this case. With a six-cavity mold, the guaranteed production rate could be achieved with $4^{1}/_{2}$ shots per minute, so that 13.5 s were available for a molding cycle. With favorable cooling possibilities for the thin-walled measuring spoon, this provided sufficient time to ensure that the runner system and six measuring spoons could drop safely out of the mold. The 1600 pieces per hour, including the runner, require a plasticating capacity of 6.4 kg/h, so that even in this regard the machine plasticating capacity of 8 kg/h provides a certain reserve.

Figures 1 to 7 show the mold design. The measuring spoons are arranged in two rows of three spoons each, with a pinpoint gate at the center of the bottom of each spoon.

In order to ensure good cooling of the cores used to form the bowls of the spoons, an inside ejector, which would have been adequate, was not used. Rather, the cavity plate on the movable half was designed to function as a stripper plate. Since, however, the parts cannot fall from this plate automatically because of the cavities engraved for the handles, a spring-loaded ejector 2 mm in diameter was provided at each handle to knock the individual spoons out of the flat handle cavities in the stripper plate after this plate had stripped the bowls of the spoons off the cores. To ensure trouble-free production of the mold, individual drawings of the mold components were prepared.

**Example 8**

**Figs. 1 to 7   Six-cavity mold for a measuring spoon**
1: nut, 2: ejector plate, 3: ejector rod, 4: movable side clamp plate, 5: core plate, 6: rear ejector plates, 7: bar, 8: front ejector plate, 9: return pin, 10: ejector housing, 11, 12: cavity plates, 13: socket head hex bolts, 14: stripper plate, 15: stationary side clamp plate, 16: socket head hex bolts, 17: locating ring, 18: sprue bushing, 19: spring bumper pads, 20: compression spring, 21: socket head hex bolts, 22/23: O-ring, 24: gasket, 25: guide strips, 26: cooling water connection, 27: round head bolts, 28: locating pin, 29: leaf spring, 30: rivet, 31: latch, 32: release bar, 33: socket head hex bolts, 34: cooling water tube (bubbler), 35: O-ring, 36: compression spring, 37: spring-loaded pin, 38: ejector pin, 39: core, 40: core pin, 41: runner insert, 42: guide pin, 43: set screw, 44: guide bushing

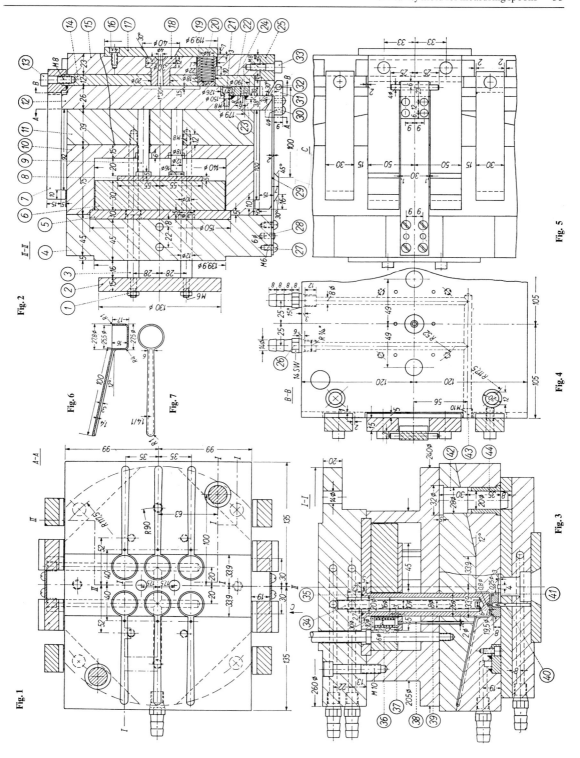

Fig. 1
Fig. 2
Fig. 3
Fig. 4
Fig. 5
Fig. 6
Fig. 7

# Example 9, Injection mold for magnifying glass frame with handle

Examples of injection moldings with inner peripheral grooves are frames for spectacles and magnifying glasses (Fig. 4). Grooves may also be required for instrument housings that have to be glazed. In standard practice, two solutions exist for designing articles of this nature.

– The part of the mold in which the groove is formed (actually a plate) is divided into four segments that are withdrawn in pairs with the aid of toggles.
– While it is still capable of plastic deformation, the injection molded part is forced out of the segment of the mold in which the groove is formed.

The first case demands a mold of complicated design and therefore incurs high costs. Owing to the toggles and pivots required, it is susceptible to breakdown. In the second case, the rough treatment of the molded part may cause easily deformation of the groove. This entails high reject rates, or, if correction is possible, considerable expense.

The design shown in Figs. 1 to 3 overcomes both disadvantages. It represents a two-cavity mold for the production of magnifying glass frames. At four points on the outside of the molded part, there are small lenticular protrusions: three on the frame itself and one on the handle. They allow a grip for the ejector pins (11) and are subsequently removed.

There is a spiral slot on the plate (19) in which the peripheral groove is formed. The slotted plate is secured in the center by two bolts with hemispherical heads. A helical spring is thus formed. When the molded part is ejected, this spring is withdrawn from the peripheral groove without causing any deformation.

A mold of this comparatively simple design has given good results in practice.

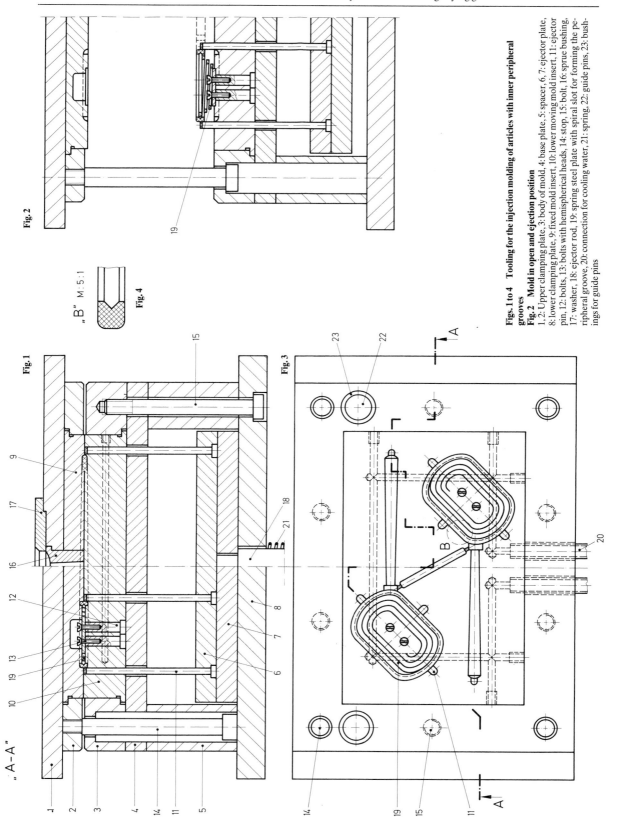

Fig. 2

Fig. 1

Fig. 3

Fig. 4

„B" M:5:1

„A–A"

**Figs. 1 to 4   Tooling for the injection molding of articles with inner peripheral grooves**

**Fig. 2   Mold in open and ejection position**

1, 2: Upper clamping plate, 3: body of mold, 4: base plate, 5: spacer, 6, 7: ejector plate, 8: lower clamping plate, 9: fixed mold insert, 10: lower moving mold insert, 11: ejector pin, 12: bolts, 13: bolts with hemispherical heads, 14: stop, 15: bolt, 16: sprue bushing, 17: washer, 18: ejector rod, 19: spring steel plate with spiral slot for forming the peripheral groove, 20: connection for cooling water, 21: spring, 22: guide pins, 23: bushings for guide pins

# Example 10, Two-cavity injection mold for a glue dispenser

A two-cavity injection mold is presented for a glue dispenser with internal and external threads. An unscrewing core forms the internal threads; the external threads are formed by a split cavity.

## Molded part

The PE-HD glue dispensers are screwed onto PE-LD bottles and have been designed for dropwise application of glue. A PE-HD cap screwed onto the dispenser seals the bottle (Figs. 1 and 2).

**Fig. 1    Glue bottle with dispenser and threaded cap**
Top: threaded cap, center: dispenser, bottom: bottle

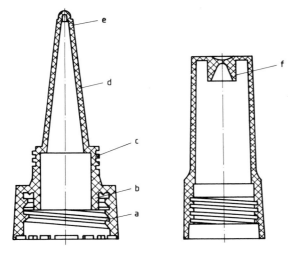

**Fig. 2    Dispenser (left) and threaded cap (right)**
a: internal thread, b: tapered seal, c: external thread, d: dispensing tube, e: tip, f: conical seal

## Mold

The two-cavity mold shown in Fig. 3 features two fixed cores (9) to shape the internal contours of the molded part. These are located within rotating threaded sleeves (10) with integral gearing engaged by a pinion (20).

The threaded cores (10) are guided axially by threaded bushings (12) the lead thread of which has the same pitch as that of the internal threads in the dispenser.

The pinion (20) is fitted onto a coarse-threaded bronze bushing (21) which is held in two tapered roller bearings (19) in the moving mold half for ease of turning. A steel spindle (17) is threaded into the bushing (21). The spindle is held in the stationary half of the mold.

The external thread (c) on the dispenser is formed by a split cavity (6). The split cavity halves are part of the moving mold half and open sideways. A total of four cam pins (23) which are held in the fixed mold half operate the split cavities. Heel blocks (24) hold the split cavity halves in place, thus relieving the cam pins when the mold is clamped. The cavity halves also accommodate the pinpoint-gated runners from the sprue bushing to the two cavities. A plug (Z) at the end of the sprue serves as a sprue puller.

At the end of the molding cycle, the mold opens along parting line I, because the solidified molded parts on the cores and in the cavities prevent the mold from opening at parting line II at this stage.

The spindle (17) is now moved axially inside the bushing (21) during this opening phase, turning the bushing and the pinion on it. The pinion, in turn, turns both threaded cores, which are now unscrewed from the internal threads in the molded parts. The molded parts are prevented from turning by 0.5 mm deep grooves in the faces of the two grooved bushings (7).

With the opening of parting line I, the cavity halves also begin their opening movement, so that the molded parts adhere only to the face of the grooved bushings once parting line I is fully open.

Two roller chains (25) have also become stretched with the opening of the first parting line. These chains are adjustable in position between the ejector plate (22) and the clamping plate (28) on the fixed half.

Parting line II now opens and, with the aid of the conical sleeves (8) fitted into it, the ejector plate strips the molded parts and runners off the grooved bushings. The opening stroke of parting line II is limited by the stop bolts (16).

The pinion has 100 teeth and the threaded cores 40 a piece. The axial position of each threaded core can thus be adjusted by 1/40th of the thread pitch.

To take up play in the coarse-threaded bushing, the spindle (17) can be turned by its square head and held in position by the adjustment washer (26). The play of the tapered roller bearings can be adjusted with the aid of the lock bolt clamping ring (18).

The arrangement of the unscrewing mechanism chosen has the advantage that the mold is quickly operational once it is installed in the machine. With such designs, however, care must be taken that the coarse-threaded spindle does not protrude too far from the center of the machine, because it transmits a pitching moment to the moving platen during mold opening.

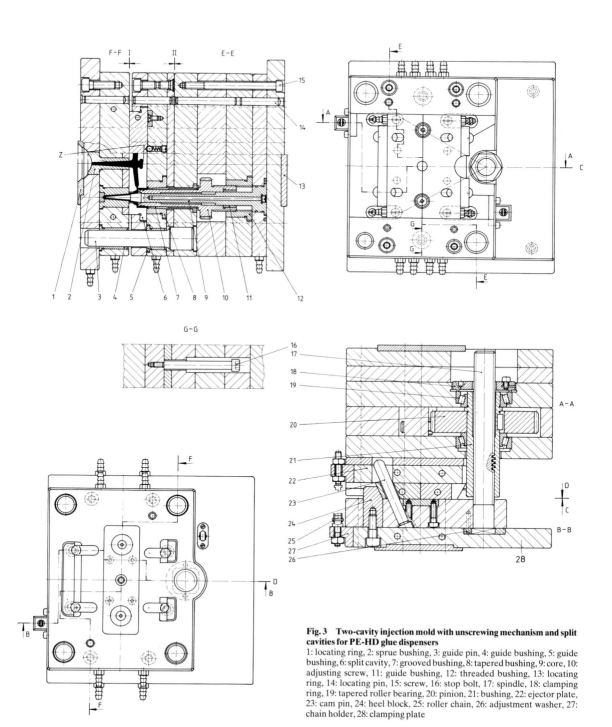

**Fig. 3  Two-cavity injection mold with unscrewing mechanism and split cavities for PE-HD glue dispensers**
1: locating ring, 2: sprue bushing, 3: guide pin, 4: guide bushing, 5: guide bushing, 6: split cavity, 7: grooved bushing, 8: tapered bushing, 9: core, 10: adjusting screw, 11: guide bushing, 12: threaded bushing, 13: locating ring, 14: locating pin, 15: screw, 16: stop bolt, 17: spindle, 18: clamping ring, 19: tapered roller bearing, 20: pinion, 21: bushing, 22: ejector plate, 23: cam pin, 24: heel block, 25: roller chain, 26: adjustment washer, 27: chain holder, 28: clamping plate

## Example 11, Four-cavity injection mold for a housing of acrylonitrile-butadiene-styrene (ABS)

The four-cavity mold is used to produce two each of the upper and lower half of a cosmetic device housing. The two halves of the housing are joined together by means of snap fits. These hook-shaped connections form internal and external undercuts on both parts that are released by lifters.

### Mold (Figs. 1 to 3)

The four cavities are arranged in a rectangle at the mold parting line (Fig. 3). The mold inserts (11, 14) are made of hardened steel; the lifters (7, 8, 20) are case-hardened.

The lifters move sideways in the ejector plates (9, 10) and are attached to slide blocks (12) that run in corresponding guide grooves. The four leader pins for the two mold halves as well as the guide pins for the ejector plates are not shown in the drawing.

Mold dimensions are 296 mm × 547 mm, with a mold height of 290 mm. The mold weighs approximately 280 kg.

### Runner system/gating

The melt flows from a heated sprue bushing (13) through an H-shaped runner system to the four submarine gates feeding into the cavities (Figs. 1, 3).

### Mold temperature control

The cavity inserts are provided with cooling channels for temperature control, while the cores contain bubblers in which baffles (19) assure that the cooling water is directed to the tip of the bubbler well. The temperature in the cavity inserts is monitored with the aid of thermocouples (16).

### Part release/ejection

Upon opening of the mold, the molded parts and runner system are retained on the core half. As soon as the machine ejector actuates the ejector plates (9, 10), the runner system and molded parts are released and pushed off the cores by the lifters (7, 8, 20) and ejectors (17). The submarine gates shear off, while the lifters release the undercuts formed by them.

Inside the housing halves (H) there is an undercut boss formed by the end of a core pin (18) and the surrounding hole in the core insert. The core pin (18) is fitted into the core insert with a certain play (V). As the parts are ejected, this pin is carried along by the molded part until the boss is clear of the hole in the core insert. The core pin (18) now stops and the boss is stripped off the end of the core pin by the remaining ejector motion. Before the mold closes, the ejectors must be pulled back.

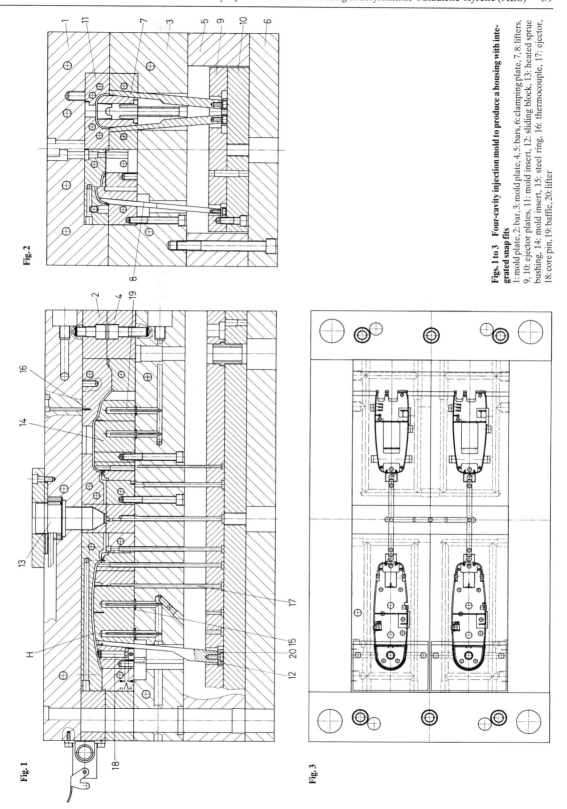

Fig. 2

Fig. 1

Fig. 3

**Figs. 1 to 3   Four-cavity injection mold to produce a housing with inte-
grated snap fits**

1: mold plate, 2: bar, 3: mold plate, 4, 5: bars, 6: clamping plate, 7, 8: lifters,
9, 10: ejector plates, 11: mold insert, 12: sliding block, 13: heated sprue
bushing, 14: mold insert, 15: steel ring, 16: thermocouple, 17: ejector,
18: core pin, 19: baffle, 20: lifter

## Example 12, Four-cavity injection mold for a nozzle housing of polyamide (nylon)

The nozzle housing for a windshield washer system has three interconnected channels and two external mounting clips. Core pulls and slides are required to release the molded parts.

The nozzle housing (Fig. 1) is used to distribute the water coming from the water pump to the two spray nozzles of an automobile windshield washer system. The hose from the pump is slipped over the conical tip on the end of a tubular extension A. The channel in this extension divides inside the housing into two channels D that lead to the spray nozzles. A hook H and a snap spring F are used to attach the housing. The ribs R serve to stiffen the tubular extension.

### Mold

The mold (Figs. 2 to 4) contains four cavities. To release the hook and snap springs, four pairs of slides (12, 13) actuated by cam pins (28) are used. The cavity surface is formed by the slide inserts (32). The slides are held in place in the closed mold by the heel blocks (9) and wear plates (10).

The channels D are formed by core pins that are attached to a total of eight slides (22). The cam pins (18) are employed to actuate the slides, while the pins (26) hold the slide (22) in place when the mold is closed.

The channel in the tubular extension A is formed by the core pin (19), the conical tip of the extension by the bushing (23). The adjacent core pins (19) and bushings (23) on one side of the mold are attached to a bridge (15, 16). The base of the cylinder (24) is also bolted to the center of the bridge between the two core pins. The rod of cylinder (24) is attached to the backup plate (4). To pull the core pins (19) the piston in the cylinder is pressurized and the cylinder, along with the bridge and core pins, moves away from the mold. The bushings are held in place by the pins (25).

The cavity insert (21) is made of through-hardened steel, while the slide inserts (32) and slides (22) utilize case-hardened steel.

The drawings were produced on a CAD system; Figs. 2 to 4 two dimensionally (2 D), Fig. 1 three dimensionally (3 D).

### Runner system/gating

The melt flows from the sprue bushing (11) into the mold via an H-shaped runner system through the cavity insert (21) to a pinpoint gate at the parting line associated with each pair of slides and enters the cavity at the hook H of the molded part (Fig. 3).

### Mold temperature control

Cooling channels in the plates (1, 3 and 4) are provided for mold temperature control.

### Venting

The ejector pin (31) is located in the cavity where air entrapment may occur. It thus also aids in venting.

### Part release/ejection

Part release and ejection are accomplished by means of a latch mechanism (17) and stripper bolt (27) not described in further detail.

The mold first opens at parting line I, at which point the gates shear off the molded parts and are pulled out of the cavity insert (21). The runner system is held on the sucker pins (30). The cam pins (18) actuate the slides (22), which withdraw the short core pins from the molded parts.

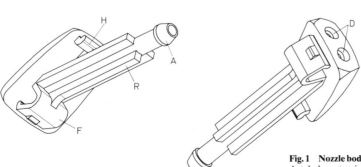

**Fig. 1   Nozzle body for an automobile windshield washer system**
A: tubular extension, D: channels, F: snap spring, H: hook, R: rib

As the mold opens at parting line II, the slides (12, 13) on mold plate (4) are spread apart by the cam pins (28). At the same time, the undercuts on the hooks and the snap springs are released along with the pins (25) blocking the hydraulic side cores, so that the core pins (19) can now be withdrawn. The parts are now ejected by ejectors (29) and (31).

Finally, the runner stripper plate (2) is actuated by the stripper bolts (27) (parting line III) and the runner system is stripped off the sucker pins (30).
Before the mold closes, the ejectors must first be retracted and then the hydraulic cores set.

**Fig. 2**

**Fig. 4**

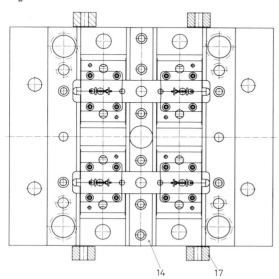

**Fig. 3**

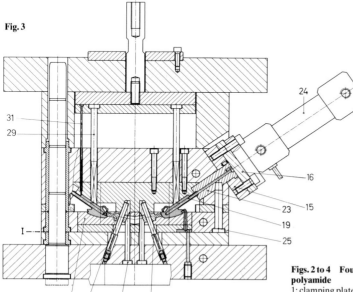

**Figs. 2 to 4    Four-cavity injection mold for a nozzle housing of polyamide**
1: clamping plate, 2: runner stripper plate, 3: mold plate, 4: backup plate, 5: bar, 6: clamping plate, 7, 8: ejector plates, 9: heel block, 10: wear plate, 11: sprue bushing, 12, 13: slides, 14: slide guides, 15, 16: bridge, 17: latch mechanism, 18: cam pin, 19: core pin, 20: runner plate, 21: cavity insert, 22: slide, 23: bushing, 24: hydraulic cylinder, 25, 26: locking pins, 27: stripper bolt, 28: cam pin, 29: ejector, 30: sucker pin, 31: ejector pin, 32: slide insert

# Example 13, Single split cavity mold for a threaded plug of polyoxymethylene

The threaded plug is a cylindrical body 65 mm in diameter and 23 mm high with a trapezoidal thread having a pitch of 3.5 mm. A split cavity is used to form the threads. The necessary number of split cavity segments depends on the thread pitch and its profile as well as on the material used to mold the part.

Fig. 1 shows the plan view of a thread having a rectangular profile. If one attempted to form this thread in a split cavity with two halves, i. e. the parting line lay in the plane of the figure, the mold would damage the thread upon opening, because of the undercuts at the positions H.

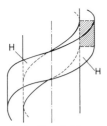

Fig. 1    Thread with rectangular profile (plan view)

The more the flanks of the thread profile are angled (trapezoidal/triangular thread), the smaller are these undercuts. With injection molding, the size of the undercut is decreased by the shrinkage of the resin up to the moment of ejection. In addition, many resins are still elastic enough to withstand minor deformation without damage. If in spite of all these factors the undercut is still too large, the number of segments forming the split cavity must be increased.

The investigation of the situation with regard to undercuts and the determination of the necessary number of cavity segments is best carried out with the aid of a computer which can be used to search out the regions endangered by the undercuts on the basis of the thread geometry.

## Mold

The present mold (Figs. 2, 3) has four cavity segments (1) each of which is actuated by two cam pins (2). The cavity segments are guided on the mold plate (3) and when closed are held in position by means of wear plates (4) attached to the mold plate (5). The mold is constructed of standard mold components.

## Runner system/gating

The part is gated centrally via the pneumatic nozzle (6).

Operation of the nozzle is described in Example 97. The sprue (8) in the nozzle tip (7) is attached to the molded parts via 2 pinpoint gates next to the central hole.

Before the mold opens, the sprue (8) is separated from the molded part and ejected by actuating the pneumatic nozzle (6).

## Part release/ejection

As the mold opens, the four cavity segments (1) are spread apart by the eight cam pins (2) and the threads are released. Now the ejectors (9) can strip the molded part off the core.

Ejection takes place hydraulically via the molding machine. The molded part is blown off the ejectors (9) by a blast of air.

## Mold temperature control

The mold plates (3) and (5) as well as the cavity segments (1) are provided with cooling channels. The hollow core (10) contains a cooling insert (11) with grooves to guide the cooling water.

**Fig. 2**

A – B

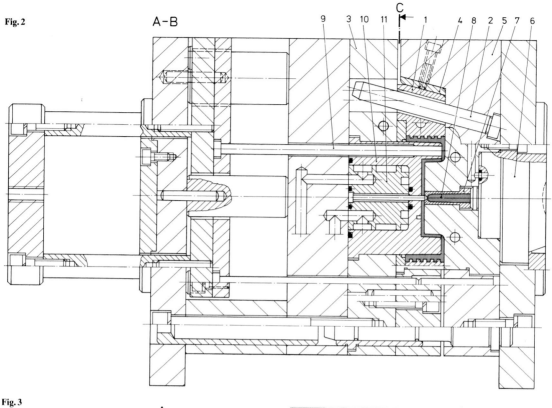

**Fig. 3**

view C

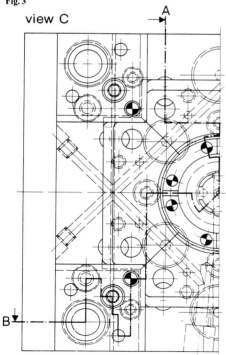

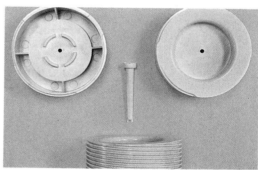

**Fig. 4  Threaded plug with sprue**

**Figs. 2 and 3    Single split cavity mold for a threaded plug of POM**
1: cavity segments, 2: cam pin, 3: mold plate, 4: wear plate, 5: mold plate,
6: pneumatic nozzle, 7: nozzle tip, 8: sprue, 9: ejector, 10: hollow core,
11: cooling insert

## Example 14, Molding a container with external undercuts

The twenty-liter container (US Patent 4648834) shown in the mold drawing (Fig. 1) has several external rims that normally require side action in the mold to be released.

Such side action increases the cost of a mold considerably and this example shows that with clever use of the shrinkage of the molded part and for moderate undercut depth mold costs and manufacturing time can be saved while simplifying mold handling (weight, volume, mechanics).

### Mold

The mold consists of a cavity half (1) and a core half (2) which are guided by means of leader pins (3) and aligned with respect to one another by means of a taper lock (4).

A ring (5) that forms the underside of the rim on the outside of the container is attached to the cavity half (1).

Stripper rings (7, 8) that give the shape of the external undercuts move on guide pins (6) attached to the core (2) and passing through the tapered alignment section (4). Stripper ring (7) is actuated by ejector rods (9), while stripper ring (8) is attached to stop bolts (10) that limit its motion.

### Part release/ejection

Part release and ejection are described in Fig. 2 in four steps.

### Step I

The mold has opened. The molded part and core have separated from the cavity.

### Step II

The stripper ring (7) is pushed forward by the ejector rod (9). The molded part is pushed off the core, while

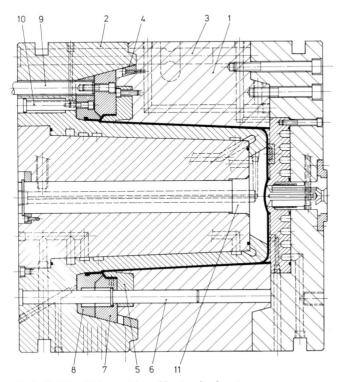

**Fig. 1    Mold for a 20-liter container with external undercuts**
1: cavity half, 2: core half, 3: leader pin, 4: taper lock, 5: ring, 6: leader pin, 7: stripper ring, 8: stripper ring, 9: ejector rod, 10: stripper bolt, 11: valve insert

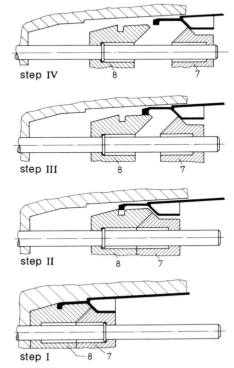

**Fig. 2    Ejection sequence**

the undercuts continue to pull stripper ring (8) along. The taper of the core now releases the inner surface of the molded part, the diameter of which decreases as the result of shrinkage, so that the rim formed in the ring (8) can now be snapped out of the recess. The ring (8) now stops.

## Step III

Stripper ring (7) now completely pulls the rim on the molded part out of the ring (8).

## Step IV

Ring (7) comes to a stop. The molded part is ejected by air.

The air used to eject the part is directed to the inside through the valve insert (11). Before the mold opens, compressed air is forced under the bottom edge of the container through the cavity half in order to facilitate removal from the cavity.

## Example 15, Injection mold with reduced opening stroke for milk crates

Beverage crates (US Patent 4731014) usually have a grid-like structure of their exterior surfaces as a result of the stacking rim, reinforcing ribs and handles, the release of which requires the injection mold to have external slides (side action). If the slides are located in the stationary cavity half of the mold, the opening stroke required equals twice the crate height plus the axial stroke of these slides in order to be able to eject the molded part.

The ejection principle described here needs less opening stroke. It is thus well suited for especially deep parts or for stack molds.

The milk crate shown in Fig. 1 has dimensions of 300 mm × 300 mm and a height of 280 mm. Its grid-like structure forms external undercuts.

Figs. 2 to 4 illustrate the ejection principle along with the additional possibility of releasing internal undercuts (on the core).

The mold (Fig. 2) consists of the core (1) with core lifters (2), cavity bottom plate (3) with sprue bushing (4) and the cavity frame (5) with movable external slides (6). The cavity frame (5) can be moved in the direction of mold opening by means of hydraulic cylinders (7).

During opening (Fig. 3), the cylinders (7) hold the bottom plate of the cavity (3) and cavity frame (5) together. The molded part (8) is held in the cavity by virtue of its external undercuts; the core (1) is withdrawn. Any

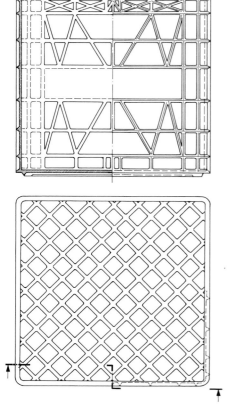

**Fig. 1   Milk crate**

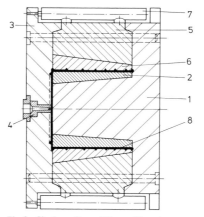

**Fig. 2   Single-cavity mold for a milk crate**
1: core, 2: core lifters, 3: bottom plate of cavity, 4: sprue bushing, 5: cavity frame, 6: external slides, 7: hydraulic cylinders, 8: molded part

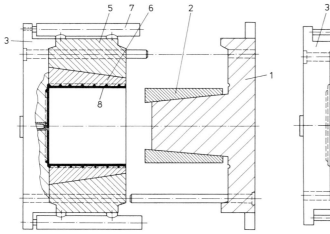 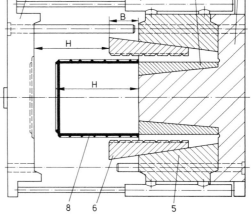

**Figs. 3 and 4    Single-cavity mold for a milk crate**
1: core, 2: core lifters, 3: bottom plate of cavity, 4: sprue bushing, 5: cavity frame, 6: external slides, 7: hydraulic cylinders, 8: molded part

undercuts on the inside of the molded part are released by the displacement of the core lifters (2) on the core (1). The molded part can now shrink freely and now becomes smaller than the cross section of the core. The cylinders (7) now push the cavity frame (5) toward the core (Fig. 4). The rim of the molded part – which is now smaller – now pushes against the core lifters (2) or core (1) in which case the core lifters (2) – if present – are pushed back.

The external slides (6) located in the cavity frame (5) do not follow the axial movement of the frame until they are far enough apart to release the exterior contour of the molded part (8). The molded part can now drop free.

The opening stroke of the mold is thus only somewhat larger than the crate height H plus the distance B required for the side action.

**Stack mold**

If this ejection principle is employed with a stack mold, the reduced opening stroke can be used twice.

A two-cavity stack mold is shown in Figs. 5 to 7. The bottom surfaces of the molded parts face one another at the center of the mold. Melt reaches the hot runner manifold (9) at the center of the mold via an extended shutoff nozzle (10) that extends through a core and an opening in the bottom of a crate. Each crate is gated along the bottom at four locations.

The opening motion of the mold is controlled by means of racks (11) and pinions (12).

The mold has dimensions of 813 mm × 813 mm with a height of 864 mm (crate height: 280 mm). The opening stroke is 660 mm. The maximum open daylight required in the molding machine is thus 1524 mm.

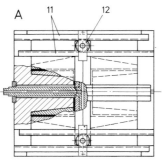  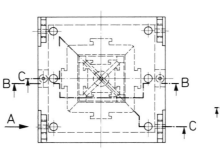 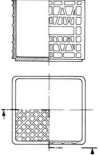

**Fig. 5    Two-cavity stack mold for milk crates**
11: rack, 12: pinions

B–B

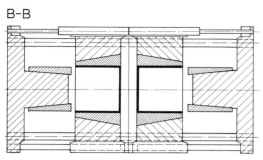

**Fig. 6   Opened mold**

C–C

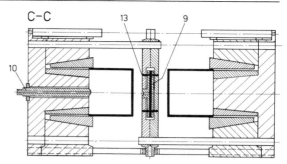

**Fig. 7   Part demolded**
9: hot runner, 10: shutoff nozzle, 13: gate

# Example 16, Two-cavity injection mold for recessed refrigerator handles of polyamide

A two-cavity injection mold had to be made for injection molding recessed handles for refrigerators of polyamide reinforced with 35 wt. % glass fibres. The recessed handles (Fig. 1) have a grooved internal structure, three flat channels from the outside to the inside, two metal inserts to be encapsulated, and recesses, into which the case of the refrigerator door engages when the handle is mounted.

## Construction of the mold (Figs. 2 to 5)

Because of the function of the molded part the main axis of the handle indentation is set at an angle of 45°

to the recesses which engage with the case walls. Since the recesses and the attached and encapsulated metal inserts are to demold on opening the mold (Fig. 2), an ejection motion with an angle of less than 45° to the handle must release the molding from the core (11). Further, a mechanical slide (13) is required for releasing the flat channels and the beaded edge of the mold.

## Ejector mechanism

The handles must be pushed away from cores (11) without any tilting; thus, hydraulically operated ejectors are not acceptable since, because of possible differences in forward motion, they do not guarantee exactly parallel guidance. It was decided to operate the ejector by means of rack and pinion mechanisms (23), which are driven through pinions (19), shaft (25), external gear wheel (21), and racks (24), by the opening movement of the mold. In order to ensure the necessary delay in the ejector motion until release of the molding by the mechanical slide (13), the block (39) in the top half of the mold, which encloses the outer racks (24), runs

**Fig. 1   Recessed refrigerators handles of polyamide reinforced with 35 wt. % glass fibres and two metal inserts**
top: front, bottom: rear

freely along a distance of 24 mm in the recess in the mold plate on the nozzle side, until meeting the stop. The loosely inserted spring (42), which is tensioned by mounting the mold on the machine, acts as support. Only when the block (39) is stopped by the spring (42) on the opposite side does the relative movement of the outer rack (24) begin, rotating the outer gear wheels (21), which again operate the internal rack drive.

The block (39), outer racks (24), outer gear wheels (21), and spring (42) were economically mounted in milled grooves on the top side of the mold, partially enclosed by the cover plate (41). The shafts (25) were mounted in bearings (36) under the outer gear wheels (21) to maintain a low bending moment in the spindles. Their exact position is achieved by bearings, fitting the inner racks (23) to the actual ejector (32); as well as by mutual displacement of the outer racks (24) made possible by means of slotted holes in these. The racks are finally connected to the block (39) by pins (40). Subsequently, the outer racks are finally calibrated along their length in order to ensure a precisely defined ejector position in the case of a closed mold.

The slides (13) are made of steel with material no. 1.2541, while the mold components (10, 11, 12) utilize steel no. 1.2343.

## Runner

The sprue opens into an S-shaped runner formed in the cavity block (12). The S-shape provides a central sprue for both cavities, which are displaced because of the rack and pinion ejector mechanism. An overlapping gate connects with a central lug of the respective molded part, which is concealed when the handle is mounted, so that the mark caused by this is not obtrusive.

## Mold operation

As the opening motion begins the mechanical slides (13) are moved outwards by the cam pins (15) and release the three flat channels. Simultaneously, the sprue begins to be released from the sprue bushing (31). After an opening distance of 24 mm the open recesses of the molded part and the metal inserts are withdrawn from their cores. Then the motion of the outer racks (24) begins relative to the ejector-side mold half. The ejectors (32) are advanced, effecting a movement of the molded part at an angle of 45° to the mold axis. The resulting movement vertical to the mold axis pulls off the overlapping gate. The axial component of the ejection movement carries with it the strip (10), such that after a distance of 14 mm the recesses formed by the strip (10) are also released. The moldings are now pushed further until they fall from the core (11). Finally the sprue, which in the meantime has also been fully released, is also ejected by the machine ejector through the sprue ejector (27).

On closing the mold, the spring (42) ensures that the ejectors (32) have returned before the mold finally closes. The return pins (28) for the sprue ejector have the same effect, but in this case synchronously with the closing action.

## Example 16

Figs. 1 Two-cavity injection mold for recessed refrigerator handles of polyamide
Figs. 2 to 6  Two-cavity injection mold for recessed handles for refrigerators

1: moving-half base plate, 2: ejector frame, 3: moving-half mold plate, 4: core retainer plate, 5: fixed-half mold plate, 6: fixed-half base plate, 7: ejector plate, 8: fixed-half locating ring, 9: ejector retaining plate, 10: strip, 11: core, 12: cavity block, 13: slide, 14: ejector plate, 15: cam pin, 16: guide pin, 17, 18: guide bushing, 19: pinion, 20: spring, 21: gear wheel, 22: feather key, 23, 24: rack, 25: shaft, 26: sliding block, 27: sprue ejector, 28: return pins, 29: ejector rod, 30: retainer, 31: sprue bushing, 32: ejector, 33: bolt, 34, 35, 36: bearing, 37: stop screw, 38: locating slide, 39: block, 40: pin, 41: cover plate, 42: spring, 43: stop, 45: spacer block

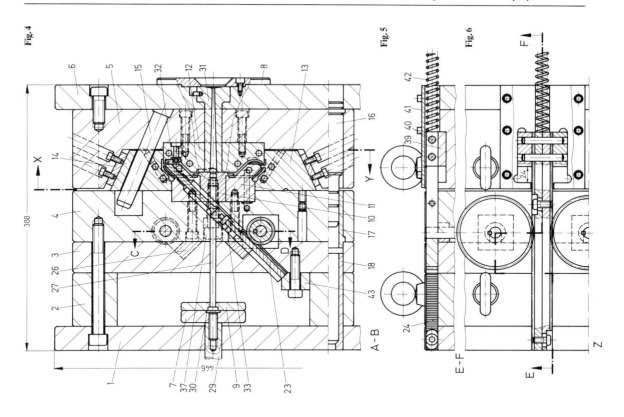

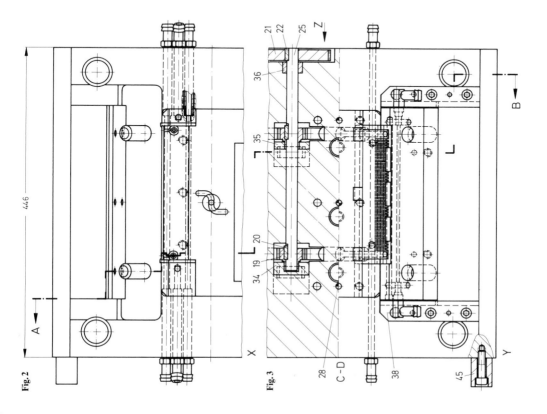

# Example 17, Injection mold for a grass catcher of polypropylene

The grass catcher consists of two halves that are produced in a common mold and joined to one another by means of snap fits. A metal rod that functions as a hinge for the grass catcher cover is inserted when assembling the two part halves. The plug-in connection at the handle is secured by means of a self-tapping screw. The weight of the molded grass catcher (without steel rod and screw) is 1525 g, with wall thicknesses ranging between 2.5 and 4.5 mm. The outside dimensions are 440 mm × 370 mm × 315 mm. Injection molding machines with a clamping force of 10,000 kN are required to produce the grass catcher halves.

**Fig. 1    Grass catcher of polypropylene for a lawn mower**
Company photo: IBS-Brocke

The injection mold shown in Fig. 2 is 1100 mm high, 790 mm wide and 884 mm long. The opening stroke is approximately 800 mm. With about 300 individual components, the total weight is 4.3 t.
Both grass catcher halves have been oriented in the mold in such a manner that the interiors are formed by cores (5, 6). The ejectors are located on the core half.
The screen-like sections at the back of the grass catcher are formed by two mechanically actuated slides (39). In addition, two small slides (41) that are also mechanically actuated serve to release the undercuts associated with the snap hooks in this area. Two additional snap hooks for the rear screen-like section are formed by the slide in this mold half. Undercuts in the direction of draw in the interior of the grass catcher are released by a total of six lifters (26, 27) which simultaneously push the parts off the cores (5, 6) during ejection.

## Runner system/gating

Each grass catcher half is filled via two submarine gates located on the outside lower surface and connected to a four-arm runner system. This runner system is machined into the core half and connected to the machine nozzle via a heated sprue bushing (35, 36). The heated sprue bushing has five heaterbands (37) with a total heating capacity of 500 W.

## Mold temperature control

Water lines 15 mm in diameter are provided wherever possible for mold temperature control. Connections to this system of water lines are made via quick-disconnect fittings. Sections in which it was not possible to place water lines are cooled via bubblers.
An insulating plate is attached to the mold clamping plate (1) on the stationary half in order to avoid the undesirable heating of the machine platen by the heat lost from the heated sprue bushing (35, 36).

## Part release/ejection

In addition to the lifters (25, 27) already mentioned above, (34) ejector pins have been provided. The ejector plates (9) and (10) are located and guided by means of guide pins (19) and bushings (20). To increase the rigidity of the mold, the ejector housing contains seven support pillars (21) in addition to the spacer bars (7).

**Fig. 2    Injection mold for producing both halves of a grass catcher simultaneously**
1: mold clamping plate, 2, 3: cavity insert, 4: core retainer plate, 5, 6: core insert, 7: spacer bar, 8: base plate, 9: ejector plate, 10: ejector retainer plate, 11: stationary-side locating ring, 12: movable-side locating ring, 13: ejector rod, 14: leader pin, 15: guide bushing, 16: insert, 17: return pin, 18: spring washers, 19: guide pin, 20: guide bushing, 21: support pillar, 22, 23, 24, 25: sliding plate, 26, 27: lifters, 28: guide block, 29: sliding stone, 30: insert, 31: ejector, 32: sleeve, 33: extension, 34: ejector retainer bushing, 35, 36: heated sprue bushing, 37: heater band, 38: insert, 39: slide, 40: cam pin, 41: slide
*a:* shown without insert

**Fig. 2**

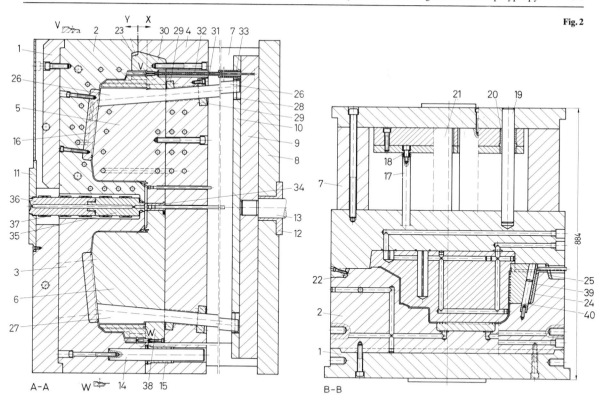

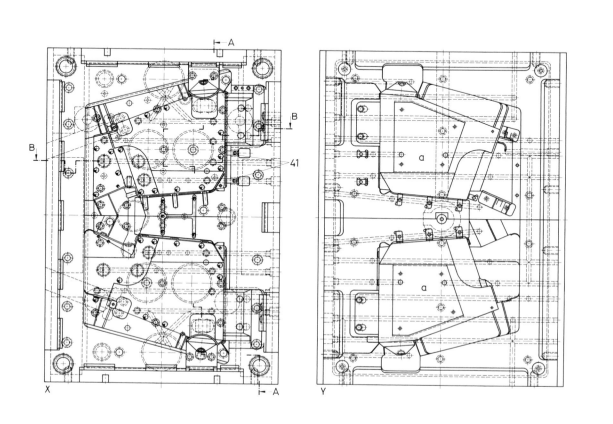

# Example 18, Injection mold for hose connectors of polyamide (nylon) 6.6

The object of the hose connector illustrated in Fig. 1 is to connect extensions to garden or household hoses which are too short or to repair broken ones. It consists of a center section and two compression nuts. The center section is designed as an outer cylinder with a concentric inner segment attached to it by means of a ring-shaped rib midway along the length of the part. Starting at this rib, the inner segment tapers conically to each end. The outer cylinder is provided with internal threads at either end (see Section C–D, Fig. 4). The ends of the hose are pushed over the conical section, to be compressed against them and clamped by the compression nuts. A single-cavity mold is used to produce this center section on an injection molding machine with a vertical injection unit.

## Mold

Threaded cores (13, 14) are installed in the fixed as well as in the moving half of the mold (Figs. 3 to 6). These cores can be synchronously operated by means of the gears (35, 36, 37) and splined shaft (38), which extends through both mold halves. They are driven by an unscrewing unit attached to the shaft of the threaded core (13), which protrudes centrally from the fixed mold half. Slides (11, 12) are moved by cam pins (41) to release the outer surface of the molded part. The cavity is filled from above through a sprue machined into the mold parting line and the faces of the slides.

## Operation of the mold

Once the molding compound has cooled sufficiently, the threaded core (13) is driven directly by the unscrewing unit via the shaft (19) and is unscrewed from the internal thread of the molded part with the aid of the threaded bushing (17) and lead threads on the threaded core (13). The turning motion of the core (13) is simultaneously transmitted to the core (14) by gears (35 to 37) and the splined shaft (38). Through the action of core (14), whose direction of rotation is opposite that of core (13) due to the idler gear (36), and with the aid of threaded bushing (23) and the lead threads on the core (14), the threads in the moving half of the mold are released.

Upon completion of unscrewing, the mold opens, the slides (11) and (12) releasing the outer surface of the molded part and the sprue. Finally, the molded part – still sitting on the cooled inner core (22) – is stripped off the latter by the stripper plate (15) and ejected. Once the stripper plate (15) has been returned by the hydraulic ejector of the molding machine and the cores (13) and (14) have been reset, the mold closes and another cycle begins.

**Fig. 1    Three-piece hose connection**

**Fig. 2    Single-cavity injection mold for the center section of a hose connector**

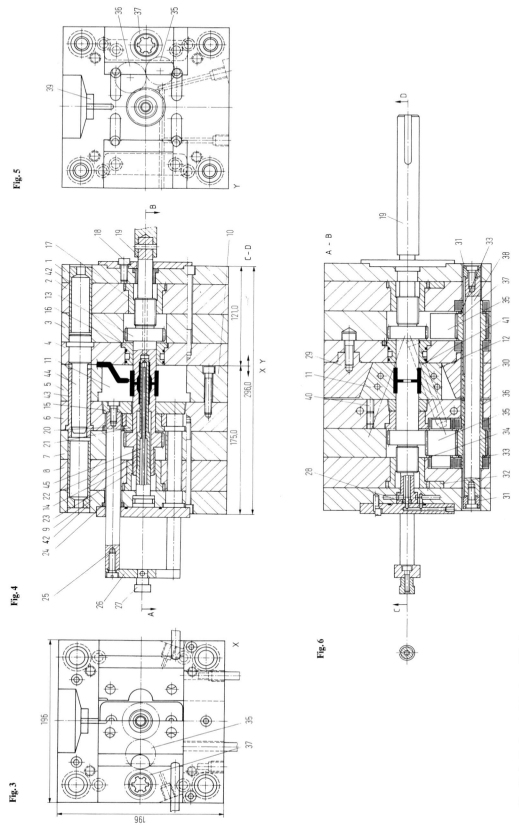

**Fig. 5**

**Fig. 4**

**Fig. 3**

**Fig. 6**

**Figs. 3 to 6  Single-cavity injection mold for the center section of a hose connector**

11, 12: slides, 13, 14: threaded cores, 15: stripper plate, 17: threaded cores, 19: shaft, 22: inner core, 23: threaded bushing, 35, 36, 37: gears, 38: splined shaft, 41: cam pin

# Example 19, Two-cavity injection mold for the coil form of an auxiliary relay

On the coil form for an auxiliary relay, sharp-edged guidance of wires and feed-through openings as well as parting line flash on the coil form surface had to be avoided. Since the flange edges of the coil form must not be distorted, large square ejectors were employed. Flash formation in the coil area can only be prevented from occurring at the parting line between the slides (16) and (17) by precision guidance and completeness

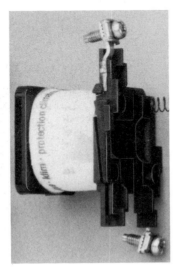

Fig. 1    Coil form for an auxiliary relay

of shutoff. Wear plates (18) and (19) have been provided to compensate for any possible wear during the time the mold is in operation; if required, these plates can be replaced.

## Mold operation

Operation of the slides is essential for forming the area taken up by the coil as well as for releasing the undercuts on the connecting flange of the coil. The ejector system of the molding machine is actuated only after the mold has opened completely at the parting line D/E, when the slides (16) and (17) are retained in their final position by the detents (15). The coil forms, now resting freely on the mold cores (13), can be ejected by the large square ejectors (24). These ensure that the coil form is not distorted during ejection. The sprue, which still adheres to the coil form and also lies in the parting line between the slides, is simultaneously ejected by the ejector pins (25). By being interlocked with the machine controls, the microswitch (32) mounted on the ejector housing (5) prevents the injection molding machine from closing the mold before the ejectors (24) and (25) have been retracted completely. Only then is the microswitch actuated by the stop (33) connected with the ejector plates (7) and (8). This precaution prevents still protruding ejectors from being bent over by the slides with the result that the mold cavity surface in the slide would be destroyed. In addition, check scales verify that the sprue and molded parts have been completely ejected from the mold.

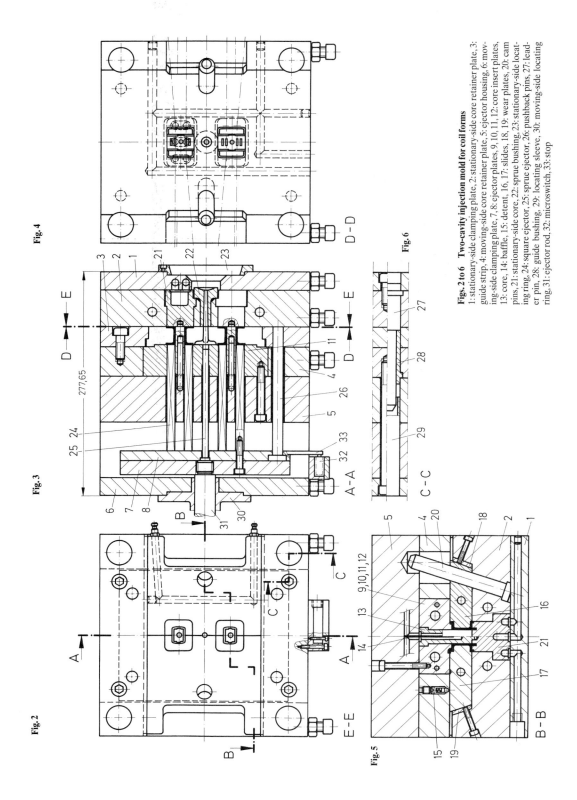

Fig. 4

D - D

Fig. 6

Fig. 3

Fig. 2

Fig. 5

A - A

C - C

B - B

E - E

**Figs. 2 to 6    Two-cavity injection mold for coil forms**

1: stationary-side clamping plate, 2: stationary-side core retainer plate, 3: guide strip, 4: moving-side core retainer plate, 5: ejector housing, 6: moving-side clamping plate, 7, 8: ejector plates, 9, 10, 11, 12: core insert plates, 13: core, 14: baffle, 15: detent, 16, 17: slides, 18, 19: wear plates, 20: cam pins, 21: stationary-side core, 22: sprue bushing, 23: stationary-side locating ring, 24: square ejector, 25: sprue ejector, 26: pushback pins, 27: leader pin, 28: guide bushing, 29: locating sleeve, 30: moving-side locating ring, 31: ejector rod, 32: microswitch, 33: stop

# Example 20, Injection mold for a housing of polypropylene

The housing is relatively complicated in design and must furthermore be molded with high dimensional accuracy. Four mounting holes are positioned around the outer edge and together with the sealing lip around the edge are ribbed to improve rigidity. Two rounded partitions are located inside the housing, the larger of which is slotted on the sides. In addition, the side of the housing has a rectangular opening with a lip for welding. The material to be used is polypropylene.

The two-cavity mold is shown in Figs. 1 to 7 and has two slides (a) that form the rectangular openings in the side of the housings by means of the side cores (b) and an interconnecting opening between the curved partitions by a cylindrical core pin (c). The inside surface faces the injection side and is formed primarily by the core insert (d), which is held against the core plate (f) by the core retainer plate (e). Inserts (g) and (h) are used to form the curved partitions and are held against the clamping plate (j) by the insert retainer plate (i). The outside of the housing faces the ejector side and is formed by the cavity insert (k). The parts are molded via a sprue (l) and a conventional runner system in the main parting line I–I and are edge-gated.

It should be noted above all that, because of the sealing lip around the edge, the slide (a) must pass through the cavity insert (k) on the movable side. The resulting bridge (m) is designed as a separate component and is screwed to the insert (k).

The mold uses three cooling circuits.

Cooling circuit A:
This circuit consists of the channels in the movable-side cavity inserts (k) and is reached via extension tubes.

Cooling circuit B:
This circuit is located in the stationary-side core inserts and consists of several channels.

Cooling circuit C:
The inserts (g) and (h) used to form the curved partitions are cooled by channels with baffles (n). The cooling medium for the series-connected core cooling circuit is supplied through channels in the clamping plate (j).

The mold first opens at parting line II–II, since the latch (o) holds plates (e) and (f) together. In this manner, the curved partitions are released first while the mold is closed (main parting line). This measure is necessary because the wall thickness of the partitions and their shape do not permit the use of sleeve ejectors. After the curved partitions have been released, the latch (o) is disengaged and permits the mold to open at the main parting line I-I. To facilitate the opening motion of the slides, four spring-loaded rods (p) providing a force of 1000 N each act on the core retainer plate (e). The slides (a) are actuated by the cam pins (q) and release the molded parts after a stroke of 50 mm. The upper slide is held by a spring catch (r), which is actuated by a rod (s).

The molded parts are ejected by a number of ejector pins (t) and ejector sleeves (u). The ejector sleeves (u) act at the mounting holes. Mold plates (e) and (f) move along the guide pin (w) and are held by the stop bolt (v) after being unlatched. Stop bolt (v) must be of adequate size, since it must withstand the entire opening force of the slide (a).

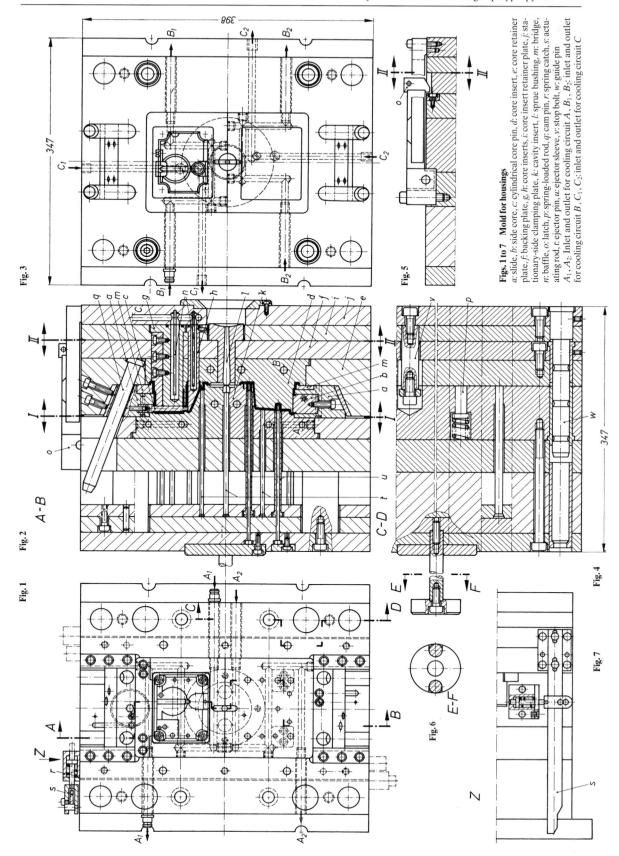

Fig. 3

Fig. 5

Fig. 2    A - B

Fig. 1

Fig. 4    C-D

Fig. 6    E-F

Fig. 7

**Figs. 1 to 7   Mold for housings**

a: slide, b: side core, c: cylindrical core pin, d: core insert, e: core retainer plate, f: backing plate, g, h: core inserts, i: core insert retainer plate, j: stationary-side clamping plate, k: cavity insert, l: sprue bushing, m: bridge, n: baffle, o: latch, p: spring-loaded rod, q: cam pin, r: spring catch, s: actuating rod, t: ejector pin, u: ejector sleeve, v: stop bolt, w: guide pin $A_1$, $A_2$: Inlet and outlet for cooling circuit A, $B_1$, $B_2$: inlet and outlet for cooling circuit B, $C_1$, $C_2$: inlet and outlet for cooling circuit C

# Example 21, Four-cavity injection mold for producing a thrust screw of polyacetal[1]

A thrust screw with a 1″ pipe thread (Fig. 1) had to be produced out of polyacetal (POM). Mechanical rigidity and dimensional accuracy were required, but above all, a low unit price was of importance. Due to the price constraints and also for the sake of transferring the

**Fig. 1   Sprue and runner system of the four-cavity mold (left) for producing the 1″ pressure nut**
Company photo: Arcu, Altermo/Sweden

melt in good condition, four mold cavities were arranged in a square for these externally threaded parts, contrary to the usual in-line arrangement. In this way, the volume of melt in the runner system could be reduced considerably below half of that required for the in-line system.

In the case where mold cavities are arranged in-line, the molded parts are released by having the two slides move apart symetrically with respect to the center line. Cavities arranged in a square, however, require an additional movement to release the threads. An unconventional solution has been found in a delay mechanism with angled guide (29) which retains the molded parts in their position during the first stage of the opening sequence, while the cores (31) are being withdrawn. During the next phase of ejection, the outer slides (27) are pulled and the outer halves of the threads on the four nuts are released. In the third phase, the outer slides pull a slide plate (25) to one side, demolding the thrust screws from the shared center bar (26).

1  from Plastforum 12 (1981) 3, pp. 50/53

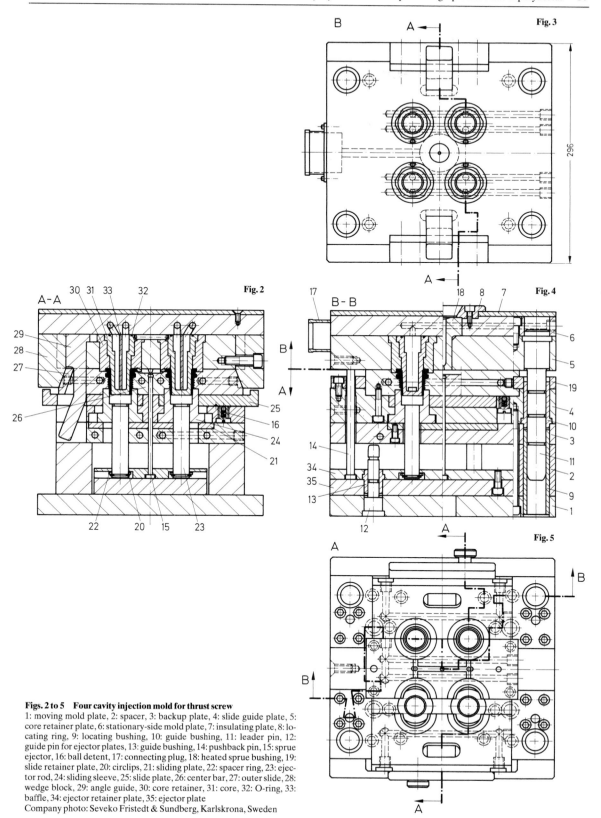

B    A ◄ ⋯    **Fig. 3**

296

A ◄ ⋯

**Fig. 2**

A–A

30  31  33    32

29
28
27

26

25
16
24
21

22    20   15    23

17    **Fig. 4**

B–B    18   8   7

6

5

19

4
10
3
11
2
9
1

14

34
35
13

12

A    **Fig. 5**

A

B

B

B

A

**Figs. 2 to 5    Four cavity injection mold for thrust screw**
1: moving mold plate, 2: spacer, 3: backup plate, 4: slide guide plate, 5:
core retainer plate, 6: stationary-side mold plate, 7: insulating plate, 8: locating ring, 9: locating bushing, 10: guide bushing, 11: leader pin, 12:
guide pin for ejector plates, 13: guide bushing, 14: pushback pin, 15: sprue
ejector, 16: ball detent, 17: connecting plug, 18: heated sprue bushing, 19:
slide retainer plate, 20: circlips, 21: sliding plate, 22: spacer ring, 23: ejector rod, 24: sliding sleeve, 25: slide plate, 26: center bar, 27: outer slide, 28:
wedge block, 29: angle guide, 30: core retainer, 31: core, 32: O-ring, 33:
baffle, 34: ejector retainer plate, 35: ejector plate
Company photo: Seveko Fristedt & Sundberg, Karlskrona, Sweden

## Example 22, Mold for a pump housing and pump piston of polyacetal

The pump housing (a) and the pump piston (b) are rotationally symmetrical parts with various external undercuts and lateral perforations. The molding material is polyacetal. Due to the similarity of both parts, a mold has been constructed (Figs. 1 to 9) in which the piston (b) and the pump housing (a) can be produced simultaneously. The outer surfaces of the molded parts are formed exclusively by a split cavity arrangement consisting of the cavity insert retainers (c) and the cavity inserts (d). When damaged, only the inserts have to be replaced. Various lateral perforations are molded by core inserts (e) housed in the cavity inserts.

Due to the height of the split cavity arrangement (146 mm, danger of tilting) and to achieve a large supporting cross section for the taper lock (f), the cam pins (g) have been mounted outside the taper lock area. The split cavity halves are guided by the stripper plate (h). A cylinder secured on one side (i) of the split-cavity parting line additionally serves to locate the split cavity half. The runner (k) and the center gate (l) for the molded parts are also located in the split-cavity parting line. The inner surfaces of the molded parts are formed by the cores (n, o) held in the core retainer plate (m). They are secured against rotating by pins. Because of their liability to damage, the core tips (p) are screwed in and are thus replaceable. They, too, are secured against rotating by fixing.

Bushings (q) that are wear parts are fitted into the stripper plate (h). To ensure the reliability of the stripping operation, the bushings (q) and the fixed cores (n, o) have conical seating surfaces.

The temperature of the mold is controlled by five independent systems:

System A + B: temperature control of the fixed cores (n, o) by means of bubblers.

System C + D: temperature control of the split-cavity inserts (d) takes place via several channels linked together into a large-area circuit.

System E: temperature control of the mold plate (r) is by means of two parallel channels connected to each other by a cross channel. The mold opens at the parting line I–I. The split cavity arrangement is simultaneously opened by the cam pins (g), thereby releasing the external undercuts and lateral perforations. A relative movement of the cavity-insert-guiding stripper plate (h) with respect to the core retainer plate (m) is prevented by coupling the mold ejector bar (v) to the hydraulic ejector on the molding machine (not shown). Ejection takes place through the operation of the hydraulic ejector on the machine and the stripping action of the two stripper bushings (q) in the stripper plate (h). Discharge of the molded part is additionally ensured by an air blast (s).

The bubblers have different diameters as a result of the different core diameters. The supply line for the temperature control fluid should be equal to or greater in cross sectional area than the remaining cross sectional area for the return flow.

This is a function of the heat transmission coefficient a, which obtains its highest values at high flow rates (turbulence). The bubbler in core (n) illustrates that the discharge opening of small diameter supply lines should be cut at an angle to enlarge the cross sectional area. With the pump piston, the stripper bushing contacts the piston skirt (t), the outside diameter of which is considerably larger than that of the piston itself. This could have lead to severe deformation when ejecting the piston. To create a more favorable flow of forces, nonfunctional ribs were placed at (u).

**Figs. 1 to 9   Mold for a pump housing and pump piston**
a: pump housing, b: pump piston, c: split-cavity retainers, d: split-cavity inserts, e: core inserts, f: supporting cross section for the taper lock, g: cam pins, h: stripper plate, i: cylinder, k: runner, l: gate, m: core retainer plate, n, o: pinned cores, p: core tip, q: stripper bushing, r: mold plate, s: connection for air blast, t: piston skirt, u: rib, v: ejector bar on mold
x: illustrated without split cavity arrangement, y: shown offset by 45°

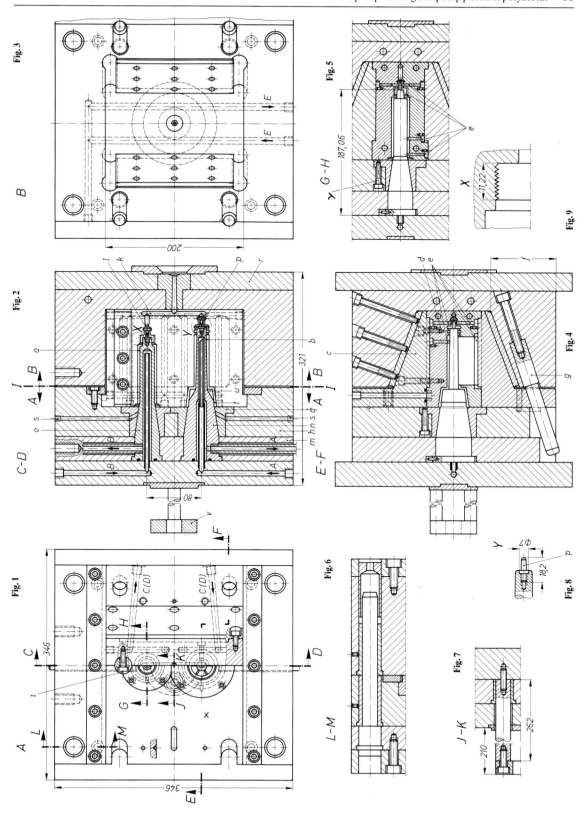

Fig.3

Fig.5

G-H

187,06

X

11,22

Fig.9

B

200

Fig.2

l

k

p

r

X

Y

a

b

321

I

B

A

c

B

A

I

A

o

s

t

u

m h n s q

C-D

B

B

A

A

E-F

80

v

F

d

e

f

c

g

Fig.4

Fig.1

C(D)

C(D)

H

346

C

i

r

L

D

K

G

J

X

A

L

M

E

346

L-M

Fig.6

Y

Φ7

p

18,2

Fig.8

Fig.7

J-K

210

262

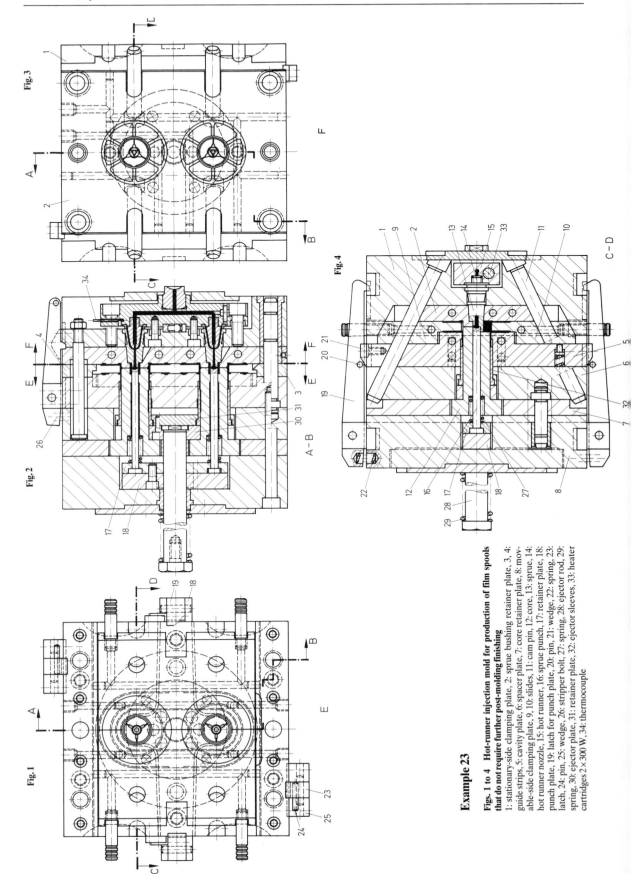

Fig. 3

Fig. 2

Fig. 1

Fig. 4

A – B

C – D

## Example 23

**Figs. 1 to 4   Hot-runner injection mold for production of film spools that do not require further post-molding finishing**

1: stationary-side clamping plate, 2: sprue bushing retainer plate, 3, 4: guide strips, 5: cavity plate, 6: spacer plate, 7: core retainer plate, 8: movable-side clamping plate, 9, 10: slides, 11: cam pin, 12: core, 13: sprue, 14: hot runner nozzle, 15: hot runner, 16: sprue punch, 17: retainer plate, 18: punch plate, 19: latch for punch plate, 20: pin, 21: wedge, 22: spring, 23: latch, 24: pin, 25: wedge, 26: stripper bolt, 27: spring, 28: ejector bolt, 29: spring, 30: ejector plate, 31: retainer plate, 32: ejector sleeves, 33: heater cartridges 2×300 W, 34: thermocouple

# Example 23, Hot-runner injection mold for two film spools of high-impact polystyrene

Because of their geometrical shape, film spools require injection molds (Figs. 1 to 4) with slides (9, 10) which, in their closed state in the mold cavity, form the inner surface of the spool on which the film will later be wound. Suitable cores (2, 12) project inward into the double-walled spool from both sides to form the spokes and drive rosettes. The center holes in the spools are formed in the ejector side of the mold by movable cores that later function as sprue punches (16). A hot-runner system (15) with indirectly heated BeCu nozzles (14) is used to feed melt to the sprues (13) with three pinpoint gates.

Ejection of the spools takes place in such a way that first the sprues are separated from the nozzles (Fig. 5). Next the sprue is punched out of the hole in the hub (Fig. 6) before the spool itself is finally released (Fig. 7). This ensures that any further work on the spool is eliminated. Because of the need to punch out the sprues in the mold and thereby reduce finishing costs, it is only possible to use a hot-runner system with this two-cavity mold. A conventional three-plate mold with multiple cavities and a normal runner system would increase costs to an unacceptable level. At the same time, the hot-runner system reduces the material losses arising from a normal runner system.

On opening, the mold components and plates (4 to 8) that are bolted togehter and attached to the movable platen as well as plate (2), which is held by latch (23), move away from the mold half attached to the stationary platen of the molding machine. In this way, the sprues (13) are withdrawn from the sprue bushings. During this opening movement, the slides (9) and (10), which are guided on plate (5) by strips (3) and (4), are forced apart by the cam pins (11) so that each film spool is released around its circumference. At the same time, the hook at the end of latch (19) reaches the end of the groove cut in plate (1) and pulls the sprue punches (16) forward against the force of the springs (27) by means of punch plate (18). This pushes the sprues and runners out of the holes in the spool hubs until the hook at the end of latch (19) is lifted out of the groove by pin (20) moving onto the wedge (21). Further opening of the mold causes wedge (25) to engage pin (24), which then lifts latch (23), thus freeing plate (2), which has served to hold the molded parts. Stripper bolts (26) finally open the mold completely by drawing plate (2) away from the mold cavities. Lastly, actuation of the ejector (28) against the force of spring (29) pushes the film spools off the cores (12) through the action of ejector plate (30) and the attached ejector sleeves (32).

Fig. 5                          Fig. 6                          Fig. 7

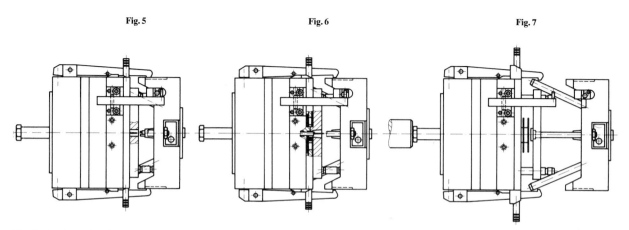

**Figs. 5 to 7    Operation of the mold during ejection**
Fig. 5: sprue tears away
Fig. 6: sprue is punched out of the spool
Fig. 7: spool is ejected

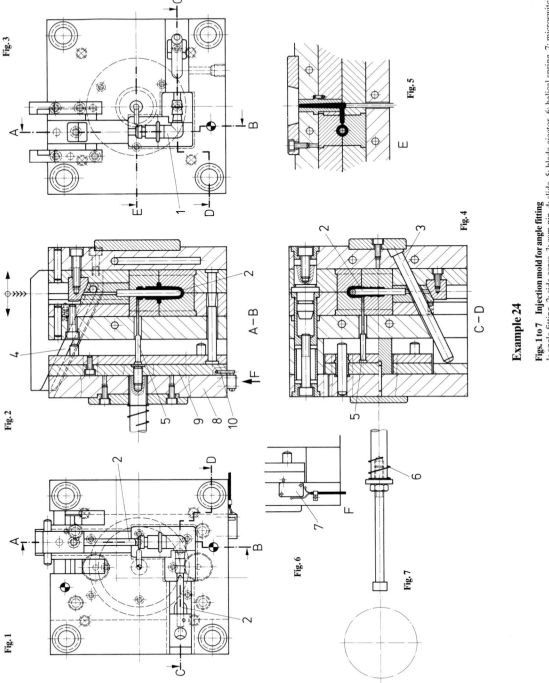

**Example 24**

**Figs. 1 to 7    Injection mold for angle fitting**
1: angle fitting, 2: side cores, 3: cam pin, 4: slide, 5: blade ejector, 6: helical spring, 7: microswitch, 8: clamping plate, 9: ejector plate, 10: pin

# Example 24, Injection mold for an angle fitting

If ejectors are located behind movable side cores or slides, the ejector plate return safety checks whether the ejectors have been returned to the molding position. If this is not the case, the molding cycle is interrupted.

This safety requires a receptacle on the movable clamping plate along with a switch on the mold that is actuated when the ejector plate is in the retracted position. The ejector plate return safety thus functions only if the molding cycle utilizes platen preposition, i. e., after the molded parts have been ejected, the clamping unit closes to the point at which the ejector plate is returned to the molding position by spring force. Only then does the control system issue the "close mold" command. In molds requiring a long ejector stroke, spring return of the ejector plate is often not sure enough. For such cases, there is an ejector return mechanism that fulfills this function. Attachment of the ejector plate return safety is shown in Figs. 1 to 7.

This single-cavity mold is used to produce an angle fitting (1). Two long side cores (2) meet at an angle of 90°. The somewhat shorter side core is pulled by a cam pin (3), while the longer core is pulled by a slide (4). The difficulty is that blade ejectors (5) are located under the two cores and must be returned to the molding position after having ejected the finished part before the two cores are set as the mold closes and possibly damage the blade ejectors. Possible consequences include not only broken blade ejectors but also a damaged cavity. Either of these could result in a lengthy interruption of production. For this reason, a helical spring (6) that permits operation with platen preposition is placed on the ejector rod. This spring then returns the ejector plate.

To ensure proper operation, a microswitch (7) is mounted to the clamping plate (8), while a pin (10) that actuates the switch is mounted in the ejector plate (9). After connecting the cable with the switch housing of the movable clamping plate, the ejector plate return safety is complete.

# Example 25, Mold for bushings with concealed gating

A flanged bushing is to be injection molded in such a way that any remnants of the gate are concealed or as little noticeable as possible. The bushing would normally require a two-plate mold with a single parting line. The molded part would then be released and ejected along its axis, which coincides with the opening direction of the mold. The gate would be located on the outer surface of the flange since it is in contact with the mold parting line.

In order to satisfy the requirement for an "invisible" gate, the cavities (two rows of four) are placed between slides carrying the cores (Fig. 1) even though there are no undercuts. From a central sprue the melt flows through conical runners in the cores to pinpoint gates located on the inner surface of the bushings. As the slides move during opening of the mold the gates are cleanly sheared off flush with the adjacent part surface. The flexibility of the plastic selected is sufficient to permit release of the end of the runner from the angled runner channel. The parts are now free and can drop out of the mold.

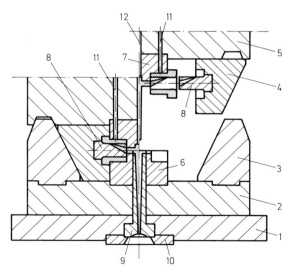

**Fig. 1    Mold for bushings with concealed gating**
Illustration: Erikssons Verktygsindustri, Gislaved/Sweden
1: stationary-side clamping plate, 2: stationary-side backing plate, 3: wedge, 4: slide, 5: movable-side backing plate, 6: injection-side cavity half, 7: ejector-side cavity half, 8: core, 9: sprue bushing, 10: locating ring, 11: part ejector, 12: sprue ejector

# Example 26, Injection mold for the valve housing of a water-mixing tap[1] made from polyacetal

A valve housing (Figs. 1 and 2) had to be designed and produced for a water-mixing tap. The problem when designing the tool (Figs. 3 to 7) resulted from the undercuts in four directions. Originally occurring considerable differences in wall thicknesses have been eliminated during optimization. Demands for high precision of the cylindrical valve seat in particular were negatively influenced by various recesses in the wall and adjoining partitions, which favored sink marks and ovalness.

**Fig. 1    View of the interior of the valve housing, showing the places of core penetration**
Company photo: ARCU, Altermo/Sweden

**Fig. 2    View of the exterior of the valve housing**
Company photo: ARCU, Altermo/Sweden

Polyacetal (POM) had been chosen as molding material. The complete molded part had to have homogeneous walls, free from flow lines if at all possible, as it would be subjected to ever changing contact with hot and cold water during an estimated long life span. Inadequately fused weld lines would be capable of developing into weak spots and were therefore to be avoided at all cost.

Provision has been made for an electrically heated sprue bushing (30) (Fig. 6) in order to avoid a long sprue, provide better movement energies for the melt and maintain its temperature until it enters the cavity. The resultant very short runner leads to the gate on the edge of the pipelike housing, to be hidden by a part that is subsequently fitted to cover it. The gating, the predetermined mold temperature, the wall thickness at the critical positions and the resultant shrinkage have been employed as the basis for dimensioning the part-forming components.

Two cores each cross in the pipe-shaped housing, i. e. one core (16) each penetrates another core (19). This obviously presents a danger spot should the minutest deviation occur from the specified time- and movement-based coordination as well as from the accuracy in the mold.

The hollow cores (19) are kept in position by mechanical delay during the first phase of mold opening, while the crossing cores (16) are withdrawn by an angle pin each (31). Mechanical actuation has been preferred over a hydraulic or pneumatic one in this case in order to exclude the danger of a sequencing error (the so-called human factor) during set-up and operation.

The cores (16, 33) consist of a beryllium-copper alloy. They are cooled by heat conducting pins (27, 28).

1 From Plastforum 12 (1981) 3, pp. 54–57

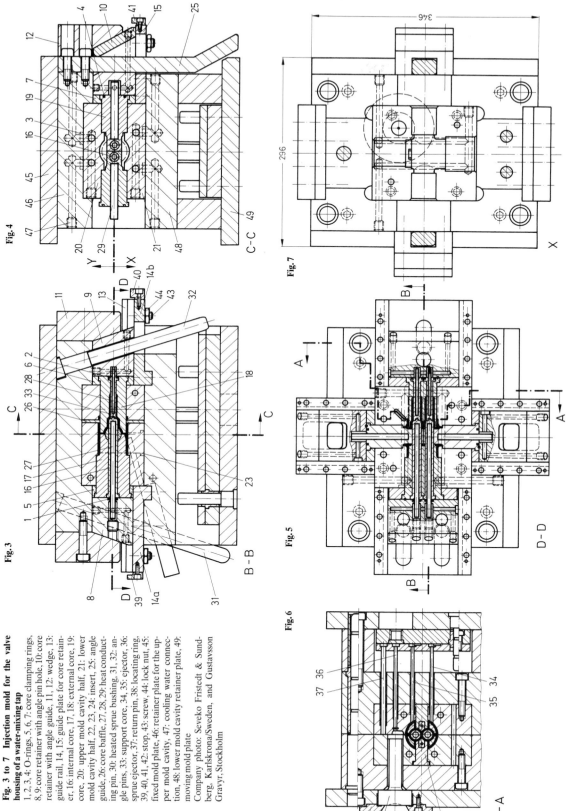

**Fig. 3 to 7  Injection mold for the valve housing of a water-mixing tap**

1, 2, 3, 4: O-rings, 5, 6, 7: core clamping rings, 8, 9: core retainer with angle pin hole, 10: core retainer with angle guide, 11, 12: wedge, 13: guide rail, 14, 15: guide plate for core retainer, 16: internal core, 17, 18: external core, 19: core, 20: upper mold cavity half, 21: lower mold cavity half, 22, 23, 24: insert, 25: angle guide, 26: core baffle, 27, 28, 29: heat conducting pin, 30: heated sprue bushing, 31, 32: angle pins, 33: support core, 34, 35: ejector, 36: sprue ejector, 37: return pin, 38: locating ring, 39, 40, 41, 42: stop, 43: screw, 44: lock nut, 45: fixed mold plate, 46: retainer plate for the upper mold cavity, 47: cooling water connection, 48: lower mold cavity retainer plate, 49: moving mold plate

Company photo: Seveko Fristedt & Sundberg, Karlskrona/Sweden, and Gustavsson Gravyr, Stockholm

# Example 27, Mold for a lid with three threads

The lid is a rotationally symmetrical part with three threads. Threads *I* and *II* are of the same pitch and can be formed by a single threaded core. The material employed is polyacetal. The size of the order (total number of units to be produced) is small.

The mold (Figs. 1 to 5) is of simple design. The external shape of the molded part is formed by an insert (*c*), which is housed in mold plate (*b*) and secured against rotating. The temperature of this insert is controlled via a ring channel (heating/cooling system *A*). Thread *III* is formed by two slides (*d*). The part is injected through a diaphragm gate (*e*). The internal shape of the lid is obtained from a main core (*f*), which is housed in the mold plate (*p*) and is secured against rotating. The temperature of this core is controlled via an internal tube (heating/cooling system *B*). Its effectiveness is increased by the soldered-on spiral (*g*). The threads *I* and *II* are formed by a single threaded core (*h*). Because of the low number of moldings required, the mold has been designed for the threaded core (*h*) to be unscrewed outside the tool. The threaded core is inserted into an ejector ring (*i*) and is retained by three spring-loaded detents (*k*). It is located by the cone (*l*) of the fixed core (*f*). The mold opens at parting plane *I–I* positively assisted by two latches (*m*). The thread-forming slides (*d*) are moved outward by this action. After a distance of 18 mm the latches are released by the control strips (*n*) and the mold opens at the main parting plane *II–II*. By actuation of the machine ejector the threaded core (*h*) is pushed in the direction of the fixed half by three ejector pins (*o*) and the ejector ring (*i*) for a distance of 90 mm (height of the molding plus 10 mm). During the movement the threaded core strips the molding off the fixed core (*f*). Then the molded part, with the threaded core (*h*), is pulled manually out of the stripping ring (*i*) without any danger of damaging the fixed main core (*f*). Unscrewing takes place outside the mold with the aid of an unscrewing device. To shorten the cycle time, several threaded cores are employed. While one part is being unscrewed, the next molded part is being produced.

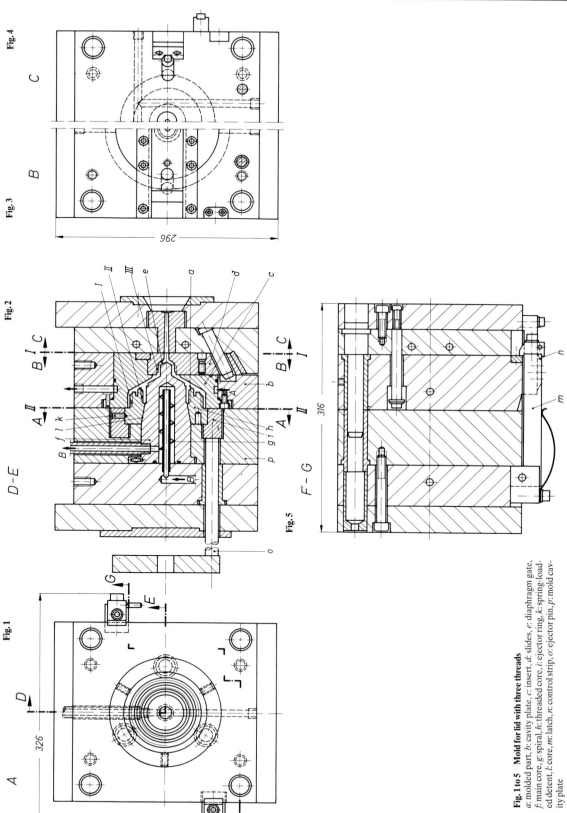

**Fig. 1 to 5    Mold for lid with three threads**

*a*: molded part, *b*: cavity plate, *c*: insert, *d*: slides, *e*: diaphragm gate, *f*: main core, *g*: spiral, *h*: threaded core, *i*: ejector ring, *k*: spring-loaded detent, *l*: core, *m*: latch, *n*: control strip, *o*: ejector pin, *p*: mold cavity plate

## Example 28, Two-cavity injection mold for coupling sleeves of polyamide

The coupling sleeve in Figs. 1 to 5 had to be produced in a PA 66 with 30 % by weight glass fiber reinforcement. The injection molded part has a center hole, entered by tapped M 10 holes that, starting from the peripheral surface, are opposite each other. As set screws are screwed into each tapped hole to push against the centrally fitted shaft, it is not necessary to have a continuous thread in both holes, which would have called for a bridging threaded core that would have had to cross the center core. Apart from problems with sealing, the unscrewing device also would have caused difficulty, as it would have had to perform a larger stroke. Use of the molded part allows for two separate threaded cores to be operated

independently of each other, however, so that they can be driven by one rack each. To avoid further core pulls for the remaining shape of the molded part, it is put perpendicular into the parting line of the mold by its axis of symmetry.

Concerning direct operation of the threaded cores by racks, a check must be made to ascertain that adequate transmission can be achieved or if intermediate stages are required to avoid an excessively long rack stroke.

The pitch of the metric thread M 10 is h = 1.5 mm. Allowing for a certain safety, an unscrewing distance of 11 mm must be taken up, which results in 11/1.5 = 7.33 rotations of the threaded core. At a pitch circle

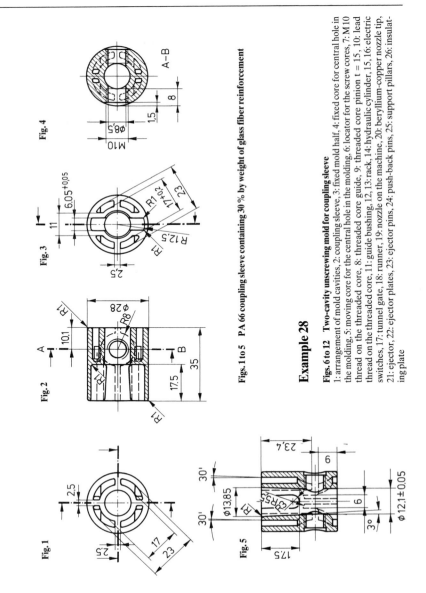

Figs. 1 to 5   PA 66 coupling sleeve containing 30 % by weight of glass fiber reinforcement

## Example 28

Figs. 6 to 12   Two-cavity unscrewing mold for coupling sleeve
1: arrangement of mold cavities, 2: coupling sleeve. 3: fixed mold half, 4: fixed core for central hole in the molding, 5: moving core for the central hole in the molding, 6: locator for the screw cores, 7: M 10 thread on the threaded core, 8: threaded core guide, 9: threaded core pinion t = 15, 10: lead thread on the threaded core, 11: guide bushing, 12, 13: rack, 14: hydraulic cylinder, 15, 16: electric switches, 17: tunnel gate, 18: runner, 19: nozzle on the machine, 20: beryllium-copper nozzle tip, 21: ejector, 22: ejector plates, 23: ejector pins, 24: push-back pins, 25: support pillars, 26: insulating plate

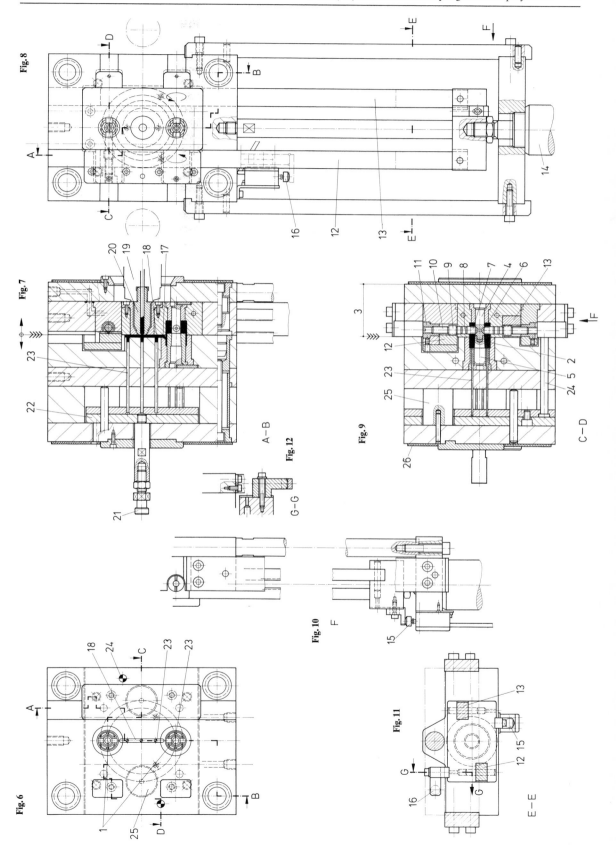

Fig. 8

Fig. 7

A – B

Fig. 12

G – G

Fig. 9

C – D

Fig. 10

Fig. 6

Fig. 11

E – E

7.33 rotations of the threaded core. At a pitch circle diameter of $d_0 = 12$ mm and a modulus of $m = 0.8$ mm, the pinion of the threaded core works out at $t = 12/0.8 = 15$ teeth and a pitch circle circumference of $12 \times \pi = 37.68$ mm. At 7.33 turns this results in a required rack stroke of $7.33 \times 37.68 = 276.19$ mm.

Standard hydraulic cylinders of 280 mm stroke are available. Divided by the pitch $d = \pi \times m = 2.5$ mm of the gear tooth system, this corresponds to 112 teeth on the rack, which with 15 teeth on the pinion turns the latter 7.46 times during one stroke. From this results an unscrewing distance of 11.19 mm, which is sufficient. It must be checked whether the space available on the injection molding machine allows the installation of the mounting hardware and the hydraulic cylinder under the mold.

The mold design (Figs. 6 to 12) is such that two sleeves (1) can be produced at the same time. The unscrewing equipment has been installed in the fixed mold half (3) so that the hydraulic cylinder (14) does not have to participate in the opening and closing movement but can remain in its position.

The center bore of the coupling, which tapers toward the moving mold half, is formed by two cores (4) and (5) which are self-centering.

The locators (6) for the threaded cores enter the core (4), which is held in the stationary side of the clamping plate, from both sides. The threaded cores are made up of the locators (6), the M 10 thread (7), a guide (8), the 15 gear teeth (9), and the guide thread (10) at the

other end, which runs in the fixed guide bushing (11). The two racks (12) and (13) have been arranged offset to each other so that opposite directions of rotation can be transmitted to the opposing threaded cores. The hydraulic cylinder pushes the racks (12) and (13) up to unscrew the threaded cores. The upper racks protrude from the mold and need to be guarded by a screen. For interlocking with the machine's control circuit for the cycle sequence, the racks contact switch (15) in the lower and switch (16) in the upper position. By employing lateral submarine gating (17), the coupling sleeves are automatically degated from the runner (18). This is fed directly through a beryllium-copper nozzle tip (20), which is screwed into the female thread of the nozzle on the machine (19) to avoid the conventional tapered sprue penetrating the fixed mold half (3).

The operating sequence of the unscrewing mold takes place as follows:

The racks are moved in by the hydraulic cylinders, unscrewing the threaded cores from the molded parts. Then the opening movement of the mold starts. When finished, the hydraulic ejector of the machine, to which the ejector bar is coupled (21), pushes forward the ejector plates (22) and through them the ejector pins (23) for the coupling sleeves and runner. For safety, the push-back pins (24) also move out simultaneously. They have to return the ejector plate to the starting position in any case when the mold closes. Once the mold is closed, the racks are pulled up again and the new cycle can start with injection.

## Example 29, Four-cavity injection mold for producing tapered tubes

Tapered tubes closed at one end and approximately 150 mm in length and 35 mm in diameter had to be produced with a flange on the open end and channels in the closed end as well as in the circumference. An injection molding machine with 300 mm maximum mold height and an opening stroke also of 300 mm was available.

Normally such tubes are accommodated in the mold in such a way that the core is located on the moving half, with the molded part being stripped off the core by a stripper plate or ejector sleeve. With this type of construction, however, neither mold height nor opening stroke of the machine would have sufficed. Therefore a design had to be found that resulted in the shortest possible mold height and a short ejector stroke. The solution was found by siting the cores on the fixed half and machining the outer shape into the slides. The tubes are released from the cores while the slides re-

main in the closed position. They then open sufficiently far to allow the tubes to drop out between the open slides. As the flange is 50 mm in diameter, the slides have to open at least 26 mm to each side so that the tubes can drop out. The mold is shown in Figs. 1 and 2. The mold clamping plate (a) of the fixed half of the tool contains the cooling water supply and return channels for two cores each. A right-hand and a left-hand wedge plate (b) are bolted to the clamping plate. These wedge plates are supported on their open side by wedge strips (c), which are tapered longitudinally by 1°, thereby facilitating adjustment of the tapered slides seating, avoiding flash on the molded parts in the parting line. The slides (d) themselves, containing the outer shape of the molded parts, are guided by bolted on guide plates (e) on a plate, which is accommodated in the moving half mold clamping plate (h) and can be displaced on rods (g).

Two further guide plates ($i$) are bolted to the wedge plates ($b$). They contain guide grooves for the guide pins ($k$), which are firmly fitted in the guide plate ($e$). These guide grooves are fashioned in such a way that they initially keep the slides closed over a distance of 20 mm when the mold opens. Over that distance the molded parts are disengaged from the cores. During further opening the slides are pulled appart sufficiently far to allow the molded parts to drop down between them when pulled off the core. So that the molded parts do not get stuck on one side during opening of the slides, the round closed end of the tubes has been machined into an insert ($l$), which also contains the core pins for the holes. At the end

of the opening movement the molded part is ejected from these inserts by ejectors ($m$).

The ejectors are moved via ejector bars ($n$), which are actuated at the conclusion of the opening movement by pushing plate ($f$) forward with the push rods ($g$). The plate ($o$) is retracted by powerful spring washers ($p$) when the mold closes. This seemingly somewhat complicated actuation of the ejectors becomes necessary, as there is not sufficient space available for standard ejector plates within the mold height at disposal. It is self-evident that the mold must never be opened to such an extent that the slides ($d$) leave the guide plates.

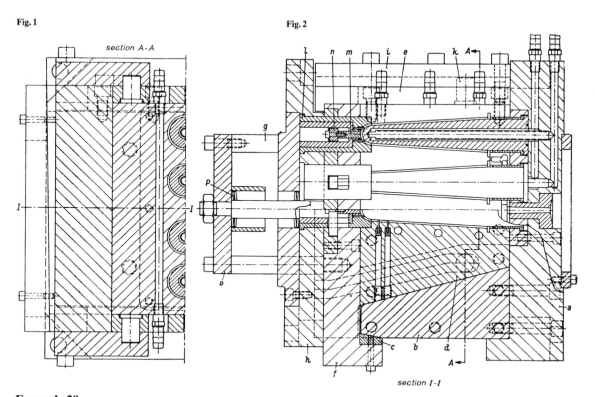

Fig. 1   section A-A

Fig. 2

section I-I

## Example 29

**Figs. 1 and 2   Four-cavity injection mold for the production of 150 mm-long tubes; cores on the fixed half**
$a$: fixed-half clamping plate, $b$: wedge plate, $c$: wear plates, $d$: slides, $e$: guide plate, $f$: plate, $g$: rod, $h$: moving-half clamping plate, $i$: guide plate, $k$: guide pin, $l$: insert, $m$: ejector, $n$: ejector bar, $o$: plate, $p$: spring washers

# Example 30, Four-cavity mold for box and lid

Example 30 involves a small, round box with an offset lip so that the lid fits flush with the side. Ejection by means of individual ejector pins is difficult for such parts especially when the parts are deep and the walls thin. The offset lip is held in the mold so tightly that, unless a stripper plate is used, puncturing of the molded parts by the ejector pins is to be feared. The offset lip is thus best placed in a stripper plate. While the box is now cleanly stripped off the core by the stripper plate, it is retained in the stripper plate by the offset lip and must be removed by hand.

The question therefore arises as to how the parts that have been stripped off the core but are still retained in the stripper plate can be reliably ejected fully automatically.

This is possible if the stripper plate stops after a certain distance and ejector pins located inside the box are then extended to eject it from the stripper plate. This two-stage ejection must be performed by the central ejector rod, however, if the mold is not to become too complicated.

In the following a solution to this problem is described that has proved successful and offers the further advantage of not using any latches involving springs, which operate unreliably and easily give rise to trouble when high ejector forces are needed.

Figures 1 to 4 show an injection mold in which two boxes and matching lids are molded. To eliminate any need for secondary operations, the box and lid are submarine-gated so that on opening the approximately 1 mm diameter gate is cleanly sheared. The molded parts and runner system thus drop out of the mold separately.

On opening of the mold, both parts are retained on the cores $(a)$ and $(b)$ from which they are stripped by the stripper plate $(c)$ at the end of the opening stroke. While the lid on core $(b)$ can drop after the stripper plate has been actuated, the box itself is retained in the stripper plate $(c)$ by the approximately 3 mm high offset lip. The motion of the stripper plate is stopped after a certain distance by ejector plate $(d)$, which is connected to the stripper plate $(c)$ by four sleeves $(e)$. The ejector pins $(f)$, which until now had accompanied the motion of the stripper plate $(c)$, do not stop, but rather continue their forward motion and thereby eject the boxes from the stripper plate. How does the sequential actuation of stripper plate and ejector pins occur?

First, there are two sets of ejector plates. The front plates $(g)$ and $(d)$ are connected to the stripper plate. Plates $(h)$ and $(i)$ actuate the ejector pins $(f)$. For actuation of the stripper plate, ejector plates $(g)$ and $(d)$ have a central actuating sleeve $(k)$ slotted like a collet. The relaxed condition of this actuating sleeve is shown in Fig. 4, whereas Fig. 3 illustrates the spread condition. The sleeve is spread as the mold closes by the action of the push-back sleeves $(e)$, which displace the actuating sleeves $(k)$ with respect to the spreader $(l)$ so that the slotted actuating sleeve $(k)$ is spread by the shoulder on the spreader $(l)$.

The two rear ejector plates $(h)$ and $(i)$, which actuate the ejector pins $(f)$, are connected to the central ejector sleeves $(m)$. With the mold closed (Fig. 3), the slotted actuating sleeve $(k)$ rests against a shoulder inside ejector sleeve $(m)$. As the ejector sleeve $(m)$ is actuated via the spring pack $(n)$, ejector sleeve $(m)$ and the rear ejector plates $(h)$ and $(i)$ with attached ejector pins $(f)$ are extended together with the front ejector plates $(g)$ and $(d)$ with the attached stripper plate $(c)$. Since a considerable amount of force is necessary to strip the parts from the cores, the spring pack $(o)$ becomes compressed during this motion. As soon as the parts are stripped off the cores, the spring pack $(o)$ can relax, which causes a sudden forward motion of the stripper plate. This sudden motion is sure to knock the lids off the stripper plate. The front ejector plate $(d)$ is now up against the backing plate so that the stripper plate can no longer move.

As a result of the motion of the stripper plate, the actuating sleeve $(k)$ has moved in relation to the shoulder on the spreader $(l)$, permitting the previously spread sleeve $(k)$ to relax as shown in Fig. 4. In this relaxed position, however, the positive connection between actuating sleeve $(k)$ and ejector sleeve $(m)$ is interrupted, so that with further forward motion of the ejector sleeve $(m)$ only the ejector pins $(f)$ are extended, while the stripper plate is held stationary.

As the mold closes, the rear ejector plate $(h)$ is first returned by the push-back pins $(p)$ while the front ejector plate $(g)$ is subsequently returned by the push-back sleeve $(e)$. The actuating sleeve $(k)$ is thereby once again spread in the ejector sleeve $(m)$ as shown in Fig. 3.

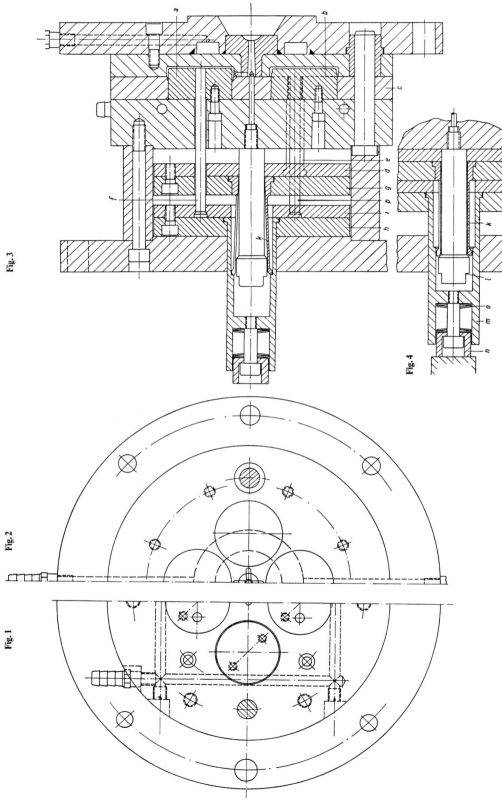

**Figs. 1 to 4   Four-cavity mold for box and lid**
a, b: cores, c: stripper plate, d, g: front ejector plates, e: four sleeves, f: ejector pins, h, i: rear ejector plates, k: slotted actuating sleeve, l: spreader, m: ejector sleeve, n: spring-loaded pad, o: spring, p: push-back pins
**Fig. 4   Mold during ejection**
actuating sleeve k relaxed

# Example 31, Two-cavity side-action injection mold for wire bobbins

Side-action molds have already been described in which the slides are opened by the advancing ejectors. However, this principle is not applicable to all molded parts. Many molded parts have to be retained in position on the cores during the opening movement of the slides, and ejection from the cores must only take place at the conclusion of the slides opening movement. This stipulates that on mold opening the slides open fully and only then are the cores pulled out of the molded parts.

In principle this sequence of movements is covered by so-called side-action molds, in which the slides for the outer shape of the molded parts are opened by cam pins during the initial opening movement. If, however, the molded parts have a relatively large surface area in the plane of the slides, assured mold clamping can be a problem with such molds. In this instance the mold design according to Figs. 1 and 2 has proved effective. The mold contains two wire bobbins to DIN 46 399, which are pinpoint-gated on a flange. The outer shapes are molded in replaceable inserts $(a)$ which are bolted to the slides $(b)$. Guides $(c)$ are screwed on top and bottom to guide the slides on the stripper plate $(d)$. These guides themselves are guided in the direction of the taper angle in guide plates $(e)$, which are bolted to the clamping plate $(g)$ of the fixed mold half through the wedges $(f)$. The stripper plate $(d)$ is connected with the ejector plate $(i)$ through the ejector rods $(h)$. When the ejector plate $(i)$ moves against the machine ejector, the stripper plate, complete with slides, is pushed forward. The correct sequence of slide movements during mold opening is dependent on the stipulation that core $(k)$ and slides $(a)$ are firmly connected to each other via the material-filled mold cavity. During mold opening the slides $(a)$ are opened so far by the time the ejector plate $(i)$ has contacted the machine ejector that the distance between them is a little larger than the diameter of the bobbins to allow the latter to drop off the core. The slides $(a)$ remain in the open position during further mold opening, while cores $(l)$ and $(k)$ are withdrawn from the bobbin. Slides $(b)$ are still engaged in the guide plate $(e)$ with their guides $(c)$ in this position, so that the ejector rods $(h)$ are relieved of the weight of the slides when the mold is open.

This design ensures trouble-free shutoff of the slides even with molded parts having large surfae areas requiring 1000 kN clamping force and more in the plane of the slides. If the wedge strip $(m)$ has been made adjustable by slight tapering, then positive shutoff can easily be regained by resetting when the wedge surface becomes worn.

Very high demands regarding absence of flash are made on wire bobbins in particular. These can only be accomplished with this type of design, ensuring extremely solid and positive shut-off.

This design also offers particular advantages regarding cooling of the slides. As the slides are unencumbered top and bottom, in contrast to the closed tapered split-cavity mold, one or several cooling channels can be included.

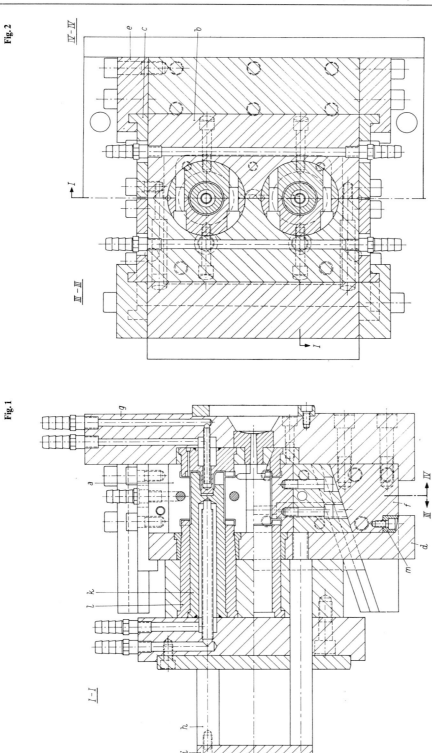

**Figs. 1 and 2    Two-cavity side-action injection mold for wire bobbins**
*a*: inserts, *b*: slides, *c*: guides, *d*: stripper plates, *e*: guide plates, *f*: wedge, *g*: clamping plate, *h*: ejector rod, *i*: ejector plate, *k*, *l*: cores, *m*: wedge strip

# Example 32, Injection mold for a polypropylene container with a threaded neck

This is the description of a three-plate injection mold for a polypropylene container that does not show any witness lines from slides. Sprue and ejectors are designed for automatic operation.

## Specifications

When the development of a household appliance had been concluded, the task of constructing a tool for the container of the appliance arose. A molded part drawing served as the basis on which the geometrical shape, dimensions, permissible tolerances and polypropylene as material had been firmly established. The container concerned is a largely rotationally symmetrical high-quality molded part with relatively high demands on the surface, on dimensional accuracy (required for assembly and operation) and on the mechanical loading of the polypropylene.

## Mold design

The design shown in Figs. 1 to 4 is a three-plate mold (parting line *I* and *II*) with stripper plate (*p*). When the injection molding machine opens, the mold is forced to open at *I* by the latches (*b*). Through this movement the two thread-forming slides (*c*) are pulled out of the thread by the cam pins (*d*), thereby releasing the undercuts formed by the thread. The latches are guided by the cam strips (*e*) and they release after 28 mm of travel. Mold plate (*f*) stops. The mold opens in the main parting line (*II* ). The cavity retainer plate is guided by four additional guide pins (*g*). This plate is secured by end-stops (*h*).

## Runner system

The molding material is fed into the cavity via sprue, conventional runners and gates (*i*). Despite the relatively high wall thickness of the molded part (3.5 mm) attempts were successfully made to inject via four submarine gates (*i*) of 1.8 mm diameter each. The gates are sheared off during mold opening (*I* ). The gates are in the upper mold cavity. The choice of this gating system and its position offer the following advantages:
– Central gating. This ensures even mold filling.
– Position of the gate is outside the functional and visible areas of the molded part.

– Feasibility of automatic production without post-molding finishing of the gate area.

## Temperature control

Uniform mold temperature control to 50 °C is necessary to satisfy the quality requirements. Effective temperature control had also been asked for in order to achieve short cycle times. The mold was therefore equipped with five temperature control systems TS, independent of one another:

System 1:    Temperature control of the main core (*k*)
System 2:    Temperature control of the cavity (insert) (*l*)
System 3 + 4:    Temperature control of the thread-forming slides (*c*)
System 5:    Temperature control of the contour-forming sprue bushing (*m*) and the auxiliary core (*n*). The effectiveness of temperature control in the auxiliary core is increased by a copper pin (*o*).

## Ejector systems

The molded part is stripped off the core by the stripper plate (*p*). This movement is effected by a hydraulically operated ejector on the machine. The stroke of the ejector plate (*p*) is limited by two bolts (*q*) with end stops (*r*) . The molding bead (*s*) in the ejector plate could cause it to stick on demolding. For that reason the air blast (*t*) has been provided, which is charged with compressed air at the end of the ejection process. This ensures certain discharge of the molded part. The sprue is pushed out of the retaining undercut and ejected by a separate ejector system (*u*). The movement of this ejector is actuated by contact of the bolt head (*v*). This bolt serves to couple the machine's ejector with the ejector plate (*w*).

## Materials used in the mold

The following materials were chosen for the individual parts of the mold:
– Part-forming inserts: case-hardening steel, case hardened
– Cavity retainer plate and stripper plate: nitrided annealed steel
– Mold base: tool steel, unalloyed

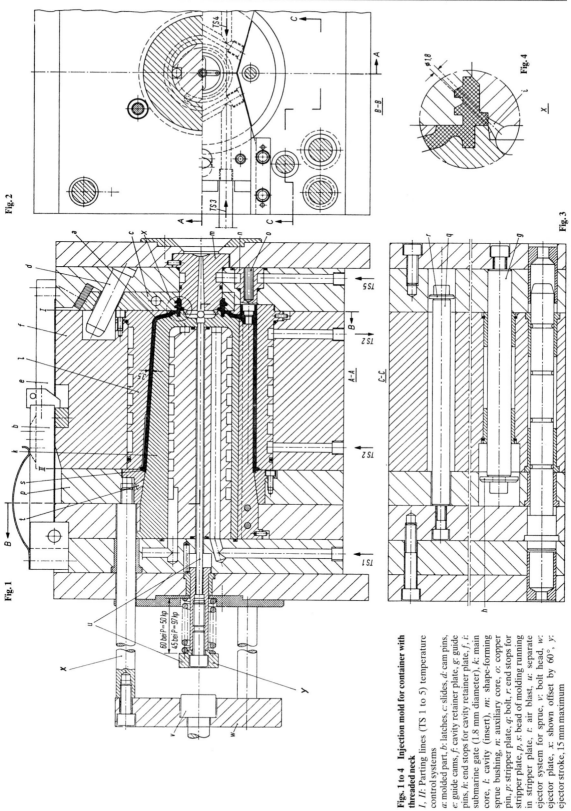

**Fig. 2**

**Fig. 1**

**Fig. 4**

**Fig. 3**

**Figs. 1 to 4   Injection mold for container with threaded neck**

*I, II*: Parting lines (TS 1 to 5) temperature control systems

*a*: molded part, *b*: latches, *c*: slides, *d*: cam pins, *e*: guide cams, *f*: cavity retainer plate, *g*: guide pins, *h*: end stops for cavity retainer plate, *f, i*: submarine gate (1.8 mm diameter), *k*: main core, *l*: cavity (insert), *m*: shape-forming sprue bushing, *n*: auxiliary core, *o*: copper pin, *p*: stripper plate, *q*: bolt, *r*: end stops for stripper plate, *p, s*: bead of molding running in stripper plate, *t*: air blast, *u*: separate ejector system for sprue, *v*: bolt head, *w*: ejector plate, *x*: shown offset by 60°, *y*: ejector stroke, 15 mm maximum

# Example 33, Three-plate injection mold with stripping device for a precision magazine

Integrated circuits (IC) are generally mounted automatically during production of electronic devices. This requires that they be stored in magazines. The magazine shown in Fig. 1 has an undercut U-shaped groove to hold the IC's and a recessed bottom that is reinforced by transverse ribs. Snap fits and mounting holes are located at either end of the magazine.

**Fig. 1    Precision magazine to hold 50 integrated circuits**
top: view from above with undercut groove to hold the IC's, bottom: view from below showing the stiffening ribs by which the magazine is pulled off the groove-forming core

## Mold

In the mold (Figs. 2 to 11), the longitudinal axis of the molded part is transverse to the opening direction of the mold. The ribbed bottom faces the runner system. The cavity is filled via two pinpoint gates from a runner system and a heated sprue nozzle (16) in a 3-plate design.

## Mold operation

### Parting line I
After a partial opening stroke of approx. 7 mm, the spring-loaded bolts (69) cause the gate to shear off. The sucker pins (22) hold the runner in the runner plate (5) and the snap fits as well as the mounting holes of the molded part are released by retraction of the slides (33). Mold plates (3) and (4) remain closed during this time.

### Parting line II (mold opening)
Parting line II (between plates 3 and 4) is opened during further opening of the injection mold. This phase of opening is concluded after a distance of 80 mm. During this opening motion, the ejector pin (36) is pushed into the eject position by the lever (29) with the aid of a stripper bolt (38). This lifts the hook-shaped detent on the molded part so that it can subsequently be stripped off the mold core.

### Parting line III
After a further opening stroke of 60 mm, parting line I opens completely through the action of stripper bolt (67). Two further stripper bolts (66) engage mold plate (4), pulling the runner plate (5) forward. The complete

runner system is now pulled off the sucker pins (22) and away from the heated sprue bushing (16), dropping out of the mold. The spring-loaded strippers (72) prevent the runner from sticking to the runner plate (5). Shoulder bolts (68) prevent the mold plates from being pulled off the guide pins completely. They do not, however, serve as a mechanical stop. This is found on the molding machine.

## Ejection (stripping) of the molded part

During the opening sequence of the mold, the stripping device, which is mounted on the moving half of the mold, has moved into the ejection position. Only in this position will the limit switch initiate operation of the stripping device.

During the inward movement, the guide blocks (56) glide under the guide strips (31), the carefully adjusted latches (54) slide over the transverse stiffening ribs of the molded part and, once the stripping device is fully inserted, engage behind two of these ribs. A limit switch (58) is actuated simultaneously in this position to initiate the stripping operation. The molded part is now stripped off the entire length of the mold core (27), which is 162 mm long, and then drops out of the mold. Once the stripping device has returned to its starting position, limit switch (59) is actuated and another cycle can start, if the infrared mold safety has also cleared the start.

The infrared mold safety monitors the lower mold half and checks whether the molded part and stripping device have cleared the tool area. Only when both conditions have been fulfilled are the machine controls able to initiate another molding cycle.

**Figs. 2 to 11    Three-plate injection mold with stripping device for a precision magazine**
1: movable-side mold base plate, 2: spacer plate, 3, 4: mold plate, 5: runner plate, 6: cam pin retainer plate, 7: stationary-side mold base plate, 8, 9: leader pins, 10, 11, 12, 13, 14, 15: guide bushings, 16: heated sprue bushing, 17: movable-side locating ring, 18: insulating plate, 19: junction box for heated sprue bushing, 20: locating sleeve, 21: cam pin, 22: sucker pins, 23: spring, 24: mold core, 25, 26: core insert, 27: core, 28: wedge, 29: lever, 30: cavity end insert, 31: guide strip, 32: slide guide, 33: slide, 34: core, 35: articulated head and guide for ejector pin 36, 36: ejector pin, 37: fulcrum for lever 29, 38: stripper bolt, 39: spring-loaded bolt, 40: spring, 41: pivot pin, 42: housing for sensor, 43: sensor, 44: microswitch, 45: housing for microswitch 44, 46: mechanical stop for slide 33, 47: spring, 48: stripper head, 49: base plate for stripping device, 50: bearing support for guide, 51: sheet metal reinforcement, 52: support plate for stripping device, 53: outboard bearing for guide, 54: latch, 55: latch spring, 56: guide block, 57: mechanical limit for inward movement, 58, 59: limit switches, 60: cylinder connection, 61: spring, 62: hydraulic cylinder, 63: linear bearing, 64: guide rod, 65: circlip, 66, 67, 68: stripper bolts, 69: spring-loaded bolt, 70: runner ejector, 71: adjustment screw, 72: stripper, 73: stationary-side locating ring

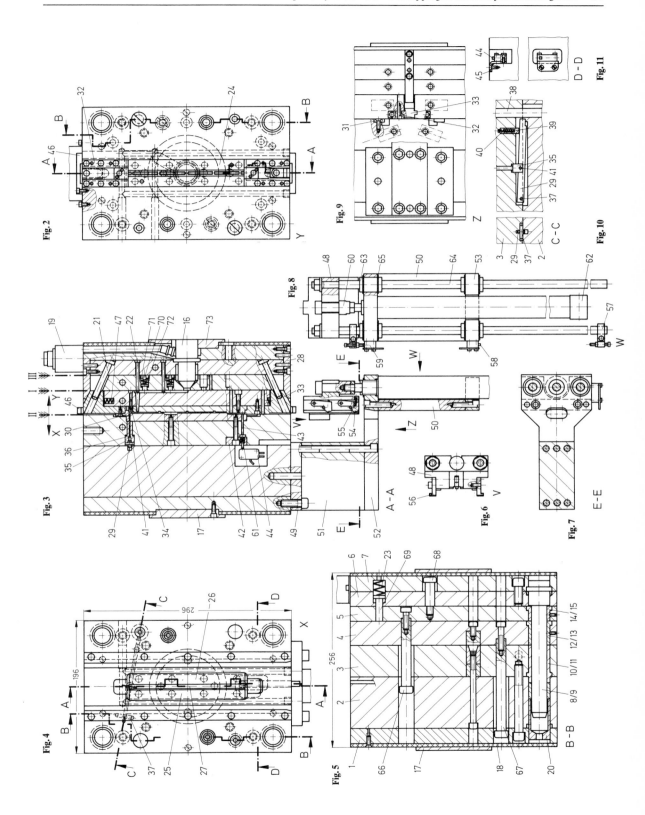

Fig. 2
Fig. 3
Fig. 4
Fig. 5
Fig. 6
Fig. 7
Fig. 8
Fig. 9
Fig. 10
Fig. 11

# Example 34, Three-cavity injection mold for a cosmetic cream container with a threaded lid

A fine-threaded lid is usually used for the closure of cosmetic cream containers. When these are containers molded in plastic, the injection molding tool must usually, for aesthetic reasons, be such that no markings on the surface of the molded part caused by the different mold parts are visible. Such marks are left behind on the piece when a simple two-piece mold cavity is used. Tools with an unscrewing mechanism prevent this disadvantage, but they are complicated and expensive.

The three-cavity mold shown in Figs. 1 and 2 shows an alternative economical solution to this problem: the container wall is molded in a nonseparating cavity and a cavity separation takes place only in the area of the outer thread at the edge of the molded part. The thread is molded by means of a three-part ring (15), which is held together in the closed mold by wedge-shaped pieces (16) (as shown in region *I* of the main sectional drawing, or in the plan view, *left,* Figs. 1 and 2). The three-plate mold is so constructed that on opening, the first separation between plates (2) and (3) causes the sprue and runner to be ejected by means of the spring (33) and the pin (32) (illustrated in region *II* on the main sectional drawing). The striking of plate (4) against the head of stroke limiting screw (22) causes the separation of plates (4) and (5) to commence. This in turn causes the thread-forming ring segments (15) to be drawn away from the wedges (16) and to be separated from each other by the springs (25), thus releasing the molded thread. Finally, the ejector (19) causes ejection of the molded part (as illustrated in region *III* of the main sectional drawing and the plan view, *right,* Figs. 1 and 2). Internal cooling of the core (13) and external cooling of plate (5) result in short cycle times.

**Figs. 1 and 2  Three-cavity injection mold for a cosmetic cream container with a threaded lid**
1, 2: fixed mold plates, 3, 4: upper mold cavity retaining plate, 5: mold cavity plate, 6, 7: base plates, 8: spacer ring, 9, 10: ejector plates, 11, 12: movable mold plates, 13: cooled core, 14: insert to form bottom, 15: three-part thread forming ring, 16: wedge, 17: guide pin, 18: cooling water connection, 19: ejector sleeve, 20: ejector rod, 21: cooling water connection for core cooling, 22: stroke limiting screw, 23: sprue bushing, 24: locating ring, 25: spring, 26: guide pin, 27: guide bushing, 28: packing ring, 29: dowel pin, 30: connection screw, 31: spring, 32: ejector pin for runner, 33: spring

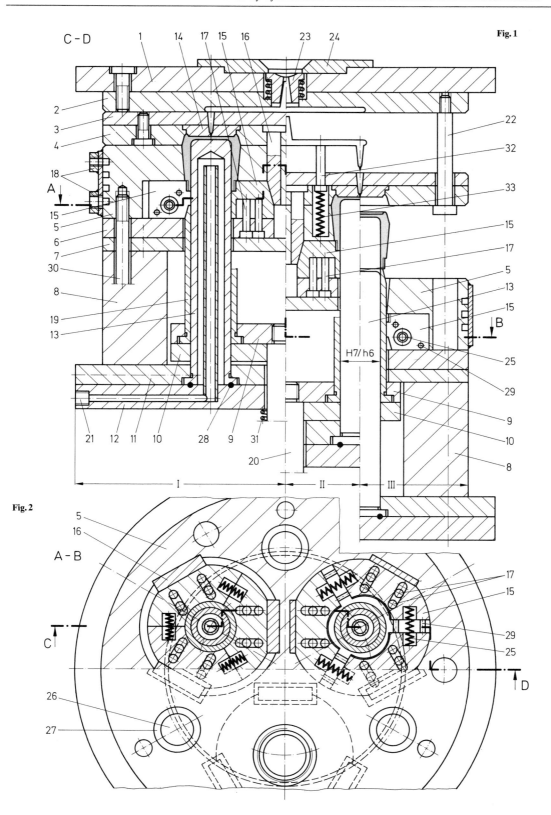

C - D

Fig. 1

H7/ h6

Fig. 2

A - B

# Example 35, Mold for a polyamide V-belt pulley

Internal and external undercuts on injection molded parts cause the costs for both mold making and mold maintenance to increase considerably, since slides and their actuating mechanisms become necessary. More-

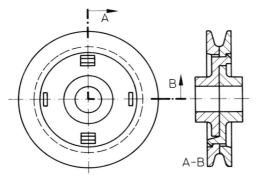

**Fig. 1  Nylon V-belt pulley, assembled from two identical parts by means of a snap connection**

over, with increasing use of the mold, the reliability drops due to the wear of precisely these additional components.

The nylon V-belt pulley shown in Fig. 1 is an example of a practical design showing how slides in the mold can be avoided. If the V-belt pulley were of a one-piece design, two or three slides per cavity would be required to form the V-belt groove in the pulley. Any flash formed in the groove with this mold design could be removed only with a great deal of effort. If the flash were not carefully removed, there would be a danger of damaging the V-belt. By dividing the pulley across the axis of rotation, the mold design shown in Fig. 2 becomes possible. Furthermore, the snap fit required for assembly may also be achieved without the use of slides. The two halves of the pulley were designed to be identical, so that the mold inserts are identical and any two pulley halves may be assembled together.

The three-plate mold (Fig. 2) operates fully automatically. Opening begins at parting line *I*, since plates (3) and (4) are held together by pin (25) and latch (24) until the bar (23) releases the latch (24) via the adjustment screw (27). Further opening movement of (3) and (4) is prevented by the stop bolts, so that parting line *II* also opens, and the molded parts may be ejected by the ejector pins (17). After removing the diaphragm gates, the molded parts may be snapped together to form the V-belt pulleys.

**Figs. 2 to 5   Four-cavity injection mold for nylon V-belt pulley halves**
1, 2: stationary-side clamp plates, 3: upper cooling plates, 4: upper cavity retainer plate, 5: lower cavity retainer plate, 6: support plate, 7, 8: ejector plates, 9, 10: movable-side clamp plates, 11: support pillar, 12: lower cavity insert, 13: upper cavity insert, 14: core pin, 15: insert, 16: flat bar, 17: ejector pin, 18: sprue bushing, 19: locating ring, 20: O-ring, 21: sprue ejector, 22: guide pin, 23: release bar, 24: latch, 25: latch pin, 26: pivot pin, 27: adjustment screw, 28: spring, 29: screw, 30: cooling water connection, 31: stop bolt, 32: ejector rod, 33: spring, 34: pin

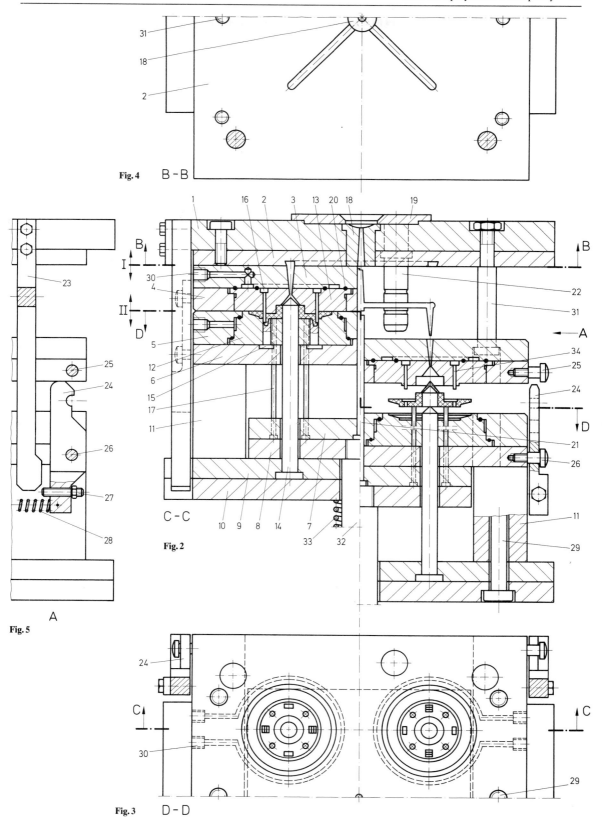

Fig. 4    B - B

Fig. 5

A

Fig. 2    C - C

Fig. 3    D - D

## Example 36, 8+8-cavity hot-runner stack mold for yoghurt cups of polypropylene

Stack molds for thin-walled cups must be built extremely ruggedly and precisely in order to avoid variations in wall thickness. Air ejection eliminates the need for mechanical ejector mechanisms and involves little wear.

Stack molds are employed whenever parts with low weight, minimal wall thickness and large projected area have to be produced in large numbers.

These polypropylene yoghurt cups weigh 13.4 g and have a wall thickness of 0.63 mm. A unique feature of these cups is the bottom rim (raised bottom), which requires special release techniques. Depending on the molding material used, yoghurt cups have wall thicknesses of 0.4 to 0.65 mm. The wall thickness within the cavity requires great accuracy, i. e. positioning of core and cavity must be extremely precise, so that the melt does not advance down one side, displacing the core in relation to the cavity. Should this be the case, it will be impossible to obtain properly filled parts.

### Mold

Figs. 1 and 2 show how ruggedly the entire mold, including core and cavity, has been dimensioned. Each core (1) and its alloted cavity (2) are aligned by the ring (3). All part-forming components are hardened, while the mold plates are nickel-plated. The mold has been designed with the aid of a CAD system and its components have been produced by means of CAM techniques.

### Mold temperature control

The minimal wall thickness of the molded parts allows for rapid cooling if the cooling system in the mold has been laid out correspondingly. As is customary with such cup molds, the cooling channels in core and cavity lie close together just below the mold surface. The cores are capped (8) with beryllium copper.

The paths of the cooling channels are shown in Fig. 3.

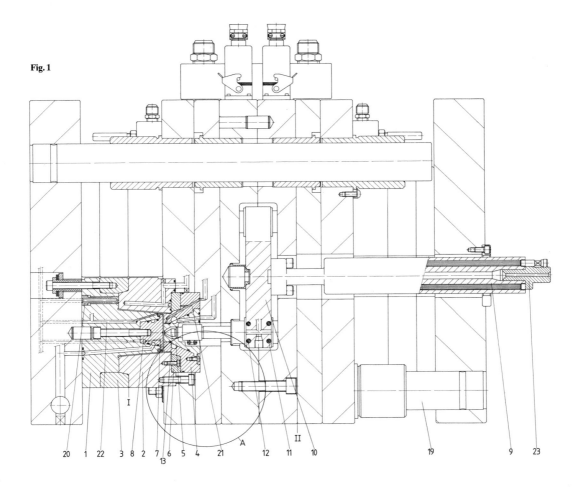

**Fig. 1**

**Fig. 2**

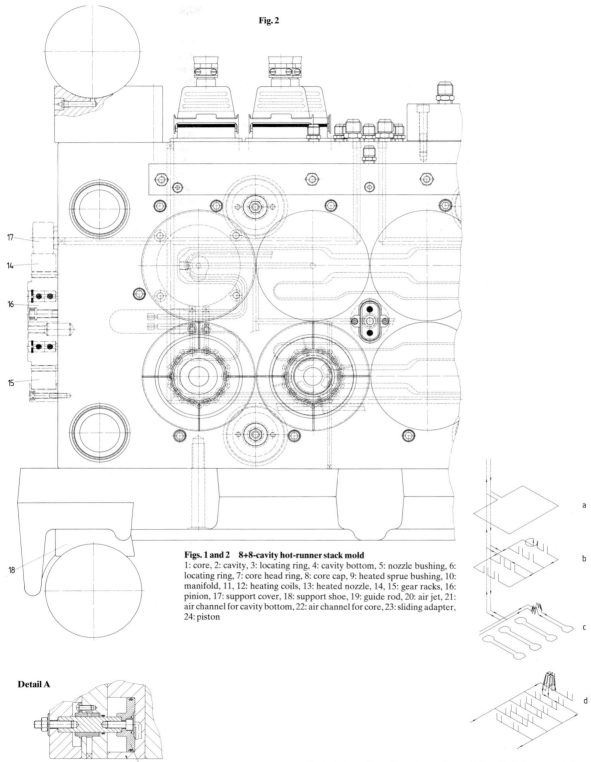

**Figs. 1 and 2    8+8-cavity hot-runner stack mold**
1: core, 2: cavity, 3: locating ring, 4: cavity bottom, 5: nozzle bushing, 6: locating ring, 7: core head ring, 8: core cap, 9: heated sprue bushing, 10: manifold, 11, 12: heating coils, 13: heated nozzle, 14, 15: gear racks, 16: pinion, 17: support cover, 18: support shoe, 19: guide rod, 20: air jet, 21: air channel for cavity bottom, 22: air channel for core, 23: sliding adapter, 24: piston

**Detail A**

24

**Fig. 4    Air cylinder for releasing the bottom rim**

a

b

c

d

**Fig. 3    Schematic cooling diagram for the 8+8-cavity hot-runner stack mold for yoghurt cups**
a: cooling for hot-runner plate, b: cooling for gate insert plate, c: cavity cooling, d: core cooling

## Runner system/gating

The melt to be injected flows to the cavities through a heated sprue bushing (9), which is screwed on to the manifold (10). The manifold itself is heated by two heating coils (11) and (12) embedded in it. Eight heated nozzles (13) lead to the cavities from the manifold (10).

There is a sliding adapter piece (23) where the melt enters the heated sprue bushing (9). When the molding machine's nozzle lifts off after injection, the adapter piece follows the nozzle, thereby increasing the volume of the manifold. The melt in it is allowed to expand, thus stopping the sprue bushing from drooling.

## Guides and supports

A pair of racks (14, 15) is mounted on either side of the mold, with a pinion (16) in between. They ensure the synchronous movement of the two parting lines when the mold opens or closes. Support pillars (17) above and below the racks absorb the radial forces transmitted by the meshed teeth when in operation. The mold

weighs 2330 kg and is supported on the machine's tie bars by shoes (18). There are also four guide rods inside the mold (19).

## Part release/ejection

The rim on the bottom of the cup can only be safely released if the cups are freed from the cavity bottom before the main parting line I opens. This is achieved with compressed air pistons (24), which push the mold apart first at parting line II on mold opening (Fig. 4). In order to prevent suction from occuring at the cup bottom, air is blown in. The cups now remain between the cavity insert (2) and core (1) until parting line I opens. The molded cups are now pulled out of their cavities and then blown off the cores by compressed air. This is achieved via two annular gaps between core head ring (7) and the adjacent components (1) or (8). There is a moving air jet (20) at the base of each core. As the mold opens, compressed air enters the air channel (21), the air jet (20) moves forward and an air blast blows the falling cups in a downward direction out of the mold.

# Example 37, 2+2-cavity stack mold for covers of polypropylene

The cover for a coffee maker has a diameter of 135 mm and is 13 mm high. Two small depressions are located on the outside edge, while two snap fits are found on the inside. In addition, and "ear" is found on the side of the cover.

## Mold (Figs. 1 to 3)

The mold has dimensions of 646 mm × 390 mm and a shut height of 736 mm, with a weight of 1000 kg.

The part-forming inserts are made of through-hardened steel (material no. 1.2767).

For such a cover (large projected area, minimal height, minimal weight), it makes sense to use a stack mold.

The four cavity inserts (2) are arranged in opposite pairs in the center plate (1) of the mold. One pair of cores (3) is located in the stationary mold plate, while the other pair is located in the moveable mold plate.

## Runner system/gating

The center plate also holds the four externally heated hot-runner nozzles (4) and the hot-runner manifold (6), that is heated with heater cartridges (5). Melt is conveyed to the manifold via the heated sprue bushing (7).

The heated sprue bushing (7) follows the motions of the center block and is enclosed in a stationary protec-

tive tube (8) that prevents any melt from drooling into the stationary-side ejector housing from the bushing plate (9).

A short runner (10) connects each of the four hot-runner nozzles (4) to the "ear" of the cover via a submarine gate.

Sucker pins (11) pull the solidified runners away from the hot-runner nozzles and out of the tunnel gates upon mold opening and then eject them.

## Mold temperature control

The cores and cavity inserts are provided with a system of cooling channels that cover their respective surfaces. Additional cooling lines are located in the center plate (1) to remove the unavoidable heat radiated by the hot-runner system.

## Part release/ejection

To release the outer depressions, each cavity has two slides (13) actuated by cam pins (12) attached to the cavity insert and guided along the core. The inner snap fits are released by lifters (14).

Ejector pins (15) are used to eject the molded part from the core. Three moveable core pins (17) position the cover during ejection. After a stroke "X", the cover is stripped off the core pin by a sleeve ejector (16).

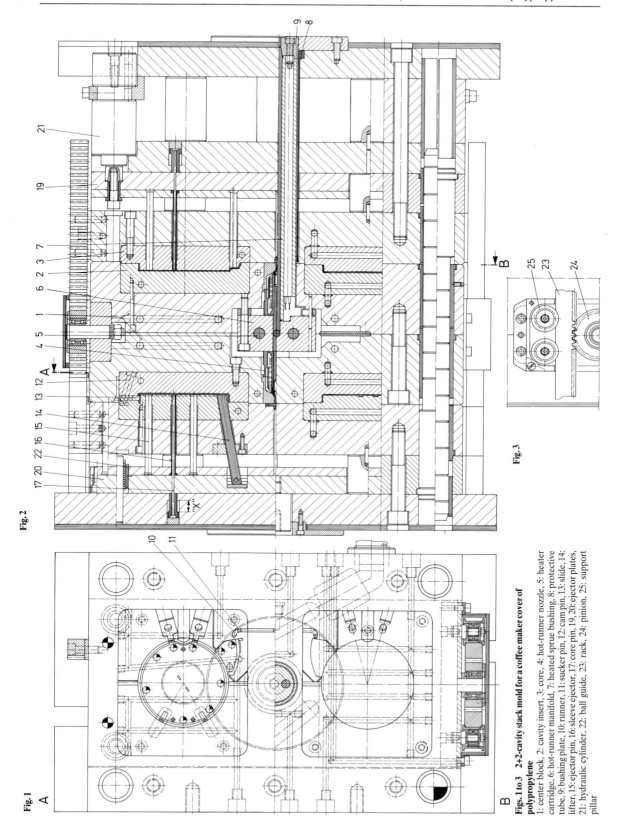

**Fig. 1**

**Fig. 2**

**Fig. 3**

**Figs. 1 to 3   2+2-cavity stack mold for a coffee maker cover of polypropylene**

1: center block, 2: cavity insert, 3: core, 4: hot-runner nozzle, 5: heater cartridge, 6: hot-runner manifold, 7: heated sprue bushing, 8: protective tube, 9: bushing plate, 10: runner, 11: sucker pin, 12: cam pin, 13: slide, 14: lifter, 15: ejector pin, 16: sleeve ejector, 17: core pin, 19, 20: ejector plates, 21: hydraulic cylinder, 22: ball guide, 23: rack, 24: pinion, 25: support pillar

The stationary-side ejector plate (19) is operated by hydraulic cylinders (21), while the moveable-side ejector plate (20) is operated by the machine's ejector. Both ejector plates run in ball guides (22).

Two racks (23) connected to each other by means of a pinion (24) are provided on the two narrow sides of the mold to assure synchronous opening and closing of both parting lines.

## Example 38, 5+5-cavity stack mold for a case of polypropylene

For a case in which the base and lid are connected by an integral hinge (Fig. 1), a stack mold (Fig. 2) has been designed with five mold cavities in each of the two parting lines. This means that each shot produces 10 complete cases. Due to the surface quality specified for the outside, the molded parts are gated on the inside surface; base and lid each require a separate gate.

Fig. 1    Case in which the base and lid are connected by an integral hinge (left opened, right closed)

Fig. 2    View into the open injection mold

### Mold

The mold mounting dimensions have been so selected that it can be used on two different injection molding machines with different distances between tie bars. Because of the mold's weight, it is also supported by shoes that fit over the tie bars of the injection molding machine in addition to its own four guide columns. The mold shown in Figs. 3 to 6 can be adapted to either tie bar spacing with the aid of the reversible adaptor (10) and the two semi-circular bearings (28) contained therein.

The moving central section of the mold accommodates the hot-runner manifold (5), which is heated by heater elements (63) cast into aluminium. The melt flows from the hot-runner manifold through a heated nozzle (42) to the respective gate in the base or lid of the case. The individual cavities are formed by the inserts (17) and (18). For appearance reasons, the gates are positioned asymmetrically. The hot-runner manifold (5) is fed by the machine's nozzle through a sprue bushing (20) which is heated by the tubular heater (64).

The total installed heating capacity amounts to about 13.5 kW. It is divided up as follows: $20 \times 300$ W for the hot-runner probes, 7000 W for the hot-runner manifold and 450 W for the tubular heater used around the sprue bushing. When in operation, the connected load is about 7.5 kW. The hot-runner probes can be independently controlled; their temperatures are monitored by built-in thermocouples. Four control circuits are provided for the hot-runner manifold. The temperature of the sprue bushing is controlled by the injection molding machine's closed-loop control in the same way as is the nozzle on the machine.

### Mold temperature control

Twenty circuits connected to a water manifold by quick disconnect couplings have been provided for cooling the molded parts.

### Part release/ejection

To eject the cooled parts, the mold opens with synchronous separation of the two parting lines assured by the action of the racks (6) and pinion (7). During the opening motion, the molded parts are retained on the central section until the racks actuate the ejector plates (3 A) and (3 B), thereby ejecting the molded cases and separating them from the gates. During mold closing, pushback pins return the ejector plates to their original positions again.

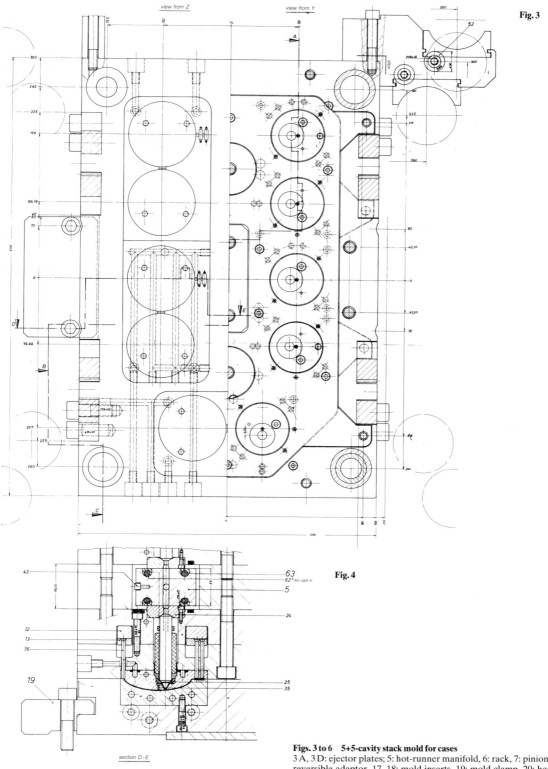

**Fig. 3**

view from Z    view from Y

section D - E

**Fig. 4**

63
62 Alu cast in
5
24
25
35

**Figs. 3 to 6    5+5-cavity stack mold for cases**
3 A, 3 D: ejector plates; 5: hot-runner manifold, 6: rack, 7: pinion, 10: reversible adaptor, 17, 18: mold inserts, 19: mold clamp, 20: heated sprue bushing, 28: semi-circular bearing, 42: hot-runner probe, 47: locating ring, 63: heater element, 64: tubular heater

**Fig. 5**

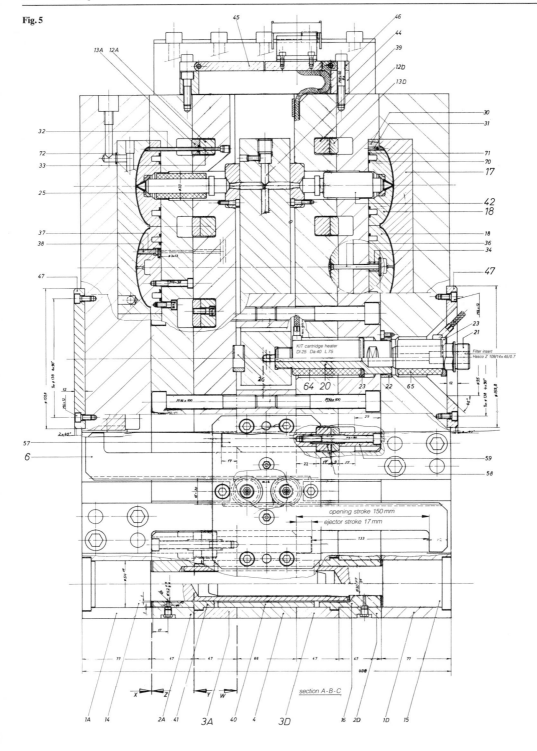

KIT cartridge heater
DI 25   Da 40   L 75

Filter insert
Hasco Z 109/14×45/0.7

opening stroke 150 mm

ejector stroke 17 mm

section A-B-C

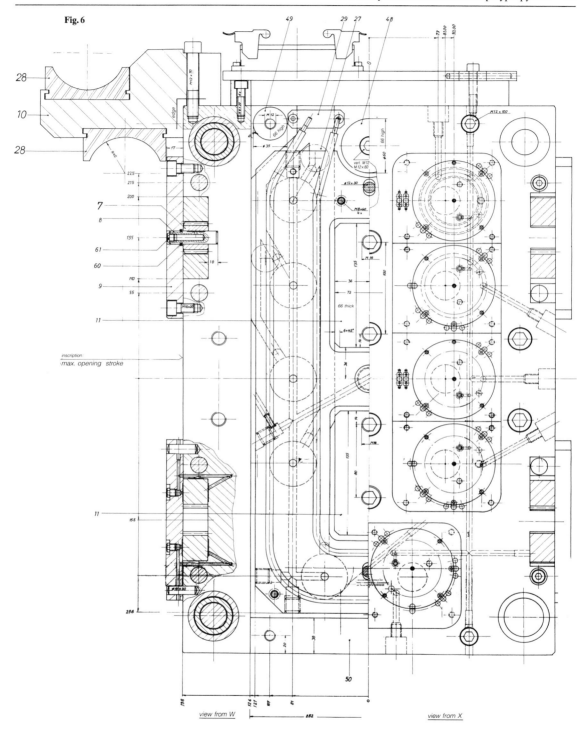

**Fig. 6**

view from W

view from X

max. opening stroke

inscription

# Example 38

**Figs. 3 to 6    5+5-cavity stack mold for cases**
3 A, 3 D: ejector plates; 5: hot-runner manifold, 6: rack, 7: pinion, 10:
reversible adaptor, 17, 18: mold inserts, 19: mold clamp, 20: heated
sprue bushing, 28: semi-circular bearing, 42: hot-runner probe, 47:
locating ring, 63: heater element, 64: tubular heater

# Example 39, Four-cavity hot-runner stack mold for producing automotive inner sill trim of polypropylene

To produce the inner sill trim used in an automobile as the transition between the carpeting and vehicle frame, a four-cavity hot-runner stack mold was designed. Interconnecting tubes with a sliding fit between the individual hot-runner manifolds eliminate the thermal expansion of the hot-runner system.

Depending on the car model, there is a left-hand and a right-hand version as well as a long and a short sill.

## General mold design

The dimensions of the inner sills are 1250 mm × 60 mm × 2.5 mm, so that the parts are relatively large in area but with comparatively little material content (Fig. 1). The molded parts weigh 180 and 150 g respectively. Producing these parts by means of a stack mold was the obvious solution, as this doubles the output of the injection molding machine although the clamping force requirements remain the same. The number of parts

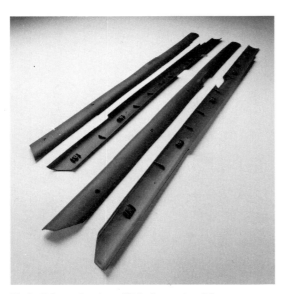

**Fig. 1   Polypropylene inner sill trim for an automobile**

needed to obtain optimum machine utilization resulted in a four-cavity mold with two different cavities for the left-hand and right-hand versions (Figs. 2 to 5). The variation in the length of the trim is taken care of by interchangeable mold inserts. To achieve warp-free molded parts with constant dimensions using the polypropylene copolymer (Hostalen PPR 1042, supplier: Hoechst AG) required that the flow lengths be limited to approximately 170 mm. Five injection points are needed along the inside of the trim.

The design of the mold provides for simultaneous opening of the two parting lines with the aid of two racks (40) and a pinion (36) for each side. As it is essential that no gate marks show on the front of the molded parts, injection had to take place on the inside. The mounting attachments and spacers for the carpeting, which require ejector assist for part release, are also lcoated in this area, however. Some of the mounting attachments are not given at right angles to the parting line, so that hydraulically operated ejectors have been incorporated in hot-runner plates (3) and (5). The cylinders have been specially designed to permit utilization in the immediate vicinity of the hot-runner manifolds at temperatures of about 260 °C.

## Mold temperature control

Three independent circuits have been provided in each of the mold plates (2) and (3) as well as (5) and (6) for mold temperature control. This permits the temperatures of the outer regions of the 1250 mm long parts to be controlled independently of the center region. At a mold width of 1500 mm and with several channels per plate, division into several circuits is also much more favorable with regard to pressure losses, which otherwise would occur.

**Figs. 2 to 5   Four-cavity hot-runner stack mold for producing inner sill trim of polypropylene for an automobile**

1: movable-side mold clamping plate, 2: movable-side cavity plate, 3: nozzle plate for the moving mold half, 4: center frame for the hot-runner manifold, 5: nozzle plate for the stationary mold half, 6: stationary-side cavity plate, 7: stationary-side mold clamping plate, 8, 9, 10: hot-runner manifolds, 11: central hot-runner manifold, 12, 13, 14: melt-conveying connecting pipes, 15: hot-runner feed pipe, 16: sliding sprue bushing, 17, 18: pressure pads, 19: thermally conductive torpedo, 20: torpedo retainer bushing, 21: gate insert, 22: insulating plates, 23, 24: lugs, 25: cartridge heater, 26: thermocouple, 27, 28, 29, 30: heater bands, 31: hydraulic ejector, 32: guide pin, 33: locating bushing, 34: guide bushing, :35: bushing retainer block, 36: pinion, 37: shaft, 38: ball bearing, 39: rack housing, 40: rack, 41: opening stop, 42: locating ring, 43: stationary-side locating ring, 44: spring, 45: insulating plate

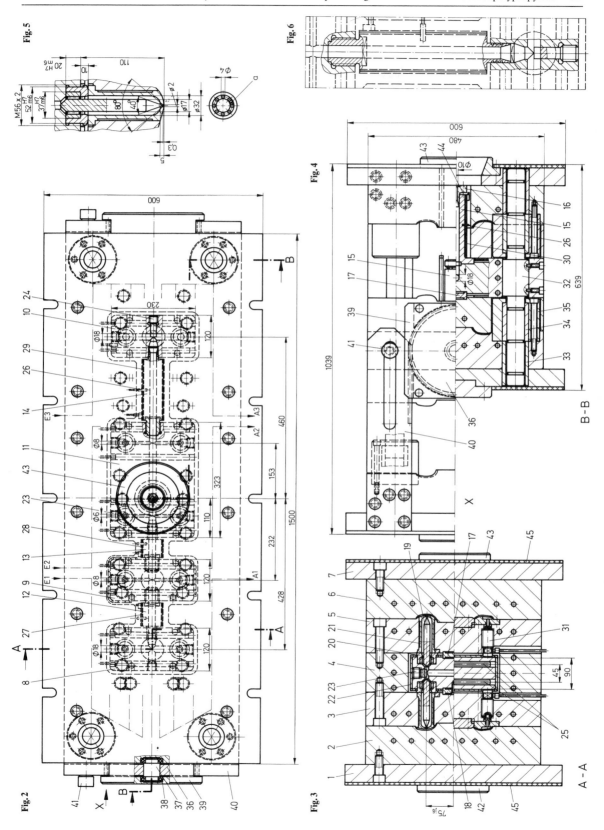

**Fig. 5**

**Fig. 6**

**Fig. 4**

B - B

**Fig. 2**

**Fig. 3**

A - A

## Hot-runner design

A hot-runner system utilizing indirectly heated thermally conductive torpedoes has been selected to distribute melt within the mold.

By incorporating the hydraulically operated ejectors in the mold plates (3) and (5) on the hot-runner side, the available space became reduced, thereby forcing a partial reduction of the torpedo diameter. By modifying other design parameters, it was possible to compensate for the resulting change in heat transfer.

The chosen injection points require the hot-runner manifold to be 888 mm long. To reduce the ensuing thermal expansion of approx. 2 mm total, four individual manifold blocks (8) to (11) that are connected to one another by means of melt-conveying pipes (12) to (14) with sliding fits have been provided. The feed pipe (15) divides the central manifold (11) into a right-hand and a left-hand half, each with its own temperature control. Each manifold contains four thermally conductive torpedoes. The left-hand side of manifold block (11) contains only three cartridge heaters, the heating for the feed pipe compensating for any possible heat loss in this area. It is thus possible to vary the temperature at each gate.

The melt-conveying pipes of the hot-runner system are fitted with commercially available heater bands with integral thermocouples. The hot-runner system thus contains five heater circuits for the manifold blocks and four heater circuits for the melt-conveying pipes. During the initial injection molding trials, it was found that heating of the melt-conveying pipes (12) and (13) was not needed. These pipes received adequate heat from the neighboring manifold blocks (8) to (11). No measurable temperature loss occurred. All of the cartridge heaters have the same dimension of 200 mm × 16 mm dia. and a heating capacity of 1250 W. The watt density in this case lies at 12.5 W/cm$^2$, a value guaranteeing long cartridge life even with negligible play in the heater cartridge well. The result is an installed heating capacity of 5000 W per manifold or heater circuit. Power is supplied via a temperature controller with thyristor control and an output current of 25 A. The four controllers for the melt-conveying pipes were chosen to have the same specifications, although an output current of 6 to 10 A would have been adequate. This means that if one temperature controller fails, operation of the most important manifold can be ensured by a simple wiring change. The total installed heating capacity thus amounts to 25 kW. The manifolds were designed to have 250 W per kg. With this specific heating capacity, balanced heating can be achieved for temperatures of up to approx. 300 °C at a mold temperature of 40 °C.

The warm-up time is approximately 15 minutes, not including the soft start provided by the controls. The integral soft start limits the supplied power to 50 % and thus protects the cartridge heaters.

The manifold pipes have been produced from hot work steel to insure that there is no loss in hardness at a possible temperature of 300 °C. The sealing lips which slide with the thermal expansion are designed to provide favorable flow characteristics. They have additionally been protected against leakage by pressure relief grooves. This design has proven to be leakproof in operation. The threaded section has been produced with a toleranced press fit. The feed pipe (15) is provided with a decompression bushing (16) at the end; this bushing has a stroke of about 5 mm. The length of the feed pipe is such that no dripping material can possibly drop into the parting line of the mold.

The melt covers a distance of 940 mm to the farthest gates. The nearest gates are 530 mm away from the decompression bushing. During operation, the hot runner is completely filled with melt. The pressure is thus transmitted almost uniformly up to the individual gates in the stationary melt (or during creep flow). The holding pressure is therefore also uniformly applied. When the melt is flowing, however, there is a pressure drop along the flow path. A Moldflow analysis conducted with the objective of providing identical pressure losses in the flowing melt up to each gate yielded different diameters for the runner channels. The primary runner channel has a diameter of 18 mm, while the vertical secondary runners have a diameter of 6 mm in the center of the mold and one of 8 mm in the outer regions.

The torpedoes are 110 mm long, 17 mm in diameter with an insulating gap of 7.5 mm. At a hot-runner manifold temperature of 260 °C, the temperature at the torpedo tip is still at least 235 °C. This value is sufficient for polypropylene. Start-up even after a prolonged production interruption does not present any problems. The gate inserts (21) are insulated from the mold plate by a 0.5 mm annular air pocket. A CuCrZr alloy (material no. 2.1293) was selected for the torpedoes (3). The torpedoes have been chemically plated with hard nickel [4] to prevent a chemical reaction between the copper and the PP and then subsequently coated with a thin layer of chrome to give better adhesive properties.

The four hot-runner manifolds (8) to (11) have been provided with central pressure pads (17) and (18) which serve to locate the manifolds and transmit the resulting forces into the adjacent mold plates. Four dowel pins in grooves prevent the manifolds from turning. The manifolds are not bolted to the adjacent nozzle plates, but are allowed to float. The distance between the torpedo retainer bushings (20) has been overdimensioned by 0.1 mm in relation to the center frame (4) to ensure that the system remains leak-proof even in the event of plate deflection or an angular displacement. It was found that, in spite of the size of the mold, the increased thermal expansion of the hot-runner system with respect to the mold frame is sufficient to provide an efficient seal.

As a result of the separation into four separate manifolds with axially sliding melt conveying pipes, thermal expansion perpendicular to the mold axis did not have to be taken into account. The torpedoes themselves were shortened by 0.4 mm when cold. As they heat up, they expand into the precalculated position. The hot-runner manifolds are covered with insulating plates (22) clad with aluminium foil to reduce radiation losses.

The total volume of melt in the system is approximately 840 $cm^3$; the volume of the four sill trim moldings is 650 $cm^3$. This assures a short residence time for the melt in the manifold system. Changing to a different color for the sill trim does not present any problems during production and can be accomplished quickly.

## Literature

1  Hot runner system with indirectly heated thermally conductive torpe-does, Technical Plastics Series "Berechnen Gestalten/Anwenden", C 2.2, company publication from Hoechst AG, 1981
2  *P. Unger:* Kunststoffe 70 (1980) p. 730/737
3  Company publication from Thyssen Edelstahlwerke AG: 1154/51 377, Elmedur X
4  Chemisch Nickel Kanigen, company publication from Schnarr OHG

# Example 40, Hot-runner stack mold for a water distribution block of polypropylene

The water distribution block for a dishwasher (Fig. 1) consists essentially of two flat parts of polypropylene that are welded together so as to be watertight. Because of the postmolding shrinkage of polypropylene, it is necessary that the two halves be welded together either after a minimum of two days storage or, better yet, immediately after molding. The latter approach is especially simple if both parts (which differ in weight and projected area) are produced together in a single mold.

The decision was made in favor of a stack mold to produce both parts. With regard to this decision, the following points had to be considered:

In a stack mold, the hot-runner manifold is always located between the two parting lines that accommodate the mold cavities. As a rule, the melt is conveyed to the manifold via a feed pipe which is coaxial with the injection and clamping units and passes through the first parting line of the mold. This is not possible here, however, because the molded part covers the entire mold surface of this parting line.

Another possibility would be to supply the melt to the manifold from the side. This requires that the injection unit of the molding machine be repositioned by 90 degrees (L position) so that the direction of injection lies in the plane formed by the runners. For plant-related reasons, this design could not be considered.

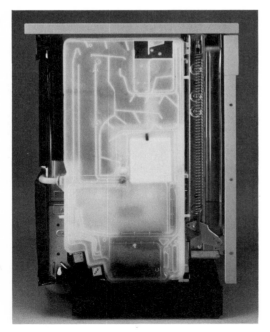

**Fig. 1    Water distribution block for a dishwasher**

## Mold

A design was selected (Fig. 2) in which the melt coming from the machine nozzle is directed from the sprue bushing (314) around the first parting line (20, 21, 22) to the hot-runner manifold (1). Such redirection of the melt flow results in an increased pressure loss during injection (Fig. 3). The arrangement shown at the bottom of Fig. 3 was finally selected.

Another unique aspect of this arrangement is that both the thickness of plate (22) as well as the opening stroke of the first parting line affect the shut height of the mold. The entire melt-conveying system (20, 21, 22) is fastened to the hot-runner manifold located in the center section of the mold and executes the same opening and closing motions. The distance H (Fig. 2) must be provided for these motions. The hot-runner plate (22) is supported against the central section (11, 12) by means of pillars (3).

A simplification of this arrangement would be possible with an injection molding machine where the injection unit is raised by the amount E (Fig. 2) so that the machine is coaxial with the melt-conveying bridge pipe (21). The shut height of the mold would then be reduced and the pressure loss in the melt-conveying system less.

## Runner system/gating

Analyses of the filling pattern (Fig. 4) resulted in the channel dimensions given in Fig. 5 for the hot-runner manifold. By varying the runner channel dimensions, it was possible to compensate for the different flow path lengths and volumes of melt in the runner system so that the 8 hot-runner nozzles (Fig. 6) could remain identical. In deviation from the standard design, the nozzle body "a" of these nozzles is steel.

## Part release/ejection

The part farther away from the machine nozzle is ejected by means of the machine's ejector system; the part closer to the nozzle is ejected by means of hydraulic cylinders (not shown) that actuate ejector plates (6 and 7).

## Heating the hot-runner system

As the result of thermal expansion, the bridge pipe (21) also increases in length. In order to avoid thermal stresses in the melt-conveying system and hot-runner manifold, and thus any possible leakage, the mounting screws between the bridge pipe (21) and hot-runner plate (22) can be tightened only after reaching the operating temperature. These screws must be loosened again before turning off the heating system.

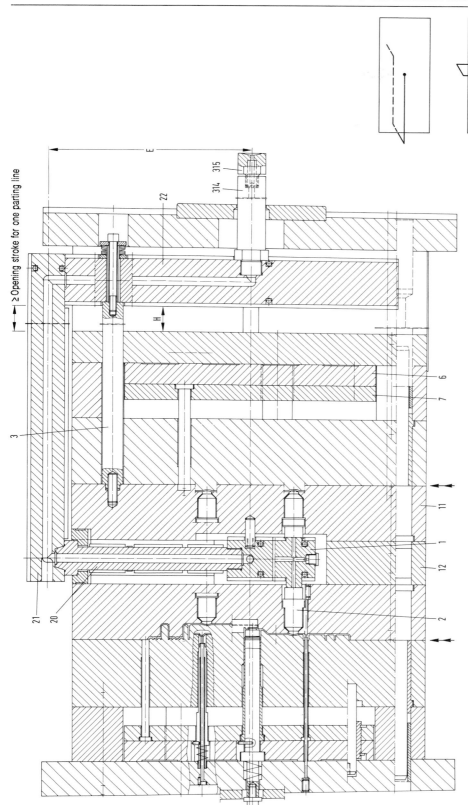

Fig. 3   Comparison of possible runner system arrangements, top; around the narrow side of the mold; bottom; around the wide side of the mold, with less pressure loss (injection time: 5 s, material; PP, type Novolen 1100 HX (manufacturer; BASF, Ludwigshafen)

Fig. 2   Connection of the mold and its central hot-runner manifold plate with the machine nozzle

1: hot-runner manifold, 2: hot-runner nozzle, 3: support pillar, 6, 7: ejector plates, 11: mold plate, 12: spacer plate, 20: feed pipe, 21: bridge pipe, 22: hot-runner, (314) heated sprue bushing, (315) adaptor

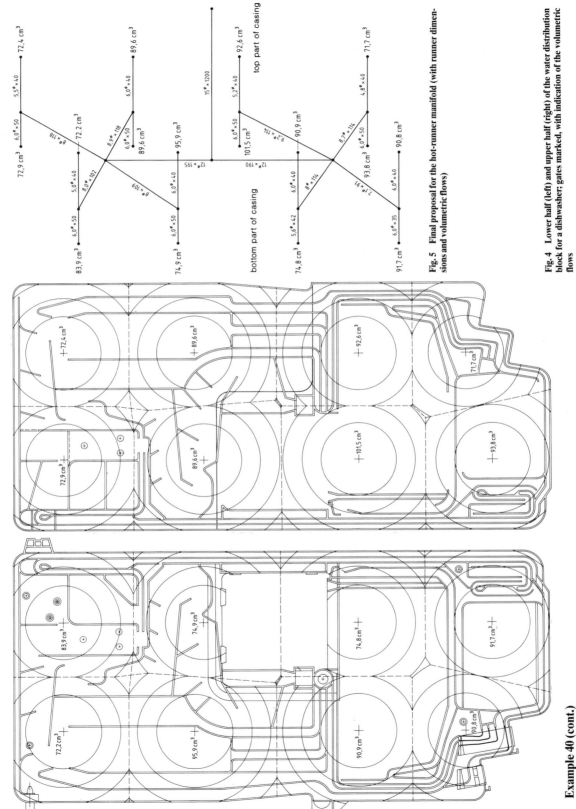

**Fig. 5   Final proposal for the hot-runner manifold (with runner dimensions and volumetric flows)**

**Fig. 4   Lower half (left) and upper half (right) of the water distribution block for a dishwasher; gates marked, with indication of the volumetric flows**

**Example 40 (cont.)**

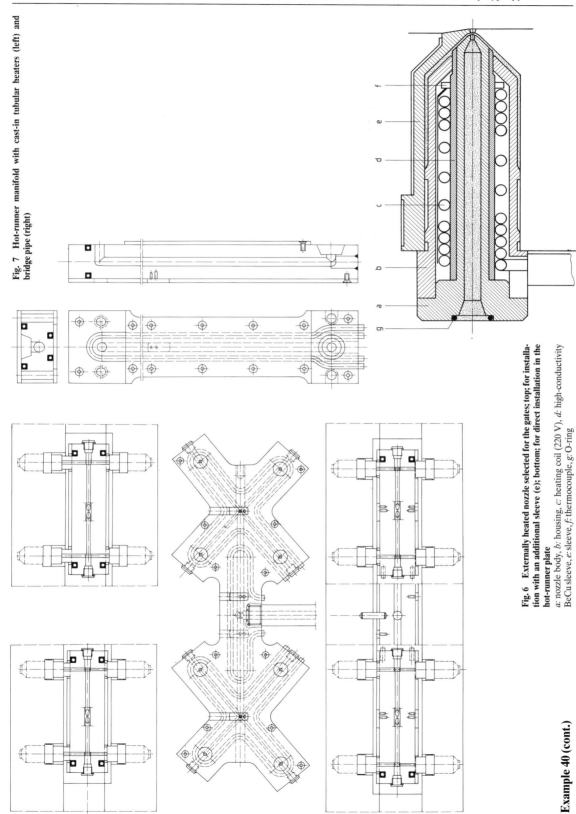

Fig. 7  Hot-runner manifold with cast-in tubular heaters (left) and bridge pipe (right)

Fig. 6  Externally heated nozzle selected for the gates; top: for installation with an additional sleeve (e); bottom; for direct installation in the hot-runner plate

a: nozzle body, b: housing, c: heating coil (220 V), d: high-conductivity BeCu sleeve, e: sleeve. f: thermocouple, g: O-ring

**Example 40 (cont.)**

## Operation

Opening and closing of the two parting lines is accomplished with the aid of two racks connected via a pinion on each side of the mold (Fig. 8). Both parting lines thus open and close synchronously.

**Fig. 8    Stack mold with racks for synchronous opening**

# Example 41, 8+8-cavity stack mold for lozenge box in polystyrene

A mold was to be designed for a transparent, thin-walled lozenge-box bottom in polystyrene. The manufacturing costs had to be kept in an acceptable relation to the production costs. An injection molding machine of sufficient daylight opening was available, hence the decision for an 8+8-cavity stack mold (Figs. 1 to 5). This mold consists of three plate assemblies with interspaced ejector plates (3) and (9). In the central plate assembly (4 to 8) are installed the hot-runner (15) with the heated sprue bushing (19), the hot-runner nozzles (14) and the mold cavities in plates (4) and (8). The latter can be cooled intensively, as can be the cores (12) fixed in the outer plate assemblies.

The H-shaped hot runner manifold (15) is heated by four cartridge heaters (30). A cartridge heater (18) installed in the torpedo (16) ensures uniform heating of the molding material in the sprue bushing (19). The specially designed nozzle from the machine's plasticizing unit extends into the sprue bushing (20). The hot-runner nozzle (14) projects its tapered tip up to the shape-forming surface of the mold cavity, so that a "runnerless" injection is feasible. The gate insert sleeve (21) required with indirectly heated thermally conductive nozzles for thermotechnical reasons had to be shortened, because a continuous gate insert sleeve would have left an unacceptable marking on the molding.

Opening and closing of the two mold parting lines is coordinated by two laterally fitted angle levers (32, 33) that are linked to the plate assemblies. When the mold opens, the central plate assembly (4 to 8) is held centered between the two outer plate assemblies (1, 2) and (10, 11) by this lever arrangement. The ejector plates (3) and (9) are set in motion simultaneously by the levers (34), so that the molded parts are pushed off the cores (12) by the ejector plates (13) during the continued opening movement.

**Figs. 1 to 5 s. p. 104/105**

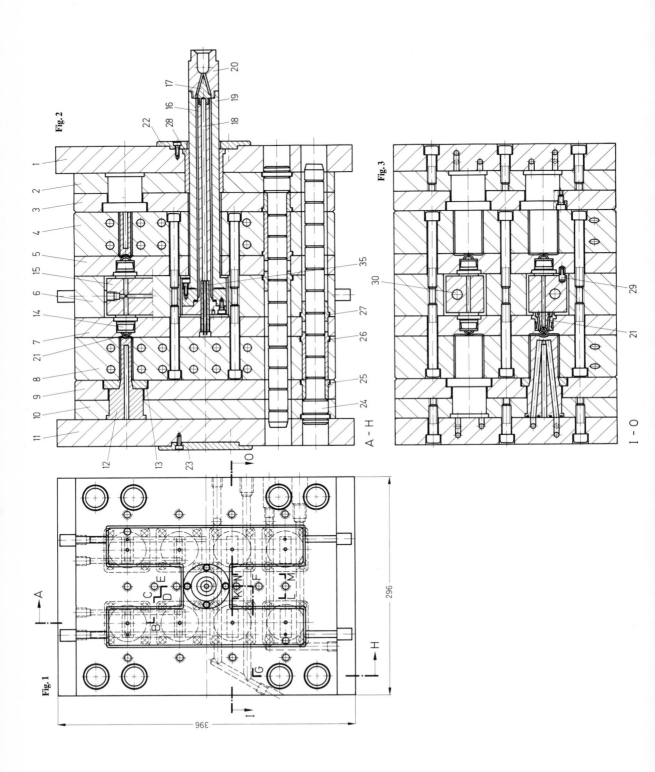

Fig. 2

Fig. 3

Fig. 1

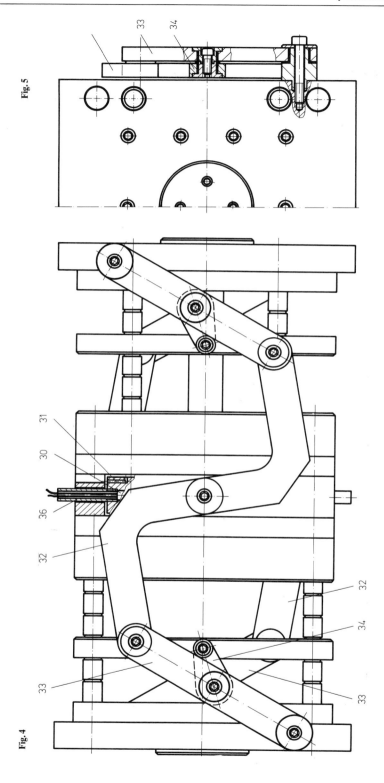

**Fig. 5**

**Fig. 4**

## Example 41

**Figs. 1 to 5   8+8-cavity stack mold for lozenge-box bottoms in polystyrene**
1: fixed-half mold mounting plate, 2: fixed core retaining plate, 3: fixed-half ejector plate, 4: fixed-half mold cavity plate, 5: fixed-half ejector plate, 6: hot-runner plate, 7: moving-half nozzle plate, 8: moving-half mold cavity plate, 9: moving-half ejector plate, 10: moving core retaining plate, 11: moving-half mounting plate, 12: core, 13: ejector insert, 14: nozzle housing, 15: hot-runner block, 16: torpedo, 17: torpedo tip, 18: cartridge heater, 19: heated sprue bushing, 20: sprue bushing, 21: hot-runner gate insert sleeve, 22, 23: locating ring, 24: leader pin, 25, 26, 27: guide bushing, 28: guide bushing, 29: locating pin, 30: cartridge heater, 31: thermocouple, 32: angle lever, 33: connecting lever, 34: pilot link, 35, 36: cartridge heater housing
lever, 33: connecting lever, 34: pilot link, 35, 36: cartridge heater housing
The cores 12: are not shown in Fig. 4

## Example 42, Two-cavity hot-runner stack mold for trays

Flat molded parts of large areas such as trays cannot be produced in customary design stack molds if only one cavity is to be provided in each one of the two parting lines. In this case the heated sprue bushing cannot be located in the central longitudinal axis of the mold as connecting body between the injection unit of the machine and the hot runner manifold. If, however, an injection molding machine is available with the plasticizing unit at a right angle to the axis of the clamping unit (L position), then the mold illustrated in Figs. 1 to 6 represents a simple solution for the above-mentioned case of application. With this design the molded material is injected from the side immediately into the hot runner manifold (7), which is situated as usual in the center of the plate assembly. Each of the two injection molded parts is injected "runnerlessly" via four pinpoint gates from the bottom. The injection molding material is fed into the star-shaped hot-runner manifold (7) from the center, so that the flow paths of the melt in the manifold to the gates are of equal length.

The mold is symmetrically constructed except for plates (4) and (5) which enclose the hot-runner manifold (7). In the completely open position the central plate assembly (4, 5) with the hot-runner manifold is placed at equal distance centrally between the two outer plate assemblies (1, 2, 3) due to the stripper bolts (18). The molded parts are ejected by the ejection device (18 to 21), which is actuated by spring (20) pressure and pushes the ejector plate (22) forward when the stripper bolts (18) make contact with plate (4) or (5). The molded parts are then ejected by the ejector pins (24). This can take place in both halves of the mold independently of each other and at different times.

The hot-runner manifolds and nozzles shown in this example no longer represent the current state of the art. They can be replaced with commercially available components from manufacturers of standard mold components.

### Literature

1  *E. Lindner, W. Hartmann:* Plastverarbeiter 28 (1977) p. 351/353
2  *T. Johnson:* Kunststoffe 70 (1980) p. 742/746

**Figs. 1 to 6   Hot-runner stack mold for trays**
1: mold mounting plate, 2: spacer, 3: core plate, 4, 5: mold cavity plate, 6: sprue bushing, 7: hot-runner manifold, 8: clamping plate for hot-runner manifold, 9, 10: spacer ring, 11: outer body of nozzle, 12: heat conducting insert for nozzle, 13: pressure ring, 14: locating ring, 15: pressure ring, 16: leader pin, 17: guide bushing, 18: stripper bolt, 19: spring bolt, 20: pressure spring, 21: washer, 22: ejector plate, 23: clamping plate for ejector pin, 24: ejector pin, 25: locating plate, 26: cartridge heater

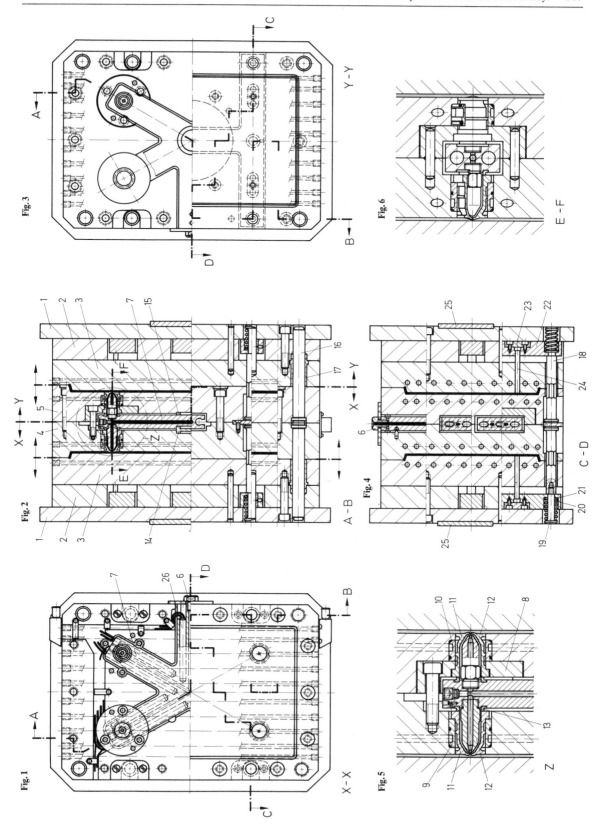

Fig. 1

Fig. 2

Fig. 3

Fig. 4

Fig. 5

Fig. 6

## Example 43, 2+2-cavity stack mold with a hot-runner system for runnerless molding of polystyrene container lids using direct edge gating

In selecting a suitable injection molding machine, the necessary clamping force, shot volume, mold height and mold opening stroke must be in a balanced ratio to each other. This, however, is achieved only partially in the production of relatively flat and thin-section parts unless the number of cavities in a mold is doubled by adopting the multidaylight design. This increases injection volume, mold height and necessary mold opening stroke while the necessary locking force remains unchanged [1].

### Stack molds for container lids

Stack molds became established to any extent only when it became possible to employ runnerless gating of the mold cavities lying in the two mold parting surfaces via hot-runner systems. With few exceptions the systems used have a common feature, namely that the gate is always parallel to the longitudinal axis of the mold.

The task was to produce polystyrene lids (Fig. 2) for a polystyrene container (Fig. 1) using a stack mold (Figs. 3 to 5, see pp. 110 and 111) so as to make better use of the machine. The outer surface of the lid must not, however, show any gate mark, so that the lids can only be gated on the inside or externally from the side.

Gating on the inside of the lid is not possible since it would be too difficult and complicated to design a hot-runner system passing through the mold core and the necessary ejector system. This means that the only solution is to provide for direct edge gating of the lid, the gate being situated on an external side wall surface.

Although standard hot-runner nozzles specially developed for the purpose are now on the market for runnerless, direct edge gating, the shape of the article will dictate whether such a hot-runner nozzle can be used. As Fig. 6 A shows, the space for hot-runner nozzles used for direct edge gating should be far enough away from the mold cavity for the cavity wall lying in between to be able to absorb the stress produced during injection. On the other hand, the thinner the cavity wall and the shorter therefore the gate land, the smaller will be the residue remaining inside the gate until the next injection molding cycle. Under no circumstances must the residue be longer than the component wall thickness.

In the present container lid this kind of runnerless edge gating of the article with a hot runner nozzle cannot be realized since this would make the gate disproportionally long (Fig. 6 B) because of the angle of the side wall relative to the lid surface.

To gate the component directly on the side wall nevertheless, the hot-runner system of the stack mold was equipped with hot-runner nozzles. In contrast to the generally used direction of installation (along the longitudinal axis of the mold), installation in this case was at right angles to the longitudinal mold axis. This hot-runner nozzle is of pointed conical shape at the front end, which fits into a conically shaped gates insert so that the nozzle tip can be flush with the cavity wall. In this way the formation of a gate vestige, which could prevent release of the component, is prevented (Fig. 7).

Fig. 1    Polystyrene packaging container

Fig. 2    Lid for the container shown in Fig. 1

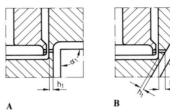

A                          B

Fig. 6  Dependence of gate height on article wall thickness for the minimum distance of the gate insert from the cavity (governed by strength considerations) for hot-runner nozzles used for direct edge gating
$h_1$ gate height for right angled position of article side wall to base and minimum distance of mold cavity from the antechamber of the hot-runner nozzle, $h_2$ gate height for non-rectangular position of article side wall to base ($a_2 \geq 95\,°$). In this case $h_2 > h_1$

**Fig. 7    Smoothed-out gate mark of container lid**

## Construction and operation of the stack mold

Two container lids (C) lie in each of the two parting surfaces (A) and (B) of the stack mold (Fig. 5). The mold consists of three plates (1, 2, 3), the cavities being in the center plate (2), formed by the cavity plates (4 a, 4 b, 5 a, 5 b) and core inserts (7) and (8). The core inserts are attached to plates (9) and (10), which form part of the plate assemblies (1) and (3).

The plate assemblies (1) and (3) are guided via leader pins (11) and guide bushings (12) (Fig. 4). The position of the three plate assemblies relative to one another is assured by means of further centering units (13), which lie in the parting surfaces (A) and (B).

The container lids (C) are injected via directly heated hot-runner nozzles (14) in the center of a longitudinal side at a distance of 10 mm from the lid bottom. Each mold cavity is filled through the annular gap of about 0.3 mm between hot-runner nozzle and gate. To keep the heat requirements for the two heated hot-runner nozzles as low as possible compared with those of the cooled mold, the nozzles are surrounded by thermally insulating gate inserts (15). These center the nozzles and at the same time support them relative to the cavity plates. Each gate insert lies centrally in an insert well and the gate linked to it. This ensures that the nozzle's tip is exactly centered in the gate.

At the center of the stack mold there is a hot-runner (16). This is rectangular; only near the band heater (650 W) (17) and the centering collar is it round. In the rectangular part of the hot-runner the cartridge heaters are accommodated by means of bars fixed to it (18). Two high-capacity cartridge heaters (19) are incorporated, each with a heating capacity of 800 W (Fig. 3).

On the outside of the mold there are clamps (20) that pull the cavity plates (4 a) and (4 b) as well as (5 a) and (5 b) toward the hot-runner over the hot-runner nozzle when the center plate assembly is being assembled. These parts are thus clamped in such a way that there is no risk of leakage between the end of the nozzle and hot-runner manifold. The surface contact pressure between nozzles and manifolds is further increased during operation because of thermal expansion.

A flangelike thickening at the hot-runner is clamped between cavity plates (4 a, 4 b) and (5 a, 5 b), so that the injection unit's nozzle contact force acting axially on the manifolds is absorbed. The manifold is centered in the intermediate plate (6) as well as by the two two-part centering pieces (23) and (24).

The mold cavities are fed with melt through the central feed channel (21) and the four runners (22) lying at right angles to it and the four hot-runner nozzles. At the front side the hot-runner is closed by a sliding shut-off nozzle (25) when the machine nozzle moves away, so as to prevent molding compound escaping, which would inevitably cause production problems after cooling and solidifying. Because of the axial displacement of the torpedo (26) when the hot-runner moves away from the machine nozzle, the melt compressed in the hot-runner system during the injection process can expand in the resultant space of the channel (21). This prevents the melt escaping through the gates when the mold opens.

The claddings (27) and (28) protect the hot-runner from major heat loss when the mold is opened and at the same time serve to protect the operator against accidental contact with the hot-runner.

When the mold is opened, the plate assembly (3) is pulled toward the left by the mold clamping plate (29), which is fixed to the moving platen of the injection molding machine, thereby opening parting line (B). During this operation, a synchronous opening movement of the two parting lines is achieved via a rack and pinion drive (30), which lies diagonally on the front and back surface of the mold (Fig. 3).

Ejection of the container lids takes place in the parting line (A) via the ejector mechanism (31), which is operated via two pneumatic cylinders (32). These lie on two opposite outer mold surfaces diagonally relative to each other. The ejector movement for the articles in parting surface (B) is carried out, as usual, via the ejector mechanism (33), which is actuated via the ejector rod (34).

The hinge holes on the component are produced by the core pins (35), which lie in the slides (36). The slides' movement at right angles to the direction of demolding is achieved by cam pins (37) (Fig. 4).

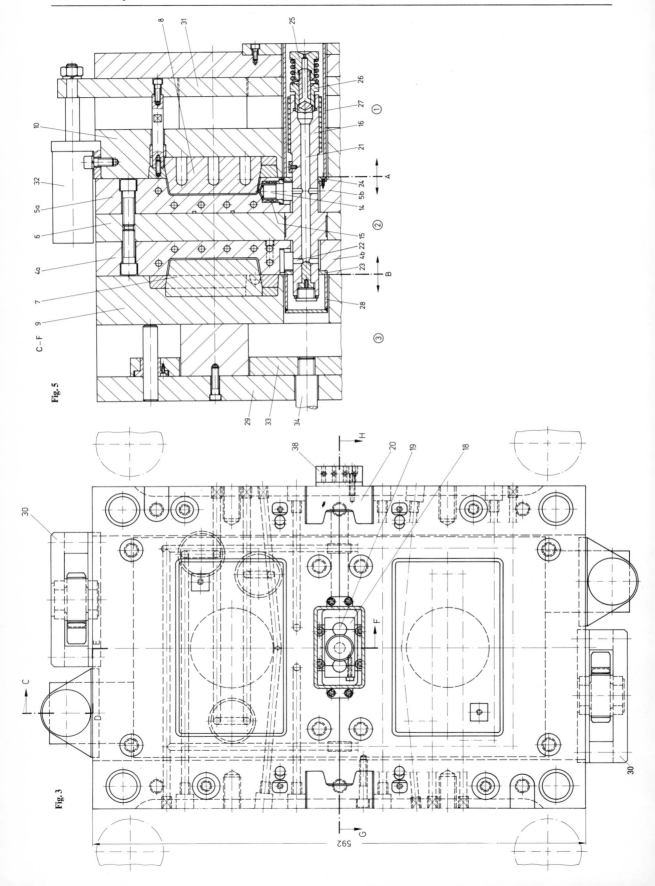

Fig. 5

Fig. 3

## Example 43

**Fig. 3 to 5   2+2-cavity stack mold with hot-runner system for direct runnerless edge gating of polystyrene container lids**

1, 2, 3: plate assembly 4 a, 4 b, 5 a, 5 b: cavity plates, 6: intermediate plate, 7, 8: core inserts, 9, 10: support plates, 11: leader pin, 12: guide bushing, 13: centering unit, 14: hot-runner nozzle, 15: gate insert, 16: hot-runner, 17: band heater (650 W), 18: cover strip, 19: high-capacity cartridge heater, 20: centering clamp, 21: principal hot-runner, 22: secondary hot-runner, 23, 24: centering piece, double-shell, 25: sliding shut-off nozzle unit, 26: torpedo, 27, 28: sheet metal cladding, 29: mold clamping plate, 30: rack-and-pinion drive, 31: ejector mechanism, 32: pneumatic cam pin, 38: electrical terminal block for hot-runner nozzles

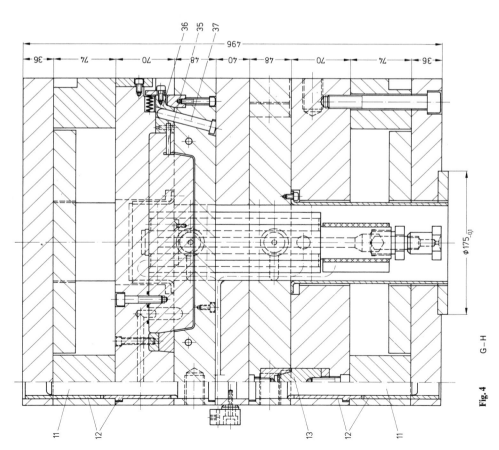

**Fig. 4**

G – H

# Example 44, 4+4-cavity hot-runner stack mold for dessert cups of polypropylene

The mold described here is used to produce polypropylene dessert cups with an average diameter of 60 mm, a height of 85 mm and a wall thickness of 0.55 mm. The cups weigh 7.5 g. The cup is footed so that an undercut that must be released by means of slides is formed between the foot and body of the cup.

## Mold

The mold weighs approx. 2200 kg, has a shut height of approx. 700 mm and is designed as a 4+4-cavity stack mold. As is customary with stack molds, it consists essentially of three sections, namely the two end sections each of which has a clamping plate (1, 11) with approx. dimensions of 540 mm × 800 mm and a core retainer plate (2, 12). The center section (5) with the two bottom retainer plates (3, 13) holds the hot-runner manifold (4).

Two cavity retainer plates (6, 16) that accommodate the cavity inserts (7) are located between the two end sections and the center section.

The core inserts (8) are held by the core retainer plates (2, 12). Rugged locating rings (9) with conical surfaces that engage and center the cavity inserts (7) are fitted over the core inserts.

Guide strips (10) in which the slides (14) move sideways are bolted to the cavity retainer plates (6, 16). Each slide forms half of the outer shape of one foot for two neighboring cavities. Cam pins (15) mounted in the center section serve to actuate the slides. The opening stroke of the mold is 2 × 200 mm.

## Runner system/gating

Melt flows from the sprue bushing (17) with an attached sliding shutoff (18) into the feed pipe (19) and from there to the hot-runner manifold (4), which is heated by four heater rods (20). The directly heated hot-runner nozzles (21) the tips of which extend to the gate openings in the bottom inserts (22) are attached to the hot-runner manifold.

The heaterbands for the feed pipe are enclosed by a protective tube (23), since the feed pipe is exposed via parting lines ( I A) and ( II A) when the mold is opened. The total installed heating capacity is approx. 6 kW.

The sliding shutoff prevents leakage of melt when the feed pipe is pulled in to the stationary section of the mold during mold opening. In addition, the increase in volume of the hot-runner system produced by the sliding shutoff when the machine nozzle backs away prevents drooling from the hot-runner nozzles.

## Mold venting

Vent gaps (32) and vent channels to remove the air displaced by the melt entering the cavity are provided at the ends of the flow paths around the rim of the cup and at the foot.

## Cooling

Thin-wall parts such as these cups transfer heat quickly to mold surfaces, so that increased expenses for the cooling system are worthwhile in molds for such parts. Cooling of the core should be given special attention. A beryllium/copper cap (24) with six radial cooling channels is placed on the core insert (8). These cooling channels require drilling of the center tube (25) leading to the cap. This drilling weakens the center tube and there is the risk of rupture if the mounting nuts (26) are tightened excessively. Compression springs (27) are provided to permit an exactly defined tightening torque.

Coolant is supplied to the cooling channels in the slides via tubes (28) threaded into the slides. Slots (29) in the guide strips (10) allow these tubes to follow the motion of the slides.

## Part release/ejection

Prior to mold opening, the hydraulic cylinders (30) are pressurized, so that the parting lines ( I A, II B) open first. The undersides of the feet are released, the slides separate. Ball detents (33) secure the opened slides in their end positions.

Once the piston in the hydraulic cylinders has completed its full stroke, the mold opens at ( I A, I B) , and the cups, still retained on the cores, are withdrawn from the cavity inserts (7).

Finally, compressed air is introduced to the annular gap between the core insert (8) and core cap (24) via the channels (31). The molded parts are now blown off. A rack and pinion arrangement not shown in the drawing is used to assure synchronous opening of the mold parting lines.

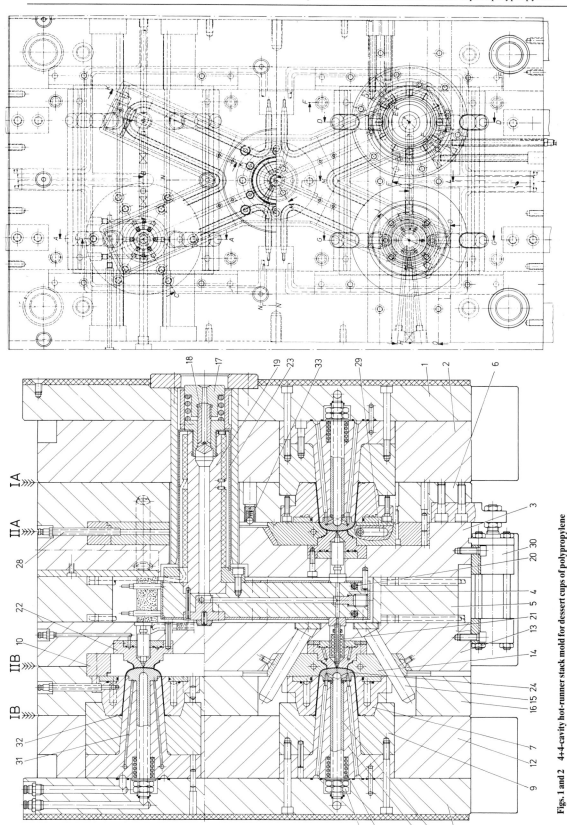

**Figs. 1 and 2    4+4-cavity hot-runner stack mold for dessert cups of polypropylene**
1: clamping plate, 2: core retainer plate, 3: bottom retainer plate, 4: hot-runner manifold, 5: center plate, 6: cavity retainer plate, 7: cavity insert, 8: core insert, 9: locating ring, 10: guide strip, 11: clamping plate, 12: core retainer plate, 13: bottom retainer plate, 14: slide, 15: cam pin, 16: cavity retainer plate, 17: sprue bushing, 18: sliding shutoff, 19: feed pipe, 20: heater rod, 21: hot-runner nozzle, 22: bottom insert, 23: protective tube, 24: core cap, 25: center tube, 26: mounting nut, 27: compression spring, 28: cooling water connection, 29: slot, 30: hydraulic cylinder, 31: air channel, 32: vent gap and vent channel, 33: ball detent

# Example 45, Hot-runner mold for bumper fascia of thermoplastic elastomer

Bumper fascias of TPE (thermoplastic elastomer) can be found today on most automobiles. To protect the vehicle, the sides of the bumper fascia wrap around to the side by a significant amount, so that in conjunction with numerous stiffening ribs, openings and mounting elements, very large molds with rather intricate part release are necessary.

The bumper has an overall width of approx. 1750 mm. With its wrap-around sides, it forms a U with a depth of 750 mm. Numerous ribs are located on the inside and the side sections have transverse and longitudinal depressions that form undercuts in the direction of draw. The lower surface of the front section contains holes.

## Mold (Figs. 1 and 2)

The mold has dimensions of 2800 mm × 1500 mm, with a shut height of 1740 mm and a weight of 32 t.

To facilitate machining and handling, the cavity and core blocks are built up from a number of parts. The cavity block (1) is bolted to the filling pieces (2). The core half consists of the core retainer plate (3) and the core proper (4). These two parts of the core are fitted together with the aid of wear strips (6) and wedges (7). When the mold is closed, the cavity and core are centered with respect to one another by means of taper locks and attached wear plates (5).

To guide the core and cavity, four guide blocks (8) are provided, one at the center of each side of the mold. In contrast to the usual round leader pins, such guide blocks permit the core and cavity to be operated at different temperatures without binding. In addition, subsequent corrections in the event of uneven wall thicknesses are possible.

The part-forming components of the mold are made from polishable steel (material no. 1.2311) heat treated to a strength of 1100 to 1200 N/mm$^2$. For the remaining components, material no. 1.2312 is employed because of its better machinability. The mold clamping plates are made of material no. 1.1730; the wear plates are made of material no. 1.2162 and case-hardened. Bronze is employed for sliding pieces and guides. The movable slide inserts in the core are also made of bronze, in part because of the better thermal conductivity. Lifters (12) that are actuated by push rods (13) are used to release the undercuts on the inside of the front surface. The push rods are movably mounted in the ejector plate (14). With these lifters, the short U-shaped sections on the inside of the top surface of the bumper fascia can be released.

The inside surface of the two wrap-around side sections is released by internal slides (15) that are also actuated via push rods attached to the ejector plate (14).

The outer surface of the wrap-around side sections is located in hydraulically (cylinder 17) actuated external slides (16). Recesses with holes on the bottom surface of the bumper fascia are formed by core pins (18). They are operated by hydraulic actuators (19) located along the lower surface of the mold.

## Runner system/gating

The part is filled from a hot-runner manifold (9) with two nozzles (11) with external heaterbands (10). Each nozzle fills a short sprue and runner with a film gate. The two sprues, runners and film gates are removed from the molded part in a subsequent operation.

## Cooling

The front surface of the molded part is cooled via cooling lines in the cavity, while the outer surfaces of the wrap-around side sections are cooled by cooling lines in the external slide (16).

Cooling lines in the lifters (12) and the internal slides (15) serve to cool the inside of the molded part. Supply and return of the coolant takes place via channels in the push rods (13). To the extent that space permits, cooling lines are also located in the stationary core components.

## Part release/ejection

The core pins (18) are pulled prior to mold opening. During opening, the cylinders (17) push the two external slides (16) in the open direction. The molded part is released from the stationary cavity surfaces as well as from the slides (16); the sprues are pulled out of the tapered orifices of the hot-runner nozzles.

After the part has been withdrawn from the cavity half, the ejector plate (14) is advanced by the cylinders (20). This actuates all lifters (12) as well as the internal slides (15) and the sprue pullers (29). The molded part is pushed off the core; the internal undercuts are released. It must be also be assured during ejection that the wrap-around side sections of the fascia do not become caught by the shape of the internal slides. Blocks (21, 22) are provided for this purpose. With the aid of guides (23, 24), they assure that the wrap-around side sections do not follow the sideways motion of the slides.

To release the molded part from the lifters that have advanced along with it, the ejector plate (25) is now actuated by hydraulic cylinder (26). With ejector plate (14) stationary, the molded part is pushed off by the ejector rods (27) and thrust blocks (28).

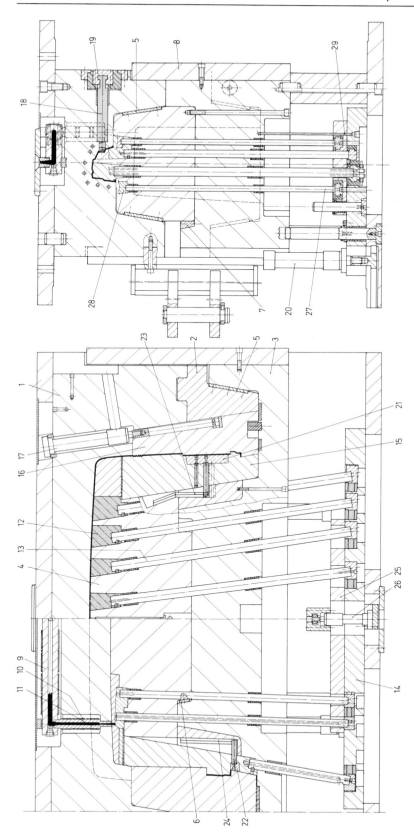

**Figs. 1 and 2    Hot-runner mold for a bumper fascia**
1: cavity block, 2: filling piece, 3: core retainer plate, 4: core assembly, 5: wear plate, 6: wear strip, 7: heel block, 8: guide block, 9: hot-runner manifold, 10: heaterband, 11: hot-runner, nozzle, 12: lifter, 13: push rod, 14: ejector plate, 15: internal slide, 16: external slide, 17: hydraulic cylinder, 18: core pin, 19: core actuator, 20: hydraulic cylinder, 21, 22: block, 23, 24: guides, 25: ejector plate, 26: hydraulic cylinder, 27: ejector rod, 28: thrust block, 29: sprue puller

## Example 46, Four-cavity hot-runner mold for threaded covers of SAN

The appearance of cosmetic containers must, as a rule, meet very high standards. Thus, no gate marks are permissable on the appearance surface of the cover for a cream jar (60 mm diameter, 15 mm high). Gating on the outside either at the center or at the edge via a submarine gate, for instance, is not allowed.

It is thus necessary to gate the part through the core that forms the threads. In such a case, it would be possible to keep the cores stationary and rotate the cavities for unscrewing. The unscrewing mechanism would be simpler; the flow paths shorter. This is not possible, however, here, because – as mentioned – the appearance surface of the cover must be completely smooth so that no elevations or depressions to assist in unscrewing can be present.

### Mold

As shown in Figs. 1 to 4, the unscrewing mechanism was thus located on the injection side.

The core inserts (1) are placed in threaded sleeves (2) that run in guide bushings (3) and are driven by drive shaft (5).

A hollow core (6) with helical cooling channel is located within the core insert (1) and accommodates within its 22 mm diameter a hot-runner nozzle (7) with a length of 150 mm.

The hot-runner system employed here is described in greater detail in Example 50 (toothpaste dispenser).

Radial grooves (i. e. ribs on the inside surface of the cover) that prevent the cover from turning during unscrewing are located on the part-forming surfaces of the core insert (1) and hollow core (6).

A drive shaft (5) extends through the movable-side mold clamping plate (8). The unscrewing motor does not follow the opening motion; the guide bushing (9) slides back and forth on the shaft (5) during opening and closing of the mold.

### Mold temperature control

Cooling water reaches the mold cores through the hollow cores (6). Cooling lines are provided in the cavity plate (10) and the stripper plate (11). Channels in the core retainer plate (12) supply the hollow cores (6) with cooling water.

### Part release/ejection

Unscrewing of the threaded sleeves is initiated upon mold opening. The molded parts are firmly held by the ribs on the core insert (1) and hollow core (6) until the latch (13) (Fig. 3) engages the stripper plate (11) and ejects the molded parts. The stripping motion is limited by the mechanical stop (14) (Fig. 4).

**Fig. 1**

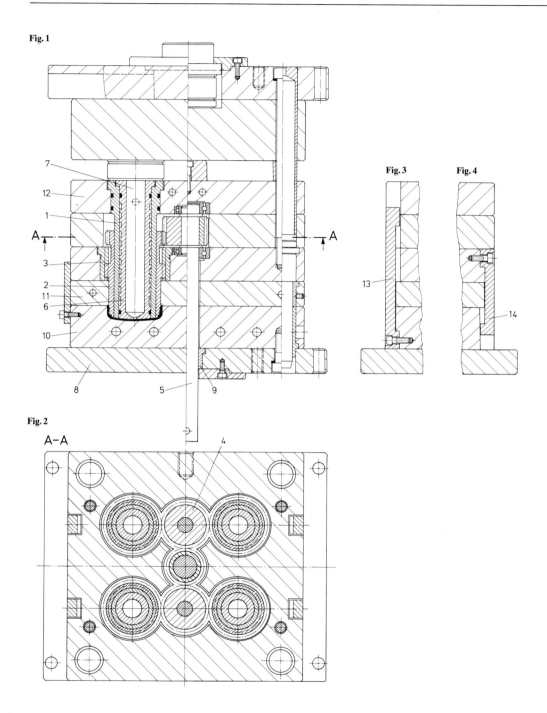

**Fig. 2**

A–A

**Fig. 3**

**Fig. 4**

## Example 46

**Figs. 1 to 4   Four-cavity hot-runner mold for threaded covers**
1: core insert, 2: threaded sleeve, 3: guide bushing, 4: gear, 5: drive shaft,
6: hollow core, 7: hot-runner nozzle (Guenther Heißkanaltechnik,
Frankenberg), 8: mold clamping plate, 9: guide bushing, 10: cavity plate,
11: stripper plate, 12: core retainer plate, 13: latch, 14: mechanical stop

# Example 47, Two-cavity hot-runner mold for trim bezels of ABS

The two trim bezels (Fig. 1) have outside dimensions of 150 mm × 155 mm × 30 mm and are to be chrome-plated. They are installed in motor vehicles in pairs. For installation, each part is provided with eight snap hooks on the installation side to snap into the vehicle body.

**Fig. 1    Automotive trim bezel**

## Mold

The mold contains a pair of parts (Figs. 2 to 4). The distance between the two mold cavities is determined by the slide (15) that must be placed between them to release the snap hooks found there. The remaining hooks are released by slides (12 to 14). Mold inserts (16, 17) attached to the slides form the part-forming surface for the snap hooks. The slides are operated by cam pins (24, 25, 33). When the mold is closed, the slides are secured by heel blocks (22, 23) and the bracket (18). The ejector pins are secured against turning (pin 32) since their ends are shaped to the part-forming surface.

The mold has dimensions of 596 mm × 396 mm with a shut height of 482 mm and a weight of 725 kg.

## Runner system/gating

Each of the parts is filled via two submarine gates at either end of a runner positioned in the opening diago-

nally between two snap hooks. Melt reaches the two mold cavities through a heated sprue bushing (4), a hot-runner manifold (20) and two attached hot-runner nozzles (21). The hot-runner manifold contains two heating coils (19). The manifold block is supported against the opening force resulting from the injection pressure by support pads (26) of a high-strength thermally insulating material.

A transducer (28) to measure the melt pressure in the runner is located behind the ejector pin (27).

## Mold temperature control

Each cavity is provided with two cooling circuits on the stationary side and one circuit on the movable side. The cooling circuits are formed by channels drilled to follow the shape of the molded parts. Thermocouples (29) to provide information on temperature changes of the coolant in the mold are provided at the inlet and outlet of the cooling circuits.

## Part release/ejection

Upon mold opening, the parts and solidified runners are retained on the movable mold half, since the snap hooks and runners are still held in the slides and sprue pullers as well as submarine gates respectively.

After the snap hooks are released by the slides, the molded parts and runners are ejected by the ejector pins. This also shears off the submarine gates.

During mold opening, the slides disengage from the cam pins required to operate them. Coil springs (30) hold the slides in the opened position. In this way, the cam pins can reenter the slides during mold closing without suffering any damage. The ejectors are retracted during closing by means of pushback pins (31).

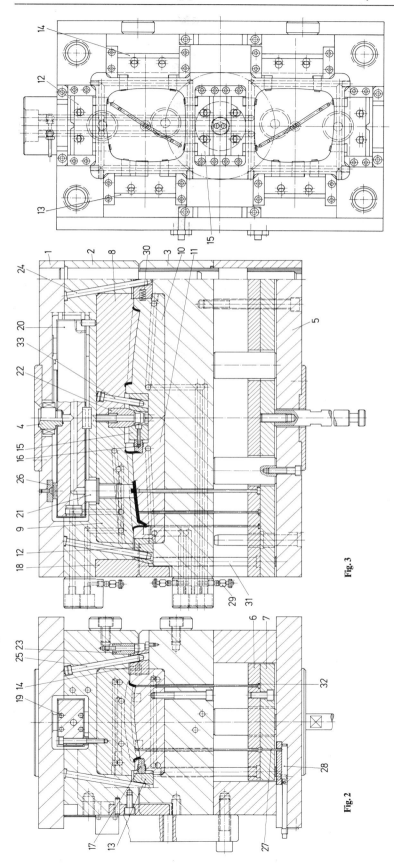

**Fig. 4**

**Fig. 3**

**Fig. 2**

**Figs. 2 to 4    Two-cavity injection mold for automotive trim bezels**
1: mold clamping plate, 2, 3: mold plate, 4: sprue bushing, 5: mold clamping plate, 6, 7: ejector plates, 8, 9, 10, 11: mold inserts, 12, 13, 14, 15: slides,
16, 17: mold inserts, 18: locking bracket, 19: heating coils, 20: hot-runner
manifold, 21: hot-runner nozzle, 22, 23: heel block, 24, 25: cam pin, 26: insulating support pad, 27: ejector, 28: transducer, 29: thermocouple, 30:
coil spring, 31: pushback pin, 32: securing pin, 33: cam pin

# Example 48, Four-cavity hot-runner mold for control flap of acetal (POM) copolymer

The control flaps (Fig. 1) are installed in pairs in the flush valve of a toilet tank and permit water-saving interruption of flushing.

The parts have approximate overall dimensions of 55 mm × 65 mm × 55 mm and consist essentially of a cup-shaped float chamber that functions also as a valve body and a number of attached spring levers.

**Fig. 1    Toilet tank flush valve of polyacetal (POM) copolymer**

## Mold

The mold has dimensions of 496 mm × 316 mm with a shut height of 427 mm and contains four cavities (Figs. 2 to 5). The four cavities are arranged in a line so that the spring levers attached to the float chambers can be molded together in a single slide (21). The slide runs in guide strips (22) and on wear strips (25) and is actuated by two cam pins (45). Wear plates (24) hold the slide in position when the mold is closed.

Four mold inserts (20) are attached to the slide. In addition, four ejector plates (27, 28) with ejector pins (54) and pushback pins (53) are located in the slide.

The cavities of the float chambers are formed by cores (23).

The ejector assembly (4) containing the ejector pins (51), blade ejectors (52) and pushback pins (47) runs in ball guides (48).

The mold halves are aligned as usual by leader pins (11) and guide bushings (12, 13). Locating strips (29) assure proper final alignment. The mold inserts (16, 17, 20) and the slide (21) are made of hardened steel (material no. 1.2767). The cores (23) are made of beryllium copper.

### Runner system/gating

Melt flows from the sprue bushing (39) through a filter insert (62) to the hot-runner manifold (30), which is heated by four heater cartridges (64) with a heating capacity of 800 W each. From there it flows to the four gate chambers where it is kept warm by the indirectly heated thermally conducting torpedoes (34). The torpedo tips extend into the gate openings so that the gate separates cleanly from the molded parts.

### Mold temperature control

The slide (21) and mold inserts (16, 17) contain cooling lines and bubblers with baffles (33) to direct the cooling water. The BeCu cores (23) transmit the heat they absorb to the surrounding, directly cooled components via conduction.

### Part release/ejection

As soon as the mold opens, the slide (21) moves sideways away from the molded parts, allowing the ejector plates (27, 28) with the attached ejectors (54) to push the spring levers out of the recesses in the mold inserts (20) through the action of the compression springs (57). The slide is secured in the opened position by spring-loaded ball detents (59). Pushback pins (53) return the ejectors (54) to the molding position as the mold closes.

The ejector pins (51, 52) eject the molded parts from the cores (23) and from the recesses in the inserts (17).

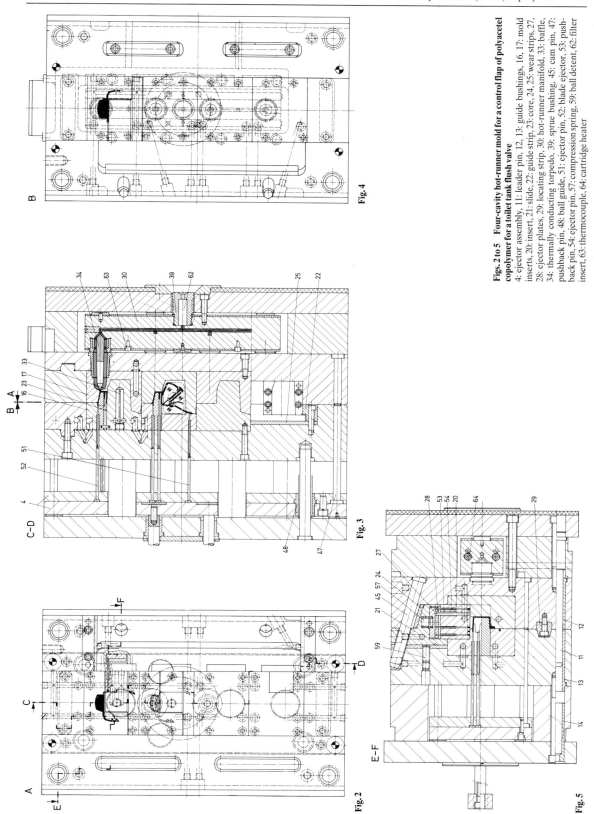

**Figs. 2 to 5   Four-cavity hot-runner mold for a control flap of polyacetel copolymer for a toilet tank flush valve**

4: ejector assembly, 11: leader pin, 12, 13: guide bushings, 16, 17: mold inserts, 20: insert, 21: slide, 22: guide strip, 23: core, 24, 25: wear strips, 27, 28: ejector plates, 29: locating strip, 30: hot-runner manifold, 33: baffle, 34: thermally conducting torpedo, 39: sprue bushing, 45: cam pin, 47: pushback pin, 48: ball guide, 51: ejector pin, 52: blade ejector, 53: pushback pin, 54: ejector pin, 57: compression spring, 59: ball detent, 62: filter insert, 63: thermocouple, 64: cartridge heater

Fig. 2

Fig. 3

Fig. 4

Fig. 5

Fig. 6 gives a view of the ejectors in the open mold. The mold inserts (20) in the slide (21) can be seen at the right, a core (23) is visible at the top left and a molded part being ejected by the ejector pins (51, 52) can be seen at the lower left.

**Fig. 6   Ejection of the control flap**

## Example 49, 64-cavity hot-runner mold for seals of thermoplastic elastomer (TPE)

Seals for disposable injection syringes (Fig. 1) are increasingly being produced from thermoplastic elastomers (TPE), whose processability by the injection molding method has advantages over the rubber hitherto employed. In the mold introduced here 64 seals of 14 mm diameter, 8 mm high are produced in a runnerless manner. The cycle time is about 20 s.

The external mold dimensions are 740 mm × 550 mm, mold height amounts to 463 mm. The 64 cavities have been arranged in four blocks of 16 each. They are supplied with melt through a hot-runner system. The cavity inserts (22), cores (23) and ejector sleeves (24) are identical and interchangeable with each other (Fig. 2 and 3).

### Runner system/gating

The hot-runner manifold block is of two-storey construction, so that the runners leading to the mold cav-

**Fig. 1   Seal for disposable syringes**

ities can all be of equal length. Thus a natural balancing of the flow resistances in the manifold is achieved.

The melt arriving from the machine's nozzle enters the manifold block A (12) through the sprue bushing (25). The manifold block is in the shape of a St. Andrew's cross, guiding the melt through four channels of equal length into the center of the four distributors B (13). From there bores – also of equal length – lead to individual heated nozzles (14) of the spear torpedo type. Steel O-rings (17) serve as seals between the manifold blocks, the heated nozzles and the sprue bush. The two manifold blocks are heated by cartridges (18, 19). The block A on the fixed half has been divided into two heating zones; the blocks on the torpedo side form one heating zone each. Every heating zone is controlled within itself. The torpedoes have two different heating zones. Whereas heating (20) in the torpedo shaft has a constant effect, heating in the torpedo tips (21) is switched ON and OFF in such a manner during the injection cycle, that a thermal opening and closing of the gates is achieved. By closed-loop controlling the shaft-heating it is possible to achieve fine-tuning of the melt volume entering individual mold cavities. This has the advantage that these changes in temperature have no influence on the opening and closing of the gate passages.

In order to achieve a clean break at the gates, the diameter of the gate orifice must not be larger than 0.5 mm maximum and the discharge opening must have very sharp edges.

## Mold temperature control

The cavity side has been provided with numerous cooling channels (29) for removing heat from the molded parts and hot runner system dissipation. The cores are cooled by central bubbler tubes (28) housed inside them.

## Part release/ejection

When opening the mold in the parting line, molded parts and cores are withdrawn from the cavities. The machine's ejectors then push against the bushings (27), moving the ejector plate (7) together with the core plate (8) forward, so that the ejector sleeves (24) force the seals off the undercuts on the cores.

With the start of the closing movement the coil springs (26) return the ejector plate to its starting position.

**Fig. 2**

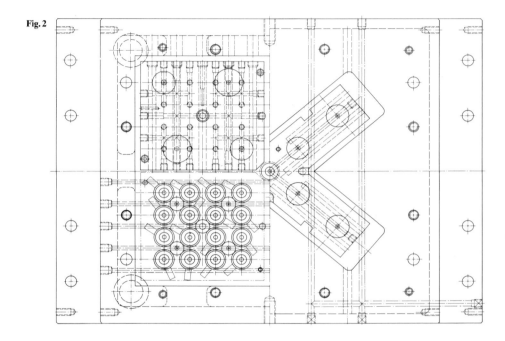

**Fig. 3**

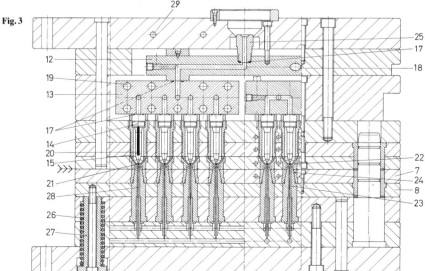

**Figs. 2 and 3    64-cavity hot-runner mold for seals of thermoplastic elastomer**

7: ejector plate, 8: ejector plate, 12: manifold block A, 13: distributor block B, 14: hot-runner nozzle, 15: insulating bushing, 17: O-ring (steel), 18, 19: cartridge heaters, 20: torpedo shaft heating, 21: torpedo tip heating, 22: cavity insert, 23: core, 24: ejector sleeve, 25: sprue bushing, 26: coil spring, 27: shoulder bushing, 28: bubbler, 29: cooling channel

# Example 50, Eight-cavity hot-runner mold for PP toothpaste dispenser

### Injection of long tubular moldings straight through the core

The polypropylene toothpaste dispenser (Fig. 1) is a cylindrical, 146 mm long article, essentially consisting of two tubular sections, the first of which is of 36 mm internal diameter, 26 mm long. The second part is 120 mm long with an internal diameter of 38 mm. There is a partition between the two sections, equipped with various functional components.

Fig. 1    Polypropylene toothpaste dispenser

Fig. 2    Hot-runner nozzle for injecting through the long tubular section

If one were to gate this molding at one point on the outside, the long core would curve due to the unilaterally entering melt: the article would not fill uniformly.

A number of gates distributed around the periphery – although preventing the core from being displaced – would leave gate marks and mean a large percentage of wasted material in the runner.

Internal gating would be a possibility with a three-plate mold and a break-away pinpoint gate. However, an even greater material loss in the form of sprue would be unavoidable, as the specific shape of the partition only allows gating through the long tubular section.

An externally heated, temperature-controlled hot-runner nozzle (Fig. 2) can be employed here to advantage, with the melt being carried in a tube electrically heated to the required processing temeprature at low voltage (3 to 5 V) and effectively insulated against heat losses. As Fig. 3 illustrates, it is thereby possible to employ a cooling spiral equipped hollow core (9) inside the long core for the tubular section of 38 mm internal diameter, which accommodates the 200 mm long hot-runner nozzle in a bore of 22 mm diameter.

This nozzle is equipped with a cone-shaped heated tip entering the gating point. Thus a small ring-shaped gate is created that ensures clean article separation. There is no interference between cooling system and hot-runner nozzle; the article is therefore allowed to cool rapidly.

The melt conveying system inside the manifold (Fig. 6) is designed differently from that in the nozzle. The melt-carrying heating tube a is electrically insulated and surrounded by a supporting tube f. This tube

system is enclosed in a stationary layer of rigid material d and rests in a bore of the manifold plate (4). The "frozen" material layer d acts as heat insulation, so that the manifold plate (4) is allowed to make full surface contact with the two adjacent mold plates without requiring any other form of heat containment. A hot-runner system so designed combines the advantages of externally heated hot-runners (thermally homogeneous melt) with those of the internally heated systems (simple manifold construction, good thermal insulation against the environment).

The bores in the manifold plate (12) (Figs. 3, 4, 5) have been arranged in two layers, one above the other. Thus the channels serving the eight cavities – grouped in two rows in the mold – can be of equal length, so that a natural balancing of the flow resistances can be achieved between sprue bushing and cavities.

### Mold temperature control

The short cores (2) (Fig. 3) are accommodated in the moving mold half. They have been equipped with an effective spiral cooling system (8). The mold cavities are formed by two cylindrical sleeves each (3, 4), around which spiral cooling grooves have been arranged. Even the stripper rings (16) have a grooved ring for cooling.

### Part release/ejection

The mold opens at parting line I. Plates (5, 6) are retained by the latches mounted on the fixed half of the mold, so that the moldings remain on the two cores (1, 2) to start with. They are only displaced in relation to the cavity (3, 4).

When the opening stroke has reached distance S the pair of plates (5, 6) stops, the moldings remains on the long core (1) and the cavities (3, 4) are further taken off. The short cores (2) are pulled, the undercut at the left hand end of the articles is demolded.

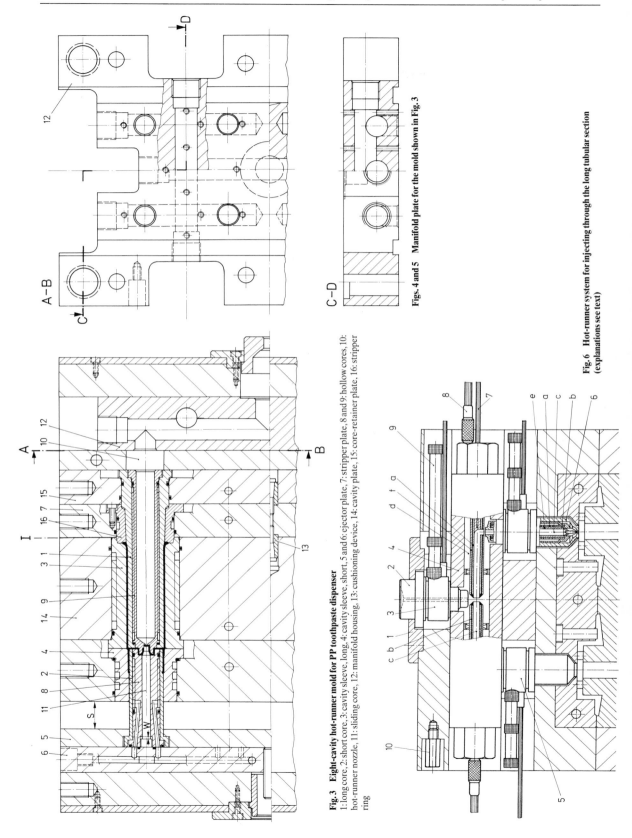

**Figs. 4 and 5 Manifold plate for the mold shown in Fig. 3**

**Fig. 6 Hot-runner system for injecting through the long tubular section (explanations see text)**

**Fig. 3 Eight-cavity hot-runner mold for PP toothpaste dispenser**

1: long core, 2: short core, 3: cavity sleeve, long, 4: cavity sleeve, short, 5 and 6: ejector plate, 7: stripper plate, 8 and 9: hollow cores, 10: hot-runner nozzle, 11: sliding core, 12: manifold housing, 13: cushioning device, 14: cavity plate, 15: core-retainer plate, 16: stripper ring

One sliding core (11) each is housed in the center of the cores (2) with a displacement stroke W . When the articles are released from the short cores (2), each core (11) travels with the departing molding for the distance of stroke W. Having reached the end of the stroke the core – which had given shape to the molding's partition – is only then released from it. Finally, the stripper plate (7) pushes the moldings off the long cores (1).

A cushioning device (13) has been fitted in the stripper plate (7). Its two ends, which protrude beyond the plate (7) enter bores in the cavity plate (14) and the core retaining plate (15) with a friction fit. This prevents the mold plates from chattering when being pushed together during mold closing. Core (1) returns the sliding core (11) to its starting position with the closing movement.

## Example 51, Two-cavity hot-runner mold for tubs of polyethylene

A tub is 50 mm in diameter, 28 mm high (Fig. 1) and must have a smooth, clean gate mark for which reason a hot-runner nozzle with needle shutoff was selected. The bead around the inside edge of the tub forms an undercut. In addition, there are four small ridges along

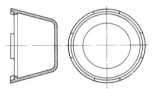

**Fig. 1    PE tub**

the rim. Accordingly, two-stage ejection was selected to assure that the parts drop out of the mold cleanly. The mold is shown in Fig. 2 to 5.

### Runner system/gating

The melt flows from the sprue bushing (43) through the hot-runner manifold (56) and two hot-runner nozzles (37) into the cavities. The hot-runner manifold is heated by means of four cartridge heaters (39) inserted in pairs at either end. The patented cartridge heaters and their installation wells are tapered to facilitate installation/removal and assure good heat transfer.
The shutoff needle of a pneumatically operated valve (41) located behind the manifold passes through each hot-runner nozzle. This shutoff needle extends into the gate orifice, which it opens or closes when operated.
In addition to the already mentioned advantage of providing smooth gate marks on molded parts, needle shutoffs require less injection pressure than pinpoint gates because of the larger orifice available for mold

filling. They are also less sensitive to impurities in the molding compound (regrind).
An insulating plate (14) that prevents heating of the machine platen by the hot-runner manifold is located behind the stationary-side mold clamping plate (1).

### Mold temperature control

A standardized double-flighted helical core (46) is employed in the hollow core (59) to direct the flow of coolant.
The cavity insert (58) has an annular cooling channel. Particular attention should be given to the two O-rings (49, 50) used to seal this cooling channel. Ring (49) is smaller in diameter than ring (50) and its seat. This ensures that damage to ring (49) is avoided when it is pushed past the openings K during insertion of the cavity insert.

### Part release/ejection

The mold opens at parting line I ; the molded part is withdrawn from the cavity. When the standardized two-stage ejector (53) is actuated by the machine ejector, ejector plates (10, 11, 12) advance. Ejector plate (10) actuates the two stripper plates (5, 6) (parting line II ) and the stripper ring (60) by means of sleeve (23). Ejector plates (11, 12) advance the ejector pins (51).
After the molded part has been freed from the undercut on the core, ejector plate (10) and stripper ring (60) come to a stop; ejector (51) continues moving and releases the part from the stripper ring. The part drops out.
As the mold closes, the pushback pin (52) returns the ejector system to the molding position.
A transducer (54) to monitor the cavity pressure is located behind an ejector pin (51).

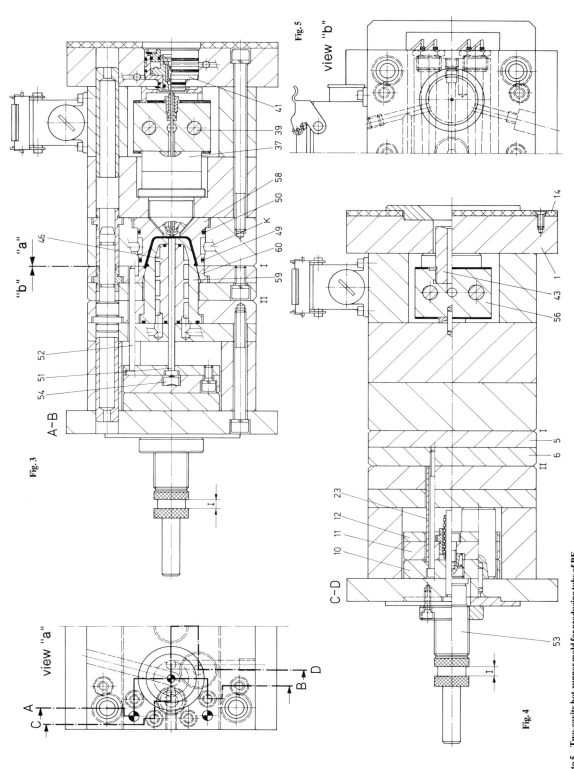

**Fig.2**

view "a"

**Fig.3**

A–B

"b"  "a"

46

52

54  51

41

37  39

50  58

60  49

59

K

I

II

**Fig.5**

view "b"

**Fig.4**

C–D

10  11  12

23

53

14

43  1

56

I

5

6

II

**Figs. 2 to 5    Two-cavity hot-runner mold for producing tubs of PE**
1: mold clamping plate, 5, 6: stripper plates, 10, 11, 12: ejector plates, 14: insulating plate, 23: sleeve, 37: hot-runner nozzle, 39: cartridge heater, 41: pneumatically operated needle valve, 43: sprue bushing, 46: spiral core, 49, 50: Viton O-rings, 51: ejector pin, 52: pushback pin, 53: two-stage ejector, 54: transducer, 56: hot-runner manifold, 58: cavity insert, 59: core, 60: stripper ring

## Example 52, Two-cavity hot-runner mold for production of connectors of polycarbonate

A connector shell (Fig. 1) was supposed to be molded in glass-fiber-reinforced, flame-retardant polycarbonate.

**Fig. 1   Connector shell (upper and lower halves) of glass-fiber-reinforced polycarbonate**

The two different parts (upper and lower halves) were to be produced in a single mold (Fig. 1). Prior to the start of production, the question arose as to whether a second gate might not be required to fill the part. To avoid weld lines and entrapped air, however, it might also be necessary to use only a single gate. This flexibility as to gating was supposed to be possible simply by switching on or off a hot-runner nozzle. A further difficulty resulted from the small amount of space in which the gates were to be located on the face of the molded part. All of these requirements were satisfied through the particular arrangement of the conductive, internally heated hot-runner system.

### Mold

Fig. 2 shows the basic construction of the mold. It consists of a heated sprue bushing (2), a hot-runner manifold (1) and four hot-runner nozzles (3). The hot-runner nozzles have not been installed parallel to the longitudinal axis of the mold, but rather at an angle. In spite of the unfavorable geometric relationships, it is possible to gate each part on its face in this manner (Figs. 3). This arrangement is possible, because the solidified melt in the outer regions of the hot-runner manifold and nozzle channels precludes any possibility of leakage. Each of the hot-runner nozzles is individually controlled and can thus be switched on or off as required. It is thus possible to fill the part through either one or two gates. These measures alone, however, would not have been adequate to vary the gating possibilities. Attention also had to be given to the hot-runner manifold to assure that no melt stagnated at continuously high temperatures in the runner channels when the various gating possibilites were being employed. The installation of four manifold end pieces (1, 2, 4, 5) in addition the central heating element (3) in the hot-runner manifold solved the problem (Fig. 4). Each of these manifold end pieces is individually controlled so that switching on or off sections of the hot-runner manifold is possible without subjecting the material in regions where it is not flowing to thermal loads. Switching the hot-runner nozzles on or off produces an H-, U- or Z-shaped runner in the manifold. Activating the control circuits ( I , II , III , IV , V ) produces an H-shaped runner. Activation of control circuits ( III , IV ) and ( V ) results in a U-shaped runner, while control circuits ( I ) , ( III ) and ( V ) yield a Z-shaped runner. The H-shaped runner is a basic prerequisite for molding of both parts. The U-shaped runner permits one part to be gated at two locations. The Z-shaped runner permits both parts to be gated at only a single location. For variations U and Z , however, the corresponding hot-runner nozzles must also be switched off.

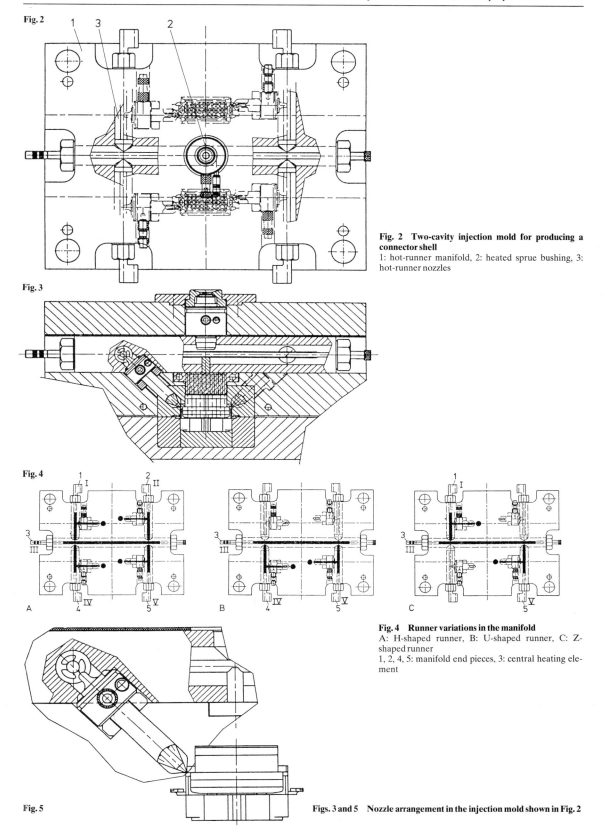

Fig. 2

**Fig. 2  Two-cavity injection mold for producing a connector shell**
1: hot-runner manifold, 2: heated sprue bushing, 3: hot-runner nozzles

Fig. 3

Fig. 4

**Fig. 4   Runner variations in the manifold**
A: H-shaped runner, B: U-shaped runner, C: Z-shaped runner
1, 2, 4, 5: manifold end pieces, 3: central heating element

Fig. 5

**Figs. 3 and 5   Nozzle arrangement in the injection mold shown in Fig. 2**

# Example 53, Four-cavity hot-runner unscrewing mold for cap nuts of polyacetal (POM)

The four cavities of the mold are arranged in line because this results in an especially space-saving arrangement for the drive mechanism for the unscrewing cores by means of an hydraulically actuated rack.

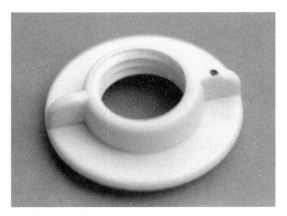

Fig. 1    POM cap nut produced in a 4-cavity hot-runner mold

The unscrewing cores are of a multi-piece design and consist of the gears (33) with journals and lead threads and the part-forming threaded cores (31). The threaded cores must be unscrewed while the mold is still closed, since the ejector side of the cap nuts is flat and offers no means to prevent rotation. An hydraulically actuated gear rack (36) drives the threaded cores. The gear forces are absorbed by the guide plate (32) and threaded bushings (34).

After unscrewing has been completed, the mold opens and the ejector sleeves (30) eject the molded parts.

The replaceable mold inserts (13), (14) are made of the polishable, through-hardened steel (material no. 1.2767); mold plates (6), (7) of pre-hardened steel (material no. 1.2312).

The cap nuts are gated on their face along one of the two ribs via an off-center pinpoint gate.

An externally heated hot-runner system is employed. As a result of identical flow cross sections and flow path lengths to the individual cavities, balanced and uniform filling is assured.

The melt flows from the heated sprue bushing (46) into the manifold (49) via a central cylindrical insert. The manifold pipe is made of hardened steel and is encased in a heating element. The steel pipe and heating element are bonded together and thermally insulated. Attached cylindrical inserts (48) direct the melt to the gates.

The slip fits permit unobstructed movement of the manifold pipe in the cylindrical inserts as it expands during heating.

From the cylindrical inserts the melt flows to the four hot-runner nozzles (45) where it is directed to the gates. The heated nozzles (Fig. 5) have a central tip that extends into the gate orifice and assures clean separation of the gate from the molded part. The cylindrical inserts and nozzles are thermally insulated from the surrounding mold components by air gaps. The manifold pipe and nozzles are fitted with replaceable thermocouples for closed-loop temperature control.

As shown in Fig. 6, nozzles built in accordance with this hot-runner system concept are available not only in the standard version used in this example (axial single gate), but also in the versions "multiple edge gates" and "multiple axial gates".

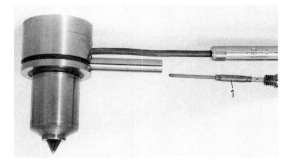

Fig. 5    Hot-runner nozzle with replaceable thermocouple (1)

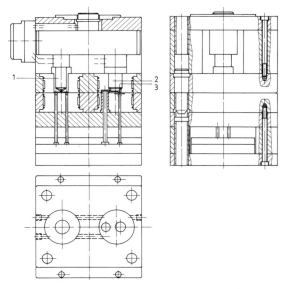

Fig. 6   Mold showing three classical applications of hot-runner technology at the same time
1: standard nozzle, 2: edge gating, 3: multiple gating

**Fig. 2**

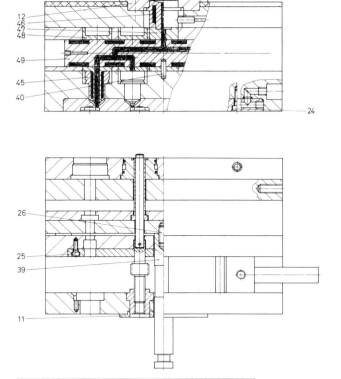

**Fig. 3**

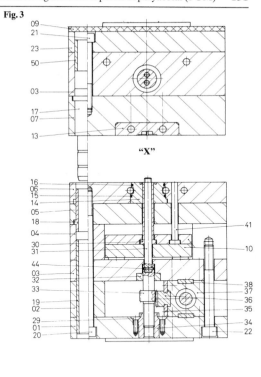

"X"

**Fig. 4**

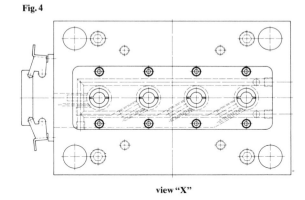

view "X"

| Item | Qty. | Designation | Dimensions | Material |
|---|---|---|---|---|
| 50 | 4 | locating bushing | Ø 30 × 60 | |
| 49 | 1 | manifold pipe | Ø 35 × 250 | |
| 48 | 4 | cylindrical insert | 01.01 K | |
| 47 | 1 | cylindrical insert | 01.01 K | |
| 46 | 1 | heated sprue bushing | 01.09.06.40 | |
| 45 | 4 | hot-runner nozzles | 01.01.20.30 K | |
| 44 | 4 | straight pin | Ø 3 × 14 | |
| 43 | 1 | flange | 25/1 | |
| 42 | 8 | cylinder head screw | M 5 × 30 | |
| 41 | 4 | push back pin | Ø 8 × 80 | 2516 |
| 40 | 1 | straight pin | Ø 6 × 20 | |
| 39 | 1 | ejector rod | Ø 18 × 200 | |
| 38 | 4 | guide plate | 25 | |
| 37 | 1 | hydraulic unscrewing mechanism | 25/300 | |
| 36 | 1 | gear rack | 25/600/1.25 | |
| 35 | 2 | guide strip | 25/300 | |
| 34 | 4 | threaded bushing | Ø 34 × 32 | Bronze |
| 33 | 4 | gear | 16/1.25 | 2767 |
| 32 | 1 | guide plate | 30 × 240 × 10 | Bronze |
| 31 | 4 | threaded core | Ø 8 × 115 | E130K |
| 30 | 4 | ejector sleeve | Ø 8 × 68 | |
| 29 | 8 | flat head bolt | M 6 × 20 | |
| 28 | 1 | cylinder head screw | M 8 × 20 | 10.9 |
| 27 | 1 | cylinder head screw | M 8 × 30 | 10.9 |
| 26 | 1 | set screw | M 10 × 20 | |
| 25 | 6 | cylinder head screw | M 5 × 16 | 10.9 |
| 24 | 8 | cylinder head screw | M 6 × 20 | 10.9 |
| 23 | 1 | clamping plate D | 196 × 296 × 27 | 1730 |
| 22 | 2 | cylinder head screw | M 12 × 100 | 10.9 |
| 21 | 4 | cylinder head screw | M 12 × 50 | 10.9 |
| 20 | 4 | cylinder head screw | M 12 × 170 | 10.9 |
| 19 | 2 | locating bushing | Ø 30 × 120 | |
| 18 | 3+1 | guide bushing | 46/22/24 | |
| 17 | 3+1 | leader pin | 46/22/24 × 65 | |
| 16 | 4 | O-ring | 36/3 | |
| 15 | 4 | O-ring | 36/3 | |
| 14 | 4 | round core | Ø 48 × 27 | 2767 |
| 13 | 1 | insert D | 80 × 16 × 250 | 2767 |
| 12 | 1 | locating ring D | Ø 110 × 13 | |
| 11 | 1 | locating ring A | Ø 110 × 8 | |
| 10 | 1 | ejector plates | 196 × 296 | 1730 |
| 09 | 1 | insulating plate | 196 × 296/5/90 | |
| 08 | 1 | manifold plate | 196 × 296/46 | 1730 |
| 07 | 1 | mold plate D | 196 × 296/46 | 2312 |
| 06 | 1 | mold plate A | 196 × 296/27 | 2312 |
| 05 | 1 | spacer plate | 196 × 296/27 | 1730 |
| 04 | 2 | strip | 196 × 296/46 | 1730 |
| 03 | 1 | spacer plate | 196 × 296/27 | 1730 |
| 02 | 1 | strip | 196 × 296/46 | 1730 |
| 01 | 1 | clamping plate A | 196 × 296/27 | 1730 |

**Figs. 2 to 4   Four-cavity hot-runner unscrewing mold for production of cap nuts**

# Example 54, Four-cavity hot-runner mold with a special ejector system for a retainer of polypropylene

A retainer for insulating material having a total length of 168 mm and a weight of 9,5 g (Fig. 1) is to be produced in polypropylene. In the axial direction the pro-

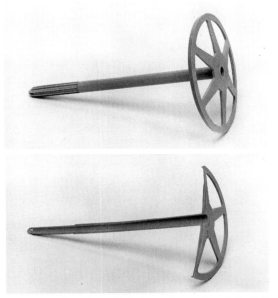

**Fig. 1    View of injection molded polypropylene retainers for insulating material, complete (top) and in section (bottom)**

jected area of one part amounts to 33,7 cm$^2$ . An injection molding machine of 1300 kN clamping force has been chosen from the available machinery for the intended four-cavity tool. This machine however has insufficient mold mounting height available and possesses too short an ejection stroke to be able to demold the injection molded article by a conventional ejection system. In order to make it possible to produce these parts on this machine despite these shortcomings, the subsequently described hot-runner mold was designed with a special ejection system.

## Four-cavity hot-runner mold

The molded part is injected at its tip via a hot-runner pinpoint gate. As can be seen in Fig. 2 the system employed is that of the "indirectly heated thermally conductive torpedo" [1, 2]. Heating is by two tubular heating elements of several bends (19) which are embedded in the hot-runner manifold by heat conducting cement. The hot-runner manifold is covered by heat protection plates to reduce heat losses and the contact areas of the nozzle bodies (9), pressure pads (12) and (18) have been kept as small as possible.
The melt compressed in the hot-runner manifold must not be allowed to expand into the cavity at the start of

mold opening, as the core (64) would otherwise be damaged on mold closing. To prevent this from happening, the manifold is relieved of pressure immediately after the injection process is finished by withdrawing the machine nozzle from the recessed sprue bushing (14).

## Cooling

Fig. 3 shows the arrangement of the cooling circuits as well as specific cooling data. Blind holes for housing the thermocouples (34) have been drilled in various places so that the temperatures of the mold plates can be checked during production.
The cores (64) had originally not been equipped with cooling pins (39). It was found during the first molding trials, however, that just the high core temperature alone can prevent a faster production cycle being achieved. New cores were produced with bores to house the cooling pin [3]. A 23 % reduction in cycle time has been achieved by this action. The heat transfer between cooling pin and temperature control medium would be improved still further by playing water directly onto the cooling pin. However, this would require a considerable reconstruction of the mold.
The frontal area of the core is additionally air-cooled during ejection. The air is supplied via three channels in the cener ejector (27) for a duration of 5 sec. (Fig. 2, section Y b).

## Part release/ejection

The core carrier plate (29) is connected to the hydraulic ejector of the injection molding machine via the ejector bar (41). The core carrier plate rests against the mold plate (23) in the injection position, i. e. the hydraulic ejector has moved forward. The force created by the hydraulic ejector suffices to hold the core in position during injection.

**Fig. 2    Four-cavity hot-runner mold for insulating material retainers**
1: mold clamping plate, 2 a , 2 b: spacer strip, 3: stationary-side mold plate, 4, 5: stationary-side mold insert, 6: sealing ring, 7: hot-runner manifold, 8: end plug, 9: nozzle body, 10: torpedo, 11: locating insert, 12: pressure pad, 13: sealing ring, 14: recessed sprue bushing, 15: heater band, 16: thermocouple, 17: locating ring, 18: pressure pad, 19: tubular heater, 20: spacer sleeve, 21: plug plate, 22 a , 22 b: plug-in connection, 23: movable-side mold plate, 24: actuating cam, 25: actuating bar, 26: pneumatic valve, 27: central ejector, 28: stop bushing, 29: core carrier plate, 30 a , 30 b , 30 c: stop strip, 31: pneumatic valve, 32: sealing ring, 33: guide bushing, 34: thermocouple, 35: sealing ring, 36: movable-side mold insert, 37: threaded plug, 38: locating ring, 39: cooling pin, 40: clamping plate, 41: ejector bar, 42, 43: sealing ring, 44: water connection, 45: cover plate, 46: sealing ring, 47: water connection, 48: piston, 49: circlip, 50: air ejector, 51: support bolt, 52: leader pin, 53: guide bushing, 54: gear, 55: cover plate, 56: gear, 57: washer, 58: shaft, 59: bearing plate, 60: draw plate, 61: nut, 62: threaded pin, 63: guide, 64: core, 65: clamping piece, 66, 67: spacer plate, 68: clamping plate, 69: guide, 70: draw plate, 71, 72: gear rack, 73: strips, 74: housing for infrared light barrier, 75: transmitter/receiver

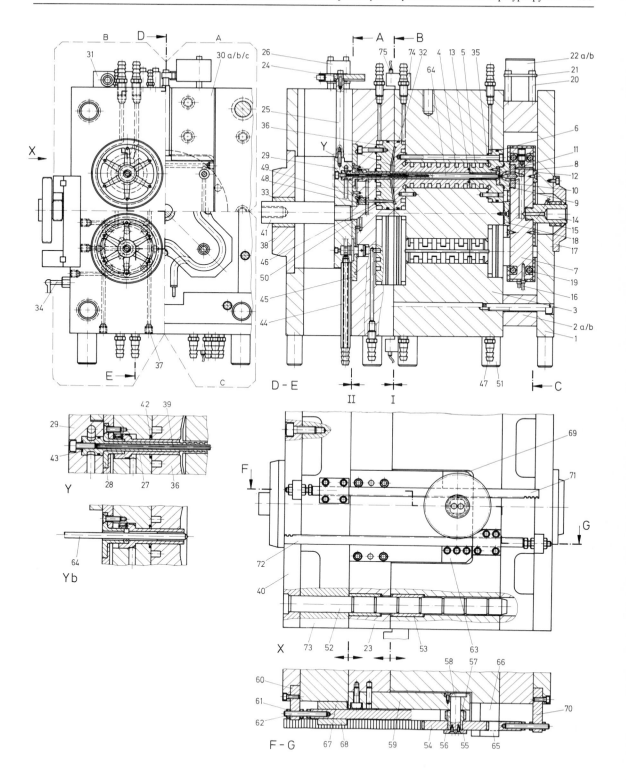

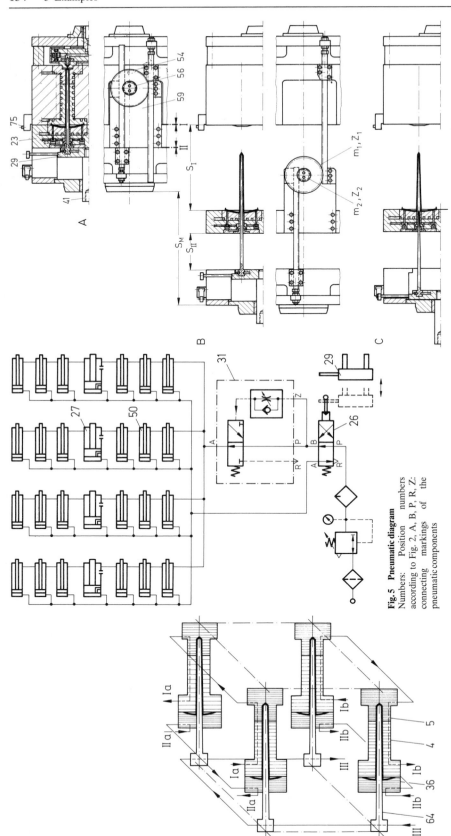

**Fig.5  Pneumatic diagram**
Numbers:    Position    numbers
according to  Fig. 2, A, B, P, R, Z:
connecting    markings    of    the
pneumatic components

**Fig.4  Ejection sequence**
Numbers:    Position    numbers
according  to  Fig. 2,  m:  gearing
modulus, S: distances, Z: number of
teeth,  I,  II:  parting  lines,  A:
injecting,  B:  mold  opening,  C:
retract core, D: ejector

| cooling circuit no | cooling medium | mean temperature of the coolant [°C] | volume-tric flow [m³/h] | flow rate [m/s] | Reynolds number | notes |
|---|---|---|---|---|---|---|
| Ia & Ib | Water | 40 | 0.5 | 3.3 | 35000 | heating/cooling unit |
| IIa & IIb | " | 40 | 0.7 | 4 | 50000 | " |
| III | " | 5.5 | 0.6 | 9.5 | 32000 | chiller |

**Fig.3  Cooling diagram**
Numbers: Position numbers according to Fig. 2, I, II, III: cooling circuits

One gear drive each is situated in each mold half. The two gears (54) and (56) which cannot be turned against each other are housed in the bearing plate (59) and connected by this to the mold plate (23).

When mold opening starts the parting lines I and II open simultaneously but at different speeds and for different distances in accordance with different pitch diameters of the gears.

The molded part is pulled out of the fixed-half cavity by its adhesion to the core, additionally aided and increased by indentations on the latter. A partial stripping from the core takes place simultaneously through the opening of parting line II (Fig. 4 B). At the conclusion of the machine opening stroke the hydraulic ejector retracts. A pneumatic control is activated at the end of the stroke so that each part is ejected from the moving mold half by six air ejectors (50) and a central ejector (27) per mold cavity. The three holes in the central ejector leave the zone of the stop bushing (28) during the ejection stroke. This allows air to pass from the pressurised cylinder area through these channels for additional core cooling (64) (Fig. 2 section Y b).

Air cooling of the cores terminates with the return stroke of the central and the air ejectors, activated by pneumatic controls as soon as the core carrier plate (29) moves from its rear position.

The pistons (48) and the central ejector (27) are not sealed against the bores. The DIN – fit $H_6/g_6$ has been chosen as tolerance between bores and pistons. This results in leakages. The supply lines and valves have therefore been dimensioned to sufficiently large nominal sizes to ensure that the pressure in the cylinder interior is high enough despite the losses through leakage. Fig. 5 shows the pneumatic controls. Ejection stroke and return stroke are initiated by the core carrier plate (29) via the valve at (26). To keep the leakage losses low, the supply line is shut off by valve (31) soon after the return stroke.

## Literature

1 *Unger, P.:* Kunststoffe 70 (1980) p. 730/737
2 *Unger, P.; Hörburger, A.:* Kunststoffe 71 (1981) p. 855/861
3 *Wübken, G.:* Kunststoffe 71 (1981) p. 850/854

## Example 55, Two-cavity hot-runner mold for fuel tank cap production in polyacetal copolymer

The mold described here utilizes a hot-runner together with a secondary runner. The molded parts are ejected from the stationary side by stripper plates.

Fuel caps in polyacetal copolymer can be produced more economically and in only one step by injection molding, compared to the metal caps, which required several steps. Good mechanical properties and imperviousness to petrol and methanol (M 15 – fuel) made employment for this application possible (Fig. 1).

**Fig. 1    Polyacetal copolymer injection molded fuel tank cap, with gate still attached (right) and completed (left)**

On a multitude of vehicles the fuel caps are placed on the outside of the vehicle without the protection of a covering lid. This exposes them to all weathering influences and above all to ultraviolet rays. To protect against the damage by ultraviolet rays special grades have been developed for outside use.

### Construction of the mold

In conjunction with the above-mentioned requirements, the surface of the cap has to be free from blemishes. In order to prevent undesirable gating and flow marks on the visible areas of the molded parts, a combination hot and conventional runner was chosen for this tool. There was a possibility of siting the conventional runner in the central bore as multiple submarine gate, which would have made automatic degating possible. However, with regard to the surface quality required, the processor decided for a small disc gate inside the bore, which has to be removed subsequently. The decision was made to employ the "indirectly heated thermally conductive torpedo" [1 to 5] when chosing the hot-runner system, because of the low production costs, the low control, operating and maintenance requirements and the possible production of that

particular system by the in-house tooling department. This system offers uniform temperatures in the hot-runner manifold and in the gate areas. The hot-runner block (1) has been positioned between mold mounting and spacer plate (2 and 4) in the bolster plate (3) in such a way, that heat losses by the so-called 'chimney effect' are eliminated. The block is supported by bushings (5) and pins (6). The pins are overdimensioned by 0.03 + 0.01 mm, which ensures that there are no leaks. The hot-runner block (1) is connected to the mounting plate (2) by dowel pins (17) and bolts (18) and thus safeguarded and located against falling out of the mold, if this is dismantled. To keep radiation losses to a minimum, the hot-runner block (1) is covered by bright aluminium sheet (8). The block is heated by four cartridge heaters (9), (of 12,5 mm diameter, 100 mm long, 600 W each). At 2,400 watts a specific heat capacity of 300 W/kg hot-runner block results. Good heat conductivity from the heater cartridges (9) to the hot-runner block (1) is ensured by the clamping strips (10). The thermocouple (11) is situated between cartridge heater and runner.

The copper thermally conductive torpedoes (12) (E-Cu, 2.0060) have been so dimensioned with their diameter of 10 mm, that the temperature drop from the block to the torpedo-tip is negligible. The uniform heat transfer from the hot-runner block (1) through the bushings (5) to the thermally conductive torpedoes (13) is assured by adhering to the tolerances H 7/m 6. By placing the leader pins (16) in the fixed half of the mold, care has also been taken that any possible damage to the torpedo tips by the bolster plate (3) is avoided when the tool is being assembled.

The gate position necessitates ejection of the molded parts from the fixed half. The links (13) pull the mold plate (14) and the stripper plates (15) forward when the mold opens, thereby ejecting the fuel caps.

### Mold temperature control

The mold incorporates five cooling circuits, which ensure intensive cooling and fast heat removal from the inserts, cores and plates. With the aid of this heating/cooling system good surface quality as well as tight tolerances of the article dimensions can be obtained at mold temperatures of $\vartheta w = 95$ °C.

### Literature

1  *Unger, P.; Hörburger, A.:* Kunststoffe 71 (1981) p. 855/861
2  *Unger, P.:* Kunststoffe 70 (1980) p. 730/737
3  *Blauert, K. H.; Unger, P.:* Kunststoffe 71 (1981) p. 209/211
4  *Kallinowski, H.; Bopp, H.:* Kunststoffe 72 (1982) p. 186/188
5  *Schulz, D.:* Kunststoffe 71 (1981) p. 864/865

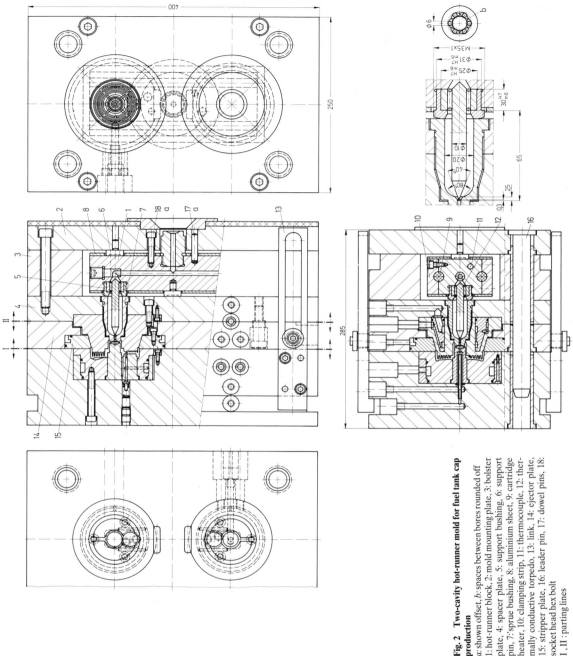

**Fig. 2   Two-cavity hot-runner mold for fuel tank cap production**

*a*: shown offset, *b*: spaces between bores rounded off
1: hot-runner block, 2: mold mounting plate, 3: bolster plate, 4: spacer plate, 5: support plate, 6: support pin, 7: sprue bushing, 8: aluminium sheet, 9: cartridge heater, 10: clamping strip, 11: thermocouple, 12: thermally conductive torpedo, 13: link, 14: ejector plate, 15: stripper plate, 16: leader pin, 17: dowel pins, 18: socket head hex bolt
I, II: parting lines

## Example 56, 32-cavity hot-runner mold for production of packings of polyethylene

A two-plate mold with a conventional runner system (Figs. 1 and 2) was used as the production mold for packings for atomizer pumps (the piston pump principle). In this mold, ejection of the molded parts and runner system took place separately via synchronized ejector mechanisms (12, 13) and (14, 15), the latter being actuated subsequent to extension of ejector mechanisms (12) and (13) which severs the molded parts from the submarine gates. To provide the most economical production possible, the mold was designed with 32 cavities. Each part is molded via a single submarine gate with a diameter of 0.8 mm. After extensive mold trials, PE-LD was selected as the suitable material for the packings (Fig. 5), which had to be produced with high precision. With a total weight of 11.2 g (= 32×0.35 g) for the molded parts, the weight of the runner system in this mold design was 10.03 g (Fig. 6). The ratio of part to runner volume was 1.1 : 1.

As part of a campaign to improve production efficiency, the mold was supposed to be redesigned at the lowest possible cost and in the least amount of time to reduce the volume of the runner system and shorten the cycle time, if possible, through use of a suitable hot-runner system. After detailed study of various hot-runner systems, the system utilizing indirectly heated probes (torpedoes) was selected for reasons of

- Simple and problem-free conversion
- Lowest temperature control requirements
- Low space requirement
- Little susceptibility to trouble
- Low maintenance requirements
- Low cost

The design is shown in Figs. 3 and 4. For space reasons, the hot-runner manifold (H-pattern) (21) was designed with eight copper probes (22) (E-Cu F 37; DIN 40 500). The probes were electroless hard-nickel-plated by the Kanisil technique. To ensure adequate integrity of the probe locating bushing in the limited space available, the probe shank was made as long as possible (18 mm).

With a weight of 12 kg for the hot-runner manifold block, a heating circuit consisting of two tubular heating elements (23) with a total heating capacity of 3.5 kW was provided. This corresponds to a specific heating capacity of about 300 W/kg of hot-runner manifold. To provide good heat transmission the tubular heating elements are embedded in thermally conductive cement. To reduce heat losses due to radiation, the surfaces of the hot-runner manifold are covered with bright-rolled aluminium plates (24). The hot-runner manifold is controlled with the aid of only one temperature controller.

As a result of the conversion of the mold, the weight of the runner system was reduced to 4.15 g (Fig. 7). This corresponds to a volume reduction of 59 %. The ratio of part to runner volume changed to 2.7 : 1. Through the reduction of recovery time and shot volume, it was possible to reduce the cycle time by 25 %.

Use of the hot-runner system in conjunction with a shortening of the flow paths led to noticeably lower pressure drop along the runner compared with that of the original mold design. This resulted in greater part density and better dimensional accuracy. The volume of the runner system could be reduced even further if the entire mold were redesigned.

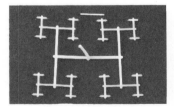

**Fig. 6    Runner system before mold conversion**

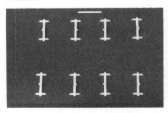

**Fig. 7    Runners between hot-runner manifold nozzles and molded parts after mold conversion**

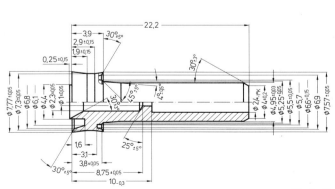

**Fig. 5    LDPE plunger packing for atomizer pump**

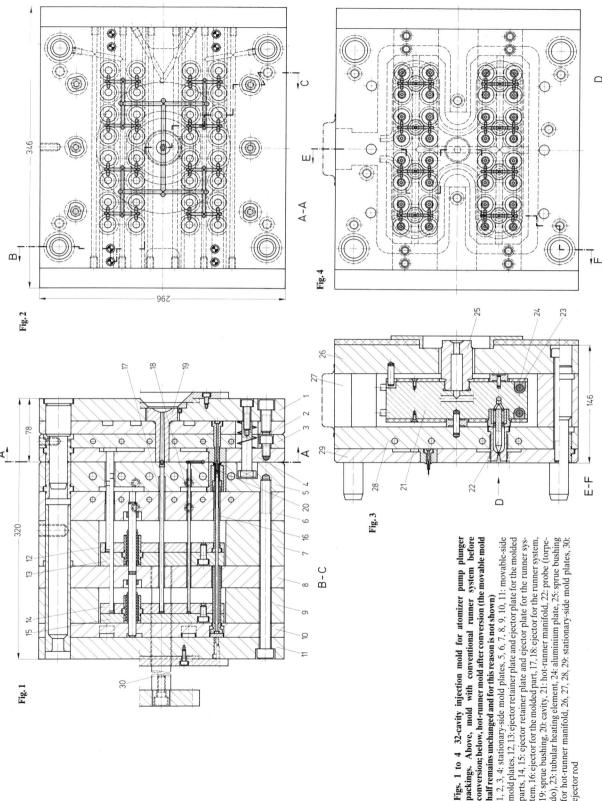

Fig. 2

Fig. 4

A–A

B–C

Fig. 1

Fig. 3

E–F

**Figs. 1 to 4   32-cavity injection mold for atomizer pump plunger packings. Above, mold with conventional runner system before conversion; below, hot-runner mold after conversion (the movable mold half remains unchanged and for this reason is not shown)**

1, 2, 3, 4: stationary-side mold plates, 5, 6, 7, 8, 9, 10, 11: movable-side mold plates, 12, 13: ejector retainer plate and ejector plate for the molded parts, 14, 15: ejector retainer plate and ejector plate for the runner system, 16: ejector for the molded part, 17, 18: ejector for the runner system, 19: sprue bushing, 20: cavity, 21: hot-runner manifold, 22: probe (torpedo), 23: tubular heating element, 24: aluminium plate, 25: sprue bushing for hot-runner manifold, 26, 27, 28, 29: stationary-side mold plates, 30: ejector rod

# Example 57, 12-cavity hot-runner mold with edge gates for bushings of polyacetal copolymer

This 12-cavity hot-runner mold was fitted with indirectly heated probes (thermally conductive torpedoes) to produce bushings of polyacetal copolymer.

**Fig. 1    Edge-gated injection molded bushings of polyacetal copolymer**

## Design features of the mold

The hot-runner block (1) is located between the mold clamping plate (2) and cavity plate (4) in the surrounding spacer plate (3) such that there is no heat loss by the so-called "chimney effect". The block is supported by bushings (5) and pads (6) which are pressed into the locating holes and ground flat on a surface grinding machine to assure a uniform reference surface, which is necessary to ensure a leak-free system. The support pads are overdimensioned by 0.03 + 0.01 mm. The end plug (8) is longer than in prior versions. This excludes the possibility that the mold maker, by chamfering the face, could unknowingly introduce an undercut into which melt would penetrate and, after a sufficiently long residence time, degrade and lead to rejects. The hot-runner block (1) is connected to the mold clamping plate (2) by dowel pins (13) and bolts (14), and thus centered and secured against falling out when the mold is disassembled. To reduce radiation losses, the hot-runner block (1) is clad with bright aluminium plate (9). The block is heated by three cartridge heaters (10)

(diameter 12.5 mm, length 160 mm, 1000 W each). At 3000 W, this gives a specific heating capacity of 250 W/kg of hot-runner block. Good heat transmission from the cartridge heaters (10) to the hot-runner block (1) is ensured if the cartridge heaters are inserted into polished wells with heat-conducting paste (tolerance H 7). The thermocouple (11) is located above the central cartridge heater and seated so deeply in the block that the measuring position lies between two gates. This guarantees that the requirements for temperature measurement and control will be met.

The probes (12) are generally of copper (E-Cu 2.0060). It is recommended that probes of smaller diameter be made of CuCrZr 2.1293 because of its greater hardness, particularly at higher processing temperatures.

Compared to standard probes, these probes have a flattened tip with two or more conical protrusions at the side to conduct heat directly to the gates. The rear end of the probe is inserted into the support bushing (5) with the tolerance H 7/m 6. This guarantees uniformly effective heat transfer from the hot-runner block (1) through the support bushing to the probe (12). The normal dimensioning rules are applicable for calculating the main probe dimensions in advance.

Upon mold opening, the gates shear off the molded parts. The thin gate residue remaining in the gate orifice is melted during the following shot. The molded parts are ejected by means of the ejector plates (15) and the ejector sleeves (16). To protect the probes when assembling the mold, the leader pins are located on the injection side and dimensioned such that the injection-side cavity plate slides on the leader pins before reaching the tips of the probes.

Usually, the mold clamping plate (2), the spacer plate (3) and the cavity plate (4) are bolted together. To permit rapid separation of the cavity plate and spacer plate, they are held together by two clamps (18) in the present design. This is of advantage for quick color changes or when processing regrind. If a contaminant plugs a gate or the color is to be changed, the clamps are released from the mold cavity plate (4) and the spacer plate (3) and used to hold mold cavity plate (4) and mold plate (19) together. On starting up the injection molding machine, the gate side of the mold opens between plates (3 and 4). The insulating material is stripped from the exposed hot probes (12), the mold closed and the clamps returned to their original position. After a few minutes, the mold is again ready for use.

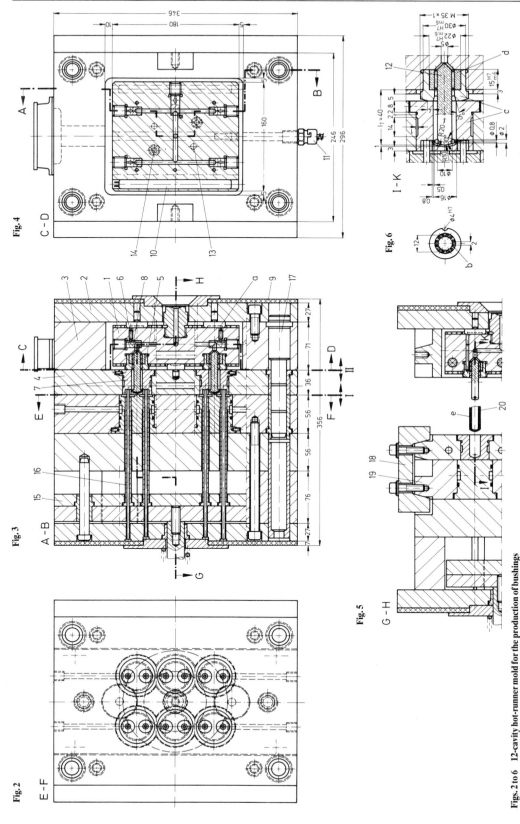

**Figs. 2 to 6   12-cavity hot-runner mold for the production of bushings**

1: hot-runner manifold, 2: mold clamping plate, 3: spacer plate, 4: cavity plate, 5: support plate, 6: support bushing, 7: gate insert, 8: end plug, 9: aluminium plate, 10: cartridge geater, 11: thermocouple, 12: probe, 13: dowel pin, 14: socket-head cap screw, 15: ejector plate, 16: leader pin, 17: ejector sleeve, 18: clamp, 19: cavity plate, 20: insulating material
*a*: interference for pressure pad 0.03 + 0.01 mm, 1.2767 hardened, *c*: 1.2767 hardened, *b*: transitions rounded, *c*: 1.2767 hardened, *d*: E-Cu, 2.0060 or CuCrZr, 2.1293, *e*: insulating material stripped, pre-hardened tool steel 1.2311, 1.2312 was used for plates and hot-runner manifold

I: operating parting line, II: parting line for cleaning, section G-H/parting line II opened

## Example 58, Hot-runner mold for a polycarbonate sight glass

For a combined dryer and conveyor for thermoplastic resin, a sight glass was needed, for which the mold shown in Figs. 1 to 5 was designed. The sight glass was supposed to exhibit good transparency and withstand temperatures of up to 110 °C, for which reasons polycarbonate was selected as the material. A special feature of the sight glass is a vertical lip running around the circumference inside the edge. Usually sight glasses are edge-gated. Studies of how the cavity fills and correction to the gate ensure that the flow front forms a line to prevent the entrapment of air that would lead to the formation of weld lines. This is assisted by an overflow opposite the gate through which the displaced air can escape.

However, with edge-gating the circumferential lip near the edge would cause the melt to first fill the edge region and then to flow together in the center. Accordingly, the present sight glass had to be center-gated.

Of the four types of gates possible in this case, the hot-runner system was selected, since a sprue gate would leave too large a gate mark and require secondary finishing operations. Furthermore, the sprue (or riser in an insulated runner mold or three-plate mold with pinpoint gating) would be too long as the molded part must be ejected from the stationary half of the mold, since the outer surface of the sight glass is required to be completely smooth. In addition, formation of waste in the form of a sprue that could not be reground and used again for transparent parts is avoided.

An open nozzle (1) with female thread is screwed into the barrel of the injection molding machine. This nozzle has a BeCu tip (2) that fits into the decompression chamber (3) of the hot sprue bushing. A decompression chamber is necessary to prevent drool out of the hot sprue bushing when the nozzle (1) is retracted.

The hot sprue bushing holds four cartridge heaters (4) with a total heating capacity of 1000 W. The heating capacity should not be too low in order to have reserve capacity available if needed. The temperature of the hot sprue bushing is sensed by a resistance thermometer with a bayonet connection (5) that is especially suited for such molds because of the great depth of penetration. This sensor is connected to a solid-state control unit that also provides the electrical power to the receptacle box (6). The controller rating is 1600 W. The contact surfaces of the hot sprue bushing must be kept as small as possible to keep heat transmission to the mold at a minimum. An insulating plate (7) prevents material from penetrating into the area of the cartridge heaters. A BeCu nozzle (8) with a tip that reaches to the cavity and forms an annular gate is screwed into the hot sprue bushing. The advantage of such nozzles is clean degating directly at the part. In conventional nozzles with a central orifice a small stub often remains on the molded part, and there is the further danger that stringing may occur because the fluid core is larger than with the present nozzle. With regard to nozzle designs for hot-runner manifolds in general, it should be pointed out that the nozzle threads should be larger in diameter than the nozzle body if possible. This will ensure better heat transfer from the hot-runner manifold to the nozzle tip.

Whenever high-quality parts are desired, the temperature of the mold should be kept as uniform as possible and sufficiently high, up to 130 °C for polycarbonate. It is known from experience, however, that this is not always possible. Inserts, for instance, often prevent an optimum solution or make it more difficult. In the present case, however, there are no such difficulties. It was possible to provide spiral channels on both sides through use of inserts (9) and (10).

After the melt has been injected through the hot sprue bushing and has solidified, the mold opens at the parting line. After an opening stroke of 45 mm, the latches (11) pull the ejector plate (12) forward so that the ejector sleeve (13) ejects the sight glass. As soon as the part has been ejected, the latches are disengaged by the release bar (14). As the machine closes, the ejector plate (12) is returned to the molding position by four push-back pins (15).

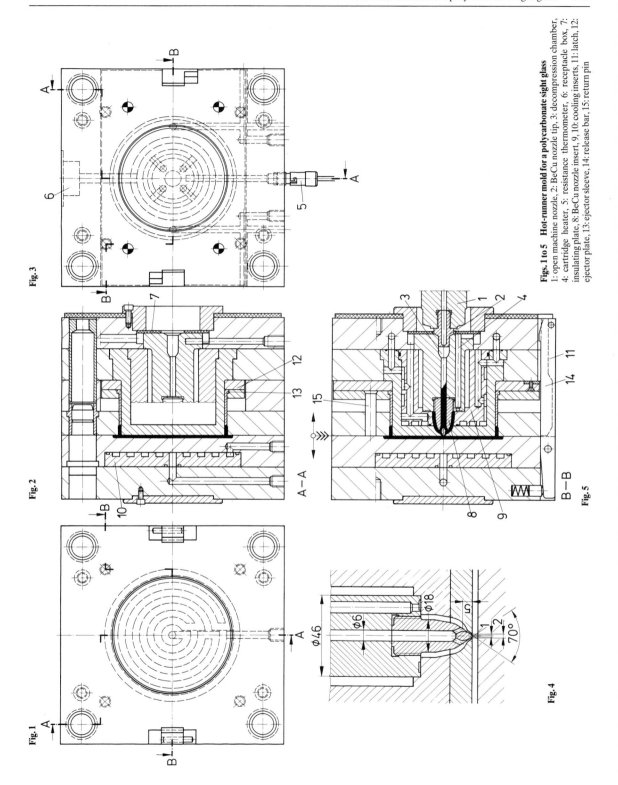

**Figs. 1 to 5    Hot-runner mold for a polycarbonate sight glass**
1: open machine nozzle, 2: BeCu nozzle tip, 3: decompression chamber, 4: cartridge heater, 5: resistance thermometer, 6: receptacle box, 7: insulating plate, 8: BeCu nozzle insert, 9, 10: cooling inserts, 11: latch, 12: ejector plate, 13: ejector sleeve, 14: release bar, 15: return pin

Fig. 3

Fig. 2

Fig. 1

Fig. 4

Fig. 5

A–A

B–B

## Example 59, Four-cavity hot-runner mold for tumblers of polyacetal copolymer

In designing a four-cavity hot-runner mold for poly-acetal copolymer tumblers weighing 21 g each (Figs. 1 to 6), a hot-runner system utilizing indirectly heated probes was chosen in preference to one with direct heating of the nozzle probe, e. g., by means of a cartridge heater [4].

The heated and temperature-controlled manifold block serves as the heat source. Heat flows to the probe and gate area, ensuring that the melt remains fluid. The indirect heating requires very little in the way of temperature control hardware. Local overheating and the resulting thermal degradation of the melt can be prevented by maintaining the specified processing conditions. The forces are transmitted from the manifold block (11) to the mold plates (1, 3) via the support pads (17) and locating bushings (18). Surface pressure adequate to ensure absence of leakage throughout the system is provided by a slight interference fit. The shank of the probe (19) is shaped like the spider die commonly used in extrusion (with spokes between the openings with air foil cross sections; Figs. 5 and 6). Compared with the performance of straight-sided probe support spokes, this results in better homogeneity of the melt stream.

This hot-runner system is comparatively simple to manufacture. In addition to its reliability, the low manufacturing costs, minimal requirement for auxiliary equipment and gentle processing capabilities constitute the major advantages in its favor. Furthermore, a large number of various thermoplastic resins may be processed with it.

The reader is referred to Example 57 for information concerning selection of material for the probe (torpedo) and its design.

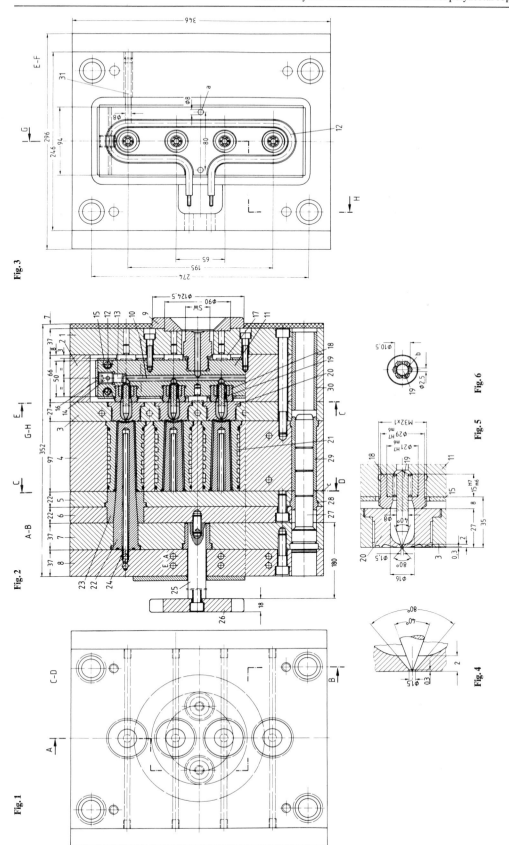

**Figs. 1 to 6   Four-cavity hot-runner mold for polyacetal copolymer tumblers**

1: stationary-side clamping plate, 2: spacer for hot-runner manifold, 3: nozzle plate, 4: cavity retainer plate, 5, 6: ejector plates, 7: core retainer plate, 8: movable-side clamping plate, 9: locating ring, 10: runner channel, 11: hot-runner manifold, 12: tubular heating element, 13: runner end plug, 14: set screw, 15, 16: aluminium cover plate, 17: support pad, 18: locating bushing, 19: probe (torpedo), 20: gate insert, 21: cavity, 22: core, 23: stripper ring, 24: bubbler tube, 25: ejector rod, 26: ejector bar, 27: guide pin, 28, 29: guide bushing, 30: locating bushing, 31: thermocouple

*a*: Hot-runner manifold pinned to mold plate, *b*: rounded openings, *c*: parting line, *A*: cooling water outlet, *E*: cooling water inlet

## Example 60, Four-cavity hot-runner mold for high-strength ski bindings of polyacetal copolymer

In the past years ski bindings have undergone a rapid development, leading to an as yet incomplete conversion of entire ski bindings from metal (aluminium die casting, sheet metal) to high-quality engineering plastics. On the basis of the previous standard, the plastic parts have to meet correspondingly high quality requirements.

Originally, plastics found application in the area of downhill ski bindings as functional components, e. g., as cams for opening or closing the binding. The present state encompasses housing components, including the inside functional components that must absorb all forces. A typical example is the ski binding shown in Fig. 1.

Fig. 1    Ski binding. In front, a housing component of the binding

On the basis of preliminary trials, four-cavity, three-plate split-cavity molds were selected to produce the components of this heel binding. This satisfies the requirement to produce four parts economically and with the same high quality. The high quality with regard to dimensional accuracy (precision injection molded parts) as well as strength (rigidity and toughness) can be achieved during long-term production only with optimum processing parameters.

The production rates provided by a conventional mold led to the investigation of the possibility of utilizing a gating system (Figs. 2 to 6). In this way it was possible to eliminate the runner system, which weighed about 50 g. With a molded part weight of about 258 g, this translates into a material savings of about 20 %. Recycling of the regrind was not possible in production of these parts, since ski bindings represent safety components as the link between an individual and ski.

On the basis of the stringent requirements to be met by the molded parts, special attention must be given not only to maintenance of the optimum machine parameters but also to the heat balance of the mold. This means that

– Temperature differences between the hot-runner manifold and probe tips should be as small as possible.
– All cavities should have optimum and uniform temperature control.

The system selected utilized indirectly heated probes (see also examples 57 and 59). On the basis of its basic design, this system provides for maintenance of a very uniform hot-runner manifold temperature. In order to eliminate the normally negligibly small effect of the unheated end portions of the tubular heating element on the region around the probes, the design shown in Figs. 5 and 6 is recommended to provide identical amounts of heat to each gate. The probe temperatures are almost identical. Uniform filling of the cavities in multiple-cavity molds is thus ensured. This feature of the system is one of the essential prerequisites for the production of high-quality injection molded parts. This applies equally to the maintenance of close dimensional and weight tolerances, but especially to the mechanical properties of the molded part.

The heating system for the hot-runner manifold (13) is controlled from only one point (thermocouple 16). The specific heating capacity is about 220 W/kg of hot-runner manifold. The tubular heating elements (15) are embedded in the hot-runner manifold (13) with thermally conducting cement. To reduce heat losses due to radiation, the manifold is covered with bright aluminium plates (14). The four probes (10) are made of copper (E-Cu F 37; DIN 40 500) and were modified slightly for the existing mold. On opening of the mold the slides (6, 7) open first and the cores (5) are then pulled hydraulically. Individual temperature control is provided for the slides, cores and mold plates.

With the conversion of a conventional mold to a design utilizing a hot-runner system, a direct comparison of the two approaches is possible. It was found that the high quality level was maintained. Further advantages resulted from a shortening of the cycle time, since the recovery time was reduced, as well as from an improvement of the thermal homogeneity of the melt due to the better degree of utilization of the machine capacity, which should only be between 40 and 70 % when high quality standards must be met.

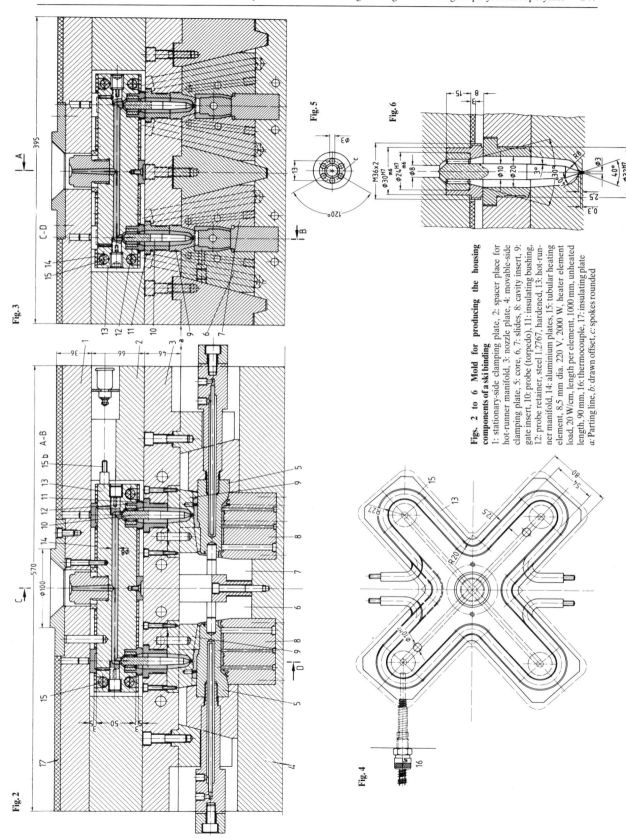

**Fig. 2**

**Fig. 3**

**Fig. 5**

**Fig. 6**

**Fig. 4**

**Figs. 2 to 6 Mold for producing the housing components of a ski binding**

1: stationary-side clamping plate, 2: spacer place for hot-runner manifold, 3: nozzle plate, 4: movable-side clamping plate, 5: core, 6, 7: slides, 8: cavity insert, 9: gate insert, 10: probe (torpedo), 11: insulating bushing, 12: probe retainer, steel 1.2767, hardened, 13: hot-runner manifold, 14: aluminium plates, 15: tubular heating element, 8.5 mm dia. 220 V, 2000 W. heater element load, 20 W/cm, length per element, 1000 mm, unheated length, 90 mm, 16: thermocouple, 17: insulating plate

*a:* Parting line, *b:* drawn offset, *c:* spokes rounded

# Example 61, Eight-cavity hot-runner mold for closure plugs

The shape of the closure plugs incorporates undercuts, which usually requires a relatively complicated mold design with slides to ensure problem-free part release and ejection.

On the mold illustrated (Figs. 1 to 3) the elasticity of the thin-walled PE molding is made use of for part release and ejection, eliminating the need for slides. It is necessary, however, that the core (13) is being pushed out of the mold cavity insert (7) to allow the molding to slide over the undercut in the side of the core.

As the ejectors (17) must only enter into operation when the core (13) has been displaced, the ejector movement is controlled by ball catches. When the mold has opened, the cores (13) as well as the ejectors (17) are pushed forward between plates (2) and (3) by means of the ejector bar (18) and the ejector plates (15, 16). The balls (21) engaged in bushing (22), which are carried along by sliding bushing (19), ensure that core (13) and ejector (17) move in parallel. The movement of core (13) is concluded and it is stopped when the core carrier plate (14) engages in catch (23). Simultaneously the balls (21) reach the screwed-in position of bolt (20). Sliding bushing (19) and bushing (22) now disengage, so that only the ejectors (17) continue on moving with the ejector bar (18). This results in the ejectors passing the face areas of the now fully extended stopped cores (13) and ejecting the molded parts. The plan view in Fig. 4 shows the final position of the opening movement. With mold closing, the ejectors (17) are pushed back by the ejector plate return pin (24) until the balls (21) are aligned with the ball raceway of bush (22). At that point plate (2) also reaches the pushback pin (25), which now also pushes back the core (13) parallel to the ejectors (17), which becomes feasible through the balls (21) being able to run into the larger diameter of bolt (20).

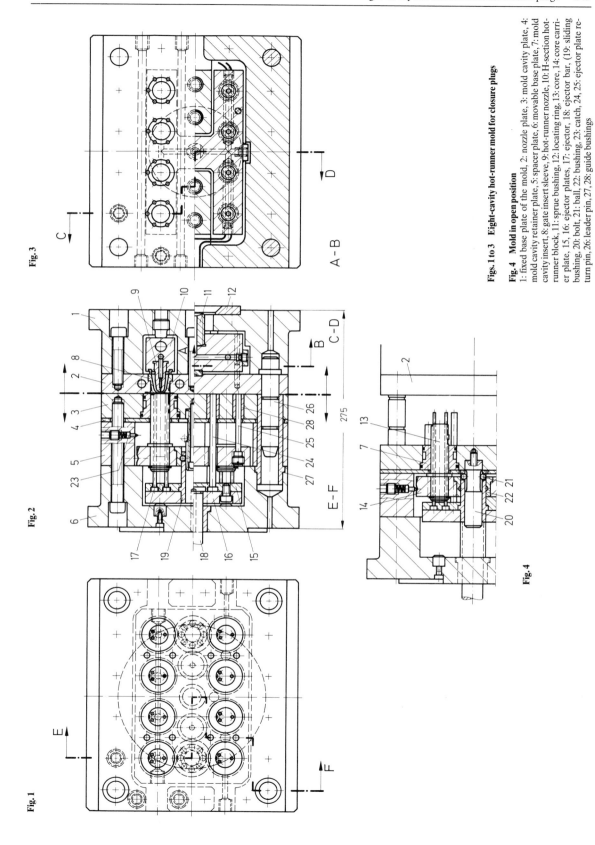

Fig. 3

Fig. 2

Fig. 1

Fig. 4

**Figs. 1 to 3   Eight-cavity hot-runner mold for closure plugs**

**Fig. 4   Mold in open position**

1: fixed base plate of the mold, 2: nozzle plate, 3: mold cavity plate, 4: mold cavity retainer plate, 5: spacer plate, 6: movable base plate, 7: mold cavity insert, 8: gate insert sleeve, 9: hot-runner nozzle, 10: H-section hot-runner block, 11: sprue bushing, 12: locating ring, 13: core, 14: core carrier plate, 15, 16: ejector plates, 17: ejector, 18: ejector bar, (19: sliding bushing, 20: bolt, 21: ball, 22: bushing, 23: catch, 24, 25: ejector plate return pin, 26: leader pin, 27, 28: guide bushings

# Example 62, Single-cavity injection compression mold for a cover plate of unsaturated polyester resin

When injection molding thermosetting resins, undesired fiber orientation in the molded part can be largely reduced by employing injection compression. If side action is also needed to release the molded part, the drive mechanism for this side action must take into account the compression movement.

The cover plate (Fig. 1) is produced from a free-flowing thermosetting resin and has a dovetail-shaped slot that must be released by means of a slide.

## Mold (Fig. 2)

The cavity is formed between the core insert (1) and cavity insert (2). The core fits into the cavity recess; the lateral shear surfaces have a slight taper to facilitate entry. The slide (3), which is attached to the piston rod (5) of an hydraulic cylinder by means of the slide retainer (4), is located in the cavity. A lock (6) fits into an opening in the slide retainer (4) to hold the slide in position. The lock fits against the wear plates (7).

## Runner system/gating

The molding material enters the mold via the jacketed sprue bushing (8). A system of cooling channels (10) in the sprue bushing keeps the molding compound within at a temperature of 90 to 100 °C to prevent curing. The insulating gap (9) assures thermal separation between the heated mold (approx. 180 °C) and the sprue bushing (8).

## Heating

Heating of the mold is accomplished with the aid of high-capacity cartridge heaters (11) that are divided into 4 heating circuits. Each heating circuit is provided with a thermocouple for individual temperature control. The power and thermocouple leads are brought to a junction box (16) in accordance with the appropriate electrical codes (VDE 0100).

## Mold steels

The mold is constructed of standard mold components. The part-forming components (core, cavity and slide) are made of hardened steel (material no. 1.2083). The slide retainer and wear plates are made of case-hardened steel (material no. 1.2764).

## Operation

Prior to mold closing, the slide is hydraulically set in the cavity so that the lock (6) enters the opening in the slide retainer (4) before the core (1) enters the cavity (2). The mold is not completely closed during injection of the molding material. The exactly metered shot volume initially fills the gap in the runner region and a portion of the cavity. During the subsequent closing motion (compression phase), molding compound fills the entire cavity and cures there under the action of heat.

During the compression stroke, the lock (6) prevents the slide (3) from being displaced outward by the molding pressure.

The molding material in the runner region also cures. The boundary between cured and uncured material in the sprue bushing is located approximately at the cavity end of the cooling channel (10). The sprue puller (13) and ejector (14) remove any remaining cured runner material. The molded part is ejected by means of four ejectors not described here.

Fig. 2   **Single-cavity injection compression mold**
1: core insert, 2: cavity insert, 3: slide, 4: slide retainer, 5: piston rod, 6: lock, 7: wear plate, 8: jacketed runner (cold runner):, 9: insulating gap, 10: cooling channel, 11: cartridge heaters, 12: insulating plate, 13: sprue puller, 14: ejector, 15: pushback pin, 16: junction box

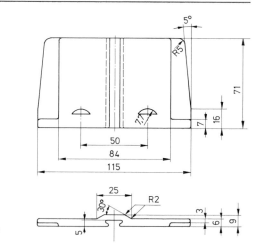

Fig. 1   Cover plate

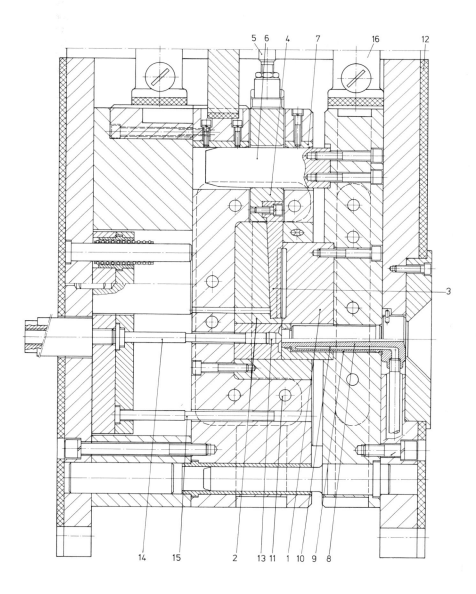

# Example 63, Two-cavity injection compression mold for a housing component of a thermosetting resin

Fiber orientation, deflashing and lost runner material are problems that result in costs especially in the area of thermoset processing. The mold presented in this example shows how expenses for the above can be reduced. A device that permits more exact metering of the molding compound to the two mold cavities is described.

The molding material is injected into the partially opened two-cavity mold (Fig. 2 and 5).

## Flow divider

Distribution of the molding material to the two cavities is accomplished with the aid of a conical flow divider (1) with appropriately designed grooves. During injection, the flow divider is opposite the discharge opening of the sprue bushing (2). After injection, the molding compound lies in the common pocket (Bakelite system) at the mold parting line in the form of two approximately equal masses.

## Compression step

With final closing of the mold, the molding compound is forced into the two cavities (3, 4), where it cures under the action of the mold temperature (approx. 180 °C). As a result of the compression step, fiber orientation in the molded part is considerably less than would have been the case with injection into a closed mold.

## Degating

The flow divider (1) protrudes into the sprue bushing (2) during compression and blocks it off from the parting line.

The standardized jacketed sprue bushing is provided with cooling channels (5), as a result of which the molding compound in the sprue bushing is held at a temperature of 90 to 100 °C, so that it does not cure ("cold runner system"). Only the protruding tip of the flow divider is warmer – as a result of mold heating – and

molding compound cures here. As a result, material lost in the form of a runner is limited to only the small amount of material in the grooves of the flow divider (1). An insulating gap (17) provides thermal separation between the sprue bushing and mold.

## Flash

During the compression step, the molding compound flows past the projected area of the mold cavities and forms flash.

The mold cavities (3, 4) are provided with flash edges (7, 8) to assure clean separation of the molded parts from the flash during ejection. Fig. 3 shows the common pocket (9) with flash edges (7, 8) located on the movable side of the mold parting line.

Fig. 4 shows the two molded parts and the associated flash.

## Common pocket

The shear edge (12) defines the size of the common pocket. Details of the shear edge configuration and gap are shown in Fig. 5. The different edge radii (0.8/2.4 mm) impart increased stiffness to the flash rim (13) and give the numerous ejector pins located behind it a good means for ejecting the flash. A slight undercut (14) holds the flash on the movable side during mold opening.

## Mold steels

The mold is constructed largely of standard mold components. The part-forming inserts are made of steel (material no. 1.2767, hardened).

## Heating

The mold is heated by means of high-capacity cartridge heaters divided into 6 control circuits. Six thermocouples control the mold temperature.

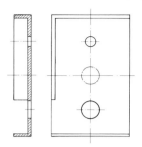

**Fig. 1    Housing component**

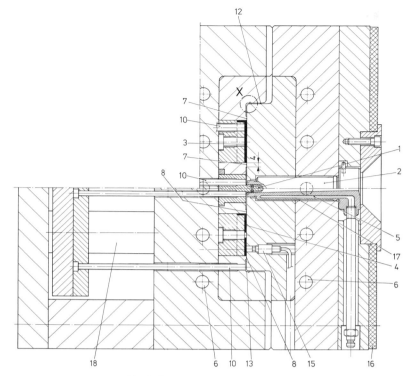

**Fig. 2    Two-cavity injection compression mold for a housing component**
1: flow divider, 2: sprue bushing, 3 and 4: mold cavity, 5: cooling channel, 6: cartridge heater, 7 and 8: flash edge, 10: ejector, 12: shear edges, 13: flash rim, 15: pressure sensor, 16: insulating plate, 17: insulating gap, 18: support

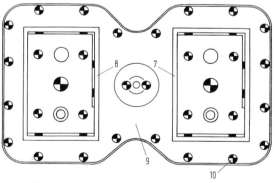

**Fig. 3    Common pocket**
7 and 8: flash edge around cavity, 9: common pocket, 10: ejector

**Fig. 4    Molded parts with separated flash**

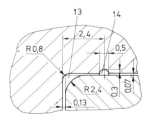

**Fig. 5    Shear edge**
13: flash rim,
14: undercut

Detail X (Fig. 2)

# Example 64, Injection compression mold for a plate of melamine resin

Plates, cups and a variety of household items are often produced of melamine resin, type 152.7. In addition to the "classical" compression molding technique, injection molding machines are employed to mass-produce such parts by means of the injection compression technique. Fig. 1 shows the mold in the three steps of production: injection ( I ) , compression ( II ) and ejection ( III ) .

The plate is molded using a pinpoint gate. When injection molding without subsequent compression with this type of gating, the melt would be subjected to severe orientation that could lead to molded-in stresses in the part and thus warpage or even cracks. With the injection compression technique utilized here, the mold is closed until a gap of only 6 to 8 mm remains and then the molding compound is injected. After injection, the machine closes the mold and compresses the molding compound in the cavity. In this way, production of warp- and stress-free molded parts is assured. To permit injection compression, the mold must have a shear edge, usually in the vicinity of the parting line. With this rotationally symmetrical part, a mold was selected in which the compression plate $c$ passes through the mold plate $b$ and forms the underside of the plate.

The mold operates as follows: the injection molding machine closes the mold until the two mold plates $a$ and $b$ contact one another and a compression gap $z$ is formed between mold plate $b$ and compression plate $c$ . After injection of the carefully metered amount of molding compound, the mold is closed completely, compressing the material in the mold cavity. As the mold opens, the spring washers $t$ initially cause plates $b$ and $c$ to separate by the amount of the compression gap $z$ , which is limited by the stripper bolts $x$ . Since the machine nozzle $d$ is still in contact with the mold at this point in time, a vacuum that holds the molded plate against mold plate $b$ is formed in the "molding chamber". After the mold has opened completely, the machine nozzle $d$ retracts from the mold. Because of the undercut $h$ , the cured sprue is pulled out of the sprue bushing and ejected from the nozzle with the aid of a pneumatically actuated device. With opening of the gate, the vacuum in the molding chamber $f$ is released. The molded plate is ejected by means of a pneumatically actuated valve ejector $v$ . During ejection, the molded parts are held by the suction cups on a part extractor and subsequently placed on a conveyor belt.

Cartridge heaters $k$ heat the mold, while the sprue bushing is heated by a heater band $m$ . Each heating circuit is individually controlled. The mold is separated from the machine platens by means of insulating plates $n$ . The gate is so designed that upon of retraction of the machine nozzle $d$ only a relatively small gate vestige remains on the molded part after the sprue breaks away. This vestige is removed mechanically in a subsequent finishing operation.

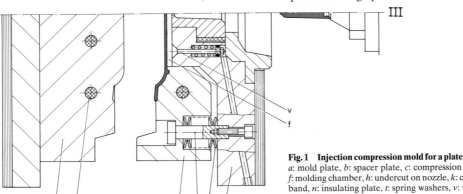

**Fig. 1    Injection compression mold for a plate**
$a$: mold plate, $b$: spacer plate, $c$: compression plate, $d$: machine nozzle, $f$: molding chamber, $h$: undercut on nozzle, $k$: cartridge heater, $m$: heater band, $n$: insulating plate, $t$: spring washers, $v$: valve ejector, $z$: compression gap, $x$: stripper bolts

# Example 65, Five-cavity unscrewing mold for ball knobs of a thermoset resin

Ball knobs of a thermoset resin, e. g. type 31, in a variety of diameters with and without internal threads are often employed for handles and levers on machinery and equipment. An alternative to compression molding as a means of producing these ball knobs is given by injection molding, which permits shorter cycle times and an automatic production cycle to be achieved. With the injection mold shown schematically in Figs. 1 to 3, it is possible to produce ball knobs with different diameters and optionally with or without internal threads. Initially, molds were produced in which a film gate was located in the parting line on the periphery of the ball knobs. During degating, however, the molded parts were often damaged and could not be repaired even in a secondary finishing operation.

With conversion to a three-plate mold with two parting

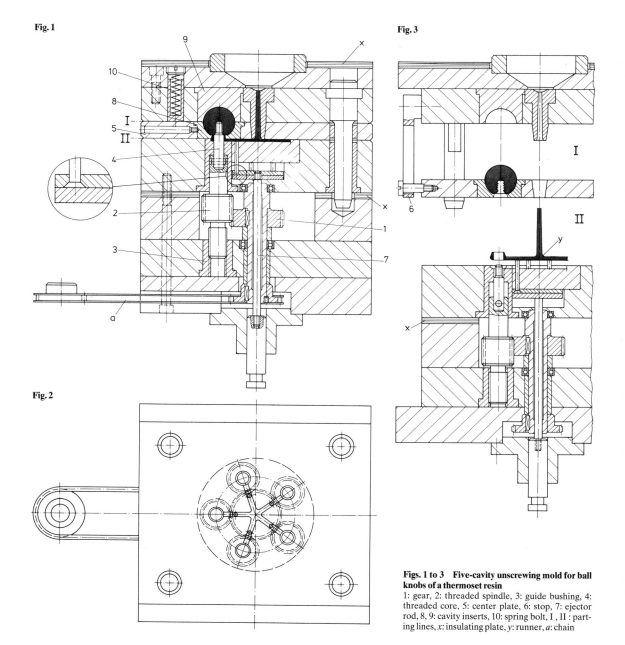

**Figs. 1 to 3    Five-cavity unscrewing mold for ball knobs of a thermoset resin**
1: gear, 2: threaded spindle, 3: guide bushing, 4: threaded core, 5: center plate, 6: stop, 7: ejector rod, 8, 9: cavity inserts, 10: spring bolt, I , II : parting lines, x: insulating plate, y: runner, a: chain

lines, it was possible to mold the ball knobs by means of a ring gate on the seating surface. Since the relatively clean gate mark after degating is not on a visible surface or functional area of the molded parts, subsequent finishing is not required. To permit production of ball knobs with different diameters, all part-forming components have been designed to be interchangeable (mold inserts (8, 9)). By replacing the threaded cores (4) with unthreaded core pins, ball knobs without internal threads can be produced. If threads with a different pitch are to be molded, the threaded spindles (2) and guide bushing (3) must also be replaced. The threads of the guide bushing (3) must always have the same pitch as the threads on the threaded cores (4). Only in this way is it possible to release the threads and assure exact positioning of the threaded cores prior to injection.

The mold is heated by cartridge heaters located in the mold plates and insert retainer plates. The heating circuits are closed-loop controlled. Insulating plates $x$ are provided to separate the mold from the machine platens and the drive mechanism.

The mold operates as follows: with the mold closed and the cores in the forward position, the molding compound is injected into the cavities via the ring gates. After the molded parts have cured, the threaded cores (4) are unscrewed from the ball knobs by an hydraulic motor that is controlled through an interface on the machine. To prevent the ball knobs from turning, unscrewing takes place while the mold is closed. The rotary motion is transmitted to the threaded spindles (2), which are displaced axially during unscrewing, by the chain $a$ and the gear (1). Upon mold opening, the spring bolts (10) separate parting line I. Following this, plate (5) continues moving until it reaches the stop (6) after parting line II has also opened. Undercuts hold the runner on the movable half of the mold after the ring gates have separated from the ball knobs. Next, the runner $y$ is ejected by the ejector rod (7) which is connected to the machine ejector. During mold closing, parting lines II and I close automatically. Following this, the threaded cores (4) are returned to the molding position by the hydraulic motor.

## Example 66, Four-cavity injection mold for a thin-walled housing of a thermosetting resin

The housing component shown in Figs. 1 to 3 was produced in a thermosetting resin by means of injection molding. The special features of this part are the thin wall sections of 0.7 mm, some of which taper down to 0.3 mm. As a result of the very slight shrinkage, there is no assurance that the molded parts will remain on the core for ejection. It was not possible to provide undercuts to hold the molded part on the core. This means that ejection poses a particular problem. Since there was also no possibility to eject the part only by means

of ejector pins because of the extremely thin wall sections, a three-plate mold was selected.

The four-cavity injection mold shown in Figs. 4 to 10 operates as follows: after the housings have been molded via the sprue (4) and runner system and the molding compound has cured, the mold opens at parting line I through the action of the spring-loaded inserts (3). This pulls the sprue (4) out of the sprue bushing, since an undercut is provided in the guide bore for the somewhat recessed center ejector. Simultaneously, the slide (5), which forms the holes in the side of the housing, is pulled by the cam pin (6) and held in position by the spring-loaded detent (7). Parting line I now opens until mold plate (8) is stopped by latch (9), whereupon parting line II opens. This pulls the core (10) out of the housing. The molded part is supported by the two ejectors (12) during this motion. The ejector plate (13) is connected to mold plate (8) by stop bolts (14) so that the ejectors (12) do not change their position with respect to the molded part during opening of parting line II. As the mold opens further, pin (16) releases latch (9) so that the movable half can now retract completely. Ejector rod (18), which is connected to the hydraulic machine ejector, now advances the ejector plates (13) so that the ejector pins (12) eject the housings from the cavities in plate (8) along with the

Figs. 1 to 3    Thin-walled housing component of a thermoset resin

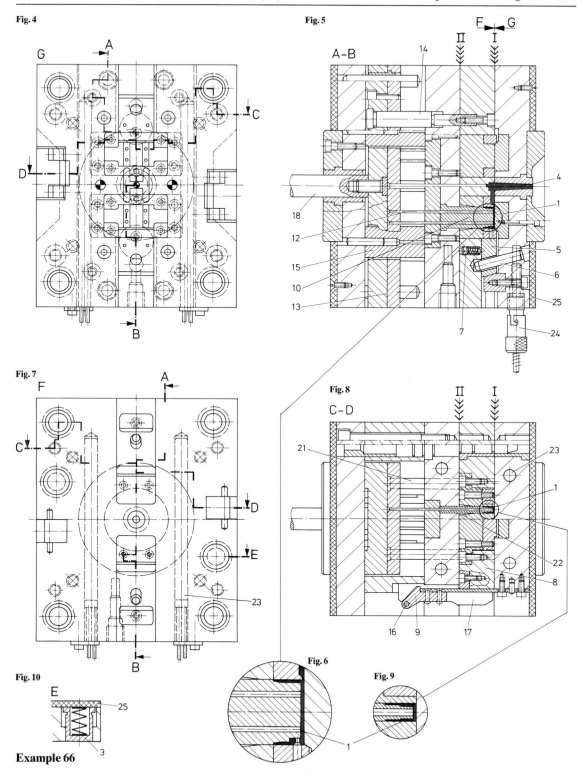

Fig. 4

Fig. 5

Fig. 7

Fig. 8

Fig. 6

Fig. 9

Fig. 10

**Example 66**

**Figs. 4 to 10    Four-cavity injection mold for a thin-walled housing component of a thermoset resin**
1: housing component, 3: spring-loaded insert, 4: sprue, 5: slide, 6: cam pin, 7: spring-loaded detent, 8: plate, 9: latch, 10: core, 11: narrow side of housing, 12: ejector, 13: ejector plates, 14: stop bolts, 15: support pillar, 16: pin, 17: ejector plate guide, 18: ejector rod, 21: pushback pin, 22: relief on core, 23: cartridge heater, 24: thermocouple, 25: insulating plate

runner system. Advancing and retracting the ejector plates several times assures that the molded parts do not stick on the ejector pins. This pulsating ejection also clears the ejector guide bores of any slight flash that might impair venting of the cavities and operation of the mold. In the present case, the parting line around the core (10) provides a good means for venting. After a short guiding surface, plate (8) is relieved

(22). In addition to functioning as a vent, this relief acts as a discharge for any thin residual flash that could otherwise cause a malfunction. The mold is heated by high-capacity cartridge heaters (23); the temperature is controlled with the aid of thermocouples (24). The insulating plates (25) prevent heat transfer to the machine platen, thereby saving energy and assuring a more accurate temperature in the mold.

## Example 67, 20-cavity injection mold with cold-runner manifold for rubber bumpers

As it is not possible to regenerate vulcanized rubber, cold-runner molds are much preferred. They permit runnerless molding and allow for a high degree of automation. The cold-runner system relies on intensive cooling within the runner region, and in this respect it represents the opposite of the well-known hot-runner system for thermoplatics molds. The cold-runner consists of three parts: the main body (1), the insulating body (2) and the half-shell (3).

The insulating body is bolted to the half-shell by four M 12 bolts, completely enclosing the main body. This contains the star-shaped runner arrangement into which the material is injected to be fed into the machined annular runner channel in parts (2) and (3). It is very important that the surface of these channels be well polished. The gates of 2 mm × 0.4 mm branch off this annular channel at chosen intervals to feed the individual mold cavities. The material that remains in the runner system is protected from heat transfer from the heated mold plates by effective cooling, which ought to be kept constant at 60 °C to ensure that the material is of a homogeneity necessary for its flow characteristics. As shown in Fig. 1 the main body is surrounded by a labyrinth of cooling channels, relieved surfaces and machined grooves, the whole of which is

sealed by O-rings. The locating of the cold-runner insert is by conical surfaces, which hold it precisely in the parting line. The insert has been relieved with machined slots to keep the contact area as small as possible against heat absorption. The cylindrical part should be a slight push fit. When the mold is open, the cold-runner is lifted off the mold mounting plate by about 10 mm through four springs (4). The movement is restricted by four bolts. This offers the advantage of the insert not contacting the hot mold mounting plate, preventing heat transfer during the opening and ejection period. When the mold closes, the insert is pushed back on its cone-shaped seat again. The injected material flows through the runner manifold into the mold cavities. After curing, the mold opens and the sleeve ejectors (5) demold the parts. The play between sleeve (5) and core pin (6) should not exceed 0.05 mm, maximum.

In case the material nevertheless should cure in the cold runner, much time can be saved if a spare insert is available. An exchange of manifolds facilitates cleaning the blocked one outside the mold. Care must be taken that the mold is always closed when injecting, to counteract the pressure within the cold-runner.

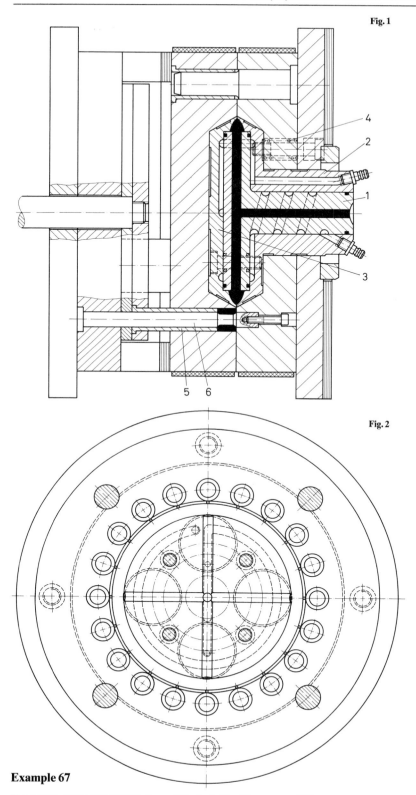

**Fig. 1**

**Fig. 2**

# Example 67

**Figs. 1 and 2    Rubber-bumper injection molding tool with cold-runner manifold**
1: main body of the cold-runner manifold, 2: insulating body, 3: half shell, 4: compression spring, 5: sleeve ejector, 6: core pin

## Example 68, Eight-cavity injection mold for manufacturing bellows of silicone rubber

Silicone rubber bellows (Fig. 1) have high heat resistance, outstanding mechanical properties, resistance to effects of aging, ozone, and weather, good electrical insulation properties, and high flexibility at low temperatures. Silicone rubber is injected as a pasty un-

**Fig. 1    Injection molded bellows of silicone rubber**

cured mass into heated mold cavities and cross-linked in the mold under the effect of heat and high pressure to yield the finished material. Before the material is injected into the mold cavity, it must be kept cool so that the cross-linking reaction does not start prematurely.

The wall thickness tolerance of the finished rubber components may not exceed 0.03 mm. Contamination of the molding material could be avoided by using the advanced cold-runner injection transfer technique. Using this process, the relatively expensive silicone rubber can be processed almost without loss.

The mold shown in Fig. 2 was conceived for use in compression molding. Silicone rubber is fed not by a screw unit, but is located in the so-called injection chamber (2) directly in the mold. This injection chamber has holes in the side facing the cavities, through which the silicone rubber is forced into the cavities (8, 9) through the channels of the nozzle plate (6). This is carried out by the piston inside the injection chamber (3, 4). The piston is connected to plate (1).

To inject the material, the top plunger of the press exerts pressure on plate (1), and thus on piston (3, 4). After the mold cavities have been thus filled, the silicone rubber in the heated mold cavity (8, 9) cross-links. When the material is fully cured, the mold is opened in the YZ plane by lifting the top part of the mold including plate (7) and cavity insert (8). Thus the sprue in the heated part of the cavity insert (8) is also demolded, to be susequently separated from the molding as slight waste.

For demolding, the bottom mold half is withdrawn from the press and conveyed to a demolding station (Fig. 3). The core (14), on which the elastomer bellows are seated, is now lifted out of the mold cavities (9). The stripper device helps to remove the molding from the cores semi-automatically. Afterwards the cores are again lowered into the cavities and are aligned by bar (15). After the top mold half has been introduced into the mold space and lowered, the next production cycle can begin by injection of the the silicone rubber.

Numerous cooling channels are located in the top half of the mold, which serve to maintain the silicone rubber at a sufficiently low temperature, and keep the nozzle plate from overheating. The nozzle plates contact the heated mold area only with their face sides. Air gaps at the side ensure that the heat transfer here is low, so that cross-linking is not initiated in the channels of the nozzle plate.

When the reserve of material in the injection chamber is used up, the piston (3, 4) is raised until the injection chamber (2) is opened and refilling is possible. When the injection chamber is closed, the air is evacuated from it by means of a vacuum pump after the piston (3, 4) is inserted. This ensures that the silicone rubber molding is free of bubbles. The air is likewise exhausted from the mold cavities before each injection cycle. This is absolutely essential for manufacturing high precision moldings.

**Fig. 3    Demolding station for fully automatic demolding of bellows**

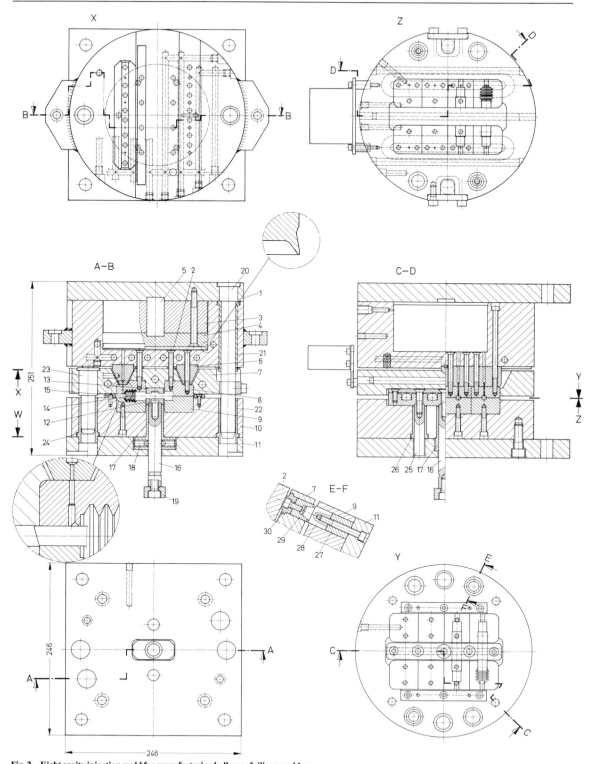

**Fig. 2    Eight cavity injection mold for manufacturing bellows of silicone rubber**
1: top mounting plate, 2: injection chamber, 3: basic piston, 4: piston cap (of polyamide), 5: alignment bolt, 6: nozzle plate, 7: front-side retainer plate,
8: front-side cavity insert, 9: ejector-side cavity insert, 10: ejector-side retainer plate, 11: lower mounting plate, 12: core support, 13: clamping bar of
core support, 14: core, 15: core alignment bar, 16: ejector bar, 17: ejector guide, 18: ball catch, 19: connection block, 20: leader pin, 21: guide bushing,
22: guide bushing, 23: leader pin, 24: guide bushing, 25: guide rod, 26: guide bushing, 27: spacer bolt, 28, 29: alignment blocks, 30: locating ring

# Example 69, Two injection molds for overmolding of nylon tubing for automobile power window operators

## Molded part

In power window operators for automobiles, the operating force is transmitted from the drive mechanism to the raising mechanism by means of a flexible gear rack that runs in plastic tubing. To hold the drive mechanism and mount it in the vehicle, two attachments of glass-fiber-reinforced nylon are molded onto a piece of nylon tubing (Fig. 1).

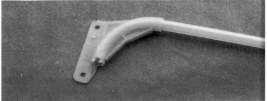

Fig. 1    **Guide tube with elbow and drive mount**

## Mold

Two pieces of tubing (for the left and right-hand versions) are placed into one injection mold for the elbows (Figs. 2 to 4) and into another for the drive mounts (Figs. 5 to 7).

Core inserts (1) are placed into the ends of the bent tubing and then into the elbow mold along with the tubing. Once this mold is closed, the core inserts are held in place by the heel blocks (2). Two sets of core inserts are available. The overhanging tubing is held in a bracket (9) attached to the side of the mold. The melt flows from a sprue through a runner system to fill each of the parts via two side gates.

For insert molding, the ejectors must be retracted to permit loading of the inserts. Accordingly, the elbow mold has a return spring (3) around the ejector rod (4). After ejection and prior to insert loading, the movable platen of the machine must be repositioned by an amount corresponding to the ejector stroke.

With the mold for the drive mounts, straight lengths of tubing are placed into the mold and overhang on either side. The overhanging tubing is held in spring-loaded retainers (1) at each end.

The parts are molded with the aid of a hot-runner system consisting of a hot-runner manifold (2) and six hot-runner nozzles (3) that feed six sprues with secondary runners. The sprue bushing (4) threaded into

Fig. 2

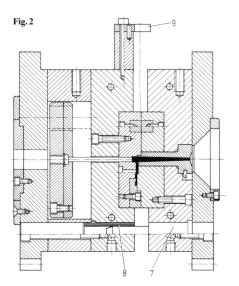

Fig. 3

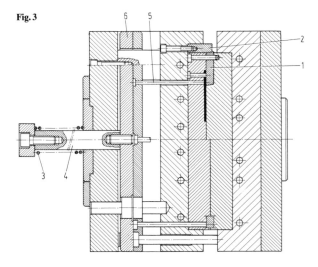

Figs. 2 to 4    **Injection mold for elbow**
1: core insert, 2: heel block, 3: return spring, 4: ejector rod, 5: ejector, 6: ejector plate, 7: leader pin, 8: guide bushing, 9: bracket

the hot-runner manifold has a decompression chamber to relieve pressure on the melt within the hot-runner system prior to opening of the mold.

The hot-runner manifold is heated by means of two cast-in heater coils (5) and is clad with insulating plates (6) to prevent heat losses.

With the gating selected, air may be entrapped at location (A) in the molded part. A date stamp (8) and vent insert (9) eliminate this danger.

In this mold as well, the ejectors must be retracted prior to loading the tubing. This is accomplished here by means of the hydraulic ejector in the machine, which is coupled to the ejector rod (10).

**Figs. 5 to 7    Injection mold for drive mounts**
1: spring-loaded retainer, 2: hot-runner manifold, 3: hot-runner nozzles, 4: sprue bushing, 5: heater coils, 6: insulating plates, 7: insulating plate, 8: date stamp, 9: thread insert, 10: ejector rod

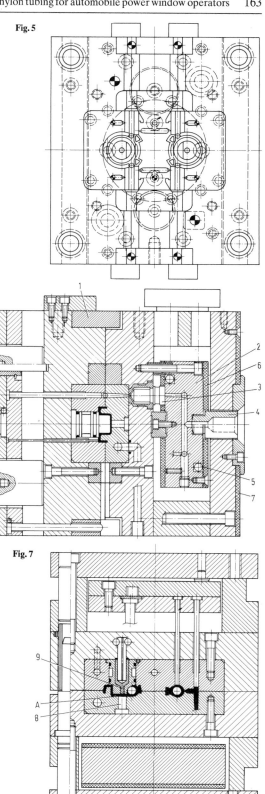

Fig. 5

Fig. 6

Fig. 4

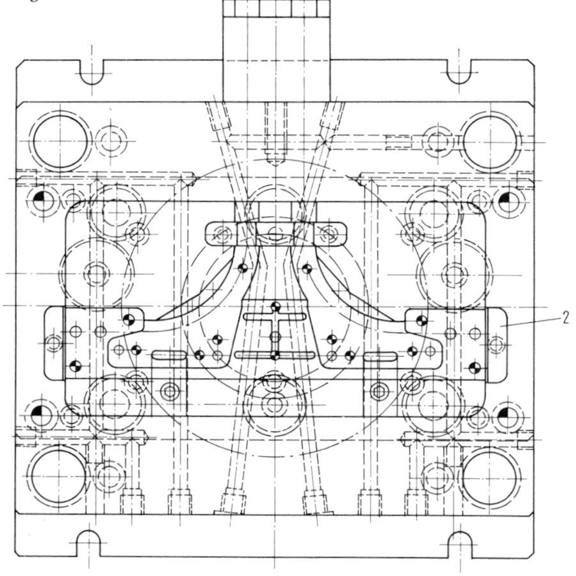

Fig. 7

## Example 70, Single-cavity injection mold for a housing base of polycarbonate

The housing (Fig. 1) has dimensions of 150 mm × 80 mm × 44 mm and has four threaded holes on its bottom and two each on the narrow ends. The narrow ends also have recesses between the threaded holes. The interior contains snap hooks, bosses and mounting eyes.

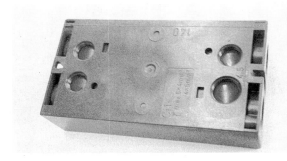

**Fig. 1    Housing base**

### Mold (Figs. 2 and 3)

The design of the part requires 8 unscrewing cores, two side cores and special measures for release of the snap hooks. Except for the part-forming components, the mold is constructed largely from standard mold components. The part is oriented in the mold with its bottom facing the injection nozzle.

The four threaded cores (105) for the side holes are placed next to one another in pairs parallel to the mold parting line. These cores rotate and are supported at one end in bronze bushings (136) and at the other by means of journals (83) in ball bearings (82). They are further guided in threaded bushings (113) and are operated in pairs by a gear (111) attached to a pinion shaft (112). A rack (126) engages the pinion shaft.

The four threaded cores (106, 107) for the bottom holes are also guided in threaded bushings (114) and are also operated in pairs by means of gear racks (125). The two gear racks (125, 126) on each side of the mold are joined by a yoke (123) into which the piston rod of an hydraulic cylinder (138) is threaded.

The threaded cores (105) turn faster than the threaded cores (106, 107) because of the transmission ratio of the gearing (111, 112). This is required by the different thread lengths.

The four threaded cores (105) on the side each have a flange that is enclosed by the slide (88) and the retaining strips (89, 90).

When one of the two hydraulic cylinders moves, the four threaded cores driven by it unscrew from the molded part, carrying along the slide (88) and thus releasing the recess on the narrow side of the part. Since the drive mechanisms for the two sides of the housing are arranged in a mirror image with respect to the axis of the housing, the two hydraulic cylinders must operate in opposite directions (Figs. 3).

The part-forming inserts and the core are made of hardened steel (material no. 1.2083 (ESR), the threaded cores are made of case-hardened steel (material no. 1.2764). The gear racks are made of inductively hardened C 45 K.

### Runner system/gating

The part is gated on its bottom and filled via a hot-runner nozzle (25) which is attached to a heated sprue bushing (108) which extends through the space required for the unscrewing mechanism in this half of the mold.

### Mold temperature control

To the extent that space permits, cooling lines and bubblers with baffles (132) are provided in the core and stationary mold inserts.

### Part release/ejection

Prior to mold opening, the piston rods of the two hydraulic cylinders (138) are moved in opposite directions so that the threaded cores unscrew from the threaded holes. The slides (88) retract from the recesses on the sides of the molded part and the mold can now open.

As the two-stage ejector (28) advances, the stripper plates (4), the ejector sleeves (30) and the mold cores (101, 102) jointly strip the molded part off the core. Mold core (103) remains stationary, thereby releasing the smooth back surface of the snap hook.

After a distance of approximately 20 mm, the ejector plates (10, 12) stop and plates (9, 11) continue moving along with the stripper plate (4) and ejector sleeve (30). The snap hooks and the core pins for the mounting eyes are released and the part is now free to drop.

Pin (37) and sleeve (99) also serve to vent the cavity for the bosses in the mold.

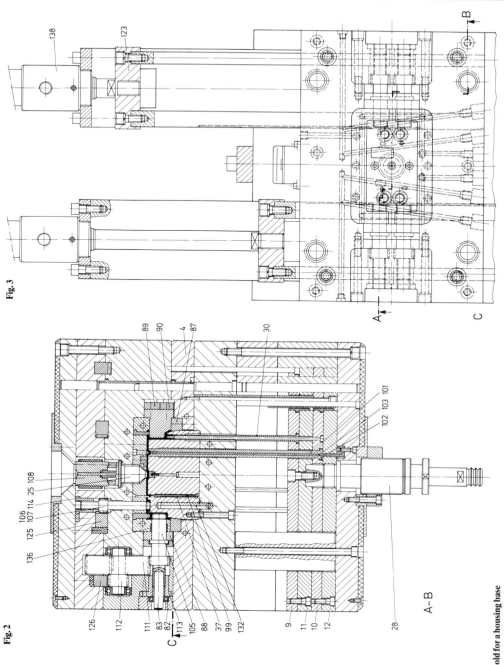

Fig. 3

Fig. 2

A–B

**Figs. 2 and 3   Single-cavity injection mold for a housing base**
4: stripper plate, 9, 10, 11, 12: ejector plates, 25: hot-runner nozzle,
28: two-stage ejector, 30: ejector sleeve, 37: pin, 82: ball bearing, 83: jour-
nal, 87: stripper ring, 88: slide, 89, 90: retaining strips, 99: mold sleeve,
101, 102, 103: mold cores, 105, 106, 107: threaded cores, 108: sprue bushing, 111: gear, 112: pinion shaft, 113, 114: threaded bushings, 123: yoke,
125, 126: gear racks, 132: baffle, 136: bushing, 138: hydraulic cylinder

# Example 71, Connector of glass-fiber-reinforced nylon with opposing female threads

The connector (Fig. 1) is 90 mm long in the direction of the through hole with the two opposing threads ($^3/_4$ in. NPT). Another hole intersects this first hole at a 90 degree angle and four additional holes pass through the connector parallel to it. The walls are 4 mm and the ribs 2 mm thick respectively.

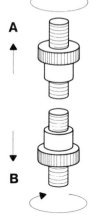

**Fig. 1    Connector of glass-fiber-reinforced nylon (PA)**

**Fig. 2    Threaded cores for releasing the two opposing threads**

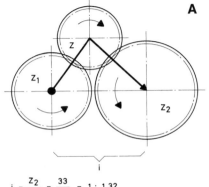

$$i = \frac{z_2}{z_1} = \frac{33}{25} = 1 : 1,32$$

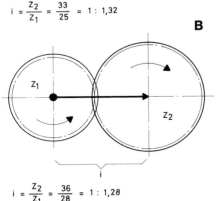

$$i = \frac{z_2}{z_1} = \frac{36}{28} = 1 : 1,28$$

**Fig. 3    Gears on the drive shafts for the threaded cores**

## Mold

### Unscrewing mechanism

To release the two opposing threads and the hole between them requires two threaded cores, one at each end of the part. Dividing the length of the hole among the two threaded cores, each must move a distance of 45 mm or, with a pitch of 1.814 mm, make 25 revolutions.

An hydraulic unscrewing mechanism was selected to drive the threaded cores.

The cores rotate in opposite directions (Fig. 2) for which reason an intermediate gear Z is incorporated in the gear set A shown in Fig. 3. The gears Z 1 sit on the common drive shaft, while the gears Z 2 are located on the threaded cores. After 34 revolutions of the unscrewing mechanism, core A has moved 46.72 mm and core B 48.18 mm. The total displacement is thus approximately 94 mm, since the two cores engage one another slightly and thus center each other.

The unscrewing mechanism is attached to the stationary mold half (Fig. 4). Each of the two threaded cores (4) has a rectangular end (3) which slides in a mating hole in the gears (6). Threaded bushings (5) provide guidance for the threaded cores. The drive gears (8, 9) are mounted on the drive shaft (10). On side A, intermediate gear (7) is located between gear (8) and gear (6).

The core (16) for the internal shape, core (24) for the side hole and two cores for the holes passing through the connector are located on the moving mold half. Two additional cores (25) are attached to the stationary mold half, because there was not sufficient space to attach them next to core (24) on the moving mold half.

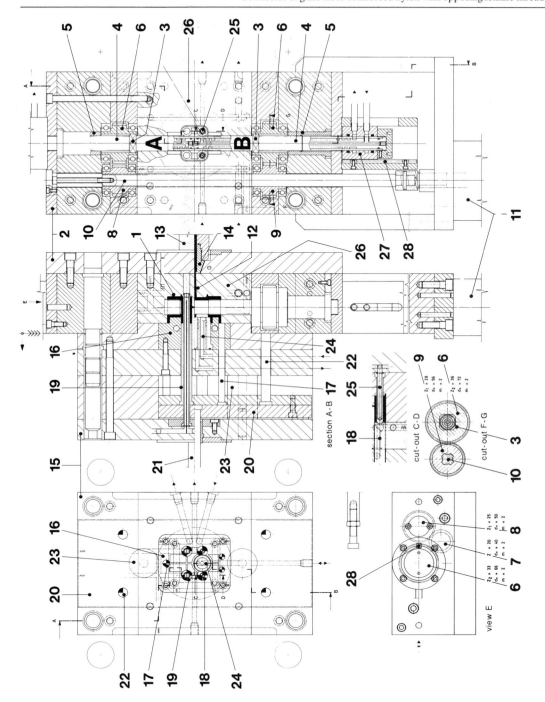

**Fig. 4   Injection mold with unscrewing mechanism for a connector**

1: molded part, 2: stationary mold half, 3: rectangular end, 4: threaded core, 5: threaded bushing, 6: gear, 7: intermediate gear, 8, 9: drive gears, 10: drive shaft, 11: unscrewing mechanism, 12: sprue, 13: nozzle, 14: extension, 15: moving mold half, 16: mold core, (17, 18: ejector pins, 19: ejector sleeves, 20: ejector plate, 21: ejector rod, 22: pushback pin, 23: support pillar, 24: core, 25: core pin, 26: cavity, 27: manifold block, 28: key

## Mold temperature control

The mold is operated at a temperature of 100 °C. Channels are provided in the mold cavity (26) for mold temperature control. The two threaded cores (4) are hollow and each contain a single-flighted helical core. The temperature control fluid is supplied and returned through manifold blocks (27) with a rotating fit to the ends of the cores (4). Keys (28) prevent the manifold blocks (27) from rotating.

Mold core (16) is provided with cooling channels. Core (24) is provided with helical cooling. The four core pins are hollow and fitted with baffles to guide the temperature control fluid.

## Part release/ejection

The ejector pins (17, 18) and ejector sleeves (19) serve to eject the molded part from the core. Ejector rod (21) advances the ejector plate (20) with the aid of the hydraulic ejector on the molding machine. Pushback pins (22) return the ejector plate to the original position. Pillars (23) support the core retainer plate.

## Runner system/gating

The part is filled through a sprue (12) with the aid of an extension (14) attached to the machine nozzle (13).
The cycle time is 98 s, the cooling time 57 s. Screwing the two cores (4) in and out each requires 10 s.

## Example 72, Cylindrical thermoplastic container with reduced-diameter opening – a study in part release

Cylindrical containers such as paint cans have an inner rim and are sealed by means of a press-fit cover. Such containers can be packed in an especially space-saving arrangement. This study shows how such a container can be manufactured by means of injection molding and how it is released in the mold.

## Mold

The mold (Figs. 1 and 2) consists of a cavity (5) and a central core (6) on which core slides (1) move along tapered surfaces. The core slides (1) can move additionally in a radial direction along a guide plate (7). When the mold is closed, the slides (3) between the core slides (1) seat against the central core (6) and together with the slides (1) form the cylindrical outer surface of the core.

The slides (3) can also move in a radial direction on guide plate (8). They are actuated by the cam pins (2) attached to the guide plate (7).

The rim of the container is formed by the stripper ring (4), which encloses the slides (1, 3) when the mold is closed.

Fig. 2 shows the guides for the slides (1) and plate (7) at the top and the guides for the slides (3) and plate (8) at the bottom.

Not shown are the actuating mechanisms that control the part release sequence described in the following. The well-known actuators (hydraulic cylinders, latch arrangements, chains etc.) are suitable for this purpose.

## Part release/ejection

1. The mold opens at parting line I ; the core and molded part are withdrawn from the cavity.
2. Plate (7) and plate (8) separate from the central core (6) (parting line II ). Because they move on guiding surfaces on the central core (6), the slides (1) move inwards radially, while the slides (3) initially retain their original position. Tangential and radial spaces (Fig. 3) form between the slides (3).
3. Plate (7) comes to a stop and plate (8) continues to move (separation at parting line III ). Now, the cam pins (2) pull the slides (3) inwards; the molded part is held only by the stripper ring (4) (Fig. 4), which ejects it from the core (Fig. 5).

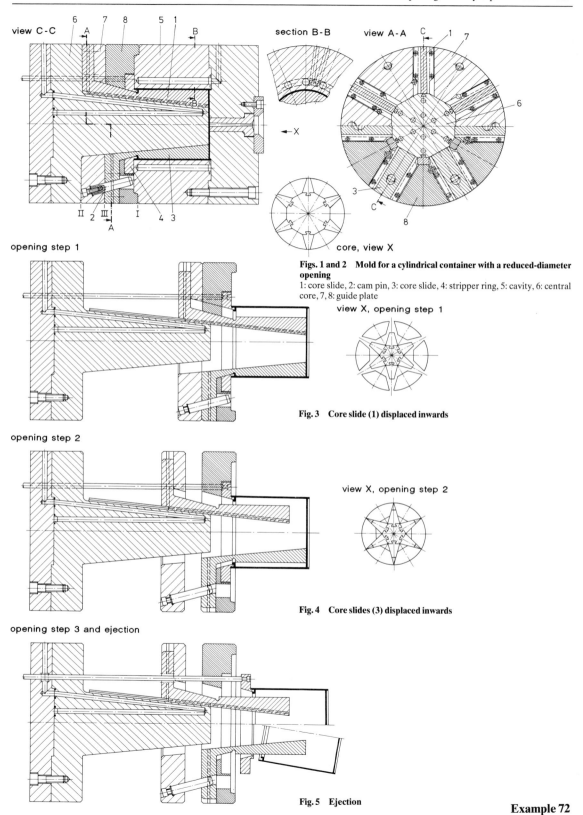

view C-C

section B-B     view A-A

view X

opening step 1

**Figs. 1 and 2    Mold for a cylindrical container with a reduced-diameter opening**
1: core slide, 2: cam pin, 3: core slide, 4: stripper ring, 5: cavity, 6: central core, 7, 8: guide plate

core, view X

view X, opening step 1

**Fig. 3    Core slide (1) displaced inwards**

opening step 2

view X, opening step 2

**Fig. 4    Core slides (3) displaced inwards**

opening step 3 and ejection

**Fig. 5    Ejection**

**Example 72**

# Example 73, Single-cavity injection mold for a lighting fixture cover of polymethylmethacrylate (PMMA)

The lighting fixture cover of PMMA with a diameter of 87 mm and a height of 76 mm (Fig. 1) is attached by means of three pockets into which hooks on the lighting fixture snap. Snapping the molded part off the core is not possible, for which reason three slides are necessary for part release.

## Mold (Figs. 2 and 3)

A pneumatically actuated nozzle (37) is used to mold the part. Such nozzles are often used on single-cavity molds, because they leave a small, clean gate mark on the molded part and do not require any heaters or temperature controllers as does a heated sprue bushing, yet still permit fully automatic operation. They do, however, produce a small sprue with each shot.

Use of a granulator directly next to the injection molding machine and immediate reintroduction of the regrind into the hopper has proven successful. The operation of the nozzle (37) is described in Example 98.

## Mold construction

The mold is constructed of standard mold components. The cavity has been machined directly into the plate (2). The three cam pins (30) that actuate the slides (43) are also attached to plate (2).

The core is machined from plate (3) and is supported against the mold clamping plate (5) by plate (4), support ring (6) and support pillars (35). The core plate (3) contains three radial grooves which accommodate the slides (43) that form the pockets in the molded part.

When the mold is closed, the slides are held in position by the conical pins (31) as well as the taper pins (44).

## Part release/ejection

As the mold opens, the following three sequences take place simultaneously:
1. The pushback pins (32) release plate (9), which can now displace the taper pins (44) with respect to the slides (43) by means of the compressed helical springs (40) such that a radial movement of the slides is now possible. Conical pins (31) release the slides (43) too.
2. With a slight delay resulting from the clearance "s", the slides (43) are displaced inwards by the cam pins (30) so that the pockets in the molded part are released.
3. The molded part is withdrawn from the cavity on the core.

Steps 1 and 2 are complete when plate (9) stops against plate (4).

Lastly, the molded part is stripped off the core by the ejector pins (33) which are actuated by the ejector plates (7, 8).

The ejectors (33) are hydraulically retracted prior to mold closing by means of the ejector plate (7, 8). In the final phase of closing, they also act as pushback pins. The taper pins (44) are pulled behind the slides (43) by the pushback pins (32) and plate (9) after the slides have been displaced outwards by the cam pins (30).

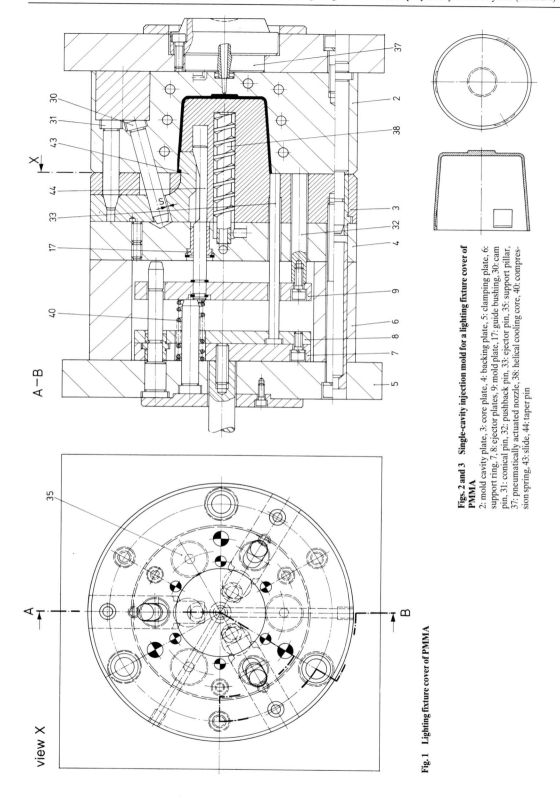

A – B

X

view X

Fig. 1   Lighting fixture cover of PMMA

**Figs. 2 and 3   Single-cavity injection mold for a lighting fixture cover of PMMA**

2: mold cavity plate, 3: core plate, 4: backing plate, 5: clamping plate, 6: support ring, 7, 8: ejector plates, 9: mold plate, 17: guide bushing, 30: cam pin, 31: conical pin, 32: pushback pin, 33: ejector pin, 35: support pillar, 37: pneumatically actuated nozzle, 38: helical cooling core, 40: compression spring, 43: slide, 44: taper pin

## Example 74, Injection mold for a housing of polycarbonate with a thread insert

The rectangular housing (Fig. 1) of polycarbonate has a neck with a thread at one end.

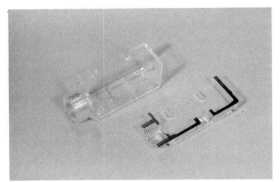

**Fig. 1   Housing with thread steel insert at one end**

### Unscrewing mechanism

The unscrewing mechanism for the thread is actuated by the mold opening motion. Since the axis of thread is perpendicular to the direction of opening, a gear rack drive mechanism was selected.

The thread have a length of 10.7 mm with a pitch of 1.41 mm. An unscrewing stroke of 11.9 mm, requiring 8.5 revolutions of the threaded core, was selected.

The pitch diameter of the drive pinion on the threaded core must be at least 20 mm, so that a stroke of 20 mm $\times \pi \times 8.5 = 534$ mm would result with direct drive by means of the gear rack. The maximum possible opening stroke of the injection mold machine available, however, was only 200 mm. It is inadvisable, though, to use the entire 200 mm stroke available on a toggle machine, because the opening force of such machines is only very low at the end of the opening stroke.

Accordingly, two pairs of gears with a transmission ratio to increase the speed were incorporated between the gear rack and theraded core (Fig. 2).

### Runner system/gating

The part is molded via a runner in the parting line which ends in a submarine gate on the end of the housing opposite the threads.

### Molds construction

The mold opens along the line a–b–c–d–e–f (Fig. 3). The gearing arrangement with the gears (6, 10, 11, 12, 13) and the threaded core (5) with the threaded bushing (8) are thus located in the moving mold half, while the gear rack (14) is attached to the stationary mold half.

With the overall transmission ratio selected (Fig. 2), the unscrewing stroke for the core is achieved with an opening stroke of 128 mm. An additional stroke of 3 mm is used for mold protection in the machine.

The stripper plate (16) is fitted around three sides of the mold core (15). It is actuated by means of rods (23) by the ejector plate (21), which is coupled to the machine hydraulic ejector by means of ejector rod (20). Pillars (19) support the core retainer plate against the mold clamping plate.

### Mold temperature control

The mold temperature is supposed to be between 75 and 130 °C. The cavity insert (17) is provided with cooling channels for the mold temperature control fluid. Bubblers with baffles (18) to direct the coolant are provided in the mold core (15).

### Part release/ejection

Upon mold opening, the molded part (1) and mold core (15) are withdrawn from the cavity. During this motion, the threaded core is unscrewed from the molded part by means of the gear rack and gearing arrangement.

Simultaneously, the submarine gate shears off the molded part. Initially, the runner is retained on the cavity half of the mold, because the sprue puller (22) has been designed with a certain amount of axial play. This feature facilitates separation of the runner from the molded part. The runner is pulled out of the submarine gate only after the mold strokes this mount.

Finally, the stripper plate (16) strips the molded part off the core and ejects the runner from the sprue puller. Prior to closing, the stripper plate is returned to its original position.

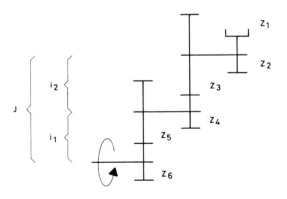

$$z_1, \ z_2 = 20, \ z_3 = 44, \ z_4 = 18, \ z_5 = 34, \ z_6 = 20$$

$$i_1 = \frac{z_5}{z_6} = \frac{34}{20} = 1,7 : 1 \qquad i_2 = \frac{z_3}{z_4} = \frac{44}{18} = 2,44 : 1$$

$$J = i_1 \cdot i_2 = \frac{1,7 \cdot 2,44}{1} = 4,14 : 1$$

**Fig. 2   Gearing arrangement**

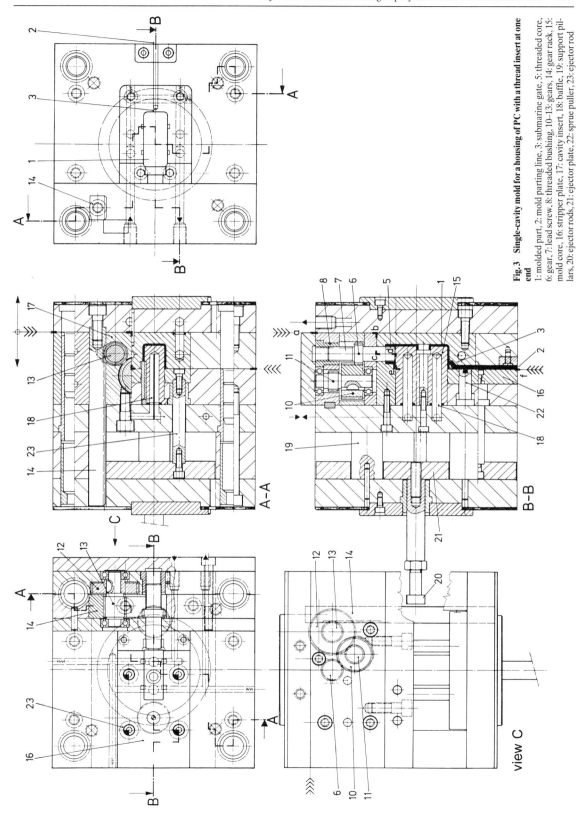

**Fig. 3   Single-cavity mold for a housing of PC with a thread insert at one end**

1: molded part, 2: mold parting line, 3: submarine gate, 5: threaded core, 6: gear, 7: lead screw, 8: threaded bushing, 10–13: gears, 14: gear rack, 15: mold core, 16: stripper plate, 17: cavity insert, 18: baffle, 19: support pillars, 20: ejector rods, 21: ejector plate, 22: sprue puller, 23: ejector rod

A–A

B–B

view C

# Example 75, Mold for long, thin, tubular parts of polystyrene

A large quantity of test-tube-like specimen tubes was to be molded in polystyrene. The tube was to have a flange at its larger end and a conical tip with axial opening at the smaller end. A four-cavity mold appeared both technically and economically reasonable. The length of the tubes, however, posed a problem. For the length of 170 mm, an opening stroke of 510 mm would have been required with a conventional mold design. Since only 40 cm³ of melt would have been needed to simultaneously mold the four tubes, a small injection molding machine would have been adequate. As a rule, however, small machines do not have such a long opening stroke. The clamping force required was slight, since the projected area amounted to only a few square centimeters, so that only a small machine would have been required from this standpoint as well. Because the outside surface of the tubes, was not permitted to show any witness lines, it was not possible to place the cavities in the plane of the parting line.

Accordingly, a mold (Figs. 1 and 2) was designed that projected through an opening in the movable platen where the ejector mechanism normally would be mounted. A further slight modification of the machine was also required: the stripper plate (20) located in the stationary mold half leaves the normal guide pins (21)

during the last portion of its stroke and thus needs an auxiliary means of guidance. Accordingly, two holes were drilled in the movable platen, through which two extended auxiliary guide pins (14) project. The stripper plate (20) runs in ball bearings (16) on these pins. To provide optimum filling, each cavity was provided with two submarine gates.

Bolts (18) and (19) are located between the cavity and auxiliary guide pin (14). Bolt (19) is mounted in the stationary-side clamping plate. Bolt (18) serves as the stripper bolt to actuate the stripper plate (20) located in the stationary mold half. This plate must not be actuated before the movable mold half has released the entire length of the molded parts. Accordingly, it is held in position by pins (22) that project into the runner system and become embedded in the solidifying melt. As soon as the movable mold half has released the molded parts, stripper bolt (18) actuates stripper sleeve (13), and the molded parts are stripped off the cores (6, 10) until the shoulder in sleeve (17) seats against the bolt (19) and stops further motion of stripper plate (20). The stripper plate is now supported on the auxiliary guide pins (14) and is returned to the molding position as the mold closes. This design proved successful both technically and economically.

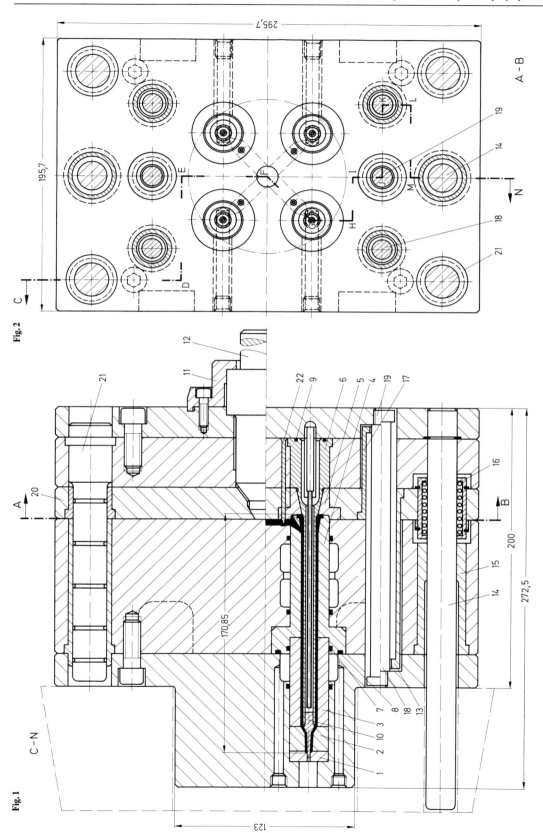

**Fig. 2**

**Fig. 1**

**Figs. 1 and 2   Four-cavity injection mold for test-tube-like polystyrene specimen tubes**
1: core tip support, 2: cavity insert for tip, 3: cavity insert for tip, 4: cavity insert for flange, 5: stripper ring, 6: core insert, 7, 8, 9: O-ring, 10: core insert tip, 11: locating ring, 12: hot sprue bushing, 13: stripper sleeve, 14: auxiliary guide pins, 15: guide bushings, 16: ball bearing, 17: stop sleeve, 18: stripper bolt, 19: stop bolt, 20: stripper plate, 21: guide pin, 22: sucker pin

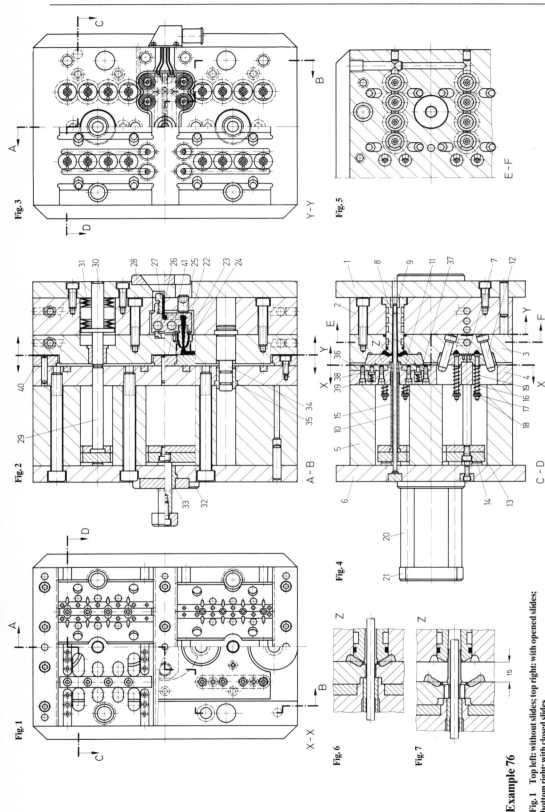

**Fig. 3**

**Fig. 5**

E – F

Y – Y

31
30
28
27
26
41
25
22
23
24

**Fig. 2**

40

29

35   34

33   32

A – B

1

2

8

9

11

37

7

12

E

Y

F

X   X

36

39   38

Z

5

6

10   15

18

17   16   19   4

14   13

20

21

C – D

**Fig. 4**

**Fig. 1**

A

C

D

B

X – X

Z

Z

15

**Fig. 6**

**Fig. 7**

## Example 76

**Fig. 1   Top left: without slides; top right: with opened slides; bottom right: with closed slides**

**Fig. 7   Detail illustration (detail Z) after 15 mm opening stroke**

**Figs. 1 to 10   16-cavity injection mold with degating for ballpoint pen barrels**

1: stationary-side mold clamping plate, 2: spacer plate with hot-runner manifold, 3: runner plate, 4: base plate for slides, 5: spacer plate, 6: movable-side mold clamping plate, 7: cover strip, 8: cavity, 9: core locator, 10: core, 11: slide, 12: cam pin, 13, 14: ejector plates, 15: ejector sleeve, 16: ejector pin, 17: stop washer, 18: shaft circlip, 19: compression spring, 20: ejector rod, 21: outer ejector plate, 22: hot-runner manifold, 23: hot-runner nozzle, 24: nozzle well insert, 25: pressure screw, 26: hot-runner manifold locator, 27: sprue bushing, 28: locating ring, 29: retaining bolt, 30: bolt with collar, 31: spring pack, 32: locating ring, 33: guide bushing, 34: locating pin, 35: locating sleeve, 36, 37: detent holder, 38: detent, 39: compression spring, 40, 41: guide for slides

# Example 76, 16-cavity injection mold with degating for ballpoint pen barrels

Edge gating of small diameter molded parts, such as ballpoint pen barrels, for instance, can nowadays be accomplished in a multi-cavity hot-runner tool with standardized hot-runner nozzles developed especially for side injection and marketed by such firms as Mold-Masters, Thermoplay and Jetform. If one does not choose this system of gating, then there only remains the combination of hot- and conventional runner systems for fully automatic production without any sizeable runner losses. This type of solution is shown with the mold in Figs. 1 to 10. A centrally placed hot-runner block (22) with eight hot-runner nozzles (23, 24) supplies four mold cavities each by way of two convention-al runners. These lead the melt into the cavities from two sides via submarine gates. This bilateral gating ensures additional core centering during injection. The gates are located on the locating ring of the ball-pen barrel and will later be covered by a decorative ring. The external threads of the ballpoint pen barrels are formed by two slides (11). These also house the runners.

It is important when demolding that axial displacement of the ballpoint pen barrels on the cores (10) is avoided until the slides (11) guided by the cam pins (12) have opened. This detaches them from the submarine gates, and the barrels are simultaneously demold-

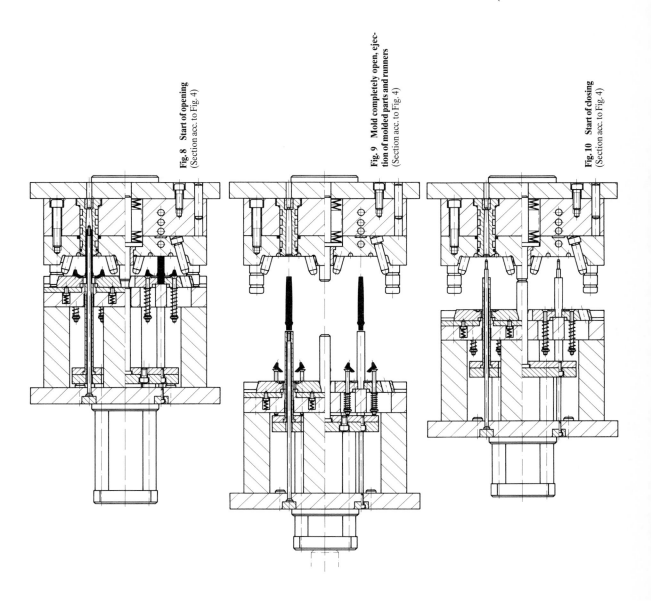

**Fig. 8   Start of opening** (Section acc. to Fig. 4)

**Fig. 9   Mold completely open, ejection of molded parts and runners** (Section acc. to Fig. 4)

**Fig. 10   Start of closing** (Section acc. to Fig. 4)

ed from the cavity (8). This sequence is assured by a spring pack (31), which retains the ejector plates (13, 14) by pushing bolt (30) against bolt (29) until the collar on the former, housed in plate (3), bottoms. Because of the length of the ballpoint pen barrels, the mold requires a long opening stroke and the cam pins (12) move out of the slides (11). They are retained in their open position by detents (37) to ensure the safe entry of the cam pins (12) into the guide holes when the mold is being closed. The ejector on the machine is adjusted so that it meets with the outer ejector plate (21) when the molded part has been withdrawn completely from the cavity. Then the ejector sleeve (15) pushes the molded part off the core (10). During the course of this movement the ejector plate (13) contacts the ejector pins (16), so that the runners are ejected by them. The illustrations in Figs. 8 to 10 show the sequence of this ejection process.

# Example 77, Injection mold for parts with several parting lines perpendicular to the direction of opening

If parts with shallow undercuts are to be produced in a multi-cavity tool, the mold will have to be furnished with multiple slides. The mold in Figs. 1 to 4 contains four little boxes, open at two sides, which have depressions in all four sides. The outer side walls of these boxes are bordered by four slides (a) , which have been set into the cavity plate (b) with a tapered fit. Into each one of these slides two guide pins (c) are firmly pressed, which are at a slightly less acute angle than the tapered fit. The taper angle of the slides must in any event exceed the self-blocking limit of 10 ° (approx.), otherwise the slides will release only with difficulty when pushed forward, as they will be pressed against the tapered contact area with great force by the injection pressure. It is also recommended to keep the angle of the tapers small enough that the slides can lodge behind the molded parts sufficiently far during that part of their travel during which the molded parts are still retained on the cores (d) to be able to demold them during their further advance. Pushback pins are not required for the ejector plate (e) , as the guid pins of the slides return the ejector plate when the mold closes.

Efficient core cooling is achieved by equipping the cores with larger bores, into which the cooling water is fed via brass tubes (f) . The cores are sealed with an O-ring (g) . A triangular groove having the same area as the diameter of the core accommodates the O-ring, which is pressed into the groove to form a watertight seal when the retaining bolts for the core are tightened. The cooling water is supplied to the brass tube through a bore in the base plate (h) . A second channel, connected to the cooling bore of the core, serves as return. The nozzle flange (i) is either cooled by a surrounding channel or a ring groove, as is the case here. The pressed-in ring (k) is sealed by the rubber ring (l) .

The runners for the mold cavities are led to the four corners of the boxes. They have been milled into the core-retainer plate (m) and reach right up to the box. The gate serving the cavity is situated on the ejector side and is cut into the slides approximately 1 mm deep.

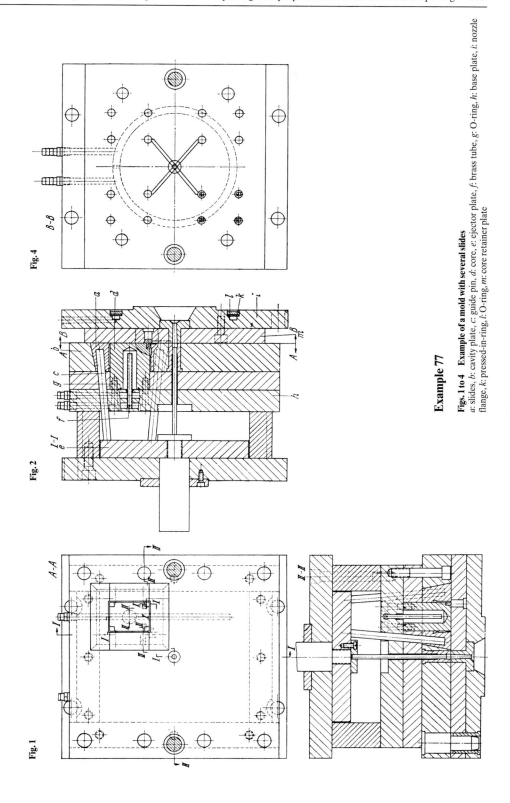

**Example 77**

**Figs. 1 to 4   Example of a mold with several slides**

*a*: slides, *b*: cavity plate, *c*: guide pin, *d*: core, *e*: ejector plate, *f*: brass tube, *g*: O-ring, *h*: base plate, *i*: nozzle flange, *k*: pressed-in-ring, *l*: O-ring, *m*: core retainer plate

# Example 78, Injection mold for battery caps with undivided external thread and sealing cone

The external thread and the sealing cone of battery caps are usually molded in splits-cavity tools, leaving a fine parting line seam.

If it has been specified that no parting line seam at all be visible, thread and sealing cone will have to be demolded by unscrewing. Figures 1 to 5 show such a tool designed as an eight-cavity mold. Its construction and operation are described below:

To avoid an externally visible gate, an easily severed pinpoint gate is situated inside the cap. The construction and operation of such molds have been described repeatedly. The external thread and the sealing cone of the caps are produced in the threaded sleeves ($a$). These are carried in bronze guide bushings ($b$), which have the same screw pitch as the battery caps. The threaded sleeves are provided with gear teeth on the other side, where they mesh with the central pinion ($c$). This pinion is driven by a central spindle ($d$), with a screw thread of low pitch, by the opening and closing movement of the mold. The mold drives the sleeves ($a$) counter-clockwise when opening and clockwise when closing. The caps grip the cores ($e$) sufficiently tightly through shrinkage during the unscrewing process, so that they remain stationary. The shape of the molded part also ensures that it does not turn.

As soon as the threads have been released, the ejector pins ($f$) push against the clamping cover ($g$) and the caps are ejected by the ejector pins ($h$).

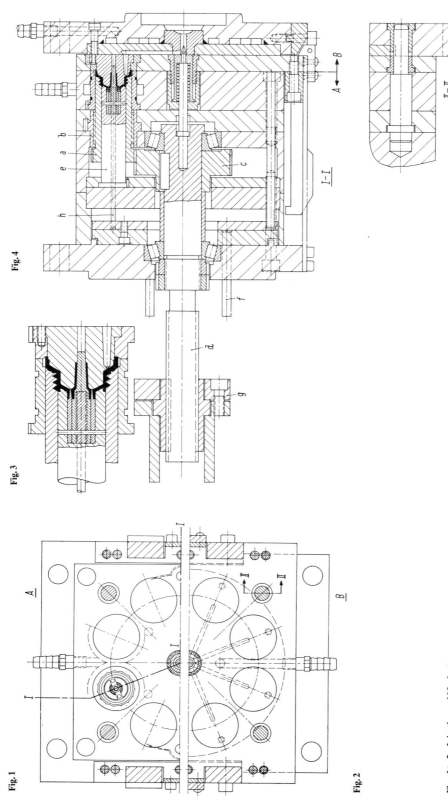

Fig. 4

Fig. 3

Fig. 1

Fig. 2

Fig. 5

$I-I$

$II-II$

**Figs. 1 to 5   Injection mold for battery caps**
*a*: thread sleeves, *b*: guide bushings, *c*: pinion, *d*: threaded spindle, *e*: cores, *f*, *h*: ejector pins, *g*: clamping
cover

## Example 79, Injection mold for a curved pouring spout

Complicated part release processes result from curved, hollow molded parts, such as a pouring spout, for example. This particular one can be fitted with a retaining nut to be screwed onto the threaded mouth of a bottle for drinks. The production of this molded part calls for a curved core, requiring a stripper plate describing an arc that is matched to the contour of the molded parts.

The mold illustrated in Figs. 1 to 4 serves to describe the production of this type of pouring spout. For part release the tool opens in the parting-line plane. To start with, the molded part remains in the moving mold cavity of the mold plate (3), with the core carrier (9) being moved along the guide pin (24) by springs (26) until stopped by the discs (27) following the opening movement. On further opening, part release takes place from this mold cavity half as well and the freed molded part rests on core (13) between the mold halves. When the hinged latch (32) housed in the retainer (31) reaches the ejector rod (20), the latter through its downward movement rotates the ejector plate (10) against the force of spring (23) down around the fulcrum pin (11). The molded part is pulled off the core. Due to the conical shape of the core an ejector stroke of approximately 5 mm suffices to drop the molded part off the core.

With the mold closing movement the latch (32) moves into the retainer (31) via ejector rod (20) without shifting the ejector rod. When the injection unit moves back, it pulls the sprue out of the mold. The sprue must be removed from the machine nozzle after each shot in the version described here.

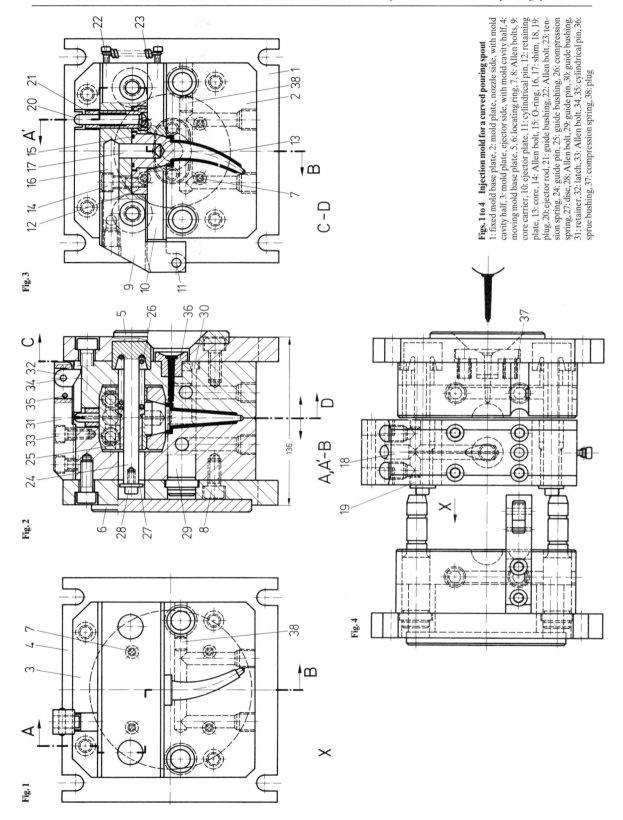

**Figs. 1 to 4    Injection mold for a curved pouring spout**
1: fixed mold base plate, 2: mold plate, nozzle side, with mold cavity half, 3: mold plate, ejector side, with mold cavity half, 4: moving mold base plate, 5, 6: locating ring, 7, 8: Allen bolts, 9: core carrier, 10: ejector plate, 11: cylindrical pin, 12: retaining plate, 13: core, 14: Allen bolt, 15: O-ring, 16, 17: shim, 18, 19: plug, 20: ejector rod, 21: guide bushing, 22: Allen bolt, 23: tension spring, 24: guide pin, 25: guide bushing, 26: compression spring, 27: disc, 28: Allen bolt, 29: guide pin, 30: guide bushing, 31: retainer, 32: latch, 33: Allen bolt, 34, 35: cylindrical pin, 36: sprue bushing, 37: compression spring, 38: plug

Fig. 3

Fig. 2

Fig. 1

Fig. 4

## Example 80, Injection mold for an ABS spectacle frame

The shape of a frame for protective goggles (Fig. 1) poses part release problems for the mold designer. Undercuts on injection molded parts are usually formed in the mold by means of split cavities or slides. The pro-

**Fig. 1    Spectacle frame for protective goggles made of ABS**
(®Teluran, made by BASF AG)

duction of the undercuts needed for subsequently fitting the lenses involves considerable design problems, especially since these slides would not lie at right angles to the direction of draw. The present design of an injection mold for making a spectacle frame (Figs. 2 and 3) shows how, by using collapsible cores, the problem can be simplified. These cores can be obtained as standard mold components.

The cavity for the frame is formed by plates 5 and 6 (Fig. 2). The lens surrounds (undercuts) are formed by the core segment sleeves (11) of the collapsible cores (9) (Fig. 4). When the mold opens (Fig. 3) the moving mold half (2) is separated from the fixed mold half (1) by the clamping plate (4), the frame being released from the cavity plate (5). During this operation, the pneumatic ram (15) of the cylinder (14) is subjected to compressed air via a control valve and the air inlet (L) of the cylinder, so that the parting line between the guide plate (13) and support plate (8) remains closed.

After a certain opening stroke the air control valve shifts and the compressed air is passed via an air inlet (R) to the second piston surface of the double-acting pneumatic cylinder. This causes the plate (7) and the collapsible core elements (9) in it to move in the opposite direction together with the support plate (8). Hence the center cores (10) of the collapsible cores (9), which move outward, are held fast by the sliding blocks (16) of the guide plate (13) and so they slide out of the core segment sleeves (11).

Before the opening stroke is limited by the pneumatic piston, the stop bolts (18) in the guide plate (13) carry along the outer sleeve (12) of the collapsible core elements via the fastening flanges (17) after a certain distance has been covered. This causes the cores of the segment sleeves (11) to drop toward the inside. The undercuts (lens surrounds) of the spectacle frame are thus released (Fig. 5).

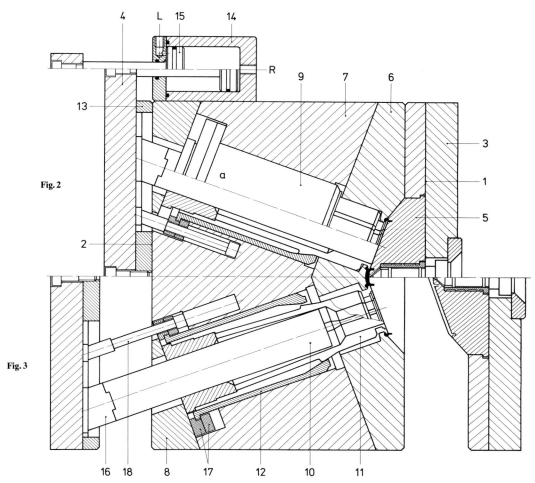

Fig. 2

Fig. 3

**Figs. 2 and 3    Injection mold for the spectacle frame**
1: fixed mold half, 2: moving mold half, 3: fixed clamping plate, 5: cavity plate, 6: cavity plate, 7: plate, 8: support plate, 9: collapsible core element, 10: center core, 11: segment sleeve, 12: outer sleeve, 13: guide plate, 14: pneumatic cylinder, 15: double-acting pneumatic piston, 16: sliding block, 17: fastening flange, 18: stop bolt
*View top:* Closed mold
*View bottom:* Mold opened with collapsed core, part release is possible
*a:* Collapsible core, L, R: air inlet holes

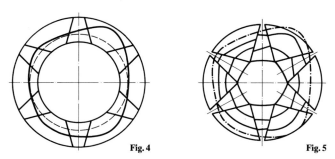

Fig. 4                    Fig. 5

**Figs. 4 and 5    Contour of spectacles near the lens surrounds on the core disc**
Fig. 4    Contour on the core during molding
Fig. 5    Contour on the core during part release

## Example 81, Eight-cavity injection mold for the upper halves of cable clamps

The fully automatic production of the well-known upper parts of cable clamps requires a rather complicated injection mold (Fig. 1). A threaded core of approximately seven turns of thread has to be unscrewed and a slide containing the retaining notches has to be pulled out. Furthermore, the mold must sever the gate cleanly from the runner when opening, so that the eight upper cable clamp halves discharge separately from the runner.

Fig. 1    Upper parts for cable clamps

To start with, the considerations leading to the construction of the mold will be examined. An injection molding machine having 225 mm mold height and a maximum opening stroke of 170 mm is available. To assure a reliable discharge of the molded parts, separated from the runner, a sleeve ejector with an ejector stroke of 25 mm has been provided over the threaded cores. The threaded cores must therefore be screwed out for a distance of $170 - 25 = 145$ mm. At an 80 mm pitch of the center spindle imparting the rotational movement to the cores, this results in 145 to $80 = 1.8$ spindle rotations which have to be transmitted to the threads so that approximately seven core rotations take place prior to the start of ejection. The transmission ratio between the central pinion, which is turned by the spindle during the opening process, and the core pinion must therefore be 4 : 1, so that with a stroke of 145 mm $4 \times 1.8 = 7.2$ turns result. Once the diameter for the inserts producing the external shape has been established at 40 mm, a distance of 75 mm for the inserts from the center of the mold results, having taken the space for the four arms of the ejector star between the inserts into consideration.

### Arrangement of the ejector

With modulus 1, which is quite adequate for the teeth of the pinions, the ratio of numbers of teeth at a 1 : 4 transmission results in 120 to 30 teeth.

As the ejector sleeves have to be arranged in a circle of 150 mm diameter but an unrestricted passage of only 90 mm is available behind the mold clamping plate on the moving half, the ejector mechanism has to be housed within the diameter of 90 mm. This calls for a

second ejector plate within the given mold height, and the connecting bars between the ejector plates must fit outside the large gear wheel. The two tandem ejector plates enlarge the mold height by approximately 50 mm. For this reason those machines are at an advantage that possess as large a free access space behind the mold clamping plate of the moving half as possible to enable ejector bars to be fitted outside the large gear diameter directly up to the ejector on the machine. On machines with a central setting nut for adjusting the mold height, which has its own advantages, this would hardly be possible, however, as the setting nut would have to be too large in diameter. These machines ought to have as large a mold height accommodation as possible in order to house the second ejector plate necessary and to account for the large ejection stroke within the mold.

### The slides

Release of the internal notches of the clamp is only possible if the slides containing these notches are pulled before ejection takes place. During this pulling operation the cores can simultaneously be unscrewed. As the inserts for the exterior shape of the clamp are arranged in a circle because of the central spur gear drive of the threaded cores, these slides have to be withdrawn radially toward eight sides. Through contact between the end face of the slides against a sturdy conical ring care is taken that no injection molding material can enter between the slides contact area and the insert surfaces, so that at that point no flash occurs.

The mold is illustrated in Figs. 2 to 4. The mold clamping plate ($a$) of the fixed half is bolted together with the conical ring ($b$) for contact with the slides ($c$). A cooling water circulation channel has been arranged between the two, as direct cooling of the inserts ($d$) is hardly possible. A second cooling water circulation channel is housed within the inserts ($d$) in the insert plate ($e$).

Insert plate ($e$) is furnished with radial T-slots, in which the slides ($c$) with the detent-machining for the upper parts of the clamps slide. These slides are moved via the guide strips ($f$), which slide in the T-slots of the slides and which have been bolted together with the conical surface of ring ($b$). In the open position, when not in contact with the molded parts, the slides ($c$) are held in their position by ball detents ($g$).

The threaded cores ($h$) mesh through their gears with the central spur gear ($i$), their free ends being carried in threaded bushings ($k$), which are of the same pitch as the cable clamps.

The central spur gear is keyed onto the spindle ($l$), whose opposite end glides in a nut ($m$) with a six-turn left-hand thread of 80 mm pitch. This nut is bolted together with a nut holder ($n$), which on its opposite side is fastened to the ejector plate ($p$) of the machine with the divided clamping cover ($o$). The clamping cover

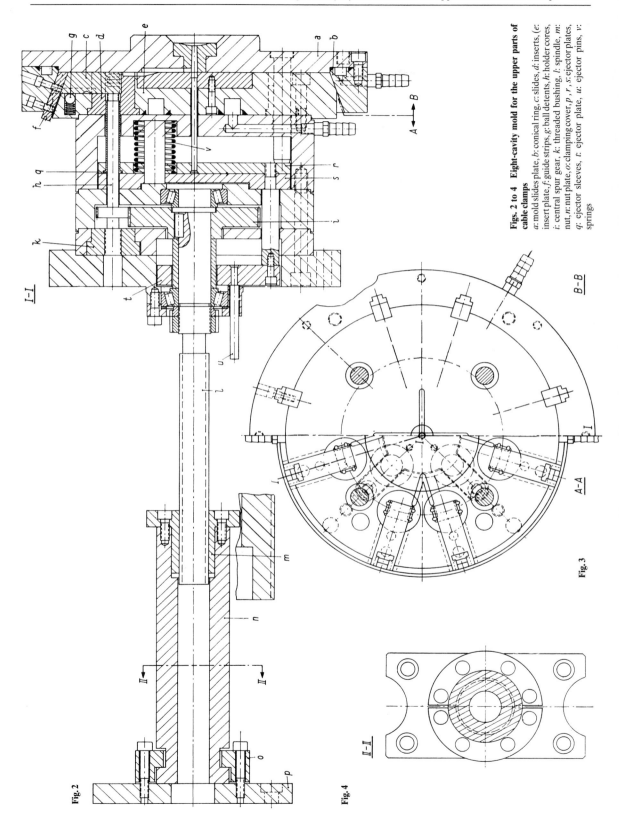

**Figs. 2 to 4    Eight-cavity mold for the upper parts of cable clamps**

*a:* mold slides plate, *b:* conical ring, *c:* slides, *d:* inserts, (*e:* insert plate, *f:* guide strips, *g:* ball detents, *h:* holder cores, *i:* central spur gear, *k:* threaded bushing, *l:* spindle, *m:* nut, *n:* nut plate, *o:* clamping cover, *p*, *r*, *s:* ejector plates, *q:* ejector sleeves, *t:* ejector plate, *u:* ejector pins, *v:* springs

*I–I*

*A* ←→ *B*

*B–B*

**Fig. 3**

*A–A*

*II–II*

**Fig. 2**

**Fig. 4**

enables the nut holder (*n*) to be turned by hand after the mold has been fitted into the machine, so that the cores (*h*) contact the slides (*c*) when the mold is closed to prevent flash from forming at the contact areas.

The eight cores can be matched by remeshing, by one or even several teeth, until all of them are flush with the contacting plane of the slides (*c*) in their end position.

The ejector sleeves (*q*) slide over the threaded cores (*h*) with a running fit. The flanged ends of the sleeves are clamped between the ejector plates (*r*) and (*s*). The ejector plates are connected to the ejector plate (*t*) by four push rods. The ejector pins (*u*), which are riveted in the ejector plate (*t*), push against the nut (*m*) after an opening stroke of 145 mm, during which the thread-ed cores have been unscrewed from the molded parts, so that the latter are ejected from the inserts (*d*) during the remaining opening stroke of 25 mm. To prevent the slides (*c*) from damaging the ejector sleeves (*q*) during mold closing, the ejector plates are pushed back by four strong springs (*v*) at the start of the closing movement. Should there be reservations that for any reason the springs might fail in pushing the ejector sleeves back in time, a microswitch can be fitted into the mold, which only closes when the ejector plates (*s*) and (*r*) are fully back. The control wiring for the "mold closing" directional solenoid valve is then fed through this microswitch. Then the mold can close only when the ejectors are in the fully retracted position. Severing of the injection point is achieved by submarine gating.

# Example 82, Two-cavity injection mold for pistol grips of polyamide

There are molded parts with internal threads in the parting line. These can be produced practically only by cores. Where it is a question of short runs, manually inserted threaded cores which will then be demolded by hand will probably be employed for the sake of economy. As the cores stick tightly inside the molded parts due to shrinkage, they are best unscrewed by a motorized device.

In the subsequently described injection mold (Figs. 1 to 5) air pistol grips are to be produced in large numbers. The mold therefore has to operate fully automatically. What makes the operation more difficult is the requirement for core pulling coaxial to the bilateral internal threads. These cores are for relatively long bores, apart from which there is also a rectangular opening for the valve-actuating lever in the parting plane that also has to be demolded via a slide within that plane. The simplest way for driving threaded cores in the parting-line is the gear rack drive, which is employed in this case as well.

The polyamide pistol grip weighs approximately 45 g. The longest core pull coaxial to the thread is 65 mm. Only two grips can be housed in one mold, as the runners would become too long for these rather thickwalled molded parts (up to 10 mm in wall thickness).

Bolt-on guides for the slides are required, as the guide length would otherwise need unnecessarily large tiebar spacing on the injection molding machine. The length of the internal thread is limited with direct rack drive by the total length of the rack, which cannot exceed the mold height. The active length of the rack is reduced by the thickness of the fixed half mounting plate up to the parting line and by the ejector stroke, if the gear rack is to remain permanently in mesh with the core pinion.

With the smallest number of teeth on the core pinion being 13 and modulus 1, one core rotation requires a rack length of $13 \pi = 40.8$ mm. At a distance of the parting line from the mold mounting plate on the fixed half of 65 mm and a maximum mold height of 360 mm, an active rack length of 280 mm results after deduction of the ejector stroke ($360 - 65 - 15$ mm = 280 mm). During this opening stroke the threaded core has to be unscrewed from the molding before it can be ejected. According to this calculation $280/40.8 = 6.9$ turns can be completed.

A $^3/_8$ " BSP thread has a pitch of 1.34 mm. The length of thread must therefore not be more than $1.34 \times 6.9 = 9.3$

mm. The thread on the right-hand side is of $^3/_4$ " in BSP = 1.81 mm pitch. To be able to eject the part, however, altogether 21 mm will have to be unscrewed, as there is a cylindrical step present from the internal diameter of the thread that can only be demolded by unscrewing the core.

Therefore $21/1.81 = 11.6$ rotations are required. The gear rack length is inadequate for a direct drive; hence the pinion driven by the rack must transmit a greater number of rotations.

Accordingly a gear rack, which drives the threaded pinions of $^3/_4$ " BSP through an idler gear with a small and a large number of teeth suffices as driving force for both screw cores.

If the small pinion of the idler gear is designed with 13 teeth, modulus 1.5, then for one rotation $13 \times 1.5 \times \pi$ = 61 mm are required. The large drive gear therefore has to do $280/61 = 4.6$ turns if the rack is to stay in mesh. The transmission ratio from the large gear to the threaded pinion must then amount to $11.6/4.6 = 2.5$ to 1. A ratio of 60/22 teeth has been chosen, equaling 2.8 : 1.

The mold is shown in Figs. 1 to 5. The inserts (c) and (d) for the mold cavities are fitted into the retainer plates (a) of the moving half and (b) of the fixed half. The insert strip (e) also contains a needle bearing (f) for the large gear and threaded bushing (g). The gear plate (a) furthermore accommodates the gear wheel housing (h) and a bearing insert (i) for the second needle bearing (f).

The gear rack (l) is meshed with the small pinion of the double gear wheel (k), so that on mold opening the core sleeve (m) for the $^3/_4$ " BSP thread is rotated counterclockwise, thereby unscrewing the molded part.

The two racks (n) drive the $^3/_4$ " threaded pinions (o), which are carried in bronze threaded bushings (p) in the same way. Coaxial core pins, which are fixed in the slides (q) and (r) to be pulled by the cam pins (s) and (t) in the usual manner when the mold opens, are led through both threaded sleeves (m) and (p).

The upper openings $17 \times 5$ mm in the pistol grips are created by the slides (u), which are actuated by the cam pins (v). All three slides are secured in their end position by ball detents. At the end of core pulling the molded part is ejected by ejector pins (w), which partially act directly on the molded part and partially on the runner. The ejectors are returned by two pushback pins when the mold closes.

**Figures on page 190/191**

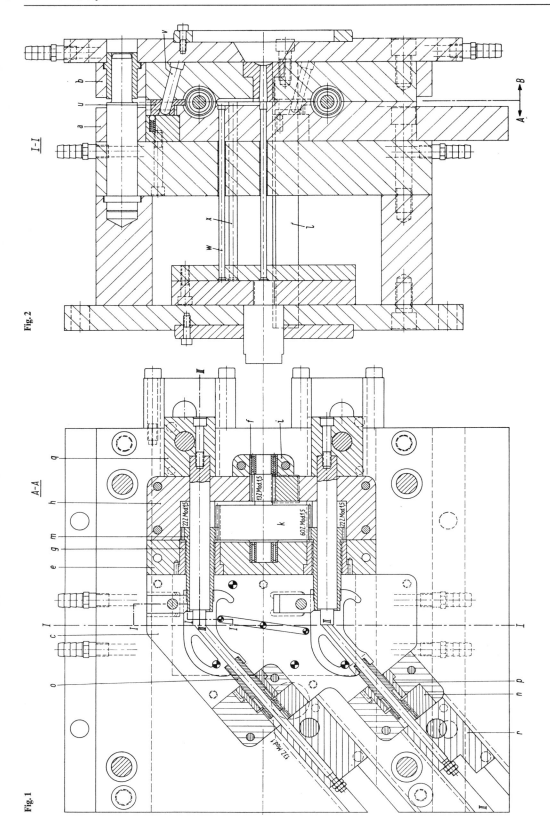

Fig. 2

Fig. 1

**Example 82**

Figs. 1 and 2    Injection mold for two polyamide pistol grips. For explanation of the reference letters refer to Figs. 3 to 5

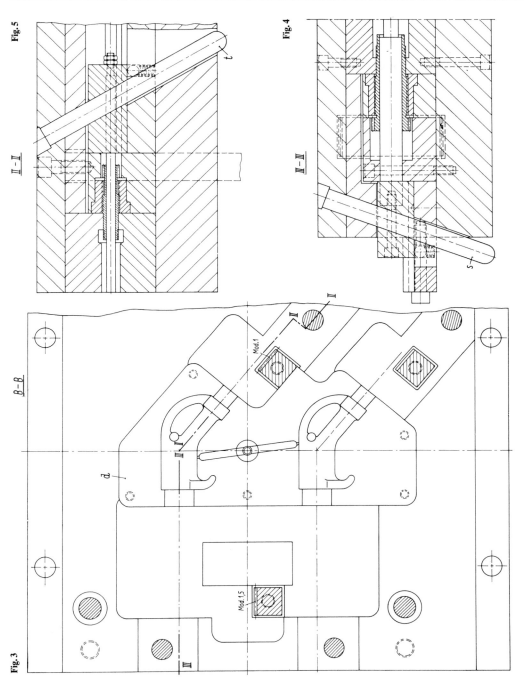

Fig. 5

II – II

Fig. 4

II – II

B – B

Mod. 1

Mod. 1,5

Fig. 3

**Example 82**

**Figs. 3 to 5   Injection mold for two polyamide pistol grips, weight of each grip approximately 45 g**
*a:* moving-side insert retainer plate, *b:* stationary-side insert retainer plate, *c* , *d:* cavity inserts, *e:* insert strip, *f:* needle bearing for 60 tooth gear, *g:* threaded bushings, *h:* spur-gear housing, *i:* insert for needle bearing, *k:* spur gear and pinion, *l:* rack, modulus 1.5, *m:* core sleeve, *n:* rack modulus 1.0, *o:* threaded pinion, $^3/_8$ " in BSP, *p:* threaded bushings, *q* , *r* , *u:* slides, *s* , *t* , *v:* cam pins, *w:* ejector pins, *x:* pushback pins

# Example 83, Injection mold for pipe fittings

It is expedient to operate long-stroke core pulling as required for pipe fittings, for instance, hydraulically. As core pulling strokes of up to 400 mm are required and cores have to be pulled sequentially, mechanical actuation through cams, as often described, has to be dismissed. Hydraulic operation has the added advantage that the movement sequences for mold opening, core pulling, ejector operation, etc., can readily be interlocked through limit switches. The respective hydraulic cylinders are actuated by directional solenoid valves, which can be interlocked electrically through these limit switches until a certain sequence is concluded.

As there is a great variety of soil pipe fittings (different diameters, various branch angles and differing designs such as bends, single branches, double branches and pipe sockets), a mold frame (Figs. 1 and 2) with swiveling hydraulic cylinders has been designed, so that in principle fittings of any type and diameter can be produced in just one basic tool by an exchange of inserts and cores.

A mold frame for fittings basically consists of a base plate (a) on the moving mold half, the T-slots for the mounting bolts for the cavity inserts (b) and the annular grooves for the bolts of the swivel carrier (c) for the hydraulic cylinders. If the finished molded parts are not to be removed manually but are to be ejected automatically, sufficiently large ejector plates (d) and (e) have to be provided additionally. Care must be taken with the latter, however, as ejector actuation must lie in the center line of the machine, but the center of the mother mold is usually offset laterally to enable the fitting to be gated at its center of gravity. An interchangeable locating plate (f) is required to equalize this eccentricity between the machine center and the center of the mold frame. A microswitch (g) is built into the locating plate. The switch is only closed when the ejector return spring (h) has retracted the ejector (i) completely. Only then is the control solenoid for "core in" energized. This prevents the core from being pushed onto protruding ejectors, protecting both from damage.

The second major item of the mold frame is the base plate (k) on the fixed half, with corresponding annular grooves for fastening the cavity inserts (l) on that side. There is also an eccentric locating plate (m) for centering the sprue bushing (n) . Further components of the mold frame are the swivel carrier (c) for the hydraulic cylinders (o) and (p) and the core-guide block (q) , which slides in the carrier. The various cores can easily be mounted in this guide support and coupled firmly with the piston rod of the cylinder at the same time.

Limit switches are mounted at top and bottom of the carrier (c) . The core movements are switched off or the next control sequence is interlocked through them, as the case may be. Actuation of the upper limit switch should, if possible, be adjustable so that the strokes of the same cylinder can be set for longer or shorter distances.

## Interchangeable inserts for the mold frame

Only the following inserts are then still required for the mold frame to produce the single branch Y-piece illustrated: the two cores (r) and (s) with cover (t) and cooling insert, the cavity plates (b) and (l) with guide pins, cooling insert, sprue bushing (n) and mechanical core interlock (u) and (v) , the ejectors (i) with ejector plates (d) and (e) as well as the locating plates (f) and (m) . The cylinder carriers (c) are only loosened off and tightened up again with the new setting corresponding to the core angles. Where applicable, the upper limit switches have to be reset according to the stroke requirements of the cores. The bottom limit switches will not have to be altered, as the lower core position is always at full stroke.

The movement sequence must follow to a predetermined control program. Starting with injection, the following movement sequence applies for the single branch fittings, controlled by the appropriate limit switches:

1. Injection;
2. Holding pressure of plasticized material during cooling;
3. Screw return;
4. Cooling time without holding pressure;
5. Mold opening until the sprue has been released and the core interlock (u) or (v) has been disengaged;
6. Withdraw the long (r) and the short (s) core completely from the fitting;
7. Open mold till it contacts the machine stop and the fitting is ejected by ejector (i);
8. Close mold until the ejector (i) has been retracted completely, whereupon the limit switch (g) will be actuated to initiate core pulling;
9. The long core (r) must be brought into the molding position at step 8;
10. When the main core is in position, move the short core (s) into place for molding;
11. Close mold completely when the mechanical interlocks (u) and (v) engage the cores;
12. = 1 , Injection.

**Figs. 1 and 2   Mold frame with insert for a fitting (branch) 100/100/45 mm incorporating hydraulic core pulling**

a: moving-side base plate, b: cavity inserts, c: swivel carriers, d, e: ejector plates, f: locating plate, g: microswitch, h: ejector-return spring, i: ejector, k: Stationary-side base plate, l: cavity inserts, m: locating plate, n: sprue bushing, o, p: hydraulic cylinder, q: guide block, r: long core, s: short core, t: cover, u, v: core interlock

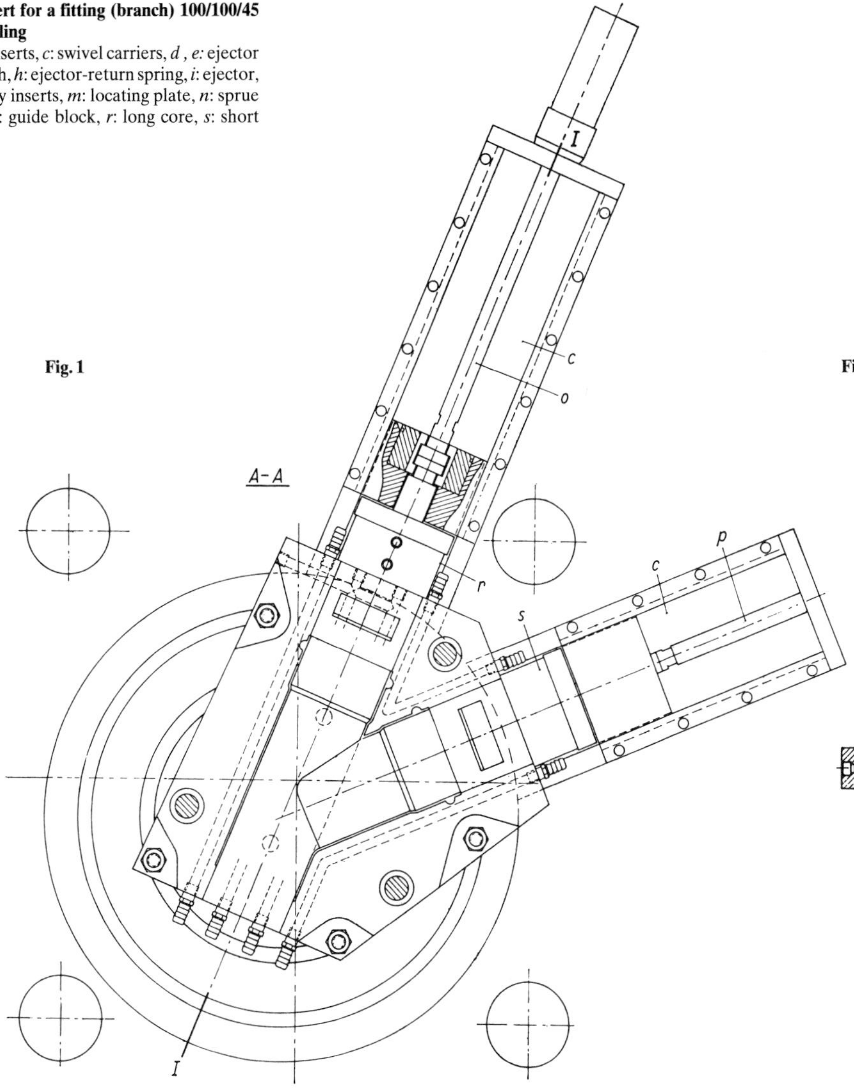

Fig. 2

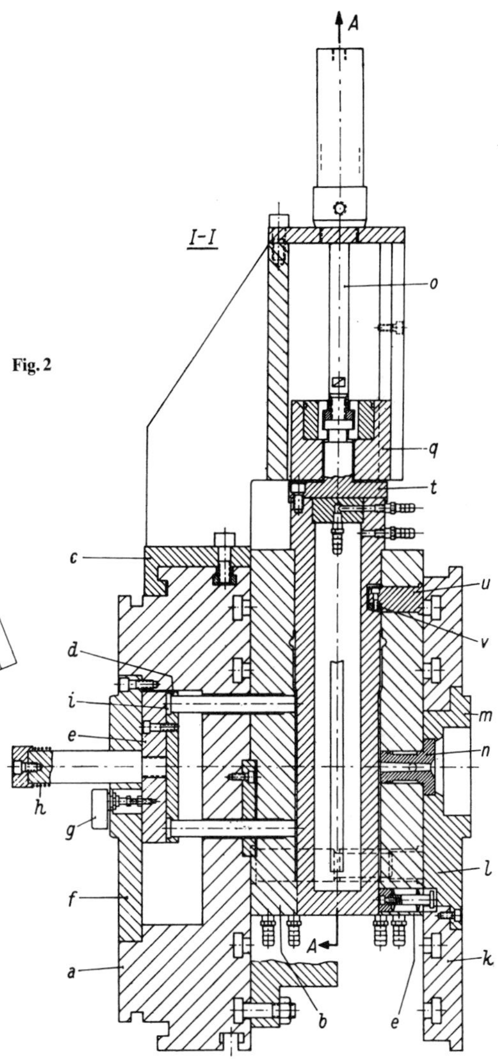

Fig. 1

## Example 84, Injection mold with hydraulic core pull for a cable socket

Hydraulic core pulling equipment is usually required when long cores have to be pulled for which mechanical core pulling devices provide insufficient length of stroke. There are applications, however, which could be adequately served by mechanical core pulling, but where the employment of a hydraulically pulled core results in simplification of the mold design and therefore in economical advantages. This presupposes that the injection molding machine can be equipped with ancillary hydraulic equipment.

The two principles of design will be compared in the example of molds for cable sockets (Fig. 1). Figure 2 shows the mold construction incorporating mechanically operated slides, which has been chosen to give a better comparison with this example. The parting line

**Fig. 1    Cable sockets of varying sizes**

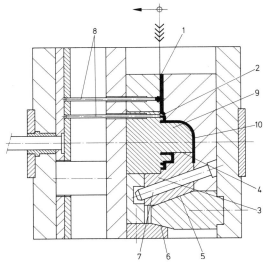

**Fig. 2    Cable socket injection mold with mechanical core pulling (slide)**
1: parting line and point of injection, 2: tunnel gate, 3: slide, 4: opening, 5: wedge surface on the slide, 6: opposite wedge surface, 7: cam pin, 8: ejector pins, 9: core, 10: surface with manufacturer's lettering

of the mold runs vertically to the plane of the drawing along line (1) to the slide (3). As this molding is exposed to view and meant to carry the manufacturer's name on the back of elbow (10), it is injected through a submarine gate (2) on the peripheral rim in the parting line (1). However, to be able to demold the part, half of the lower part of the molding had to be machined into slide (3), although a cylindrical plug would have been quite adequate for the opening itself (4).

When the mold opens, the angled surface (6) releases, so that the pressure on the slide (3) is released via the wedge area (5). The slide moves down, guided by cam pin (7) and sliding on the surface of wedge (5). This leaves the molding resting freely on the core (9), to be pushed off by the ejector pins (8).

Figures 3 to 8 show the employment of hydraulic core pulling. The mold lies in the part line, which runs vertically to the plane of the drawing from top to bottom. Gating is also via tunnel gate (2), and injection takes place in the part line. Instead of the complicated slide arrangement, a cylindrical plug forms the opening in the mold. The plug is moved by a small hydraulic cylinder (4) that is mounted below the mold on an adaptor (5). The two electrical switches (8) and (9) are fitted to plate (6). They are actuated by an S-shaped switching rod (7), signaling the upper and lower position of cylinder (4) to the machine controls. As a guide for a slide is not required on the moving half of the mold, the possibility of surrounding core (10) by a stripper plate (11) is given. This is linked with the ejector plates (13) by tie rods (12). Plate (11) acts simultaneously as pushback plate for the ejectors when the mold closes. The hollow space in the ejection system is well supported by the pillars (14). Core (3) does not have to be mechanically interlocked, as the effective area for the injection pressure is not very large. This force can be absorbed solely by the hydraulic pressure of the cylinder (4), which is cushioned in both end positions.

The operating sequence starts with mold closing. Then the core (3) is moved in by the hydraulic cylinder (4). This is followed by the injection and cooling times. When they have elapsed, core (3) is withdrawn from the mold. The mold moves into the open position, and the hydraulic ejector – coupled with the tool through the ejector bar (15) – actuates the ejector plates (13) and pushes the mold part off the core (10) with the aid of the stripper plate (11) and the ejector pins (16). The mold is cooled in the mold cavity plate (17) as well as in the core (10).

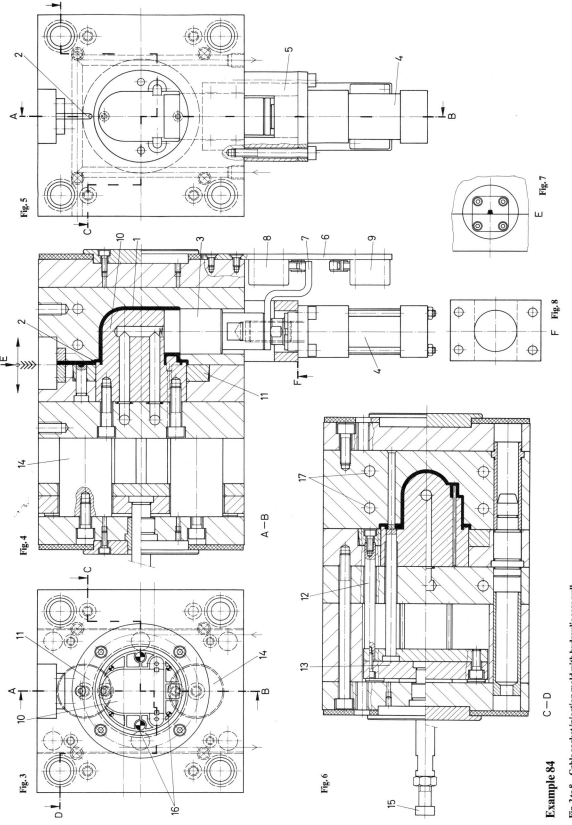

**Example 84 Cable socket injection mold with hydraulic core pull**

**Fig. 3 to 8** Cable socket injection mold with hydraulic core pull

1: molded part, 2: tunnel gate, 3: cylindrical plug for forming the opening in the molded part, 4: hydraulic cylinder, 5: adaptor, 6: plate, 7: switching rod, 8, 9: electrical switches, 10: core, 11: stripper plate, 12: tie rods, 13: ejector plates, 14: support pillars, 15: ejector bar, 16: ejector pins, 17: mold cavity plate

Fig. 5

Fig. 4

Fig. 3

Fig. 6

Fig. 7

Fig. 8

A – B

C – D

E

F

## Example 85, Two-cavity injection mold for hose connectors

A proven mold design for molded parts with external undercuts and a through hole, as represented by hose connectors, for instance, is subsequently described. The construction of this split-cavity mold offers considerable advantages with longer slides in particular, as the slides do not require an all-enclosing jacket as did split-cavity molds described earlier.

The advantage lies especially in the fact that the clamping wedges for the slides can have ground contact surfaces and that the slides themselves can be equipped with intensive cooling. They are accessible top and bottom in the direction of the clamping areas, so that cooling channels can be continuous along the full length of the slides.

A further feature arising from this design is the possibility of designing adjustable clamping force in the direction of the parting line between the slides for this mold. A considerable advantage is gained in being able to open the slides so wide that sufficient space is created to allow the molded parts to drop out between them. For that reason considerably longer molded parts can be accommodated in such a tool than is possible in split-cavity molds with closed clamping jackets.

Figure 1 shows the two-cavity mold in section along the line $I - I$ of Fig. 2. In Fig. 2 a section is shown in direction $(A)$, Fig. 3 shows one in direction $(B)$ and Fig. 4 illustrates a cross section in direction $II - II$. Figure 5 reproduces the ejector assembly in the advanced position.

The external shape of the hose connectors has been machined into slides $(a)$. Inserts $(b)$ in these slides contain the threaded part of the hose connectors for the sake of easier machining. The slides $(a)$ are held together by the wedges $(c)$, which are bolted together with the ejector side of the mold. Wedge strips $(d)$ have been provided to press these adjustable wedges against the slides. These wedge strips have been produced with a 1 ° taper to transfer the clamping pressure to the contact area of plates $(e)$. On the opposite end, the wedges $(c)$ are in contact with the hardened and ground wedge strips $(f)$, also adjustable, and support-ed by the shoulder of the mold clamping plate $(g)$ on the fixed half. Slides $(a)$ are guided on the open facing sides by plates $(h)$, which are bolted together with the wedges $(c)$. These plates $(h)$ grip the slides $(a)$ through a tongue or inserted wedge and guide these slides when advancing in the direction of the clamping taper.

Therefore, the mold opens first in parting plane $(A - B)$ while the slides are closed and the sprue is withdrawn from the sprue bushing $(i)$. After a certain opening distance in this plane the slides $(a)$ have to be propelled forward sufficiently far to free the existing undercuts on the external shape. The slides then have to be stopped and the molded parts ejected off the cores. This means that two successive ejection strokes are required upon contacting the machine ejector. This *two-stage ejection process* is achieved by the following device:

The ejector rod $(k)$ of the mold has been designed as a trip sleeve. Figure 1 shows the trip sleeve $(k)$ in position, rigidly connected to sleeve $(l)$ and thus through plate $(m)$ and push rod $(n)$ to stripper plate $(o)$. By moving the stripper plate $(o)$ forward the slides $(a)$, guided by plates $(h)$, are advanced and opened first. After an approximately 50 mm stroke the slides are opened sufficiently far to release the undercuts. This movement also trips the lock between trip sleeve $(k)$ and sleeve $(l)$ positively by the locking mandrel $(p)$, which is screwed into the moving-half mold plate $(q)$. The eight spring ends of the trip sleeve $(k)$ collapse inward and the trip sleeve $(k)$ can be pushed further forward, whereas plate $(m)$ remains stationary. In this position the hose connectors remain only loosely on the slightly tapered cores $(r)$, from which they have already been stripped by about 50 mm. They can then be stripped off the cores completely by an ejector $(s)$ acting on the central sprue, as they are still firmly connect-ed to each other by a relatively thick runner and gate. The central ejector $(s)$ is bolted to the trip sleeve $(k)$, so that by advancing the trip sleeve the hose connectors will be thrown off the cores. Figure 5 shows the final position of the trip sleeve.

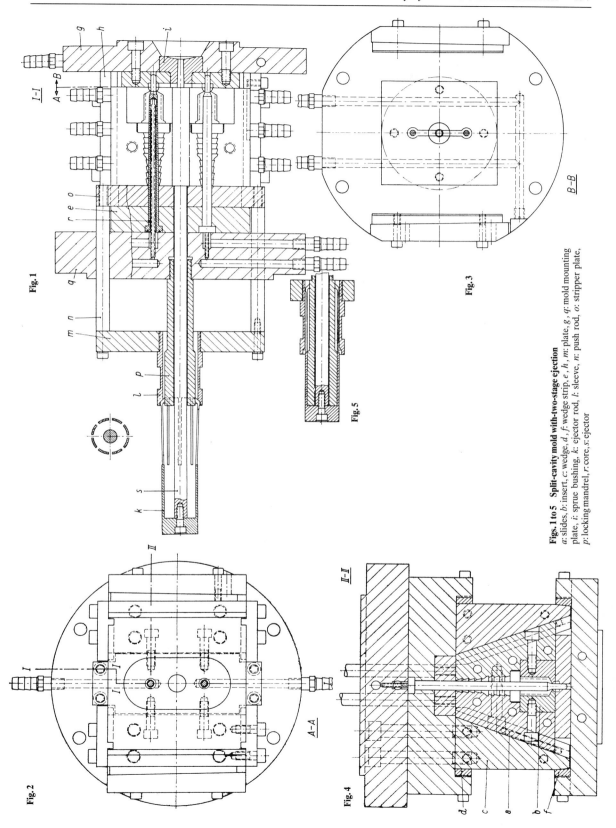

**Figs. 1 to 5   Split-cavity mold with two-stage ejection**
*a*: slides, *b*: insert, *c*: wedge, *d*, *f*: wedge strip, *e*, *h*, *m*: plate, *g*, *q*: mold mounting plate, *i*: sprue bushing, *k*: ejector rod, *l*: sleeve, *n*: push rod, *o*: stripper plate, *p*: locking mandrel, *r*: core, *s*: ejector

Fig. 1

Fig. 2

Fig. 3

Fig. 4

Fig. 5

## Example 86, Eight-cavity injection mold for fountain pen caps

Caps for fountain pens usually possess an internal thread at one end and an external one at the other for fastening the clip. To prevent harmful weld lines they ought to be gated at the closed end with the external thread. This requirement can only be fulfilled in the multi-cavity version by a self-degating mold. The difficulty lies in the pinpoint gate having to be in the slides containing the external threads for the cap.

If the threaded cores for the internal thread are to be driven by a central spur gear, then it is not possible to arrange the caps in line, which would be expedient for the release of the divided external threads. In an eight-cavity mold eight pairs of slides are required, which house the external thread and the drop for the molded part. The male thread on the caps has been cut into the pair of slides $(a)$, which have been fitted at a taper of approximately $10°$ into moving plate $(c)$, which moves in guide strips $(b)$. Cam pins $(d)$ are set into plate $(c)$ on the facing sides of the slides, with the larger part of their circumference pointing in the direction of the wedge taper. They are secured by set screws $(e)$ with plate $(c)$. Springs $(f)$ push the slides against the collar of the guide pins in the direction of opening when the mold opens, releasing the thread in that open position.

The inserts $(g)$ for the external contours of the caps have been fitted to the insert plate $(h)$ and cover plate $(i)$. Both plates are guided on guide strips $(b)$. These guide strips are provided with two stops. After an opening stroke of 72 mm between plates $(c)$ and $(i)$ the plate $(c)$ is retained by the first stop and the latch between this plate and the mold flange $(l)$ on the moving half is released simultaneously. This is managed by the release pins $(m)$ running up on the cams of the guide strips $(b)$. With the initial opening of the runner parting line the narrowest part of the gate is torn off the caps. The drop is withdrawn from its bore by this action, aided by an undercut at the end of the runners, while the tapered slides are still closed. At the same time the central sprue, held by the sprue puller $(n)$, is withdrawn from the sprue bushing $(o)$. Sprue puller $(n)$ and ejector sleeve $(p)$ run through an idle stroke initially, which is approximately equal to the sprue length for the mold, under pressure of spring $(q)$ until the movement is terminated by a collar. During the continuing opening movement the retaining pin of the sprue puller $(n)$ is forcibly withdrawn from the center sprue. During this operation the bushing $(p)$ is initially pulled back against the tension of spring $(q)$ in the opening direction. As soon as the retaining pin has been withdrawn from the sprue, spring $(q)$ can relax, thereby forcibly ejecting the runner system. At the end

of a total opening stroke of 84 mm the cover plate $(i)$ of the insert plate $(h)$ contacts the second stop on guide strips $(b)$ and is retained by them. During further mold opening the caps, which are retained firmly by cores $(r)$, are withdrawn form the inserts $(g)$. The mold now opens in the second parting line between stripper plate $(s)$ and insert plate $(h)$ until the stripper plate $(s)$ is pushed forward, stripping the molded parts off the cores $(r)$.

Before the mold parts can be stripped off, however, the internal threads have to be released. This is managed by rotating the threaded sleeves $(t)$ counter-clockwise through the central spur gear $(u)$, so that the mold parts have been released by the start of the ejector stroke. The central spur gear is driven by a threaded spindle, running in a fixed nut mounted in the machine. In the closed mold position the threaded sleeves must contact a collar on cores $(r)$ without leaving a gap. As the drive to all threaded sleeves is positive, it is hardly possible to match all cores so accurately in length that this requirement can be satisfied. To correct for this inaccuracy in length, powerful sets of disc springs $(v)$ therefore support the cores $(r)$. Slight differences in the lengths of the cores $(r)$ are corrected by these springs, so that gap-free contact of the threaded sleeves with the collar on the cores is ensured.

Prerequisite for the high output of an injection mold is efficient removal of the heat transmitted to the mold by the material melt. The most efficient cooling always results if the cooling water flows around the inserts. To fulfill these requirements, the inserts $(g)$ are sealed by rubber or plastic O-rings and provided with a cooling water groove. The cooling water is fed through channels in insert plate $(h)$ from insert to insert, ensuring extremely efficient cooling.

*Cooling of the cores* is difficult. Just that, however, is particularly important for the efficiency of the mold, as the heat from the long cores can be conducted away only with difficulty. Although the cores are fixed, water cooling can hardly be accommodated.

In such cases air cooling has proved extremely effective. Compressed air of 5 to 6 bar is available in most factories. The stripping inserts $(w)$ are provided with a machined groove, which is supplied with air instead of water in a manner similar to insert plate $(h)$. Three channels of approximately 1 mm diameter lead to the internal diameter of these inserts, which are closed off by the threaded sleeves $(t)$ when the mold is shut. As soon as the stripper plate $(s)$ is pushed forward, compressed air is blown at high speed through these channels onto the cores $(r)$, giving intensive cooling.

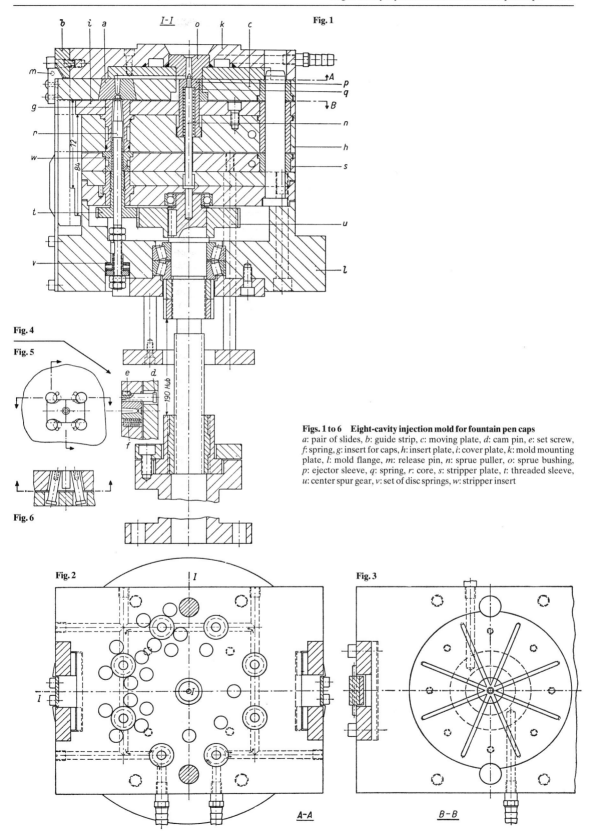

**Figs. 1 to 6   Eight-cavity injection mold for fountain pen caps**
a: pair of slides, b: guide strip, c: moving plate, d: cam pin, e: set screw, f: spring, g: insert for caps, h: insert plate, i: cover plate, k: mold mounting plate, l: mold flange, m: release pin, n: sprue puller, o: sprue bushing, p: ejector sleeve, q: spring, r: core, s: stripper plate, t: threaded sleeve, u: center spur gear, v: set of disc springs, w: stripper insert

Fig. 1

Fig. 4

Fig. 5

Fig. 6

Fig. 2

Fig. 3

A-A

B-B

# Example 87, Two-cavity mold for water tap handles

Decorative bathroom fittings are frequently made with transparent handles in which there is a second layer made from a nontransparent material. The mold illustrated in Figs. 1 to 5 is designed for the production of this type of part. Both of the differently colored materials are injected one after the other at two stations on the mold, thus enabling the part to be produced in one operation. It is also necessary, however, to use an injection molding machine that has two injection units arranged at right angles to each other.

The main view (Fig. 2) shows the mold in its closed position. At the left mold station, the molding of the colored inner component of the handle is carried out by the injection unit on axis (a). At the same time, the outer transparent part of the handle is molded over this part using the unit on axis (b) through the sprue bushing (22). The wall thickness of the outer layer of the molding needs to be rapidly cooled and hence the

mold cavity insert (15) is made with a narrowly machined helical cooling channel. On solidification of the molded part the mold is opened and the part is ejected. This occurs in position II, as shown in the right-hand side of the drawing (Fig. 4), by advancing the ejector bar (12) with the help of the pneumatic cylinder (20). Only after this first step can plate (4) be freed, and held in the appropriate position by the stop screw (30). The core retainer plates (5) and (6) with the cores (11), which carry the molded colored inner parts of the handle, move out of the plate (4) only so far as necessary to allow them to be turned through 180° under plate (4), so that on reclosing the mold the empty cores will reengage with the initial molding station and the cores containing the inner part will engage the final molding station. The turning movement is made by a four-cornered spindle (16), whose gear wheel (17) engages a pinion (18) moved by the pneumatic cylinder (19).

**Figs. 1 to 5   Injection mold for a transparent water tap handle containing a colored inner layer**

1, 2: stationary-side plates, 3: mold cavity for interior molding, 4: mold cavity mounting plate, 5, 6: rotary plates, 7: guiding ring, 8: base plate, 9: spacer ring, 10: movable-side clamping plate, 11: collars, 12: ejector pins, 13: spring, 14: mold cavity retainer ring, 15: mold cavity insert, 16: spindle with four-sided head, 17: gear wheel, 18: pinion, 19: pneumatic cylinder for rotary plates 5, 6, 20: pneumatic cylinder for ejector of finished molded parts, 21: locating ring, 22: sprue bushing, 23: spring, 24: rod, 25: hook, 26: cross pin, 27: bearing housing, 28: spring, 29: cooling water connection, 30, 31: stop screws, 32: guide pin, 33: cross bolts, 34: fitting rings, 35: ring, 36: bushing, 37: nuts for 12., 38: seal ring, 39: O-rings, 40: telescoping sleeve for 30:

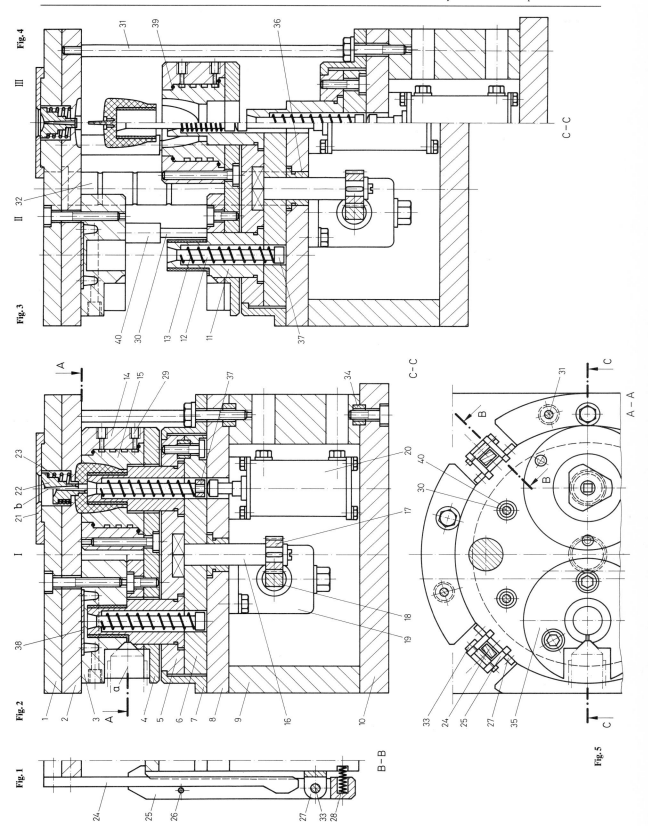

Fig.4

Fig.3

Fig.2

Fig.1

Fig.5

# Example 88, Two-cavity injection mold for the automatic molding of conveyor plates onto a wire cable

Such granular materials as plastics pellets or grain can be transported by pipe conveyor systems. A conveying cable fitted with conveyor plates at fixed intervals runs through the pipe. These plates match the inside diameter of the pipe (Fig. 1).

The mold shown in Fig. 2 to 4 was developed for the production of these conveying cables. Plates are molded simultaneously onto two parallel cables to increase productivity. There is no problem guiding the cables through the mold if the mold parting line is in the horizontal plane and the injection unit is mounted vertically on the machine.

**Fig. 1   Conveying cable with plastic conveyor plates for mechanical pipe conveyor system**

To start production the two cables are pulled through the bores in part (8) and placed in the grooves in part (9). Automatic production can only commence once two plates each have been molded onto both cables. Up to that time the cables have to be advanced by hand. Thereafter the paddles (11) situated on the roll (10), which are rotated with each machine opening stroke, engage the molded plates and advance them by

one division. To achieve this the cable (19) fixed to the bolt (30) lifts the double lever (13) against the resistance of spring (17) on bolt (16). The pawl (14) rotates the wheel (27) by engaging in its ratchet teeth, advancing the paddles (11) fitted to shaft (12) by 90 °. The turning movement must only be allowed to start when the newly molded plates have been released from the lower cavity half (7) by lifting the mold components (8) and (9), followed with continued mold opening with release from the upper cavity half (6). Only then is the cable (19) put under tension. Therefore a total mold opening distance of at least 110 mm is required for part release and cable advancement. The length of cable (19) must therefore be matched to the opening movement of the injection molding machine.

Fully automatic operation of the mold necessitates interlocking with the injection molding machine controls. The functions of the mold and the presence of melt are supervised by switches $K_1$ to $K_4$. The siting of these switches is shown schematically in Figs. 2 and 3. Figure 5 shows the wiring diagram into which these switches have been integrated. With melt present, the switch $K_3$ is actuated during each cycle by the mold plates, closing relay $J_1$. Subsequently $K_4$ is also actuated (by the mold plates) as is $K_1$ (via the moving mold plate I ), causing a relay in the injection molding machine control to indicate the end of the cycle so that a new sequence can be started. Should switch $K_2$ not be actuated due to a lack of melt, a subsequent machine cycle cannot take place. During mold closing the parts (8) and (9) are pushed back into the frame (3) again. Switch $K_2$ is thereby opened, which in turn opens relay $J_1$ so that the switching sequence for the next cycle is set up. Figure 6 shows the time sequence of these functions.

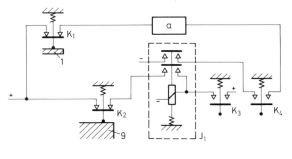

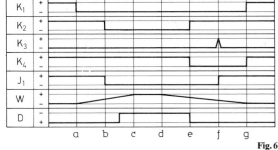

**Fig. 5   Wiring diagram**
($K_1$ to $K_4$) switches, ($J_1$) relay
(a) injection molding machine controls, (1, 9) mold components (refer to Figs. 2 to 4)

**Fig. 6**

**Fig. 6   Sequence diagram of the controls**
a: mold fully opened, start of mold closing movement, b: mold halves are touching, so that $K_2$ and $J_1$ open, c: mold closed, d: start of mold opening, e: mold halves separate, cable advance starts, $K_4$: opens, $K_2$: closes, f: new plate temporarily closes $K_3$: g: advanced plate closes $K_4$: mold is open, h: wire cable, ($J_1$) , relay, $K_1$ to $K_4$: switches, W: mold
+ closed or tensioned, − open or relaxed

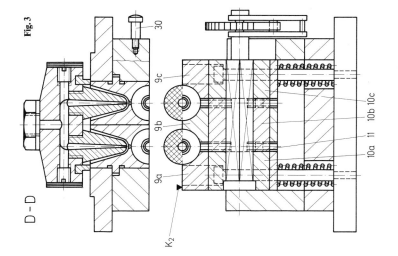

**Fig. 3**

D-D

**Fig. 2**

C-C

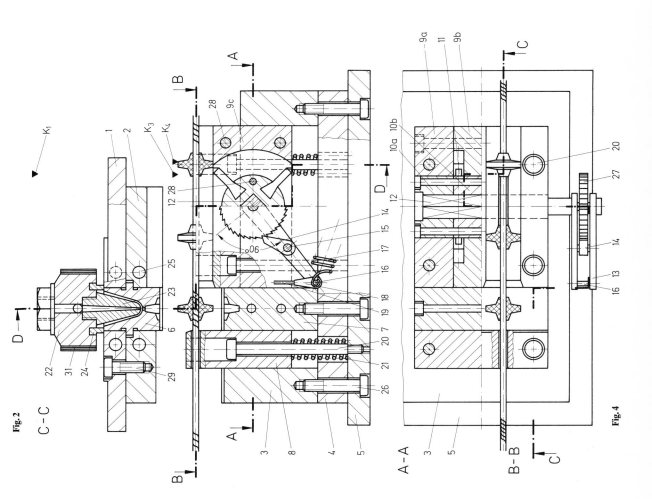

**Fig. 4**

A-A

B-B

**Figs. 2 to 4   Injection mold for the automatic molding of conveyor plates onto conveying cables for mechanical pipe conveyors**

1: upper mold clamping plate, 2: upper mold cavity retainer plate, 3: lower mold frame, 4: mold base plate, 5: lower mold clamping plate, 6: upper mold cavity half, 7: lower mold cavity half, 8: moving cable feed, 9: moving cable discharge, 10: rotation cylinder, 11: paddles, 12: square shaft, 13: double lever, 14: pawl, 15: pawl shaft, 16: cross pin, 17: spring, 18: eye on the draw cable, 19: draw cable, 20: screw, 21: spring, 22: injection head, 23: beryllium copper nozzle, 24: pressure ring, 25: cooling water channels, 26: connecting bolt, 27: ratchet wheel with buttress teeth, 28, 29: connecting bolts, 30: bolts, 31: heating element ($K_1$ to $K_4$) electrical switches

# Example 89, 20-cavity hot-runner mold for producing curtain-ring rollers of polyacetal copolymer

Curtain-ring rollers (Fig. 1) are "penny articles". Nevertheless, their production requires considerable expenditure as far as the injection mold is concerned, which has to incorporate slides for forming the shafts carrying the small rollers and by requiring assembly of these rollers. These conditions are met with the present mold (Fig. 2) through the use of a hot-runner system that results in low manufacturing expenses and puts into practice a concept which already assembles the individual parts into finished ring rollers inside the mold itself (Fig. 3).

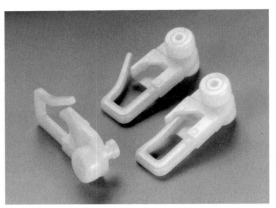

**Fig. 1    Curtain-ring rollers of polyacetal copolymer**
left: curtain roller, shown with rear roller removed, centre: curtain-ring roller with open hook, right: curtain-ring roller with closed hook

## Mold design

When calculating the mold, an optimum number $n = 60$ of cavities became established. Related to the number of complete curtain-ring rollers produced in the mold, this corresponds to a 20 cavity tool.
Gating between hot runner and molded parts is via small sub-runners with two submarine gates each of 0.8 mm diameter (Fig. 4). When dimensioning and designing the hot-runner system, reference was made to [1] (also refer to Fig. 36 there). The main dimensions

arrived at for the torpedo were $d_T = 8$ mm for the torpedo diameter and $l_T = 52$ mm for the torpedo length. Six cavities each are fed by one torpedo (material specification 2.0060). The installed heating capacity amounts to 250 W/kg of hot-runner block, the latter being provided with two heating circuits each. In order to obtain intensive cooling of the cavities, copper cooling pins are employed. The mold is built up of standard components to material specification. 1.1730 , whereas 1.2162 with a surface hardness of HRC = 60 ± 1 has been chosen for the cavities and wearing parts.

## Assembly of the curtain-ring rollers inside the mold

The mold is technically interesting because of the fully automatic assembly of the curtain-ring rollers inside the tool, this being the subject of a patent [2].
In this case the rollers and the roller-carrier are injection molded spearately within the same tool. The shafts of the roller carrier have been provided with cylindrical clearances in the area of the undercut, so that there is as much elastic deformation as possible when the rollers are being fitted onto the shafts. The connection between roller and roller carrier is of the non-releasing cylindrical snap-fit type with a retaining angle of $\alpha_2 = 90$ ° [3].
Once the cooling period has timed out, the roller carrier (c) (Fig. 3) is released by the mold-opening movement and in a subsequent step the rollers (a) and (b) are pushed home by the spring force acting on the ejector sleeves (d) and (e) (Fig. 3).
After assembly the finished article and the sheared-off runner are ejected, once the ejector sleeves and pins have been returned to their starting positions. Molded parts and runners are separated on the conveyor belt. The cycle time is 12 s.

## Literature

1 Heißkanalsystem indirekt beheizter Wärmeleittorpedo, in: Berechnen, Gestalten, Anwenden (C.2.1), Schriftenreihe der Hoechst AG, 1982
2 DE-PS 2 528 903 (1979) F. & G. Hachtel
3 Berechnen von Schnappverbindungen mit Kunststoffteilen. In: Berechnen, Gestalten, Anwenden (B.3.1), Schriftenreihe der Hoechst AG, 1982

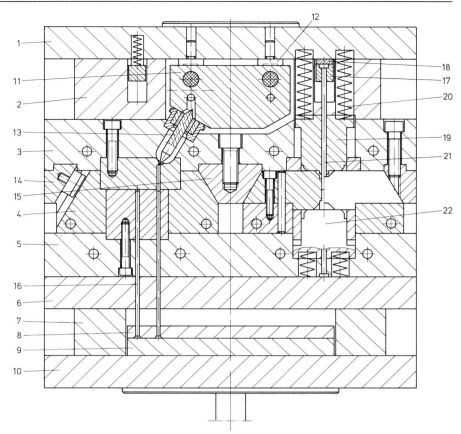

**Fig. 2  Section through the 20-cavity injection mold with hot-runner manifold and indirectly heated (thermally conductive) torpedo as well as an assembling facility for fitting the curtian-ring rollers together inside the mold**

1: mounting plate, 2: strip, 3: mold bolster, 4: slide, 5: mold plate, 6: ejector plate, 7: strip, 8: ejector retainer plate, 9: ejector plate, 10: clamping plate, 11: hot-runner manifold, 12: support pad, 13: indirectly heated (thermally conductive) torpedo, 14, 15: heel block, 16: ejector pin, 17: insert, 18: strip, 19: stepped pressure piece, 20: compression spring, 21: ejector, 22: pressure slides

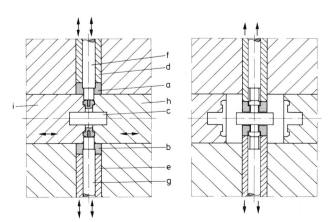

**Fig. 3  Assembling procedure for the curtain-ring rollers inside the mold**
left: before assembly, right: after completed assembly
*a, b:* roller, *c:* roller carriers, *d, e:* ejector sleeves, *f, g:* ejector pins, *h, i:* slides

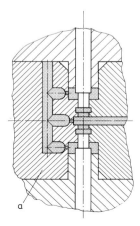

**Fig. 4  Gating to the molded parts in the mold**
*a:* turned through 90 ° around the drawing plane

## Example 90, Injection mold with attached hydraulic core pull for automatic measuring tube production

A measuring tube for a liquid-distributing manifold was to be produced fully automatically. The molded part had to be comparatively thick walled, as operating pressures of up to 10 bar and operating temperatures of up to almost 100 °C occur. It proved expedient to inject from one face end to prevent unilateral stresses that would distort the tube to an unwelcome degree. In this case an injection molding machine capable of parting line injection is advisable. The smallest possible machine suitable can be employed without having to arrange the molded part eccentrically in the tool (Fig. 1), which would only result in long flow paths and unfavorable one-sided machine loading. Hydraulic core pulling is employed, as mechanical cores are unsuitable for such lengths of stroke. Insert cores would be unacceptable, because the requirement is for automatic production of the molded part.

The mold design (Figs. 2 to 7) starts with central posi-

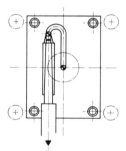

Fig. 1    Required positioning of the molded part in the parting plane of the mold with the greatest possible utilization of the machine size and central injection

tioning of the measuring tube in the parting line. To obtain the clean scale graduation surface necessary for reading off the flow rate, these divisions have been machined into the fixed mold half. The core of the measuring tube is now located precisely in the center of the mold cavity inserts. It is centered at the end of the tube as well as at the entrance.

The sprue approaches the measuring tube via the end of the core in three adequately dimensioned sections. The melt flows around the core uniformly with this type of gating and is furthermore centered accurately. Below the mold on the moving half, core (3) is housed in a yoke (5), which is fixed in its direction precisely by guide rods (6). A cross plate (7), into which the hydraulic cylinder (8) has been screwed, is fitted to the end of the guide rods. The cylinder (8) has been additionally supported (9), to avoid any excessive vibra-

tions from this long substructure during the travel movements of the mold. The piston rod (10) of the cylinder is coupled to the yoke (5). Heating/cooling channels (11) have been provided on the fixed as well as on the moving mold halves. Of great importance also is the possibility of core coling. The core has been drilled for this purpose and divided into two chambers with a cascade by a separating baffle (12).

Hydraulic cylinders as well as connecting hoses to the hydraulic circuit of the machine are not part and parcel of the core pulling equipment, as is often assumed. The size of the cylinders has to be matched to the pressures occurring in the mold. This then also becomes the decisive factor in establishing whether the core to be pulled can be held just by the cylinder pressure or if it has to be mechanically interlocked as well. In the example presented interlocking is not necessary. It has been proved advantageous for the cylinders to be equipped with cushioned end positions in both movement directions. A considerably gentler operation can be obtained in this way.

It is essential for the operating sequence of the controls to monitor the position of core (3) in its most forward and rearmost position electrically through limit switches (13, 14) and pass this information on to the machine control.

To describe the operating sequence, it is assumed that the mold is fully open and void of molded parts, i. e., in the starting position:

Core (3) is moved into the mold by hydraulic cylinder (8). The mold closes and the injection process starts. As soon as the injection, holding pressure and cooling times have elapsed the mold is opened for a few millimeters only. Due to the core (3) being mounted on the moving mold half, the measuring tube (1) with its scale (2) is released positively from the fixed mold half. Now core (3) is retracted completely from the measuring tube (1). The mold moves to the opened position and the hydraulic ejector of the machine moves forward. This is coupled with the ejector bar (15), which pushes the ejector plates with their built-in ejector pins (16) for the measuring tube and the sprue forward, ejecting the completed molded part from the mold. The core is moved in again and another cycle starts.

To make the mold more solid the hollow space required for the ejector plates contains support pillars (17). An essential feature of this mold is the quartz-crystal pressure transducer (18) in the vicinity of the gate for assessing the mold cavity pressure, which is then controlled in accordance with the data received to prevent sink marks and to reduce internal stresses in the molded part.

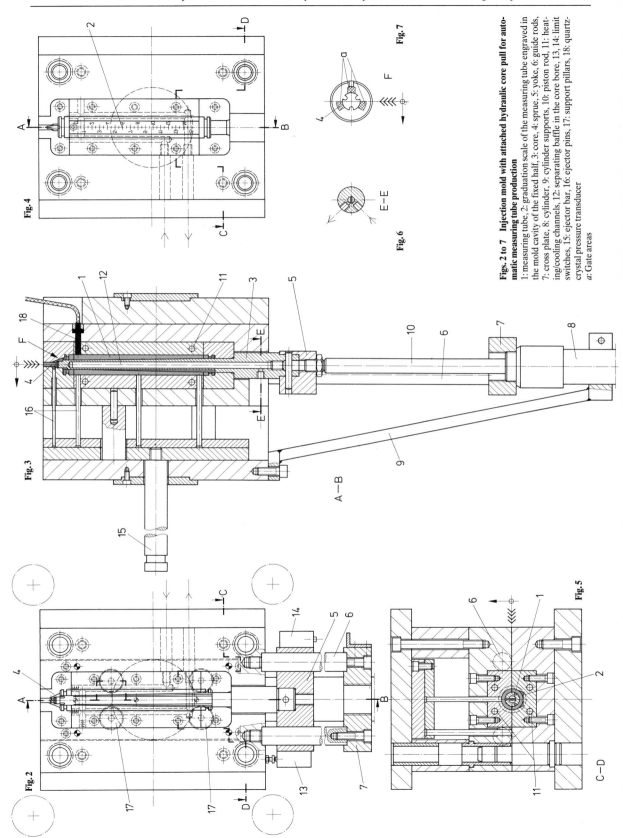

**Figs. 2 to 7   Injection mold with attached hydraulic core pull for automatic measuring tube production**

1: measuring tube, 2: graduation scale of the measuring tube engraved in the mold cavity of the fixed half, 3: core, 4: sprue, 5: yoke, 6: guide rods, 7: cross plate, 8: cylinder, 9: cylinder supports, 10: piston rod, 11: heating/cooling channels, 12: separating baffle in the core bore, 13, 14: limit switches, 15: ejector bar, 16: ejector pins, 17: support pillars, 18: quartz-crystal pressure transducer

*a*: Gate areas

Fig. 2

Fig. 3

Fig. 4

Fig. 5

Fig. 6

Fig. 7

A–B

C–D

E–E

## Example 91, Three-cavity injection mold for liquid-measuring cylinders

An injection mold had to be designed for manufacturing a measuring cylinder for liquids. Owing to the low wall thickness of 1.2 mm the wall-thickness tolerances were not to exceed 0.1 mm. This stipulation is very difficult to comply with for slim components.

For reasons of stability the core is fixed at both ends, at the top in the mold clamping plates (1) and (2) and at the bottom by a collar (8), which fits into a recess of the lower mold half (5) with a sliding fit (H 7/h 6).

At the start of injection the spring washers (9) push the collar (8) against the mold body (3). Once the plastic material has filled the cylinder jacket, it flows into the annular gap between the collar (8) and the mold body (3), pushing the collar away from the body. This end of the core is now no longer held (7) by the collar (8), and the plastic material is allowed to fill out the bottom of the measuring cylinder. During mold opening the shoulder bolts (16) and (17) pull the three-plate mold apart. The spring (14) separates the sprue from the molded part. Compressed air is admitted, which opens the mushroom valve (21), blowing the molded part off the core (7).

**Fig. 1   Injection mold for liquid-measuring cylinder**
1, 2: upper mold clamping plate, 3: mold body, 4: jacket, 5: lower mold half, 6: lower mold clamping plate, 7: core, 8: collars, 9: spring washers, 10: set screws, 11: sprue bushing, 12: spring, 13: sprue ejector collar, 14: spring, 15, 16, 17: shoulder bolts, 18: guide pins, 19: cooling water connection, 20: compressed air connection, 21: valve

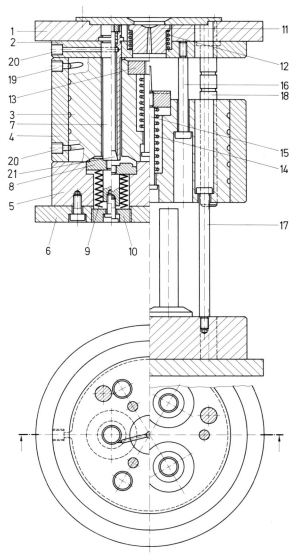

## Example 92, 16-cavity injection mold for production of tube caps

The gate on molded parts, i. e., the spot where the melt from the runner enters the mold cavity, should be as unobtrusive as possible, so that the looks of the molded parts are not spoiled. By injecting the material through a small hole on the circumference of the article, clean, automatic degating can be obtained on mold opening. However, this pinpoint gate is visible on the finished molded parts and can be a nuisance. One therefore endeavors to hide the gate as much as possible. One possibility is offered by pinpoint gating inside a threaded cap. This method of injecting also has the great advantage that the melt enters the cavity centrally without leaving any weld lines on the molded part, which is of importance particularly with larger threaded caps and lids. The 16-cavity mold illustrated in Figs. 1 to 3 distinguishes itself by the particularly suitable design of the degating feature, which no longer requires a sandwich plate for stripping the runner from the nozzle side of the mold. A much more reliable method for ejecting the runner can be employed with this design.

To achieve as short a drop as possible, the parting line for the star-shaped runner is slightly conical. This results in a saving of runner weight and a considerable shortening of the main sprue (sprue bushing). Space is also gained for a reliably operating runner-ejector system.

The threaded inserts (a) are fixed in this mold. The runners to the gates of the individual molded parts are positioned centrally in the inserts. The 16 inserts are retained between the cover plate (b) and the insert plate (c), which are bolted together. A cooling water channel that runs around the inserts ensures intensive cooling of the threaded cores.

Plates (b) and (c) are bolted together and slide on the guide strips (d) for a distance of 90 mm during opening. These guide strips are connected with mold clamping plate (e) on the nozzle half of the mold. During this travel of 90 mm the moving-half mold clamping plate (f) is rigidly locked with plates (b) and (c) through the leaf springs (g) and the latches (h), so that the mold opens first in the parting line of the runner. Plates (b) and (c) are retained by the stops on the guide strips (d) after 90 mm of travel. Simultaneously, the latches (h) are released through the unlatching pins (i) running up onto release bars on guide strips (d), thereby allowing the tool to open now in the main parting plane between plates (k) and (b).

The gates are severed from the molded parts during the initial opening of the mold in the runner parting line as follows: After injection the drops are retained by severe undercuts in the sucker pins (l) in the fixed mold half, so that they are pulled out of the threaded inserts (a), severing from the molded parts at their weakest point. Spring (o) pressing against the ejector sleeve (m) causes the ejector sleeve (m) and the sucker pin (n) to follow the initial opening stroke up to certain distance, limited by a stop, which approximately corresponds to the length of the drops.

Thus the drops to the individual molded parts are

Fig. 1

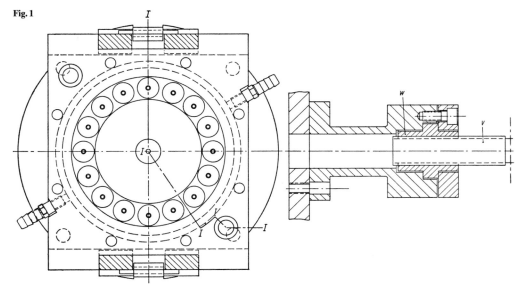

**Figs. 1 to 3   16-cavity mold for tube caps, internally center gated. The point of injection is not visible externally**

a: threaded inserts, b: cover plate, c: insert plate, d: guide strips, e: mold clamping plate, f: mold clamping plate, g: leaf springs, h: latches, i: delatching pins, j: springs, k: plate, l: sucker pins, m: ejector sleeve, n: sucker pin, o: spring, (p: sprue, q: spindles, r: guide bushing, s: plate, t: pinion, u: drive gear, v: drive shaft, w: nut, x: ejector pins, y: springs, z: spring-loaded stops (for reasons of clarity the drive shaft v: has been separated at the dotted line)

pulled out of the channels. On further opening of the runner parting line the individual runners, centrally retained by the sucker pin (*n*) are pulled from the undercuts in the sucker pins (*l*). At the same time the main sprue is released from sprue bushing (*p*). After an opening stroke of 90 mm of the runner parting line, plates (*b*) and (*c*) are held by stops on the guide strips (*d*). The moving half of the mold, starting with plate (*k*) to the mold fixing plate (*f*), however, continues opening, carrying sucker pin (*n*) along by its collar. Now the sucker pin (*n*) is forced to release from the undercut in the center sprue. Caused by the resistance of the pull, the ejector sleeve (*m*) is moved back slightly against the force of spring (*o*). At that moment, when the pin releases from the undercut of the sprue, the ejector sleeve (*m*) shoots forward, ejecting the star-shaped runner. A ring groove in the mold clamping plate (*e*) on the nozzle side provides cooling for the main sprue and the runners.

The external shapes of the threaded caps have been cut into the spindles (*q*), whose external thread corresponds to the pitch of the threaded caps. These spindles run in bronze guide bushings (*r*), which are housed in plate (*s*). They are secured against rotating by

flats. These spindles are in mesh with the central drive gear (*u*) via pinions (*t*), which are keyed onto them. When the mold opens, drive gear (*u*) is turned by the central drive shaft (*v*), which runs in a fixed nut (*w*).

On the initial mold opening in the runner parting line by 90 mm, the threaded caps are unscrewed from the fixed threaded cores (*a*). The distance of 90 mm corresponds precisely to the number of turns in the threaded cap. As plates (*b*) and (*c*) are latched to the ejector plate of the moving half, the threaded caps are not released from their cavities. After a little more than the 90 mm opening stroke, the ejector pins (*x*), pushed back by springs (*y*), contact the spring-loaded stop (*z*). During the continuing opening movement of the mold beyond the 90 mm, the stops (*z*) are pushed back until the spring force overcomes the adhesion of the molded parts in the cavities. Should the adhesion be greater than the spring force, the stops (*z*) will eventually bottom toward the end of the mold opening movement. During the remaining movement, the ejector pins (*x*) advance relative to the spindles (*q*), releasing the molded parts from their cavities in any case. The springs (*j*) can then relax and the threaded caps are forcefully ejected from their cavities.

Fig. 2    Fig. 3

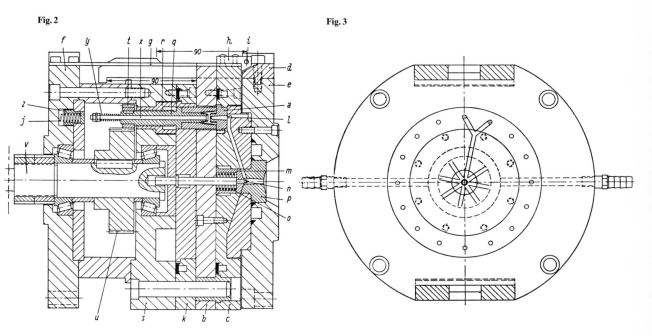

# Example 93, Four-cavity injection mold for dials

If, for instance, dials with a central hole are to be produced, edge gating is not satisfactory for high-quality requirements. A weld line would result behind the core used to form the central hole, and the surface quality and strength of the dial would be reduced. In this case, there is no other possibility than to mold a solid dial and then make the hole subsequently. Edge gating is also unacceptable if a thicker edge is required on the dial as in the present case. With edge gating of such a part, the melt would flow preferentially around the edge. The result is that during final filling the melt flows toward the center of the dial and the air cannot escape from this area. Accordingly, a dial having a thicker edge must be gated in the center. If, however, a hole is required exactly at this location in the dial, this hole must be produced subsequently.

A solution is provided in the mold designed in the following, where central gating is used for the part and the required hole is automatically produced by punch-action degating during opening of the mold.

Externally, the mold shown in Figs. 1 and 2 resembles the molds with two parting lines that have been repeatedly described previously. The runners are located in parting line $(A)$. The mold first opens at this parting line as long as the latches $(a)$ hold plates $(b)$ and $(c)$ together. The two mold halves are unlatched as the release pins $(d)$ travel along the release bars $(e)$. After this opening of the runner parting line, plate $(c)$ is held by stops on the release bars $(e)$, and the mold opens at the second parting line between plates $(b)$ and $(c)$.

The difference with respect to a pinpoint-gated mold is that the dial is gated over the entire cross section of the future hole, whereby a concentration of stress such as that which results around a pinpoint gate is largely avoided. The punch-action degating and simultaneous creation of the hole occur during the initial opening at the runner parting line $(A)$ by having the spring $(g)$ extend the punch $(f)$ toward the nozzle while plates $(b)$ and $(c)$ are still latched. During this motion of the punch, the portion of the runner around the sucker pin $(h)$ is simultaneously released from its tapered channel. The runner system is initially released from the sucker pin by the action of the strong spring washers $(i)$ on the stripper plate $(k)$. After the spring washers have relaxed, the springs $(l)$ provide for further motion of the stripper plates $(k)$.

The runner system is initially held on the sprue puller $(m)$, which is positively pulled out of the sprue on opening of the mold at the parting line between plates $(b)$ and $(c)$ as plate $(b)$ is held by the stop on the release bar $(e)$. The runner system is then ejected at parting line $(A)$ by the sudden relaxation of spring $(n)$. The dials are ejected by the sleeve ejectors $(o)$ as ejector rod $(p)$ is actuated.

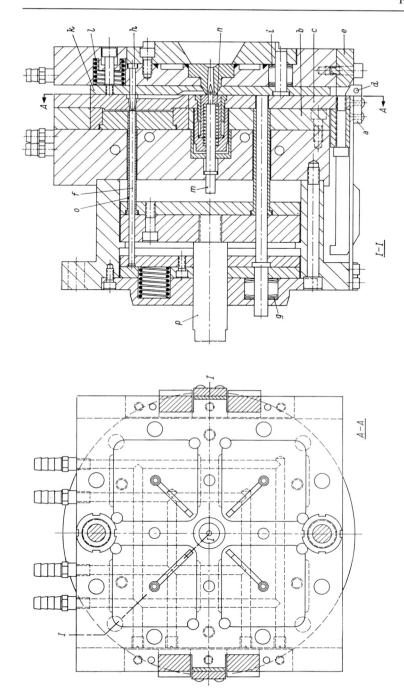

**Figs. 1 and 2 Four-cavity mold for dials**
*a*: latches, *b*, *c*: mold plates, *d*: release pin, *e*: release bar, *f*: punch, *g*, *l*, *n*: springs, *h*: sucker pin, *i*: spring washers, *k*: stripper plate, *m*: sprue puller, *o*: sleeve ejectors, *p*: ejector rod

# Example 94, Injection mold with air ejection for polypropylene cups

In developing injection molding of thin-walled polypropylene packaging items, the greatest importance by far must be attributed to mold design. Thin-walled polypropylene cups cannot be produced economically and reliably in the types of molds used for polystyrene. Because of the greater enthalpy and lower thermal conductivity compared to those of polystyrene, the cooling must be more effective when processing polypropylene. Because of its reduced rigidity during ejection and greater tendency to shrink onto the core, ejection of thin-walled polypropylene cups by means of ejector rings creates problems. While air-assisted valve ejector systems can facilitate ejection, the less effective cooling possible with such a system does not permit extremely short cycle times. Roughening or draw polishing of the surface of the core is not a suitable solution for transparent cups because of the detrimental effects on the transparency. Air ejection by means of static or dynamic air valves is only of limited use in fast-cycling single-cavity molds, since at production rates of over 20 shots per minute rapid and exact closing of the valve is hindered by the air remaining in the valve stem.

The first mold for polypropylene cups with side air ejection was built in 1978. Preliminary tests with this novel ejection system for cups were so promising that the mold makers specializing in the production fo cup molds adopted this system and improved it even further.

With side air ejection, stripper rings, which represent the most significant wearing part when producing cups by injection molding, can be eliminated. Figure 1 shows the design of such a core with side air ejection. With the mold illustrated in Fig. 2 acceptable cups were produced in a cycle time of 1.5 s using side air ejection exclusively.

This ejection system can also be employed with multiple-cavity and stack molds (see examples 36 and 44). However, exact control of the air, which is absolutely necessary for ejection, still presents certain difficulties. With polypropylene, air must also be introduced at the bottom from the cavity side. This serves not only to prevent the formation of a vacuum but also to sever the tough gate.

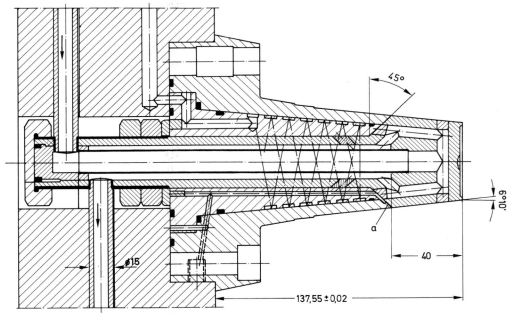

**Fig. 1    Core of a cup mold with side air ejection, dimensions in mm**
*a*: annular gap with a width of 0.01 mm
Mold drawing: Hoechst AG

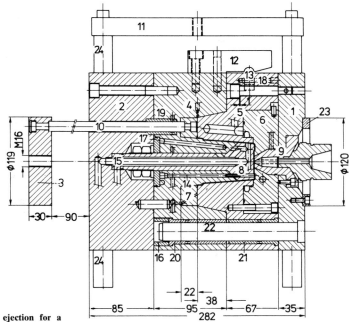

**Fig. 2   Single-cavity injection mold with side air ejection for a polypropylene dessert cup. To reduce the mold height a locating taper was provided parallel to the cavity, in constrast to the mold shown in Fig. 1, where the taper is in series with the cavity**
1: stationary-side clamping plate, 2: movable-side clamping plate, 3: ejector plate, 4: core retainer plate, 5: cavity plate, 6: cavity bottom insert, 7: stripper ring, 8: core tip with cooling channels, 9: hot sprue bushing, 10: ejector rod, 11: strap for transporting the mold, 12: latch, 13: latch bolt, 14: static air valve, 15: central cooling water tube, 16: spacer sleeve, 17: sealing plate, 18: intended cavity take off, 19: guide bushing, 20: guide bushing, 21: guide bushing, 22: guide pin, 23: locating ring, 24: strap mounting bolts

# Example 95, Molds for manufacturing optical lenses

When constructing molds for optical plastic parts, standard mold components and column-guided mold frames are used almost exclusively. This guarantees that the individual parts are interchangeable and reduces maintenance and repair times. Additional advantages include stocking of spare parts and reusability of mold components after the completion of a product.

A distinction is made between injection molds with mechanical and hydraulically operated compression.

## Injection mold for mechanical compression

Fig. 1 shows a two-cavity injection compression mold for objective lenses (meniscus lenses) that is set up for mechanical compression. The compression step in this case is carried out indirectly by the clamping unit of the injection molding machine.

## The compression sequence

The mold is closed at low pressure before the filling step, so that there is a gap of 0.2 mm between the mold mounting plate (2) and the floating plate (8). The gap is maintained by means of spring washers (19), which exert pressure through the tapered slide (14) and pin (18) on the mounting plate (2). During injection, the spring washers (19) must act against the injection pressure and keep the main parting line between the two mold plates (6 and 7) closed by their spring force, preventing the injection mold from opening. When the filling process is complete, the injection molding machine switches to full clamping pressure, which acts as compression pressure through the lense stamper after the force of the spring washers has been overcome and closes the initial gap of 0.2 mm.

## Design details

The sprue with attached runner conveys the melt to the pinpoint gate on the edge of each cavity. Ejector pins are positioned around the edge of each lens. The mold is vented through the parting line; the vent gap should not exceed 0.02 mm. The internal cavity pressure is measured piezoelectrically at a runner and stored as a measurement and control parameter.

A prerequisite for perfect lens elements is non-porous surfaces and optically perfect stamper depressions in compliance with DIN 3140. The lens thickness can be corrected by adjusting the position of the stamper via the tapered slide (14).

The mold locating means is separate for each cavity. The inserts on the stationary half are firmly fitted into the mold plate (7), while the movable-side inserts have a certain radial play to permit alignment with the stationary-side inserts.

The mold can be heated with heaterbands. A fluid circulating temperature control system with PID con-

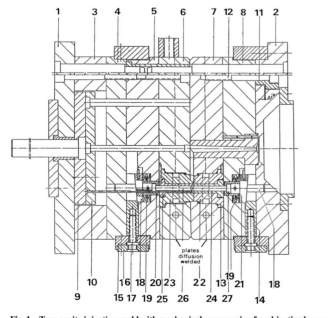
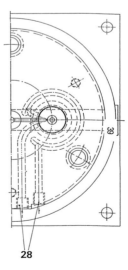

**Fig. 1    Two-cavity injection mold with mechanical compression for objective lenses**
1: clamping plate, 2: clamping plate, 3: spacer ring, 4: backing plate, 5: backing plate, 6: mold plate, 7: mold plate, 8: backing plate, 9: ejector plate, 10: ejector retainer plate, 11: spacer, 12: screw, 13: O-ring, 14: tapered slide, 15: retaining ring, 16: plate, 17: adjusting screw, 18: wedge pin, 19: spring washers, 20: cap, 21: cap, 22: mold insert, 23: mold insert, 24: mold sleeve, 25: mold sleeve, 26: lens stamper, 27: lens stamper, 28: connection for mold cooling

trols is provided for each mold cavity. The channels (28) are machined in the mold plate halves, hard chrome plated and joined to a single system by diffusion welding. O-rings (27) are used to seal the inserts (22 & 23).

All movable functional parts such as stampers and ejectors have been provided with appropriate play at their sliding surfaces so that they slip at the operating temperature of the mold and do not seize.

## Injection mold for hydraulic compression

An injection mold for hydraulic compression is shown in Fig. 2. In this case, the injection molding machine needs a pressure cushion, i. e. a separate hydraulic cylinder for the compression step. The compression step is initiated after the holding pressure stage.

## The compression sequence

After the filling step and while the injection pressure is still active (0.3 to 1.0 s), the transfer from injection pressure to holding pressure is made as a function of the filling pressure. The compression step is initiated independently of holding pressure by a pressure cushion, i. e. an additional hydraulic cylinder, with approx. 0.1 s delay.

## Design details

Here, too, the cavity is filled via a pinpoint gate. Ejector pins and ejector sleeves are used (18), which permit stress-free ejection of the lenses. The mold is also vented via the parting line.

The lens stampers (16, 17) are made of ESR steel (material no. 1.2842, with a hardness of 63 Rockwell C or as a combination of a steel holder with a ceramic insert. Repositioning of the lens stamper, which must be carried out after final polishing or to adjust the lens thickness, is accomplished by turning the threaded spindle (12) and worm gear (13). The worm gear (13) changes the axial position of the stamper holder (14, 15) via the adjusting thread. The adjusting thread must be dimensioned to withstand the mold opening force at an injection pressure of 1000 bar.

The mold halves are located by means of three conical locating units (10). For stringent requirements with regard to the concentricity (e. g. 0.010 to 0.015 mm) and surface quality of the plastic lenses, each mold cavity has its own locating unit with short guide and very tight tolerances. With these elaborate measures, very high-precision lens radii are obtained and any lateral movement of the mold cavities that might be caused by the play between the machine tie bars and guide bushings is eliminated.

## Stamper inserts

The quality of the injection molded parts depends largely on the precision of the stamper as regards surface, centering and life expectancy during operation. A precision of 0.5 to 2 (Newton) rings (2 rings = wave length of light $\lambda$) is required at diameters of 5 to 10 mm. The stamper surface must be prepared with similar accuracy.

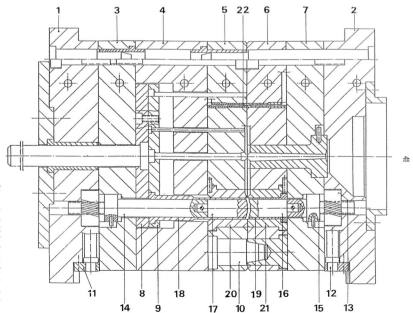

**Fig. 2 Six-cavity injection mold for meniscus lenses**
1: clamping plate, 2: clamping plate, 3: backing plate, 4: backing plate, 5: mold plate, 6: mold plate, 7: backing plate, 8: ejector plate, 9: ejector retainer plate, 10: locating unit, 11: retainer plate, 12: threaded spindle, 13: worm gear, 14: stamper holder, 15: stamper holder, 16: lens stamper, 17: lens stamper, 18: sleeve ejector, 19: sleeve, 20: mold insert, 21: mold insert, 22: thermocouple

# Example 96, Two-cavity injection mold for a polycarbonate steam iron reservoir insert

The insert for the reservoir of a steam iron (Fig. 1) is of a complicated shape due to the functions it has to fulfill. The insert serves as closure of the opening on the face of the reservoir, for instance. A spray nozzle is screwed onto the retaining thread (Fig. 2). The associated spray pump is mounted on a supporting strip. A connecting tube runs between spray pump and nozzle. This tube is pushed onto the connection stud A at the rear of the nozzle-retaining thread.

**Fig. 1    Reservoir insert of hydrolysis-resistant polycarbonate, color: transparent blue.**

## Mold

The mold has been constructed to incorporate two cavities and a conventional runner (Fig. 3). Due to the angle of the spray nozzle in relation to the plane in which the reservoir is employed, the mold is equipped with an unscrewing device for both cavities and angled lever-operated demolding mechanisms for the undercuts formed by the connecting studs and their bores. Both cavities are filled through submarine gates on the lower insert rib in a nonvisible area (arrows in Fig. 2). The gates are severed with the simultaneous ejection of the molded parts and the runner. The cavities proper have been machined into cavity inserts (41), (42) and (43).
Cooling channels have been arranged in the mold plates (9) and (11) outside the cavity inserts. Only the supporting strips of the two molded parts are served by a cooling pin (52), which penetrates through the ejector plate into the cooling sleeve (53) situated in the clamping plate (4), where it is surrounded by cooling water. The cavity inserts and the threaded cores as well as the contour cores are made of hardened steel (mat'l. no. 1. 2343).

## Mold operation

Once the mold cavities have been filled and the cooling time has elapsed, the unscrewing cores (38) are rotated

and withdrawn with the aid of the guide thread in the guide nut (37) by displacing the rack (49) via the hydraulic cylinder (50) and the pinions (61) and (62) before the two-plate tool is opened. Simultaneously with the thread-forming sleeve of the unscrewing cores (38) the contour pins (35) arranged centrically inside them are demolded. These contour pins also locate the core pins (63) at the tip. At the conclusion of the unscrewing sequence and actuation of the limit switches (51), the mold opening movement is initiated. The actuating

Flash-free holes and openings
Visible areas without sink marks, voids, scratches and striations
Part must fit into the opening on the face of the reservoir

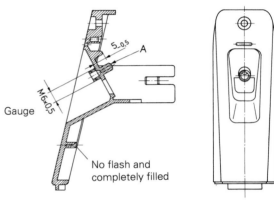

**Fig. 2    Inspection diagram for the reservoir insert**

**Fig. 3    Two-cavity injection mold with unscrewing mechanism for the reservoir insert shown in Fig. 1**

1,2: spacer rails, 3: movable-side locating ring, 4: movable-side clamping plate, 5: ejector plate, 6: ejector retainer plate, 7, 8: shoulder bolts, 9: movable-side mold place, 10: sprue puller bushing, 11: stationary-side mold plate, 12: stationary-side clamping plate, 13: sprue bushing, 14: stationary-side locating ring, 15: limit switch, unscrewing strip, 16: limit switch, base plate, 17: limit switch, unscrewing strip, 18: cylinder mounting plate, 19: limit switch support, 20: washer, 21: cylinder spacer strip, 22: cylinder unscrewing strip, 23: shim for sprue puller bushing, 24: guide bushing for ejector rod, 25: ejector rod, 26: ejector plate, 27, 28: articulated bushing, 29: rocker retainer strip, 30: rocker, 31: guide bushing, 32: spring guide bushing, 33: movable-side contour core, 34: actuating strip for rocker, 35: contour pin, 36: stationary-side contour core, 37: guide bushing, 38: unscrewing core with lead thread, 39: bearing bushing, 40, 41: movable-side contour inserts, 42: large stationary-side contour insert, 43: large movable-side contour insert, 44: bearing bushing for rocker, 45: shaft, 46: spacer bushing, 47: rack guide, 48: bearing bushing, 49: gear rack, 50: hydraulic cylinder, 51: limit switch, 52: cooling pin, 53: cooling sleeve, 54: cooling sleeve plug, 55, 56: runner ejector, 57 to 60: ejector pins, 61: pinion, 62: gear, 63: core pin, 64, 65: springs

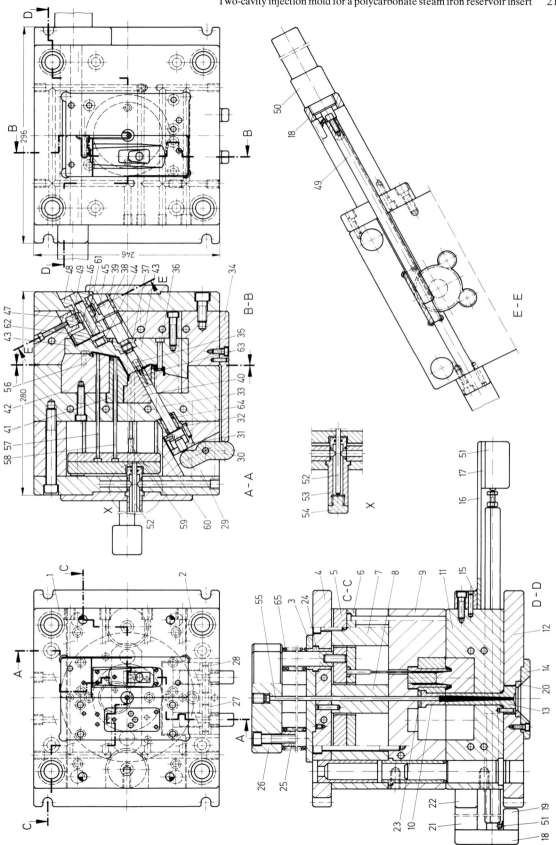

strip (34) releases the rocker (30), enabling the compression spring (64) to push the contour core (33) away from the molding, thereby allowing the tube connection on the reservoir insert to be demolded internally and externally (core pin 63).Thus the obstruction to demolding the article has been removed. Only after this release must the plate (26) at the end of the ejector bars (25) be allowed to contact the fixed machine ejec-

tor during further opening movement of the mold, thereby pushing the ejector pins forward to demold the articles as well as the runner.

Prior to mold closing, the ejectors must be retracted. During the closing motion, the contour core (33) is returned to the molding position by means of rocker (30) and actuating strip (34). The unscrewing cores (38) are advanced after the mold has closed.

## Example 97, Injection mold with pneumatic sprue bushing for headlight housing of polypropylene

The simpler the design and operation of an injection mold the more economical it is to produce smaller series. Housings for car headlights which can be retrofitted as an optional extra are parts that fall into this category. The following description will deal with a mold for these lamp housings (Fig. 1), which are produced in flame-retardant polypropylene reinforced with 15 wt. % glass fiber. The dimensions of the headlight housing are 80 mm × 170 mm × 60 mm. The wall thickness is 2 mm; part weight is 84 g. The cycle time is 12 s.

The mold was constructed with standard mold components. Using the selection tables and catalogues from standard-component manufacturers, it is possible to determine the appropriate gating system [1]. Also most of the costs and delivery dates can be calculated [2]. The decision to produce a single-cavity mold was made due to cost considerations arising from the planned production quantities. The pneumatic sprue bushing was selected in order to have a smooth running mold without the need for additional control equipment required for a hot-runner.

### Mold design

Fig. 2 shows the design of the mold, which has been assembled mostly using standard mold components. The lamp housing is gated via the pneumatic sprue bushing (25), which is available ready for installation. The part is stripped off using ejector pins. The ejector sleeves (21) are provided for the bores in the brackets which are connected with a film hinge. The internal bosses

are released and the core (34) pulled via the lifters (37), which are mounted and actuated by the ejector plates. In order to be able to accommodate the support pillars (19) as well as the ball guides (12) within the ejector plates (7, 8) of the relatively small mold, an enlarged ejector plate version has been selected. The support rails are not positioned in the usual manner, but only as corner pieces so as to allow a larger working area. For precise pressure monitoring, a pressure transducer (15) is located behind the ejector pin (16) for pressure-dependent switching from injection to holding pressure. This way the lamp housings can be produced free of flash. The ideal pressure characteristic is recorded and each mold set-up will be done in accordance with this curve [3].

The quick disconnect couplings (29) with suitable nipples allow the heating/cooling and air lines to be connected both quickly and reproducibly. This has a favorable effect on the set-up times. The helical core (26) ensures effective temperature control of the mold core.

The cavity plates (2, 3) are made of steel grade 1.2767. This through-hardening steel is very advantageous if the contours are to be hardened after rough machining and then finished via EDM; this prevents any distortion caused by subsequent hardening. For the same reason, both plates have a grinding allowance in the guide bores. The lifters (37) are produced from precision ground flat steel, also of steel grade 1.2767. This steel, machined precisely on all sides, is available in a wide range of dimensions and is particularly suitable for manufacturing mold components of these and similar types.

The adjustable date insert (32) complies with the requirement of the automobile industry for injection molded parts to be clearly marked with the manufacturing date. These new standardized date inserts can be set from the contour side of the mold using a screwdriver. They clearly show the month and year of production in raised characters on the injection molded part.

### Operation of the mold

The cavity is filled via the pneumatic sprue bushing (25) shown on the right in Fig. 3. In most cases, the front portion of the sprue is machined directly into the

**Fig. 1    Lamp housing of polypropylene, reinforced with 15 wt.-% glass fiber, flame-retardant**

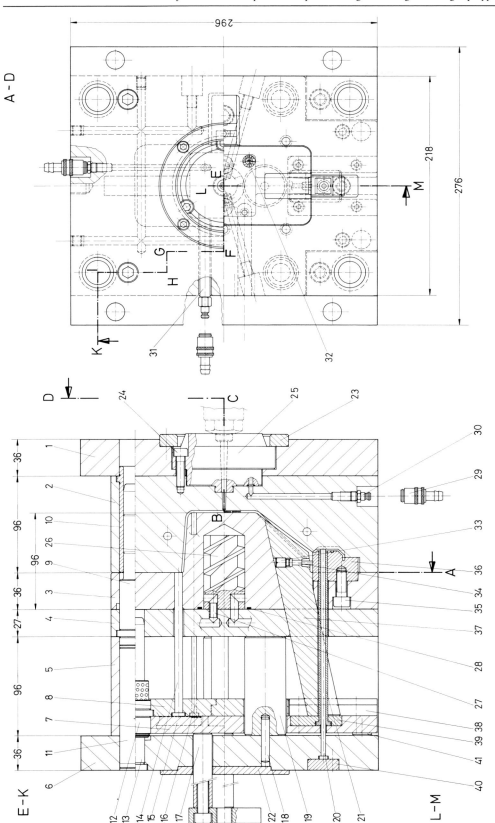

**Fig. 2  Injection mold with pneumatic sprue bushing for lamp housing**

1: clamping plate, 2: cavity plate, 3: cavity plate, 4: backing plate, 5: support rails, 6: clamping plate, 7, 8: ejector plate, 9: guide pin, 10: guide bushing, 11: centering sleeve, 12: ball guide, 13: guide pin, 14: ejector pin, 15: pressure transducer, 16: ejector pin, 17: guide sleeve, 18: dowel pin, 19: support pillar, 20: ejector pin, 21: ejector sleeve, 22, 23: locating ring, 24: socket head cap screw, 25: pneumatic sprue bushing, 26: helical core, 27: brass tube, 28: O-ring, 29: quick disconnect coupling, 30: connection nipple, 31: extension nipple, 32: date insert, 33: hexagon socket set screw, 34: core pin, 35: socket head cap screw, 36, 37, 38, 39, 40: ground flat steel, 41: stop disk

**Fig. 3   Pneumatic sprue bushing (right) and interchangeable nozzle insert (left) for thermoplastics processing**

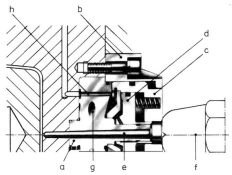

**Fig. 4   Section through the pneumatic sprue bushing (for explanations, refer to text)**

cavity plate; with very abrasive resins, a nozzle insert (Fig. 3, left) can also be used as a wear part. The pneumatic sprue bushing is an alternative to the three-plate mold and to the hot-runner and shares the advantages of the conventional sprue. Existing tools can also be converted with this sprue bushing.

Fig. 4 shows the function of the pneumatic sprue bushing, which is screwed directly to the cavity plate (2) in Fig. 2. After filling the mold and ending of the holding pressure time, the machine nozzle f retracts. Compressed air is introduced through the connection (30) in Fig. 2 and the bore *h* into the hollow piston *c* via a pilot valve. This pulls the sprue *e* from the part and releases air for the piston *d* which, aided by an air stream, ejects the sprue *e*. Before the next injection cycle starts, the machine nozzle forces the pistons *c, d* of the pneumatic sprue bushing back into their initial positions. The bore *g* allows additional temperature control for the injection area.

The ejector plates are connected to the hydraulic ejector of the machine via guide sleeves (17). When the ejector plates advances, the lifters (37) automatically move inwards and release the inner contour. The ejector plates are guided precisely via the ball guides (12). The ejectors and lifters are pulled back hydraulically before the mold closes. The lateral ejector pins (14) act as return pins in the final mold closing phase. They push the ejector plates into home position.

**Literature**

1  Heuel, O.: Kunststoffe
2  Heuel, O.: Kunststoffe 71 (1981) p. 866/869
3  Heuel, O.: Plastverarbeiter 32 (1981) p. 1496/1498

# Example 98, Unscrewing device for an injection mold for a junction box of polyamide

A polyamide junction box injection mold had to be designed for fully automatic operation. Tapped holes in the corners of the box for fastening the cover had to be taken into account. These had to be produced within the same cycle. The particularity of this design (Fig. 1) is the elimination of a lead thread for unscrewing the threaded cores. This simplifies mold construction with regard to the mechanical parts content. What had to be taken into consideration, however, is the mechanical support of the threaded core by the lead thread, preventing its axial displacement in the cavity during injection. In the case presented here, a hydraulic counterpressure is built up at the end of the core before the plastics melt is injected into the cavity. This pressure must be at least as high as the maximum available injection pressure in the mold cavity. That is the reason why this part of the core has been constructed as a hydraulic piston. Polyamide is so stiff after solidification that the molded thread just produced can serve as the lead thread when unscrewing the threaded cores.

Two each of the four threaded holes in the corners of the cover are unscrewed by hydraulic motors. Their high torque, compared with that of hydraulic cylinders, electric motors and lead-screw spindles, is transmitted through the stub shaft (10), chain sprocket (9) and roller chain (11) to the chain sprockets (12). These are connected to the threaded core (13) by a gear tooth profile, which transmits the torque to the core. The male gear shaft profile of the threaded core (13) is axially displaceable in the female tooth profile of the chain sprocket (12).

The mold operates in the following manner:

Once the mold is closed the threaded cores (13) are preloaded in the mold cavity by at least 120 bar. During injection, holding pressure and cooling this pressure is maintained to ensure the position of the threaded core (13). Then the pressure is dropped to zero and the threaded cores are uncrewed from the molded part by the hydraulic motor (8) through the chain drive (9, 11, 12). During this operation the threaded core moves back as it unscrews from the thread in the molded part. The junction box is retained in the cavity of the mold plate (2) during the subsequent opening of the mold. The box is released and ejected by pushing the cavity

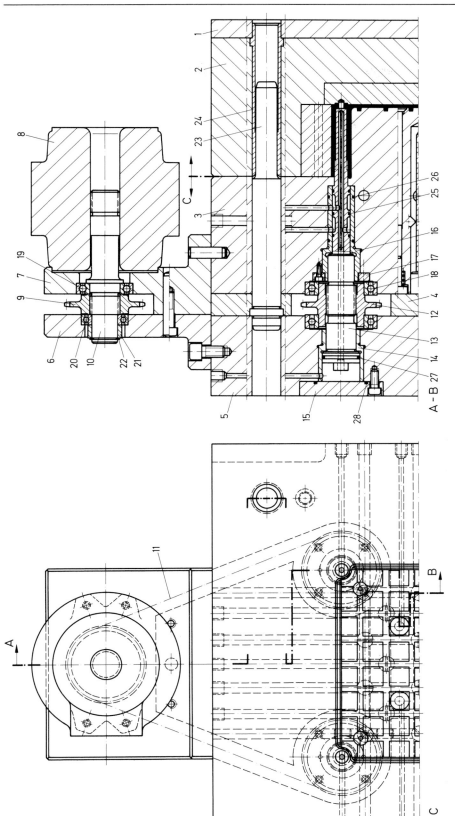

## Example 98

**Fig. 1   Unscrewing device for a junction box injection mold**

1: fixed-half mold mounting plate, 2: cavity plate, 3: core plate, 4: spacer plate, 5: moving-half mold mounting plate, 6: bearing block, 7: motor bearing, 8: hydraulic motor, 9: chain sprocket (number of teeth z = 25, chain pitch t = $^1/_2$ in, outside diameter of a gear wheel = 106.5 mm), 10: stub shaft, 11: single roller chain, 12: chain sprocket (number of teeth z = 25, chain pitch t = $^1/_2$ in, outside diameter of a gear wheel = 106.5 mm), 13: threaded core, 14: hydraulic cylinder bushing, 15: cylinder cover, 16: guide and cooling bushing, 17: ring, 18 to 20: grooved ball bearing, 21: ring, 22: circlip, 23: leader pin, 24: guide bushing, 25 to 28: sealing rings.

slides forward hydraulically. It should be noted further that such a mold requires very carefully threated cooling water, because the sealing rings (25, 26) move in a thread-like manner in the bushing (16). Rust and calcium deposits in this bushing would cause these rings to wear rapidly.

## Example 99, Alternative mold designs for a thermoplastic pump impeller

There are often several alternative mold design for injection molding of thermoplastics. An automatically operating mold with high output is not always the most favorable. Rather, the type of mold for which the sum of mold making costs and manufacturing costs for injection molding (including secondary operations) are lowest, or whether, because of a possible bottleneck in the mold making shop, another version that may have higher production costs may be more advantageous must be examined on an individual basis.

Of the costs to manufacture injection molded parts, a considerable portion is associated with mold amortization, so that lower mold costs considerably improve the economics of injection molding. The following equation applies when determining the production costs $K_M$ (in DM) of a part (without material costs)

$$K_M = \frac{n \times q \times t \times U}{3600\,Q} = \frac{n \times t \times U}{3600\,x} \tag{1}$$

where n = quantity to be produced, $q$ = volume of a part in cm$^3$, $t$ = cycle time in $s$, $U$ = machine operating costs in DM/h, $Q$ = shot volume in cm$^3$ and $x = Q/q$ = number of cavities in the mold.

The production costs $K_W$ (in DM) of the mold (as a function of the number of cavities) are

$$K_W \approx x \times K_{W1} \tag{2}$$

where $K_{W1}$ = production costs of a cavity in DM. According to the analysis in [1], that machine is most economical for which

$$\frac{U}{Q^2} = \frac{3600 \times K_{W1}}{n \times q^2 \times t} \tag{3}$$

Rearranging eq. (3) gives

$$\frac{Q^2}{q^2} = x^2 = \frac{n \times t \times U}{3600 \times K_{W1}} \tag{4}$$

Inserting the expression for $x$ obtained from eq. (4) in eq. (1) it follows that

$$K_M = \sqrt{\frac{n \times t \times U \times K_{W1}}{3600}} \tag{5}$$

If this value of x is inserted in eq- (2), it is interesting to note that the same result is obtained for $K_W$. This means that optimum conditions occur when the fraction of mold making costs proportional to the number

of cavities equals the part production costs (without material costs).

The part production costs are composed primarily of the labor costs and operating costs of the injection molding machine, and together yield a certain hourly rate. Starting with the fact that when making the molds both machine work and manual work (albeit with higher labor costs than for injection molding, but with no machine costs) are performed, it may be assumed that the hourly rate for injection molding does not differ considerably from that for mold making. The conclusion is that optimum conditions occur when the time to make a mold is approximately equal to the production time for injection molding. Expressed in another way, this means that the number employed in the mold making shop should be about equal to the number employed in the injection molding operation, assuming the same number of shifts.

This fact determines within certain limits the degree of automation for molds. The productivity of automatic molds is high, and the production time resulting from injection molding is reduced through their use. Nevertheless, the time needed to make such molds is considerably greater than that for molds that do not operate automatically.

Since the same part can be produced in molds with differing degrees of automation, the various possibilities

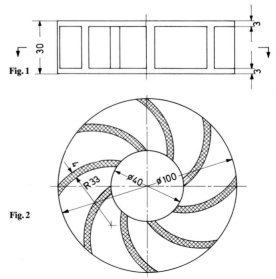

Fig. 1

Fig. 2

**Figs. 1 and 2   Pump impeller**

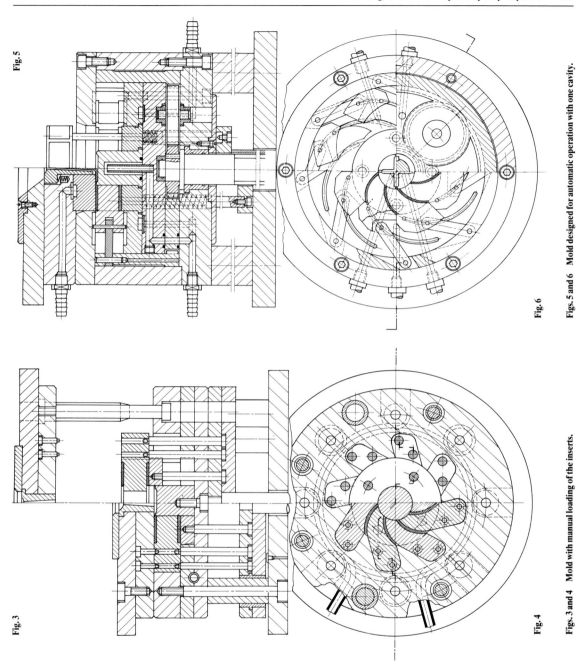

Fig. 5

Fig. 6

Figs. 5 and 6    Mold designed for automatic operation with one cavity.

Fig. 3

Fig. 4

Figs. 3 and 4    Mold with manual loading of the inserts.

must be considered and evaluated in order to achieve optimum economics. Such an evaluation starts preferably with a simple, nonautomatic mold the mold making costs of which are estimated along with the production costs of the parts to be molded (without material costs). Next, the costs incurred through use of a mold with a higher degree of automation, and perhaps a fully automatic mold, are determined in the same manner.

The mold thus determined to be optimum is not always the best in every case. The particular conditions in the plant, e.g., the available capacity of the mold making shop or injection molding department, can result in other solutions. The following example will serve to elucidate the above discussion.

A quantity of 60,000 pump impellers a shown in Figs. 1 and 2 is to be manufactured out of PVC. Figures 3 and 4 show a simple mold with a single cavity in which the spaces between the impeller blades are filled by inserts. These inserts are removed from the mold manually along with the molded part. After manually placing new inserts in the mold, the next cycle begins. The inserts are removed from the molded part with the aid of an extraction device. This relatively simple mold requires the continuous presence of an operator at the machine.

With the design shown in Figs. 5 and 6 the inserts are withdrawn by means of levers that move in internally splined cylinders. The mold operates automatically; the operator may be eliminated. The costs to make this mold, however, are more than for the first mold.

Figures 7 and 8 show a two-level stack mold with three cavities per level. The impeller is then assembled from two different parts (Figs. 9 to 12). The part with the blades has two 3 mm pins per blade, while the mating piece contains notches to accept the blades and holes for the pins. The two parts are assembled and the pins protruding through the holes are riveted. While this mold does produce three parts per cycle, they must be assembled and riveted together, which results in additional costs.

Which of these three alternatives is the most economical is indicated by an evaluation of the respective production costs and shown in Tables 1 to 3. According to

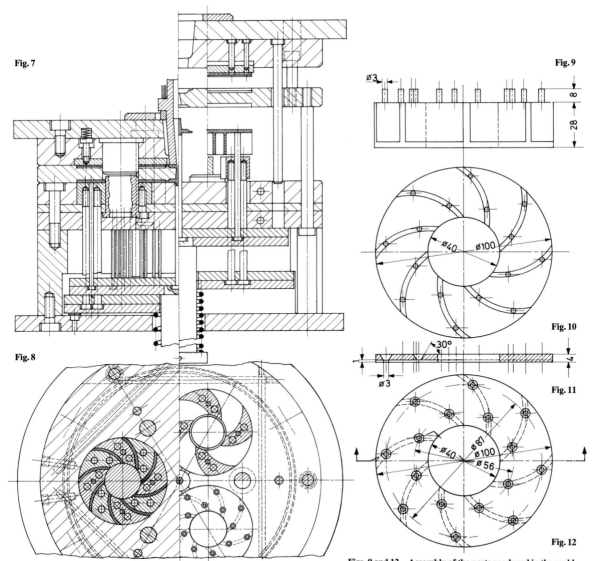

**Fig. 7**

**Fig. 8**

**Fig. 9**

**Fig. 10**

**Fig. 11**

**Fig. 12**

**Figs. 7 and 8    Two-level stack mold with 2 × 3 cavities.**

**Figs. 9 and 12    Assembly of the parts produced in the mold shown in Figs. 7 and 8.**

this evaluation, the second alternative with overall production costs of about 113,000 cost units is the most economical.

It goes without saying, of course, that under certain circumstances, e.g., limited mold making facilities or capacities for secondary operations, another version may be more advantageous for a particular operation in spite of the higher production costs. Other results are also obtained if the molds are provided by the customer. The present evaluations are based on conditions in Hungary. With other initial conditions in other countries, they could quite easily lead to different results. In any case they show that there is no universally valid economic optimum, but rather that various alternatives should always be investigated and that while economy is an important aspect, it is not always decisive.

## Literatur

1  L. Sors, *Kunststoffe*, vol. 65, 1975, pp. 120–122.

**Table 1.  Production costs corresponding to Figs. 3 and 4**

|  | Cost rate [cu/h] | Required time [h] | Cost [cu] |
|---|---|---|---|
| Quantity: 60 000 Machine time                          30 s Load 8 inserts at 3 s per insert                          24 s Cycle time                          54 s Time required for production $\left(\dfrac{60\,000 \times 54}{3600}\right)$ |  | 900 |  |
| Hourly rate for operating the injection molding machine (energy, depreciation and other incidental costs) | 80 |  |  |
| Hourly wage of the operator at the injection molding machine          16 cu (social security contributions = 25 %)          4 cu | 20 |  |  |
| Cost rate of production | 100 |  |  |
| Production costs for injection molding without material costs (900 × 100) |  |  | 90 000 |
| Time required to make the mold |  | 450 |  |
| Average hourly wage in the mold making shop (machine and manual work)          20 cu (social security contributions = 25 %)          5 cu Miscellaneous costs (= 400 %)          80 cu | 105 |  |  |
| Costs to make the mold without material costs (450 × 105) |  |  | 47 250 |
| Total production costs |  |  | 137 250 |

**Table 2.  Production costs corresponding to Figs. 5 and 6**

|  | Cost rate [cu/h] | Required time [h] | Cost [cu] |
|---|---|---|---|
| Quantity: 60 000 Machine time 30 s Time required for production $\left(\dfrac{60\,000 \times 30}{3600}\right)$ |  | 500 |  |
| Hourly rate for operating the injection molding machine (energy, depreciation and other incidental costs) | 80 |  |  |
| Production costs for injection molding without material costs (500 × 80) |  |  | 40 000 |
| Time required to make the mold |  | 700 |  |
| Average hourly wage in the mold making shop | 105 |  |  |
| Costs to make the mold without material costs (700 × 105) |  |  | 73 500 |
| Total production costs |  |  | 113 500 |

**Table 3.  Production costs corresponding to Figs. 7 and 8**

|  | Cost rate [cu/h] | Required time [h] | Cost [cu] |
|---|---|---|---|
| Quantity: 60 000 Machine time 30 s/3 part Time required for production $\left(\dfrac{60\,000 \times 30}{3 \times 3600}\right)$ |  | 166.7 |  |
| Hourly rate for operating the injection molding machine (energy, depreciation and other incidental costs) | 100 |  |  |
| Production costs for injection molding without material costs (166.7 × 100) |  |  | 16 700 |
| Time required to make the mold |  | 880 |  |
| Average hourly wage in the mold making shop | 105 |  |  |
| Costs to make the mold without material costs (880 × 105) |  |  | 92 400 |
| Time required for assembling and welding the molded pieces (30 s/piece = 60 000 × 30/3600) |  | 500 |  |
| Hourly wage for secondary operations          12 cu Social security contributions (= 25 %)          3 cu Miscellaneous costs (300 %)          36 cu | 51 |  |  |
| Costs of secondary operation (500 × 51) |  |  | 25 500 |
| Time to make the assembly and welding fixture |  | 50 |  |
| Production costs for the fixture (50 × 105) |  |  | 5 250 |
| Total production costs |  |  | 139 820 |

# Example 100, Six-cavity injection mold for watch crystals

Watch crystals with various diameters and curvatures are needed in great quantities. They are produced almost exclusively from acrylic by injection molding. The great variety of shapes forces the use of injection molds with interchangeable inserts in order to keep the mold costs within reasonable limits. In addition, it is required that these molds produce watch crystals on which the gate is as invisible as possible and where the degating occurs automatically.

By arranging the inserts in two rows, the parts can be degated on opening of the mold by shifting a slide containing the runner system and gates.

In this mold, for example, (Figs. 1 to 7), the inserts are placed in a circle and the parts are degated by rotating an insert containing the runner system as the mold opens. The inserts (*a*) for the back and (*b*) for the face of the watch crystals are fitted into slides (*c*) and (*d*) respectively and are held against the runner plate (*f*) and sprue bushing (*g*) by bolts (*e*). Since the runner plate (*f*) and sprue bushing (*g*) partially overlap the inserts (*a*) and (*b*), the inserts are prevented from falling out.

Sprue bushing (*g*) is tightly bolted to the stationary-side clamping plate (*h*), while runner plate (*f*), which contains the runner system, is mounted in bronze bushing (*i*) and may be rotated in plate (*k*). During the initial opening motion of the mold, this runner plate is actuated by means of two gear segments (*l*) and (*m*) that are operated by an offset cam (*o*). The cam is so designed that the runner plate (*f*) rotates by about 15° over an opening stroke of about 60 mm.

The runners are machined into the runner plate (*f*) and the watch crystals are gated from the back through an opening of about 1 mm. Figure 1–6 shows the cross section of the gate. The dovetail-shaped gate provides a sharp cutting edge and thus clean degating of the molded part over an area of about $1 \times 0.8$ mm.

To prevent the watch crystals from rotating as the gate is being sheared, either a small flat on the core or a few points that simultaneously identify the cavity may be provided if necessary.

In order that no ejector marks be visible on the watch crystals, they are stripped off the cores by the rotary motion. After the runner plate (*f*) rotates 15°, a cam located on the edge of the runner plate (see secs. *III–III*, Fig. 5) slips under the watch crystal and lifts it off the core (*a*) so that it may drop.

The runner system is ejected in the usual manner at the end of the opening stroke by actuating the ejector rod (*p*).

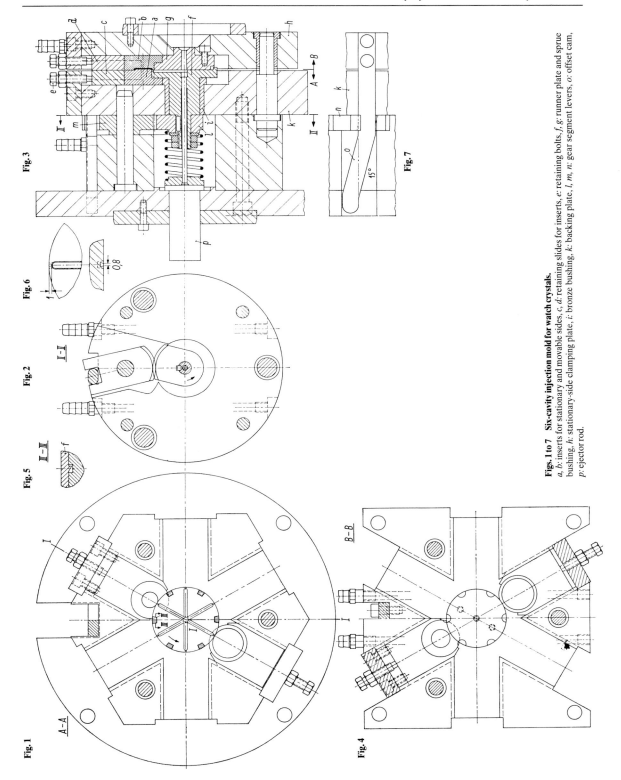

**Figs. 1 to 7    Six-cavity injection mold for watch crystals.**
a, b: inserts for stationary and movable sides, c, d: retaining slides for inserts, e: retaining bolts, f, g: runner plate and sprue bushing, h: stationary-side clamping plate, i: bronze bushing, k: backing plate, l, m, n: gear segment levers, o: offset cam, p: ejector rod.

Fig. 3

Fig. 7

Fig. 6

Fig. 2

Fig. 5

II – II

I – II

Fig. 1

A–A

Fig. 4

B–B

## Example 101, Four-cavity injection mold for thin-walled sleeves of polyester

A four-cavity mold with parting line injection was needed for a thin-walled sleeve having a wall thickness of only 0.5 mm for a length of 26 mm (Fig. 1). Parting line injection was necessary, because an extremely long hydraulic ejector was needed for the mold. The material to be molded was a polyester (polyethylene terephthalate) with good flow properties that is especially suited for thin-walled parts with a high flow length/wall thickness ratio.

are cooled by means of compressed air introduced through openings (6). As the release bar (7) disengages the latch (4), parting line (2) is opened by means of bolt (8). Parting line (3) is held closed by means of latch (9). Undercuts (10) retain the runner system and in this manner shear off the submarine gates (3). Opening at parting line (2) continues until the runner system can drop out properly. Release bar (11) then disengages latch (9) as plate (12) is held by stop (13), so that

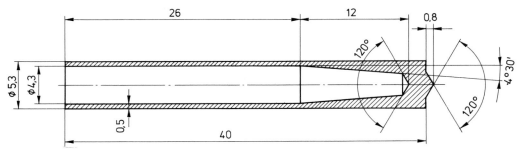

**Fig. 1    Polyester sleeve**

To permit fully automatic operation, the sleeves were to be ejected separately from the sprue and runner system. Furthermore, the outer surface of the sleeves was not permitted to have any witness line. The closed end with conical tip had to be smooth and clean. The best solution thus appeared to be to gate the sleeve at its thick-walled end by means of two submarine gates on opposite sides (Fig. 2).

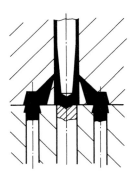

**Fig. 2    Gating of the sleeve by means of two opposite submarine gates.**

Ejection without damaging the thin walls of the molded part takes place by first withdrawing the core (5) from the sleeve (1) while it is still completely contained in the cavity. The mold (Figs. 3 to 12) first opens at parting line (1). Parting lines (2) and (3) are held closed by latch (4). During the opening stroke, the cores (5)

parting line (3) now opens. As the mold reaches the full-open position, the hydraulic ejector (14) is actuated, thereby ejecting the sleeve from the cooled cavity insert (16). Simultaneously, plate (17) actuates plate (18). The ejector pin (19) mounted in plate (18) is located behind the retaining undercut (10) for the runner system, which is now ejected. It does not drop out of the mold, however, until ejector pin (15) is retracted by the hydraulic ejector.

The position of ejector plate (17) is sensed by two roller switches, which are actuated by switch rods (20) and (21), and determine the machine sequencing. Ejector plate (18) is returned to the molding position by pushback pin (22) as the mold closes.

The closed end of the sleeve exhibits the same 120° tip as does the inner core to ensure that this inner core cannot be deflected toward one side as the sleeve is filled through the two gates (Fig. 2). In addition, the ejector pin (15) is spring-loaded (23). When the mold is closed, the end of ejector pin (15) seats against the inner core (5) and centers it in the corresponding recess. As the melt enters the cavity, the core is held centered until the cavity pressure overcomes the force of the spring located behind ejector pin (15) and forces it to its retracted position. By this time, the core (5) is surrounded by melt to such an extent that it can no longer be deflected. This precautionary measure in the mold design was found to be absolutely necessary on test molding with the completed mold.

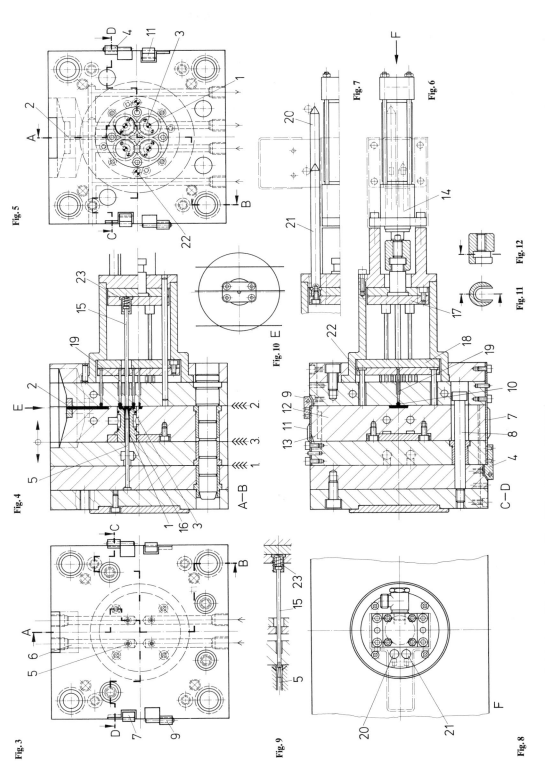

**Figs. 3 to 12    Four-cavity injection mold for automatic molding of thin-walled polyester sleeves.**
1: sleeves, 2: sprue bushing, 3: submarine gates, 4: latch, 5: core, 6: opening for cooling air, 7: release bar, 8: bolt, 9: latch, 10: undercut, 11: release bar, 12: cavity retainer plate, 13: stop, 14: hydraulic ejector, 15: ejector pin, 16: cavity insert, 17: ejector actuating plate, 18: ejector plate, 19: ejector pin, 20, 21: switch rods, 22: pushback pin, 23: spring.

# Example 102, Single-cavity injection mold for thermos bottle cups

## Comparison of rack drive vs. threaded shaft drive

The gear rack has the advantage over the threaded shaft drive described in that it is easier to produce, as the toothcutting operation can be more easily carried out than the milling of a threaded shaft with coarse pitch. However, it must be noted that worm gears, which are required for such tools in any case, can only transfer forces through point contact, so that they are incapable of transmitting large forces. Therefore a threaded shaft drive is better for the large forces required in multi-cavity tools with threaded cores, as with this type of transmission torque is transmitted through surface contact of the wedge profile of the shaft or by line contact in the case of the gears.

For single-cavity tools, and the same also applies to multi-cavity molds with threaded cores of small diameters, however, the *gear rack drive* of the cores offers considerable advantage. Without reserve, even up to six in-line cores can be driven by one gear rack. It is even possible to unscrew two rows of cores if two worm-geared shafts are provided. In principle, therefore, it is necessary that the gears are arranged in line for gear-rack drives in multi-cavity tools, whereas a threaded shaft drive requires the molded parts to be arranged in a circle, so that the threaded cores can be operated by a pinion positioned centrally in the mold.

## Single-cavity-rack-operated mold

In the following, the construction of a single-cavity mold is described, in which thermos bottle cups are produced with approximately three internal turns of thread. To avoid waste, the mold has been designed to use an insulated sprue, injecting externally in the center of the cup (Figs. 1 to 3). Intensive cooling of the cavity and the core, enabling fast cycling, is necessary so that it is possible to keep on injecting through the small gate in the insulated sprue without the material freezing at that point. As the cup is produced in high density PE, which like all types of PE is most suitable for injecting through the insulated sprue, and as the wall thickness of the cup is relatively thin, injection can take place so fast that freezing at the point of injection is prevented. The insulated sprue is kept warm internally by a heat-conducting tip of copper or beryllium bronze, as described repeatedly already. The insulated sprue pinpoint gate is sufficiently supported to degate the molded part when sprue break occurs.

Insert ($a$) on the fixed half, giving shape to the cup exterior, is centered in the stripper plate ($b$) by a cone, eliminating the need for guide pins. The stripper plate is pushed forward by four push rods ($d$) when the ejector plate ($c$) contacts the mechanical ejector in the molding machine. The threaded part must have been demolded first, though. The threaded part consists of the threaded sleeve ($e$), which is carried on core ($f$). This core is water-cooled internally by well-known methods. The threaded sleeve has a worm gear thread that is meshed with the worm gear shaft ($g$). It also possesses a lead thread at its end, whose pitch is identical to that of the molded part. The threaded sleeve is supported on its outside in the lead nut ($h$) at one end and in the bearing bushing ($i$) at the other end. The transmission of the worm gear should preferably be chosen as 1 : 1, as the degree of effectiveness is at its most favorable at that ratio for worm gear transmission.

The worm gear shaft ($g$) is supported in tapered roller bearings ($k$), and the worm gear drive is filled with grease to eliminate lubrication during operation. The worm gear shaft ($g$) is connected with the gear rack ($l$) via a transmission gear. This transmission must be so matched that the threaded parts are demolded and the molded part itself can be stripped off the core ($f$) by the stripper plate ($b$) during the sequence "mold opening" to "contacting the mechanical ejector in the molding machine".

When mold closing, the threaded sleeve must move forward till it contacts the threaded core to ensure that no gap remains at that position, which could fill with material. Care must therefore be taken that no damage can occur within the gearing, should the machine have been set. This is achieved by not fitting a key between the gear ($m$) and the worm shaft ($g$), and simply tightening bold ($n$) to obtain frictional contact. This friction coupling would slip in case of improper set-up.

A further assurance for the gapless contact of the threaded sleeve ($e$) against the collar of core ($f$) is the set of disc springs ($o$) between the mold clamping plate of the fixed half and the rack ($l$). As this spring pack compresses when the sleeve ($e$) butts up against the collar of core ($f$) in the mold closed position, it can safely be assumed that there will be no gap there and therefore injection molding material is prevented from intruding.

**Fig. 1**

**Fig. 2**

**Fig. 3**

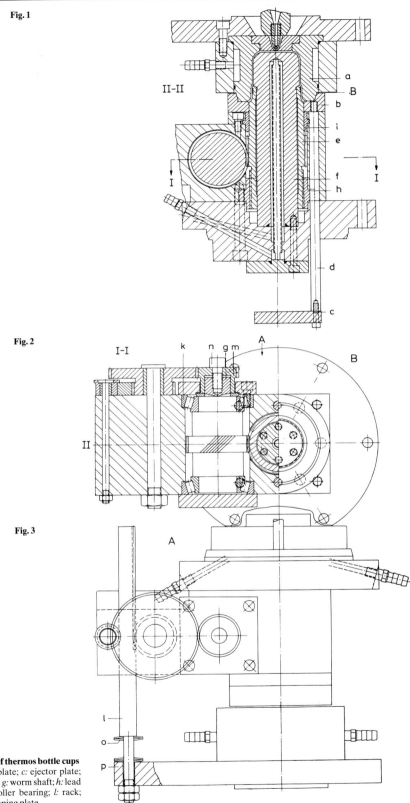

**Figs. 1 to 3   Mold for the production of thermos bottle cups**
a: insert, fixed mold half; b: stripper plate; c: ejector plate;
d: push rods; e: threaded sleeve; f: core; g: worm shaft; h: lead
nut; i: bearing bushing; k: tapered roller bearing; l: rack;
m: pinion; n: bolt; o: disc spring; p: clamping plate.

## Example 103, Eight-cavity injection mold for producing threaded sleeves

Internal threads can be demolded through a coarse threaded spindle that turns in a fixed nut in the machine during the opening sequence. The rotary movement of this spindle, centrally situated in the tool, is transmitted via gears to the threaded cores, which are arranged in a circle.

The number of threaded core rotations is limited, however, with this transmission in the same way as the rack drive or segmental rack drive is restricted, so that only a limited number of turns can be unscrewed. With more than six or seven turns of thread the direct mechanical transmission to the threaded cores fails, as the reduction ratio of at most two to three rotations of the threaded spindle to the threaded cores becomes excessive. The same applies to the gear rack drive. The rack would have to become so extended in that case that the space requirements in the machine would be inadequate. If more than six to seven rotations of the threaded cores are required for unscrewing, then the cores have to be driven by an electric motor.

It is one of the requirements for unscrewing internally threaded moldings that the injection molded parts are secured sufficiently against turning in the moving half when the cores are being unscrewed. Should this condition not be fulfilled by the external design (hexagonal profile, ribs, grooving, etc.) it could be obtained by arranging retaining ribs directly around the threaded part itself within the thickness of the walls and to a depth of 0.5 to 1 mm in the molding. This prerequisite must, in other words, be fulfilled by the design of the molding itself.

A further "must" for the mold designer's attention concerns the end positions of the threaded cores after the closing and opening movement of the mold. These precisely defined end positions of the threaded cores determine the injection process as well as the start of mold closing. This in turn means that these end positions of the threaded cores must actuate electrical contacts that initiate the injection process or the closing of the mold. It is only possible to time the unscrewing of the threaded cores independently of the mold opening through this type of electrical control. This becomes necessary, for instance, when the time for the mold opening sequence is too short for unscrewing the cores from multiple turns of thread.

If a great number of turns are to be unscrewed, it must be taken into consideration that the surface speed inside the formed thread cannot be arbitrarily high if tearing of the thread surface is to be avoided. The permissible surface speed, however, is influenced by a series of factors, which have not all been clearly defined. Conicity of the threaded cores, surface roughness of the thread and the polish as well as the influence of the various injection molding materials or their internal lubricants are among the determining factors.

Tests have shown that, surprisingly enough, a previously flawless and mirror-polished core, which had then been microscopically roughened by acid, released

considerably more easily from the molding than a highly polished core. It seems that the adhesion to the roughened surface is reduced compared with that to the polished surface. Surface speeds of 120 to 150 mm/s are obtainable if the above-mentioned conditions are fulfilled.

Determining the drive-motor capacity is still very uncertain. At present data concerning the torque required for unscrewing the threaded cores are still lacking. However, even these are determined by a series of very influential factors. Apart from the already mentioned ones concerning the speed of core rotation, the mold temperature, the injection pressure and the holding pressure time have to be added. For a start, one is forced to guess the motor capacity. However, one must have it clearly in mind that particularly with multi-cavity tools and the larger core diameters as well as a greater number of thread turns the required capacity must not be underestimated. Experience shows that capacities of 0.7 to 1.5 kW are required for larger molds if the motor is not to be stalled under unfavorable conditions, such as too long a cooling time, too low a mold temperature, etc. The latest research has for the first time established static friction coefficients as functions of the influential parameters mentioned, on which realistic calculations for the torque required can be based.

An eight-cavity injection mold for a $3/8$" threaded sleeve approximately 25 mm long is subsequently described. A $3/8$" thread has a pitch of 19 threads per inch. This means that for unscrewing the 25 mm threaded sleeve to enable it to be demolded, 19 turns of the threaded cores are required. At a thread diameter of 17 mm the circumference is $17 \times \pi = 53.3$ mm. If one calculates for 150 mm surface speed, then $150/53.3 = 2.86$ turns per second = 172 rotations per minute can be envisaged. Therefore 19 turns require $19/2.86 = 7.5$ s. Should the injection process take 2 s and the holding pressure time take 3 s, then the injection molding process takes $2+3+15 = 20$ s, provided that the unscrewing of the threaded cores starts at the time of mold opening and that the same time is taken for screwing the threaded cores in as it takes to unscrew them. This means that three injection cycles per minute can be run.

As one polystyrene threaded sleeve weighs approximately 6 g the machine would have to have a plasticizing capacity of $6 \times 3 \times 8 \times 60 = 8.7$ kg/h. With the space requirements for the injection mold-shut height approximately 300 mm – the plasticizing capacity is available anyway.

The pitch circle diameter for eight inserts results from the insert diameter of 110 mm. The threaded core pinions are equipped with 20 teeth, modulus 1.25. The common transmission gear therefore is of a 135 mm pitch circle diameter or 108 teeth of modulus 1.25. The transmission ratio is $108/20 = 5.4$. As 19 threaded core turns are required before the molding can be ejected,

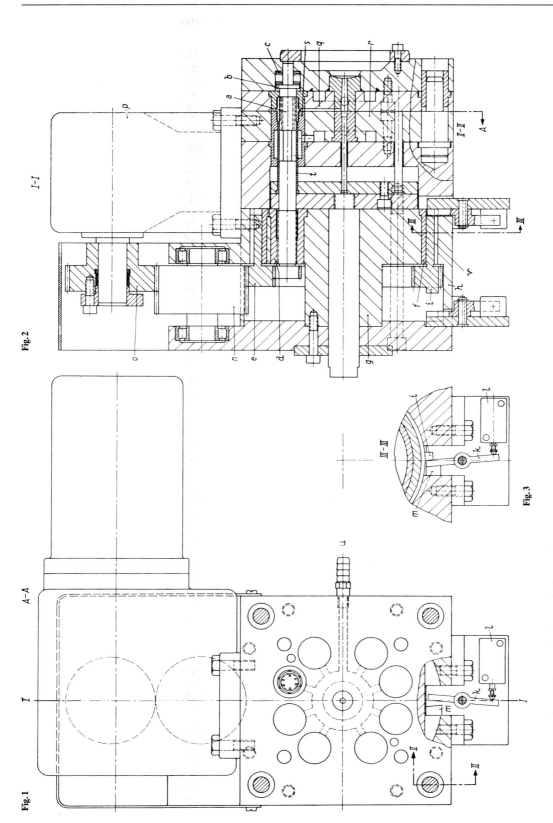

**Fig.2**

**Fig.1**

*I–I*

*A–A*

**Fig.3**

**Figs. 1 to 3    Eight-cavity threaded sleeve mold with motorized unscrewing**
*a*: threaded cores, *b*: cores on the fixed half, *c*: set of disc springs, *d*: lead nut, *e*: planet gear, *f*: bronze bearing bushing, *g*: center core, *h*: housing, *i*: stop, *k*: lever, *l*: limit switch, *m*: fixed stop, *n*: idler gear, *o*: pinion, *p*: gear box, *q*: plate, *r*: insert plate, *s*: insert, *t*: ejector sleeve, *u*: supply air, *v*: 6 mm pitch.

19/5.4 = 3.5 rotations of the gear ring are required. Four complete rotations are executed from stop to stop of the gear ring, which is equipped with 94 outside teeth, modulus 2 or 188 mm pitch circle diameter. This gear ring is driven by the drive gear with 44 teeth, modulus 2, via an idler gear. The transmission ratio of driveshaft/gear-ring therefore equals 44 to 94 = 1 to 2.14. Hence the drive shaft has to turn at 172/5.4 × 2.14 = 68 rpm if the threaded cores are to turn at 172 rpm.

For weight-saving reasons a three-phase gear motor of 2800 rpm is chosen. The gear motor is designed as a brake motor, as it has to operate from stop to stop, so that there is a little overrun as possible after switching off. It is also recommended to install a two-speed motor. It would then be possible to unscrew the cores at 172 rpm and screw them in at 344 rpm, which would shorten the cycle time by 3.7 s.

The eight-cavity threaded sleeve tool is shown in Figs. 1 to 3. The threaded sleeve is externally ribbed to se-

cure it against rotating and has been designed with a central bead connected to a submarine gate as injection point. The threaded cores (a) push against the fixed half cores (b) in the injection position. The cores at (b) are supported by substantial sets of disc springs (c). This arrangement ensures against flash across the face of the threaded cores.

The threaded cores (a) possess a lead thread on their driven side, which has the same pitch as the threaded sleeve, with which they are carried in a bronze lead nut (d); the threaded core is equipped with 20 teeth at the same end (modulus 1.25) and the pinions, arranged in a circle, are in mesh with the gear ring of the planet gear, which has 94 teeth of modulus 2 on the outside.

This planet gear is carried by a bronze bearing bushing (f) on a core (g), centrally arranged in the mold. On its outer circumference the planet gear is meshed with the housing (h) via a thread of 6 mm pitch, so that the planet gear travels 6 mm to the right or the left with one

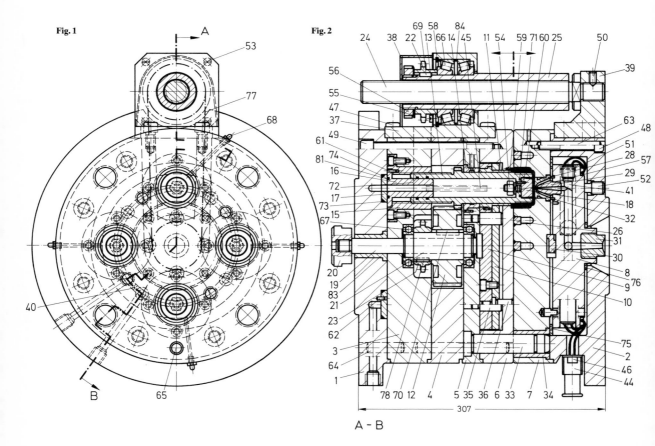

A - B

complete turn depending on the direction of rotation. This axial displacement of the planet gear suits the following purpose:

As already explained, the planet gear should complete four turns before it contacts the stop in either the one or the other direction. To achieve this, the stops ($i$) have been provided on both faces of the planet gear. They are a little lower than the pitch of the thread, so that they are overrun on the release turn after one rotation of the spur gear. The stops ($i$) move against levers ($k$), which actuate limit switches ($l$) with their opposite ends, resting solidly against supporting stops ($m$), which are fixed parts of the mold structure. In this manner the requirement has been taken care of that the two end positions of the threaded cores must be limited by stops and also that a limit switch must be actuated. It is possible, through these limit switches, to inhibit or permit the movements of the machine inde-

pendently of the final threaded core positions in the desired sequence. If required, the gear motor can even be switched to the high rotational speed by limit switch actuation. The external teeth of the planet gear mesh with the pinion ($o$) of the gear box ($p$) via the idler gear ($n$).

Plate ($q$) for the inserts on the fixed half is cooled by a ring channel for cooling water. The cores can only be cooled by compressed air. For this purpose an annular groove has been provided in the insert plate ($r$), which is supplied with compressed air. Two supply channels lead from this annulus to the hollow spaces in the inserts ($s$). The air is guided to the axial cooling channels in the cores from these hollow spaces through bores in the ejector sleeves ($t$). The high speed of the air inside the narrow bores of the cores results in an adequate cooling effect.

# Example 104, Four-cavity hot-runner injection mold for 3-liter-bottle closures

A space-saving solution for the unscrewing gear trains of a threaded closure mold has been found in the design illustrated in Figs. 1 to 3. Once again, the opening movement of the injection molding machine is utilized for operating the threaded cores. The spindle is firmly installed as a machine fixture on the mold mounting plate of the fixed half (2), whereas the coarse threaded

**Fig. 3**

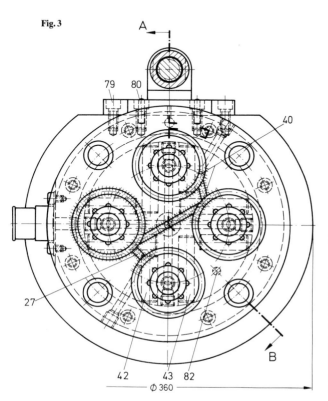

**Figs. 1 to 3    Four-cavity hot-runner 3-liter-bottle closure mold**
1: moving-half mold mounting plate, 2: fixed-half mold mounting plate, 3: retaining plate, 4: sandwich plate, 5: guide plate, 6: housing plate, 7: cavity plate, 8: manifold plate (hot-runner block), 9, 10: ejector plate, 11: ejector sleeve, 12: central gear wheel, 13: threaded core, 14: bushing, 15: coarse threaded nut, 16: core housing, 17: washer, 18: core, 19: ejector rod, 20: stop, 21: central shaft, 22, 23: chain sprocket, 24: coarse threaded spindle, 25: coarse threaded nut, 26: ring, 27: leg, 28: nozzle well insert, 29: heat-conducting nozzle, 30: spacer piece, 31: sprue bushing, 32: sealing ring, 33: guide rod, 34: guide bushing, 35: support bolt, 36: pushback pin, 37: bearing block, 38: cover, 39: spindle housing, 40: separating web, 41: plug, 42, 43: cartridge heater, 44: electrical socket connection, 45: tube, 46 to 49: Allen bolts, 50 to 52: threaded studs, 53: cylinder bolt, 54: hexagonal nut, 55: tab washer, 56: grooved ring nut, 57: spring washer, 58: circlip, 59 to 65: cylindrical pin, 66: tapered roller bearing, 67: grooved ball bearing, 68: grease nipple, 69, 70: shaft key, 71, 73, 74: O-ring, 72: sealing ring, 75, 76: gasket, 77: roller chain, 78: shaft key, 79: Allen bolt, 80: straight pin, 81: O-ring, 82: straight pin, 83: bushing, 84: spacer ring.

nut (25) is mounted in the moving half of the mold and allowed to rotate. The turning movement is transmitted by chain-drive (sprockets 22 and 23) to the center shaft (21), which carries the center pinion (12). The gear teeth of the four threaded cores (13), circularly displayed around the pinion (12), in mesh with the latter. The cores are guided in bushings (14) and lead nuts (15). The cooling water supply and return in the lead-nut zone are taken care of by the core housing (16). Two sealing rings (72) in the threaded core seal the cores and the core housings.

As the unscrewing process takes place parallel to the opening movement of the mold, the threaded closures must be secured against rotating, as they are fully withdrawn from the the cavity already on mold opening, whereas the unscrewing phase is still progressing. A pin (59), protruding into each cavity in the lower rim area of the cap, serves as antirotating device. This fea-ture subsequently requires an additional ejection movement,which is transmitted to the molding by the ejector sleeve (11), displacing the article from the pin (59). The ejector sleeve (11) is carried in the ejector plates (9) and (10). These are moved by the ejector rod (19), which is centrally housed in shaft (21). The push-back pin (36) ensures that the ejectors are returned when the mold closes.

The injection molding material is introduced into the mold cavities through a cross-shaped hot-runner manifold (8) and a copper heat-conducting nozzle(29), which extends into the nozzle well insert (28). Injection takes place through centrally positioned pinpoint gates.

The construction of the mold, which requires an opening stroke of 205 mm, is such that it does not require machine-operated core actuation, allowing the tool to be mounted in any machine of suitable size.

# Example 105, Six-cavity injection mold for retaining nuts with metal inserts

Retaining nuts on electrical instruments are provided with a threaded copper insert part to ensure good contact. To prevent the thread from becoming contaminated with the plastics material injected into the mold cavity these inserts are usually screwed onto a core. This process requires a considerable amount of time during loading as well as demolding of the finished part. Although it would be expedient to employ a rotary table injection molding machine, the loading and demolding time of a six-cavity mold determines the cycle.

A slight alteration of the insert can change this. If the insert is provided with a collar on the bearing area that rests against the locating mandrel, this can prevent plastics melt from entering the threads from below. In this case a smooth pin can be used as a holder at the upper end of the ejector (13), so that loading and demolding are greatly facilitated. The pressure bolt (11) together with the disc springs (12) compensates for the uncalibrated length of the insert, the pressure bolt sealing off the thread from the top.

**Figs. 1**

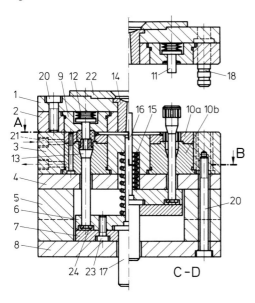

**Figs. 2**

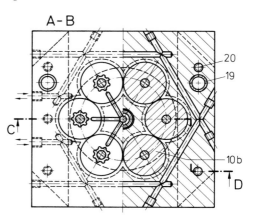

**Figs. 3**      **Figs. 4**

**Figs. 1 to 4   Six-cavity injection mold for retaining nuts with metal inserts**
1: upper clamping plate, 2: insert retainer plate, 3: mold plate, 4: base plate, 5: spacer plate, 6, 7: ejector plates, 8: lower clamping plate, 9: upper inserts, 10 a, b: cavity inserts, 11: pressure bolt, 12: spring disc, 13: ejector rod, 14: sprue bushing, 15: springs, 16: sprue ejector, 17: ejector bar, 18: guide pin, 19: guide bushing, 20: bolt, 21: cooling water connection, 22: locating ring, 23: connecting bolt, 24: slotted washer.

# Example 106, Single-cavity injection mold for a switch housing of polyacetal

Luxury cars have, among other things, a level control system that receives its information as to the vehicle orientation by means of mercury switches. The inclination in three planes is sensed, for which reason the switch housing (Fig. 1) has three obliquely positioned holes. Each of these three holes has two small openings for cable connections at its end.

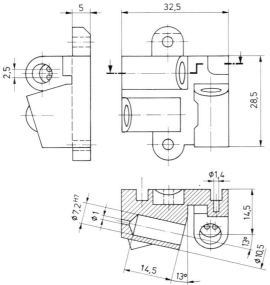

**Fig. 1    Switch housing of polyacetal**

## Mold (Figs. 2 to 5)

The orientation and position of the holes require three angled side cores (16, 17, 53) running in different directions. The cores used to form the holes visible in the sectional drawing of Fig. 1 cross one another, i.e. one penetrates the other. The slides (17, 53) for these two cores must be sequenced such that during mold opening and part release the penetrating core (17) is pulled first and the penetrated core (53) is not pulled until the first has been withdrawn.

Sequencing of the slide motions is accomplished with the aid of a cam plate (18). The shape of the cam tracks

is shown with dotted lines in Fig. 3. A cam plate is shown in the "slides withdrawn" position. Guide pins (2) attached to the slides run in the cam tracks. The slides run on obliquely positioned guide strips (10, 32, 36). When the mold is closed, they are held in the molding position by heel blocks (4). The cam plate (18) is pinned to a gear (21); both are mounted in needle bearings (20) so as to permit rotation. A gear rack (6) operated by a hydraulic cylinder (45) engages the gear (21) to rotate the cam plate. The end positions of the hydraulic cylinder and of the ejector plate (25) are monitored by limit switches (Figs. 2 to 5).

## Runner system/gating

The molded part is filled via a sprue with pinpoint gate. The sprue is held by an undercut on the machine nozzle when the injection unit retracts and is sheared off the molded part. It is subsequently removed from the machine nozzle by a special mechanism.

## Mold temperature control

The mold is operated at a temperature of 95 °C. Channels for mold temperature control have been provided in the mold plates (1, 5). Insulating plates (13) prevent heating of the machine platens.

## Materials

Mold inserts, slides, cam plate and sprue bushing are made of hardened steel, material no. 1.2718.

## Part release/ejection

The mold opens in the plane of gating; the slides are now free to move. The gear rack is now advanced into the mold so that the cam plate (18) finally reaches the position drawn in Fig. 3. From the shape of the three cam tracks, it can be seen that the slide (17) moves first and that slide (53) does not move until slide (17) has been withdrawn. Slide (16) also remains stationary for a while before it is withdrawn.

After the side cores have been pulled, the molded part is ejected with the aid of the ejector pins (24) and ejector sleeves (42).

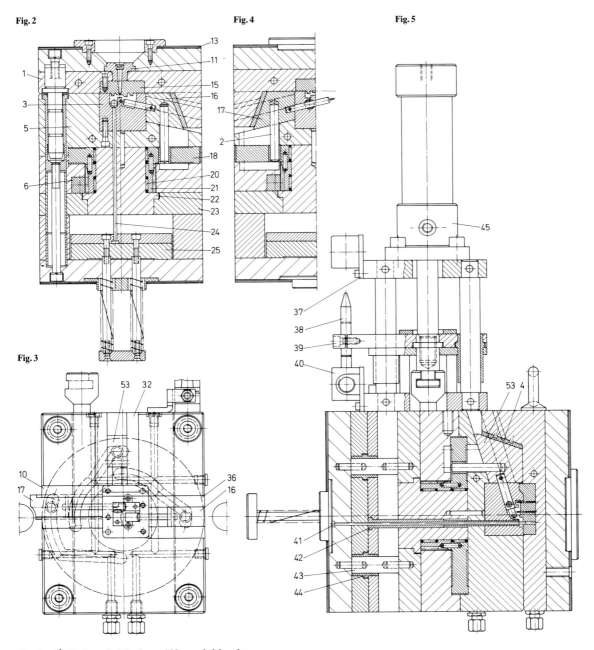

**Fig. 2**

**Fig. 4**

**Fig. 5**

**Fig. 3**

**Figs. 2 to 5    Single-cavity injection mold for a switch housing**
1: mold plate, 2: guide pin, 3: mold insert, 4: heel block, 5: mold plate, 6: gear rack, 10: guide strip, 11; sprue bushing, 13: insulating plate, 15: mold insert, 16, 17: slides, 18: cam plate, 20: needle bearing, 21: gear, 22: backing block, 23: plate, 24: ejector pin, 25: ejector plate, 32: guide strip, 36: guide strip, 37: switch holder, 38: actuating pin, 39: clamping screw, 40: limit switch, 41: core pin, 42: ejector sleeve, 43: support pillar, 44: guide bushing, 45: hydraulic cylinder, 53: slide

# Example 107, Single-cavity injection mold for a snap ring of polyacetal

The snap ring (Fig. 1) is attached to metal parts by being snapped on. Originally, the two undercuts on the ring were forcibly released, but this did not provide a satisfactory snap fit. Machining of the two undercuts was too expensive, so that a suitable split-cavity mold was designed.

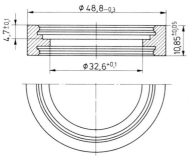

**Fig.1   Snap ring of polyacetal**

## Mold

The mold (Figs. 2 to 5) has been designed with a single-cavity. A system of slides (11, 14) that form the undercuts in the ring is located on each side of the mold cavity. Four (narrow) slides (11) each are guided on a cone (9, 17). Four (wide) slides (14) acted upon by springs (15) are located between the narrow slides. In the molding position, all eight slides on a mold half are seated on their inner surface on the guide surfaces of the cones (9, 17), while the outer surface is seated in a conical opening in the mold plate (1) and stripper plate (12). The mold opens in parting lines (I, II, III) to actuate the slides and to release the molded part. Latches (10, 31) and ball detents (20, 22) are provided for this purpose.

## Runner system/gating

With the slide arrangement chosen, injection into the parting line (II) is most favorable. The part is filled via a single submarine gate on its circumference.

## Mold temperature control

The mold must be operated at a temperature of 120 °C. The two cones (9, 17) are hollow and are fitted with "helical cores" (37). A cooling circuit is provided in mold plate (1).
Two insulating plates (2) inhibit heat transfer to the machine platens.

## Mold steel

The two cones (9, 17), the slides and the mold ring (13) are made of hardened steel, material no. 1.2718.

## Part release/ejection

The mold opens at parting line (I), because the latch (31) initially holds the mold plates to the left together. During this motion, the cone (17) is axially displaced with respect to the slides around it. The (narrow) slides (11) shift inward and make it possible for the (wide) slides (14) between them to also move inwards through the action of the springs (15). The right-hand undercut on the molded part is now free.
After the latch (31) is released the opening motion of parting line (I) is limited by the shoulder bolt (34).
Parting line (III) is held closed by the ball detents (20, 22) (Fig. 3), so that parting line (II) now opens. The molded part, held by the slides on the left, is withdrawn from the mold ring (13). The submarine gate shears off the molded part, while the sprue is held by the sprue puller (16).
As soon as the hook of latch (10) reaches plate (3), the ball detents (20, 22) are released and the mold opens at parting line (III). Cone (9) is now also axially displaced with respect to the slides around it, and the left-hand undercut on the molded part is now free. The shoulder bolt (27) limits this opening motion.
Finally, the molded part, now held loosely by the slides on the left, is ejected by the stripper plate (12). The sprue is withdrawn from the sprue puller and can drop. The increased expense for such a mold with two collapsible cores is amortized after approximately 100,000 parts as a result of the elimination of machining.

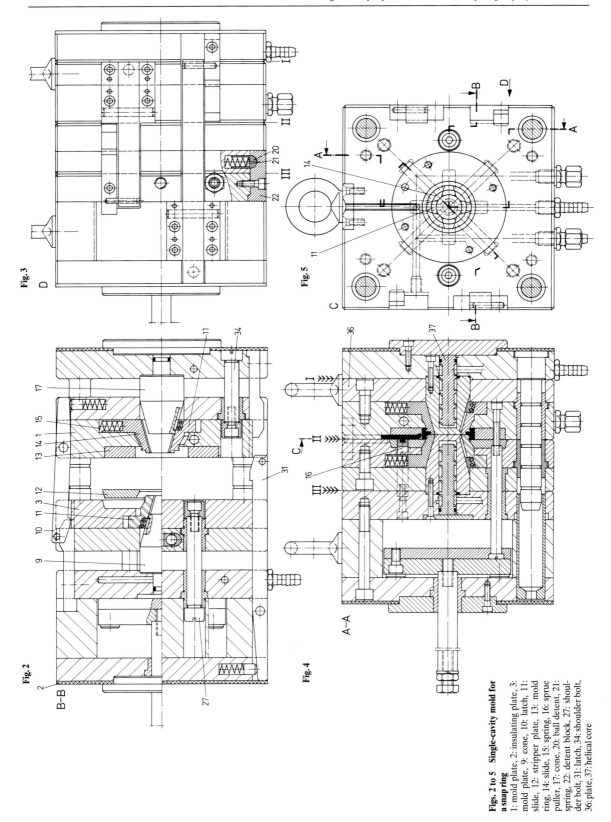

**Fig. 3**

D

**Fig. 5**

C

**Fig. 2**

B-B

2

27

**Fig. 4**

A-A

C

**Figs. 2 to 5   Single-cavity mold for a snap ring**

1: mold plate, 2: insulating plate, 3: mold plate, 9: cone, 10: latch, 11: slide, 12: stripper plate, 13: mold ring, 14: slide, 15: spring, 16: spring, 17: cone, 20: ball detent, 21: sprue puller, 22: detent block, 27: shoulder spring, 31: latch, 34: shoulder bolt, 36: plate, 37: helical core

## Example 108, Single-cavity hot-runner injection mold for an air vent housing of acrylonitrile butadiene styrene (ABS).

The frame-shaped air vent housing is part of the ventilation system for the passenger compartment of an automobile. It has dimensions of approx. 100 mm × 70 mm and must hold five adjustable vent flaps (vanes) with which the air flow is regulated. In addition, mounting points are located on the outside along the two long sides of the housing. The shafts for the air vents fit into holes also located along the two long sides. Each pair of opposite holes must be in exact alignment. The specified hole diameters do not permit the pairs of aligning holes to be formed by single long cores, regardless of the fact that this is not possible for practical reasons. Accordingly, the design shown in Figs. 1 and 2 was chosen.

### Mold

The mold is constructed largely from standard mold components. The molded part is located between cavity insert (11) and core insert (12). The cavity insert (11) and the surrounding mold plate (13) have an opening on one side for a slide (14) that runs in guide (15). Two rows of core pins (16, 17) that form the holes from both the outside of the housing (core pin 16) as well as from the inside (core pin 17) are attached to the slide (14). To accommodate core pins (17), the slide has a hook-shaped end that protrudes into a recess in the cavity insert.

The slide (14) is operated by a so-called latching cylinder (18). The piston of this cylinder is displaced by means of oil pressure and is held in the mounting position (forward) mechanically (Fig. 3).

The operation of the cylinder is illustrated schematically in Figs. 4 and 5. Fig. 4 = latched; Fig. 5 = unlatched. When the piston is in the forward position, the segments (2) are forced into the annular groove in the piston rod (1) by the latching sleeve (3), thereby holding the piston in position.

This mechanical latching is assured even in the absence of hydraulic pressure and is several times stronger than the hydraulic force.

Prior to retraction, the latching sleeve (3) is shifted by the hydraulic fluid, thereby unlatching the cylinder. The sensor pin (4) provides an exact indication of the position of the latching sleeve (3).

The cylinder (18) is threaded into the flange (19) and locked in position by the slotted nut (20).

Two slides (21, 22) actuated by cam pins (23, 24) attached to the cavity half are provided to release the mounting points on the long sides of the air vent housing.

The part-forming inserts of the mold are made of case-hardening steel, material no. 1.2764.

### Runner system/gating

The part is filled from the outside via three pinpoint gates located on one of the long sides. Since the molded part is centered in the mold, the melt flows from the sprue bushing (25) via an externally heated hot-runner manifold (26) and hot-runner nozzle (27) to a conventional runner. This runner is machined into the upper surface of the slide (21) along with the three submarine gates leading to the mold cavity. Pockets (28) and sprue puller (29) hold the runner in the slide (21) as the mold opens. A pressure sensor (32) monitors the internal cavity pressure.

### Mold temperature control

Channels for mold temperature control have been machined into the part-forming inserts as well as the two slides. Thermocouples (33) monitor the mold temperature.

### Part release/ejection

Prior to mold opening, the slide (14) is pulled outwards by the cylinder (18), thereby withdrawing the core pins (16, 17) from the molded part.

The molded part is retained on the core half as the mold opens. During this motion, the two slides (21, 22) move outwards, releasing the external mounting points on the air vent housing. Slide (21) also pulls the runner away from the molded part, shearing off the gates. The molded part is subsequently stripped off the core by ejectors.

Since the conventional runner is located in the moving slide (21), a special mechanism is needed to eject it. A runner ejector (30) that is pulled back by a spring (31) is located behind the undercut (29) that holds the runner. Once the slide (21) is in the fully opened position, the machine ejector is actuated and the ejector pin (34) strikes the end of the runner ejector (30) located in slide (21). The runner is now ejected.

The machine ejector must be retracted prior to mold closing in order to avoid damage to the ejector pin (34) by the inward moving slide (25). The position of the ejector plate is monitored by the limit switch (35).

---

**Figs. 1 and 2    Single-cavity hot-runner injection mold for an air vent housing of ABS**

11: cavity insert, 12: core insert, 13: mold plate, 14: slide, 15: guide, 16: core pin, 17: core pin, 18: latching cylinder, 19: flange, 20: slotted nut, 21 and 22: slides, 23 and 24: cam pins, 25: sprue bushing, 26: hot-runner manifold, 27: hot-runner nozzle, 28: pocket to hold runner, 29: undercut to pull runner, 30: runner ejector, 31: spring, 32: pressure sensor, 33: thermocouple, 34: ejector pin, 35: limit switch, 36: cartridge heater, 37: ejector core

**Fig. 1**

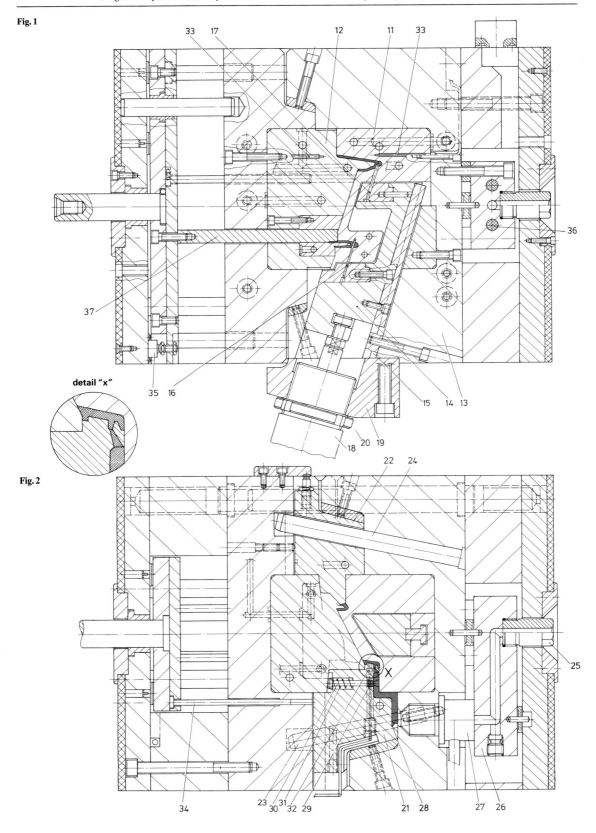

detail "x"

**Fig. 2**

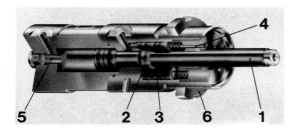

**Figs. 3 to 5    Latching cylinder**
1: piston rod, 2: segments, 3: latching sleeve, 4: sensor pin, 5: slotted nut

Fig. 3

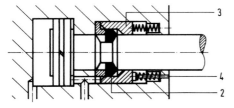

Fig. 4

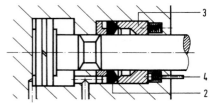

Fig. 5

# The Authors:

*H. G. Adelhard*, c/o Matthias Oechsler & Sohn, D-8800 Ansbach

*G. Bagusche*, c/o IBS Brooke, D-5222 Morsbach-Lichtenberg

*B. Bakof*, c/o Bayer AG, D-4150 Krefeld-Uerdingen

*F. Bau*, c/o Braun AG, D-6242 Kronberg

*U. Beese*, c/o Gebr. Otto KG, D-5910 Kreuztal

*K. H. Blauert*, c/o Calmar Albert GmbH, D-5870 Hemer

*H. Bopp*, c/o Hoechst AG, D-6230 Frankfurt 80

*H. Bormuth*, c/o Hoechst AG, D-6230 Frankfurt 80

*E. Braun*, c/o Braun & Keller, D-7839 Bahlingen

*L. Eberhardt*, c/o Hassenzahl & Sohn GmbH & Co KG, D-6102 Pfungstadt

*J. Gaiser*, c/o Arburg Maschinenfabrik Hehl & Söhne, D-7298 Loßburg 1

*H. Gastrow* †

*H. Gemmer*, c/o Gemmer Werkzeug- und Formenbau KG, D-8630 Coburg

*D. Geßner*, c/o Husky, D-6200 Wiesbaden-Delkheim

*H. Geyer*, D-8702 Lengfeld bei Würzburg

*R. Großmann*, c/o Formenbau + Plastic GmbH, D-7122 Besigheim

*H. Günther*, c/o Günther Heißkanaltechnik, D-3558 Frankenberg/Eder

*F. Hachtel*, c/o F. und G. Hachtel, D-7080 Aalen

*W. Hartmann*, c/o BASF AG, D-6700 Ludwigshafen

*K. Hegele*, c/o K. Hegele GmbH, D-8000 München 60

*G. Hermes*, c/o IBS Brooke, D-5222 Morsbach-Lichtenberg

*O. Heuel*, c/o Hasco, D-5880 Lüdenscheid

*G. Heyder*, c/o BASF AG, D-6700 Ludwigshafen

*A. Hörburger*, c/o Hoechst AG, D-6230 Frankfurt 80

*A. Höreth*, c/o Wilden Werkzeugbau GmbH, D-8473 Pfreimd

*J. von Holdt*, c/o Plas-Tool Company, Niles, Illinois 60648/USA

*G. Klepek*, D-8000 München

*O. Krumpschmid*, c/o Gebrüder Junghans GmbH, D-7230 Schramberg

*E. Lemmen*, c/o Bayer AG, D-5090 Leverkusen

*M. Müller*, D-7140 Ludwigsburg

*J. Nestler*, c/o Bock Plastic Karl Bock GmbH & Co., D-7233 Lauterbach/Schwarzwald

*A. Noll*, c/o BASF AG, D-6700 Ludwigshafen

*E. Oebius*, S-37101 Karlskrona

*S. Ohnuma*, c/o Spear System, D-6233 Kelkheim

*M. Pflanzl*, c/o Zimmermann Nachf., D-3554 Gladenbach-Erdhausen

*B. Romahn*, Knaufstraße 9, D-8720 Schweinfurt

*W. Sander*, c/o BASF AG, D-6700 Ludwigshafen

*F. Schauberg*, c/o Hoechst AG, D-6230 Frankfurt 80

*K. Scheuermann*, c/o Kunststoff-Ingenieurbüro Scheuermann, CH-Dietikon

*L. Schmidt*, c/o Gerhardi & Cie. GmbH & Co. KG, D-5880 Lüdenscheid

*M. Schmidt*, c/o Gebr. Otto KG, D-5910 Kreuztal

*H. Schreck*, c/o Heitec Heißkanaltechnik GmbH, D-3559 Burgwald Bottendorf

*D. Schulz*, c/o Hoechst AG, D-6230 Frankfurt 80

*I. Seres*, Fabrica de Mase Viitorul Plastice, Oradea/Rumänien

*E. Singer,* c/o Fischer Werke Artur Fischer GmbH & Co. KG, D-7244 Tumlingen/Waldachtal

*L. Sors,* Damjanich u. 12, H-1071 Budapest

*E. K. R. Strauch,* D-7143 Vaihingen

*K. Sturm,* c/o Hassenzahl & Sohn GmbH & Co. KG, D-6102 Pfungstadt

*M. M. Trapp* †

*P. Unger,* c/o Hoechst AG, D-6230 Frankfurt 80

*H. Vogel,* c/o Ewikon, D-3558 Frankenberg

*W. Weber,* c/o Fischer Werke Artur Fischer GmbH & Co. KG, D-7244 Tumlingen/Waldachtal

*W. R. Weingärtner,* c/o Hassenzahl & Sohn GmbH & Co KG, D-6102 Pfungstadt

*K. Weißenburg,* c/o DAL-Georg Rost & Söhne, D-4952 Porta Westfalica